Routledge Revivals

Leyla and Mejnun

First published in 1970, *Leyla and Mejnun* provides a thorough introduction to the Leyla and Mejnun love story and the various forms in which the story has appeared in the Islamic world. Finally, it offers for the delight of the English poetry lover, an extremely readable translation of the Turkish version of the story. This book will be of interest to students of literature and history.

Leyla and Mejnun

with a history of the poem, notes, and bibliography
by Alessio Bombaci

Fuzuli
Translated by Sofi Huri

First published by George Allen & Unwin Ltd.,
London, 1967

This edition first published in 2024 by Routledge
4 Park Square, Milton Park, Abingdon, Oxon, OX14 4RN

and by Routledge
605 Third Avenue, New York, NY 10017

Routledge is an imprint of the Taylor & Francis Group, an informa business

UNESCO Collection of Representative Works Indian Series
This book has been accepted in the Indian Translations Series of the UNESCO Collection of Representative Works, jointly sponsored by UNESCO and the Turkish National Commission for UNESCO

© UNESCO 1967, 1969

All rights reserved. No part of this book may be reprinted or reproduced or utilised in any form or by any electronic, mechanical, or other means, now known or hereafter invented, including photocopying and recording, or in any information storage or retrieval system, without permission in writing from the publishers.

Publisher's Note
The publisher has gone to great lengths to ensure the quality of this reprint but points out that some imperfections in the original copies may be apparent.

Disclaimer
The publisher has made every effort to trace copyright holders and welcomes correspondence from those they have been unable to contact.

A Library of Congress record exists under ISBN: 0048900036

ISBN: 978-1-032-77284-4 (hbk)
ISBN: 978-1-003-48226-0 (ebk)
ISBN: 978-1-032-77287-5 (pbk)

Book DOI 10.4324/9781003482260

LEYLĀ AND MEJNŪN

BY

FUZŪLĪ

———

translated from the Turkish by
SOFI HURI

with a history of the poem, notes, and bibliography
by Alessio Bombaci
(translated from the Italian by Elizabeth Davies)

London
GEORGE ALLEN & UNWIN LTD
RUSKIN HOUSE   MUSEUM STREET

FIRST PUBLISHED IN 1970

This book is copyright under the Berne Convention. All rights reserved. Apart from any fair dealing for the purpose of private study, research, criticism or review, as permitted under the Copyright Act, 1956, no part of this publication may be reproduced, stored in a retrieval system or transmitted, in any form or by any means, electronic, electric, chemical, mechanical, optical, photocopying, recording or otherwise, without the prior permission of the copyright owner. Enquiries should be addressed to the Publishers.

© UNESCO 1970

ISBN 04 890003 6

UNESCO COLLECTION OF REPRESENTATIVE WORKS
TURKISH SERIES

This book has been accepted in the Turkish Translations Series of the UNESCO Collection of Representative Works, jointly sponsored by the United Nations Educational, Scientific and Cultural Organization (UNESCO), and the Turkish National Commission for UNESCO

PRINTED IN GREAT BRITAIN
in 11 on 12 pt. *Old Style*
BY UNWIN BROTHERS LIMITED
THE GRESHAM PRESS
OLD WOKING SURREY ENGLAND

CONTENTS

PART I: THE HISTORY OF LEYLĀ
AND MEJNŪN   by Alessio Bombaci

I	The Life of Fuzūlī	11
II	The Works of Fuzūlī	22
III	The Legend of Majnūn	47
IV	Laylā and Mejnūn by Nizāmī of Ganja	64
V	Fuzūlī's Leylā and Mejnūn	84

PART II: LEYLĀ AND MEJNŪN
translated by Sofi Huri

Translator's Note	115
The Translation	122
NOTES ON PART I	333
NOTES ON PART II	339
BIBLIOGRAPHY	343
INDEX	347

PART I

THE HISTORY OF LEYLĀ AND MEJNŪN

CHAPTER ONE

THE LIFE OF FUZŪLĪ*

Fuzūlī is one of the greatest if not perhaps the greatest poet the Turks have had in the course of their literary history.[1] During his lifetime and after his death his fame spread from Mesopotamia, where he lived in the sixteenth century, to the Turks of the Ottoman Empire, of Azerbaijan, and of Central Asia. He was admired and imitated for centuries. In Turkey and Soviet Azerbaijan his life and works have been studied carefully and monographs dealing with him have recently appeared[2] in both these countries. But the subject has not yet been fully dealt with in West European languages. The publication of an English translation of *Leylā and Mejnūn* would seem to provide an excellent opportunity for introducing Fuzūlī to a body of readers who do not know Turkish, for settling some biographical details and discussing some aspects of his literary activity.

When Fuzūlī was born, probably in Najaf (in the area now known as Iraq), in the last decades of the fifteenth century (we do not know the exact date),[3] Mesopotamia had only memories of her glorious past. The poet himself recalls these glories in a poem written about 1534. This clearly indicates his intellectual horizons. Only the silent ruins of the Palace of Chosroes at Ctesiphon represent the millennia of history before the advent of Islam. Of Islam itself he recalls the outstanding moments and prominent figures in its political, religious and cultural history. He speaks of the Caliphate of 'Alī with its capital at Kūfa, of the martyrdom of Husayn, the son of 'Alī, at Karbalā'; of the learned jurist Abū Hanīfa, of the mystics Buhlūl (a legendary wise fool), Ma'rūf, Junayd, Hallāj.[4]

The splendour of the past was contrasted with the poverty of the present. Baghdad, the capital, once the heart of the Arab Islamic world, after having been sacked and destroyed by the Mongols in 1258, had fallen into the hands of the Mongol dynasty of the Jelāirids and then to the Turcomans of the White and Black Sheep. Baghdad had been a guiding light to civilization and culture for centuries, but now

* The notes to Part I will be found on pages 333–8.

great men no longer lived within its walls. Fuzūlī was, in his time, a lone star.

There is no reason to doubt the tradition which would have Fuzūlī belong to the tribe of the Bayat, one of the many Turcoman tribes scattered over Western Asia during the upheavals caused by the Seljukian and Mongol invasions. Although his ancestors were of nomadic origin, Fuzūlī's family had long been town-dwellers. The voice of Fuzūlī does not appear, as might seem today, as that of a Turk lost in an almost completely Arab world. The Bayat who had arrived in this area (other branches of the tribe are found in other regions) were not the only Turks living in the country at the time of Fuzūlī. At one time it seemed in fact that Mesopotamia was about to take the same course as Anatolia or Azerbaijan and become a Turkish country. At least this is what one would understand from the lines of Shāh Ismā'īl (d. 1524), the founder of the Safavid dynasty in Persia (often spelled *Safawid* in English encyclopaedias) whose success was in fact due to his Turcoman followers: 'As the Arab villages and dwellings gradually dwindle away so the Turcomans overrun the land of Baghdad.'[5]

We know nothing of the childhood and early youth of Muhammad ibn Suleymān (this is the poet's name and patronymic).[6] What is certain from the evidence he himself provides is that from his early years, throughout a great part of his life and into his old age, he served in the shrine of 'Alī at Najaf.[7] We know nothing of his exact duties. At one time they must have been burdensome, for while he begs to remain at Najaf, he asks to be exonerated from the duties entrusted to him in order that he may devote himself entirely to chanting the praises of 'Alī.[8] It is obvious that Fuzūlī, dedicated as he was to the cult of 'Alī, 'the dog on the threshold' of the shrine which houses 'Alī's remains and author of numerous poems in praise of him and his descendants, was a fervent Shiite even if, as we shall see below, his Shiism underwent a metamorphosis. He belonged to the 'Twelver' or Imāmī Shiites, that is to the branch most inclined to moderation and agreement with the Sunnites.

Whatever his daily duties and no matter how humble they were, Fuzūlī was a versatile and learned man, and he was both ambitious to possess these qualities, and proud of his success in possessing them. He felt himself a poet, but he understood that for a poet the wider the field of knowledge in which one soars, the greater and deeper the inspiration, since poetry without science is like 'a wall without foundations' or 'a body without a soul'.[9] Without the slightest shadow of humility he boasted of the exceptional capacities he had acquired far from courtly and academic circles: 'Although I've had little contact with eminent scholars, have not been brought up by famous and benevolent kings and have avoided travelling in other lands and towns, when it comes to discussing rational arguments my hand always grasps the various theories of the philosophers by the collar. In the problems of the traditional sciences I hold the position of an umpire sitting in judgment of the points disputed among the jurists. As far as the arts of eloquence are concerned I am master of all the arts in discussing beauty of expression—and in disputing agreeableness of style with those who are masters of one art only. Well, all this demonstrates the total "presumption" (*fuzūlī*), but also the perfection of Fuzūlī.'[10] Thus the poet explains his *nom de plume*, which literally means 'presumptuous', but which also brings to mind *fuzūl*, the plural of *fazl* meaning 'virtue'. He chose this pseudonym in order not to be confused with others and to be 'unique'. He was sure that because of its unpleasant meaning nobody else would adopt it.[11a]

From Fuzūlī's work it can be seen that he put his concept of 'learned' poetry into practice. His writings show no lack of references to various branches of knowledge, from theology to mysticism, from astronomy to medicine. However, like many poets who were also learned men, he did not leave much of a mark in the field of knowledge.

His poetic talent and his far from common scholarship justified Fuzūlī's yearning for a lot different from that to which he had fallen. He recalled the names of famous poets who had risen to favour and fame at the courts of powerful kings and this fed his hopes which were always doomed to disappointment. He wrote countless invocations to the rulers of the time begging for help and favours. In the almost complete absence of data external to his works, his biography may be based only on his almost daily supplication for acceptance as a protégé, for justice, or for material assistance.

His lines contain a procession of the names of those who were in power in Baghdad. The first historical personage that Fuzūlī had before him was Shāh Ismā'īl (1499–1524). He was the leader of tribes of Turcoman Shiites, and was venerated by his people as the incarnation of the deified 'Alī. He was also the author of erotic, mystic and religious poetry in praise of 'Alī and of the imāms, and also of warlike hymns intended to incite his followers to go on from one victory to another. In 1501 Shāh Ismā'īl had taken Tabrīz, made it his capital, and assumed the title of Shāhinshāh-i Īrān 'the king of kings of Iran'. He sent forth a decree ordering that 'the people should loosen their tongues in public in cursing and execrating Abū Bakr, 'Omar and 'Uthmān—and whoever dared to disobey would be beheaded'.[11b] In 1508 he entered Baghdad, massacred the Sunnite population, disinterred the remains of famous Sunnites, and destroyed their mausoleums. He paid his devotions at the Shiite sanctuaries of Husayn at Karbalā' and of 'Alī at Najaf, making generous offerings and providing bountifully for the upkeep of the monuments. In 1510 he defeated the Uzbek Khan Muhammad Shaybānī near the town of Merv and from his victim's skull he made a goblet for his banquets. Fuzūlī alludes to this act of medieval barbarism when he sings a hosanna to the Shāh in an allegorical poem in Turkish: 'He who for his convivial banquets fashions the cups out of the heads of emperors.'

Beng u Bāde (this is the title of Fuzūlī's poem) is not really dedicated to the Shah, as is commonly said, because there are no words of presentation in the book or even a precise appeal as in the case of proper dedications. The Shah is praised only as the reigning monarch. Probably Fuzūlī was too young and obscure a poet to dare to address his own works to the powerful monarch. Shāh Ismā'īl is perhaps 'the sovereign of time' named in an ode in Persian where a line which mentions the deification of 'Alī seems to repeat a line in Turkish written by that Shāh himself.[12]

It seems that Fuzūlī had direct contact with the Kurd Ibrāhīm Khān, the Safavid governor of Baghdad after 1514. In one of the works dedicated to this person Fuzūlī greets him on his arrival in Baghdad, describes his visit to the sacred Shiite places, speaks of his arrival in Najaf, of his benevolence to the descendants of 'Alī and the keepers of the sanctuary, and at the very end begs that he himself should be remembered.[13] According to one source Fuzūlī must have gone to Baghdad in the service of Ibrāhīm Khān.[14]

The period from the death of Ibrāhīm Khān, defeated and killed by his nephew Dhū 'l-faqar, to the setting up of the Ottoman dominion is amongst the most troubled and obscure in the history of this region. The last Safavid governor of Baghdad was Muhammad Khān Tekelü. It may be surmised that it is to him that an ode written by Fuzūlī in Persian is addressed. In this ode a lamb tells its own sad story in the first person. It tells how it found itself among a tribe of rough, disorderly, and rebellious Bedouins and how it suffered all sorts of afflictions. It managed to get away and seek refuge among the victorious hosts of the Khān, but was here set upon by troops, who threaten to kill it. It repents of having taken sides with the Arabs and, petrified with fear, it begs for mercy. It would seem obvious that the lamb represents no other than the poet himself, who found himself compromised in a revolt. The lamb-poet's mixed feelings are worthy of note. While condemning and despising the Bedouins he seems to justify their actions by the poverty of their lives. Faced by huge accumulated debts from unpaid taxes they are unable to pay a single *dīnār*. They are forced to flee hither and thither. Their cows do not calve and their sheep can hardly bear the weight of their own tails, let alone a lamb. They themselves are always alert as if afraid of surprise attacks.[15] We do not know if this is the Khān in whose household Fuzūlī declares in another Persian ode that he found peace and tranquillity.[16]

Suleymān the Magnificent's solemn entry into Baghdad on November 30, 1534, opens a new page in the history of this region. Suleymān the Magnificent stayed for four months and firmly established the Ottoman dominion. Fuzūlī enthusiastically adhered to the new regime. There are many reasons for his behaviour.

First of all he must have been dissatisfied with the Safavid domination. According to his words (which should not be taken too literally, for the attempt at flattering the conqueror is evident), 'Destiny using the hosts of calamity wanted to throw the means of existence of this kingdom into disorder. Godlessness had invaded the land and overcome Islam. Ignorance, getting the upper hand, had debased men of learning.'[17] Secondly, Suleymān, in contrast to the Shiite fanaticism of Shāh Ismā'īl, had given no indication of being a Sunnite fanatic, and so tried to capture the hearts of his new Shiite subjects. On one hand he had the remains from the profaned Sunnite tombs collected and put back again in their mausoleums. He also visited the sanctuaries of the Imāms Kāzim and Javād outside Baghdad, that of 'Alī at Najaf, that of Husayn at Karbalā', all places very dear to the Shiites. At Karbalā' in fact he ordered that a canal of water from the Euphrates should water that land where once the martyr Husayn had suffered tremendous thirst. Suleymān must have appeared to the poet as the restorer of order and justice, 'a conqueror without grudges, without greedy desire for earthly goods and wealth, seeking only the well-being of the Muslim religion'.[18]

Fuzūlī's attraction to the Ottoman sultan was not only of an idealistic order but had also a solid material basis of individual interest. Fuzūlī confesses this with surprising frankness: he longed to have a position at the court and wanted to become famous and reach a place of honour. He even gives a philosophical justification of all this. 'In the world of forms' the attributes of God are manifested and from thence infinite pleasures descend. The "world of power" (*mulk*) is not separate from the "world of the spirit" (*malakūt*) and he who has no acquaintance with power cannot arrive at the mysteries of that world; obviously, supplicating the reigning powers induces them to show bountiful largess.'[19]

Fuzūlī, who according to one source was then at Hilla,[20] greeted the arrival of the Ottoman sultan with a formal ode which opens with a list of the virtues of Baghdad and the surrounding country. The poet dared not offer it to the Sultan personally and he addresses him through Fortune (*devlet*). 'In the name of God, O Fortune, thou who art at home in his court, if the occasion should present itself do not fail to make my condition known. I have a thousand pearls of praise for the Courtyard of Sincerity but I cannot find the right moment to strew them one by one in homage to the court.'[21] Of these 'pearls' we have two other odes.[22] Besides the Sultan, Fuzūlī, coming down by degrees and beginning with the Grand Vizier Ibrāhīm, addresses his verses to the higher Ottoman dignitaries who have arrived in Baghdad.

In the first ode, dedicated to Suleymān, Fuzūlī recalls 'Alī and mentions the tragedy of Karbalā' which demonstrated the 'mystery of God' that is to say the illegitimacy of the Umayyad dynasty.[23] However he calls 'Alī the last of the 'four friends', the expression which the Sunnites used when speaking with veneration of the first four caliphs. He therefore makes honourable mention of the first three, who had been defamed by the Shiites, and he takes great care not to curse them as Shāh Ismā'īl had decreed.[24] Besides he defines the learned Sunnite Abū Hanīfa, one of those whose remains were dishonoured by Shah Ismā'īl, as 'greatest imam'. Elsewhere Suleymān is called 'Sultan of the Religion', 'chief sustainer of the Law of Islam'. He is exalted as 'successor of the successors of the Prophet', and it is stated that 'he who does not obey his orders is no Muslim'. Finally he is exalted as 'the Sultan of the Throne of the Caliphate' (*khilāfet*).[25] Fuzūlī had evidently diluted his Shiism. His position is open to diverse interpretations. It would seem reasonable to exclude his conversion to Sunnism, for later on we see him again as a fervent Shiite. It could be thought that he was masking his real beliefs following the Shiite principle of *taqiyya*, which was strictly applicable only under threat of persecution, and that does not seem to have been the case under Suleymān. From the words of the poet which have already been mentioned it would seem to be obvious that Fuzūlī allowed himself to be led by considerations of opportunism which were not at all difficult to reconcile with that form of moderate Shiism which he professed. As for the 'caliphate' of Suleymān, without taking into consideration that the title 'caliph of caliphs' had been brought by those very Safavid governors of Baghdad, it must be remembered that the Shiite imams in their time had not opposed the Abbasid caliphate, and that a theory of the caliphate different from that of the Ash'arite school formed by the philosophers, authorized the Ottoman sultan to be considered caliph.[26] In this respect it must have been of particular importance for Fuzūlī that this ruler had taken possession of Baghdad, the ancient seat of the caliphs, and that, besides promoting religion with impartiality, he was waging a holy war against the infidels. He reigned over the holy cities of Mecca and Medina and finally he was the most powerful Muslim sovereign of his time, having dominion over 'Turks,

Persians, and Arabs'.[27] On the other hand the titles which Fuzūlī attributes to the Ottoman Sultan in his literary works are after all vague and do not presuppose any theoretical conception, so much so that there is no trace of them where they should have appeared—that is in a theoretical work by Fuzūlī (see Ch. II).

What did Fuzūlī get in return for this devotion which probably never ceased to worry his conscience and for the gift of the fruits of his muse? It would seem only a pension of nine *aqches* a day on 'the surplus of the budget' (*zevā'id*) of the Shiite sanctuaries, a pension which among other things the overzealous administration refused to give him on the pretext that the budget had no surplus. The poet was obliged to appeal to the Ottoman Nishānjī, who had given him his 'award', in a subtly ironic letter in which he explains the reasons for his appeal to Suleymān 'whose rank of Sultan was ideally that of caliph and whose throne in reality was the seat of the Imam'.[28]

We do not know the result of the appeal but it is to be believed that Fuzūlī's request was met. His Ottoman biographer 'Āshīq Chelebi, who wrote in 1566, ten years after Fuzūlī's death, but who believed that he was still alive, affirms that the poet after being granted a pension which assured 'his sustenance, in fact a life of ease', had lived and was living 'in peace and prosperity'.[29] But the Ottoman writer, who had probably been anxious to point out that his own government had fittingly provided for the poet seems to exaggerate the well-being produced by the pension which was in itself pitiful.

What is certain is that one or two years after the departure of Suleymān from Baghdad in the poem *Leylā and Mejnūn* which was completed in AH 942/AD 1535–6, Fuzūlī complains that his deeds have not been recompensed and that fate was protecting the dishonest and humiliating those like himself who were faithful and honest, and lastly he makes known his own state of poverty and need. The poem is a new attempt to win the approval of the Ottoman rulers.

The subject is supposed to have been suggested by Ottoman friends. But this idea of suggestion is a convention and, even admitting its existence in this case, the intention of offering a local story to the new lords of Baghdad was probably not unconnected with the poet's choice—in fact, during the rearrangements of the legend of Mejnūn the headquarters of his tribe were moved from Najd towards Baghdad (in the poem it is said that Mejnūn's father lived 'whiles at Basra, whiles at Baghdad').[30] In the introduction Fuzūlī not only mentions 'the four friends' but praises the first three respectively for sincerity, justice and mercy. 'Alī's modesty is recalled but, in contrast to *Beng u Bāde*, the praise of 'Alī, which was customary in the works of Shiite writers, is omitted.

The poet complains of the decadence of poetry in Baghdad, that poetry is held for unbelief and nobody notices the lines which he forges by 'swallowing blood and pledging his soul'. His ambition is great. The great poets of ancient times who enjoyed high patronage have disappeared—Abū Nuwās, whose patron was Hārūn ar-Rashīd, Nizāmī patron the Shah of Shirvan, Navā'ī patron Husayn Baiqara, have all gone. Poetry was dying not only in Baghdad but everywhere, in India, in Persia, in Anatolia and in the Caucasus, and he felt it his duty to bring it back to fashion. He had great talent but he observed with bitter irony that it was not great enough to merit the attention of Suleymān. In the meantime the poem is dedicated to the second Ottoman governor of Baghdad, Üveys Pasha, to whose generosity the poet appeals in the Preface without exactly saying what he desired because the governor's generosity made that superfluous. At the end he claims to have been poorly rewarded ('Ask me then what they gave me!').

Fuzūlī knew how to adapt his words of praise to the different types of psychology of those whom he was praising. Üveys Pasha loved wine and tranquillity. An ode dedicated to him therefore opens in praise of the bottle, and in another it is said that at that time life was so safe that there was no need for walls and gates: for 'the carpenter's saw said to the bricklayer's pick: stone and wood no longer need fear our cruelty'.[31] Fuzūlī hoped for and perhaps got some assistance from the Pasha. In the first of the two odes quoted it is said: 'While at other times cruel destiny forced a thousand cups to drink blood—today favours the cup's revenge on destiny.' (Certainly the cup is a symbol for the poet.[32]) From another ode which seems to date from 1538 it appears that 'the applicant's requests were effortlessly met'.[33]

On the other hand it cannot be excluded that it is really to Üveys that the words 'constipated hearts' refer in an ode addressed to his successor Ja'fer Pasha.[34] This latter was a literary man with leanings towards mysticism. Fuzūlī exalts the pen, condemns the sword and declares his rejection of the help of the mighty—in virtue of his mystic ideals and so as not to bow before the fatuous and presumptuous. But he is ready to serve a worthy person like the Pasha and begs to be admitted to his presence ('the honey of union' alludes to the mystic union).[35] From various vague indications it would seem that he did not obtain a position (*maqām*) in the Pasha's service.[36] 'Fuzūlī was admitted to the presence of the governor. He was not, however, able to establish frequent contacts, for more than once he expresses sorrow at not being near and a desire to see him'.[37] All except the poet himself were given benefits by the Pasha: 'a whole ocean flows from Turkey to Iraq, but my parched lips remain thirsty'.[38]

The fourth Ottoman Governor of Baghdad, Ayās Pasha, used the sword rather than the cup or pen. Fuzūlī encouraged him to move against rebellious Basra in 953/1546. He sings of his departure and describes the course of events during the expedition and its victorious return. The poet sets the undertaking in the general picture of the struggle for hegemony in the Indian Ocean between the Turks and the Portuguese. He defines Basra as 'the borders of India' and he is pleased that the ambitions of the 'Franks' have been thwarted. He is also pleased about the check the Shiite sultans of Southern India, the Nizāmshāhī of Ahmadnagar and the Qutbshāhī of Golconda, have suffered. Finally he hopes that the conquest of Basra will be 'the key to peace in Persia'.[39]

At the time of Ayās Pasha Fuzūlī again showed signs of his Shiite faith. He greeted the arrival of the new Governor as he had greeted Suleymān with an ode which opens in praise of Baghdad and where for the first time in about ten years there is a reference to 'Alī, 'the cupbearer of Kauthar' (a river in Paradise), reference to the Shiite belief in the redeeming function of 'Alī.[40] The fact is that the Pasha turned out to be particularly devoted to 'Alī and while on his way to Basra paid a visit of devotion to his tomb at Najaf where Fuzūlī was. No other Ottoman Governor before him had ever done such a thing.[41]

Probably some of the odes in Persian, written with renewed fervour in praise of 'Alī the fourth caliph and of his tomb at Najaf, date from this period. The poet thanks God for having allowed him to live from the beginning to the end of his life at the venerated mausoleum and declares that he has been singing 'Alī's praises for fifty years. As an old man, on taking up again that work which he had begun in his youth, he wants to show his willingness to make amends for his past negligence and he is repentant of having sung the praise of others.[42] In the same atmosphere, as is confirmed by another mention of fifty years passed in praising 'Alī, we must place another ode in Persian in which Fuzūlī greets the emissary sent by the Indian sovereign Nizāmulmulk to Najaf and Karbalā'.[43] It seems that this person is to be identified as Burhān Nizāmshāh, the Sultan of Ahmadnagar in the Deccan (d. 961/1553) who in 1537 had solemnly embraced Shiism and like Shāh Ismā'īl imposed the execration of the first three caliphs.[44]

There is no way of putting an exact date to the ode but circumstances would suggest that it comes later than the ode which in 1546 Fuzūlī had addressed to Ayās Pasha with a malevolent allusion to the Indian sovereigns. The poet now openly exalts the Twelver Shī'a (this is the only direct declaration of faith which has so far passed unobserved) and sings the praises of the Indian monarch who lavished gifts of gold on the shrines of Najaf and of Karbalā' where later he was piously buried according to Shiite customs.

During the period when Ayās Pasha was governor, Fuzūlī moved from Najaf to Baghdad. Or at least it would seem so from an ode in Turkish addressed to the Governor. The poet declares that he has left 'his own place' because his talent was wasted there, and that he was ambitious to improve his lot. It is springtime and Fuzūlī wishes that the nightingale might enjoy the rose's company and that he himself might be able to see the rose-cheeked Pasha. In the meantime he lives alone, nobody asks for him, and he has no friends.[45]

Finally Fuzūlī addresses the usual complaints about his circumstances to Mehmed Pasha, one of the last governors of Baghdad during the poet's lifetime.[46] He was responsible and meritoriously so in the eyes of the Shiites for having taken the water to Karbalā'.[47]

It seems that Fuzūlī spent several years in the latter part of his life at Karbalā' in the attempt to collect his scattered poems[48] and to write on the orders of that very Mehmed Pasha a free reconstruction of a Persian work on the tragedy of Karbalā' by Husayn Vā'iz Kāshifī.

Besides beseeching the Ottoman governors of Baghdad Fuzūlī did not neglect even from afar to put himself forward in Constantinople. He sent Suleymān a long composition in verse entitled *Anīsu 'l-qalb*. He dedicated an ode to the Grand Vizier Rustem Pasha,[49] and by means of a friend who was going to the Bosporus he sent a message to the Grand Chancellor Mustafā Jelālzāde.[50] Fuzūlī perhaps derived greater satisfaction from the friendship of people of lower rank with whom he had dealings than from his contacts with the higher powers of the empire.

A gleam of light is thrown on to the private life of Fuzūlī in a poem in Persian in which he expresses his bitterness at the behaviour of a son who, having reached adulthood, no longer wishes his father's company. The father who is now old and weak does not feel like swallowing this bitter pill in silence; but on the other hand, should he vent his grievances, he fears he will be criticized. It will be better for both of them if the son goes away to conquer the world. When the young of the hawk can fend for itself then it is better that it should leave the nest.[51] It is believed that this son was Fazlī, a poet himself and of some merit too, but one who seems not to have had a good temperament. In an anonymous quatrain in Persian it is said satirically 'The world is upside down, the father (Fuzūlī "the presumptuous") is virtuous (*fazlī*) and the son (Fazlī "the virtuous one") is presumptuous (*fuzūlī*).'[52]

Throughout his life Fuzūlī never left Mesopotamia although he cherished the ambition to be listened to at court. As a young man he dreamt of going to Tabrīz: 'O Fuzūlī, it would seem that your heart does not want to hear of Baghdad since you would gaze fondly upon

Tabrīz the seat of pleasures.'[53] Later he turns his eyes to Constantinople and in a couplet similar to the preceding one the land of Rūm (or rather Anatolia, the Byzantine 'Rome') takes the place of Tabrīz. 'O Fuzūlī! My heart which you see a prisoner in the torment of Baghdad would prepare to go to the land of Rūm—seat of pleasures.'[54] The poet says the same thing in another couplet: 'Oh Fuzūlī! If thou shouldst wish to grow in virtue (*fazl*), turn to the land of Rūm and abandon the land of Baghdad.'[55] In times of sorrow he even expressed the idea of emigrating to India where Persian and Turkish poets were welcomed at the courts of the Moguls.[56]

Fuzūlī's humble life came to an end probably at Karbalā' in 963/1556 as the result of an epidemic of plague.[57]

It would be unjust if a picture of Fuzūlī were to be limited to the pieces of information given up to this point, which would seem to portray him as an individual who was eternally discontent and for ever begging. Above all it must be remembered that complaints of poverty, of incomprehension and hostility of others, of adverse fortune, which are spread throughout his works, always in vague terms, are commonplace to the poetic tradition to which he belonged, and he cannot be blamed for having followed the custom of his time in addressing the powerful in order to have his own merits recognized. External evidence or the contents of his writings present Fuzūlī in another light. His biographer 'Ahdī, who is well informed—as being not only a contemporary but also a fellow-countryman of the poet—describes him as being 'of a pleasant nature and pleasing in conversation'.[58] Humorous attitudes in his work, as we shall see, confirm this definition. Lines like 'The nobility of my valour would never stoop to accept even if Solomon (or Suleymān!), offered me his gifts' are certainly daring, and often his poetical satire is courageous (see Ch. II). That Shiite religious sentiment on the one hand and the ideals of Islamic mysticism on the other had deep roots in the soul of Fuzūlī is sufficiently attested by the large place they occupy in his writings. It is not without a reason that his biographer 'Āshīq Chelẹbi who has already been quoted shows him as 'prostrate on the path leading to mystic annihilation'.[59] What is certain is that his life, apart from his worries and troubles, was mainly filled with love and poetry. This is borne out in Fuzūlī's divan, and in other words of the same 'Āshīq Chelebi who says that 'his heart was ruined by love' and in the 'wind of the passion of love' he sees the reason why Fuzūlī 'fell far from the abode of wealth' and why 'his lines are enflamed'.[60]

CHAPTER TWO

THE WORKS OF FUZŪLĪ

Fuzūlī has left us writings in Turkish, Persian and Arabic. This trilingualism was not rare among Turkish writers and is explainable by their cultural formation which was based in fact on Arabic religious and scientific tradition and on Persian literary tradition. In Fuzūlī's case the use of the three languages was conditioned also by his particular environment because all three tongues were in use in Iraq in his time. The ability to write in more than one language was one of the things of which Fuzūlī was most proud and one of his favourite habits (he is not alone in this) is to use two or three languages alternately in some of his poetry and prose. However, Fuzūlī's fame rests mainly on his work in Turkish and it is of this which we shall speak first.

In the sixteenth century, at the time of Fuzūlī, Turkish literature already possessed a long history. There had already been pre-Islamic Turkish literature, which had been mainly religious and drew its inspiration from Manichaeism, from Buddhism and from Nestorianism. From the eleventh century on, an Islamic Turkish literature had developed, first in central Asia and then later in Asia Minor following on the Seljukian political expansion and the subsequent spreading of the Turks in that area. This literature had slowly evolved under the influence of Persian literature, forming schools such as the Timurid in central Asia and the Ottoman in Anatolia. Between the two, to the East of Anatolia and in Iraq itself, Fuzūlī's country, there had been no lack of literary blossoming especially of poetry. Although he lived in a remote area, a fact which he himself regrets, Fuzūlī knew at first hand the works of the Persian masters and was well-informed on the advanced Turkish literary tradition, not only the local but also the Central-Asiatic and Ottoman ones.[1] Among other people he must have met the Ottoman poet Khayālī who had come to Baghdad with the retinue of Suleymān and was greatly favoured by Suleymān, who kept him like 'a hawk which fed from his hand and never left his wrist'.[2] Fuzūlī was led to write in Turkish not only by the fact that it was his mother tongue but also by political circumstances. Shāh Ismā'īl, who conquered

Baghdad in the poet's day, has left us a divan in Turkish. After the Ottoman conquest Turkish literature acquired a greater importance in this region than it had had at the time of the Safavids. Fuzūlī expresses Turkish prestige in words which at that time were not exaggerated, 'the high ranking Turks constitute a large part of world order and a numerous category of the human species'.[3]

Nevertheless he complains that to write 'delicate' verse in Turkish rather than in Persian was difficult because the Turkish language is loath to be put into lines since the words are mostly without connection and lacking in harmony. (Perhaps the reference is to the lack of compound words and long vowels in Turkish.[4]) Even as far as prose is concerned he finds Turkish words for the most part 'sluggish' and 'disharmonious'.[5]

Fuzūlī's main works in Turkish are the divan of ghazals, the qasidas, and the poem *Leylā and Mejnūn*. To judge from the preface to the divan, the ghazals should belong to his youth. However, there are references to old age in some of the ghazals and it would seem that, although they are for the most part products of his early years, they do on the whole represent poetic activity which was carried on till old age. Altogether there are about three hundred ghazals mostly composed of seven couplets in accordance with a custom which had already been established with Fuzūlī's two masters, the Persian Jāmī and the Turk Navā'ī both from Herat. Each couplet is often quite separate from what precedes or follows it. The couplets are held together not so much by a theme or by a fundamental common source of inspiration as by the rhyme's sometimes being complemented by an echo rhyme (by the repetition of one or more suffixes or words). This gives the composition a certain unity but it is prevalently extrinsic in nature. Only in rare cases do ghazals show a certain unity of subject and inspiration. In the last couplet it was customary to mention the *makhlas*, that is, the author's *nom de plume*.

A characteristic fact is that the *Divan* opens with a ghazal dedicated to love, instead of to God as was usual, but this fact is explained because the love which is dealt with is divine love. This composition is clearly intended by the poet to be the keystone to the whole collection.

Love shone upon the way of revelation for lovers. He who travelleth along the way of truth hath love for a guide.
Love is that perfect intoxication from which the manifestation of the warmth of wine and the effect of the sound of the flute come.
The vale of unity is in reality the station of love, since in that vale the Sultan differeth not from the beggar.

The initiated in the retreat of the mystery of Unity doth not separate the lover from the beloved or the beloved from the lover.
O thou who urgest the people of love to avoid prejudice, answer 'Is it ever possible to change our destiny pre-ordained by the Lord?'
The pen of love hath thus traced these letters on the table of the existence of the lover: Be firm in the affirmation of the Truth [God's] and in the negation of all that is not He!
O Fuzūlī! Thou hast found infinite pleasure in love and so be it with everything which thou beginneth in the name of God!

A word or two of explanation is necessary for those who have no knowledge of Muslim mysticism, the so-called Sufism both in Persian and Turkish literary conventions. The ghazal translated above bears the stamp of a particular theory which had been elaborated among the Sufis and was largely accepted in poetry. This theory is singularly akin to the theory of Platonic love, which among other things is expressed in the following passage from Plato's *Phaedrus*:

When the newly-initiated, one of those who have gazed on high, seeth a face, of appearance divine and reflecting that beauty well, or a beautiful person, he first trembles, his ancient fear seizes him and then turning his eyes towards this beauty he admires him as if he were a god. If he feared not to seem a complete fool, he would do sacrifice to the beloved as if he were an idol or as if he were a god. (251a)

It is not certain however that Sufic love derives from the Platonic conception of love. To the formation of the Sufic myth various elements have contributed in various degrees. These elements exalted and spiritualized love, such as the so-called 'Udhrite Arabic poetic ideal of love which swore the lover to chastity and death, either the ideas of twin souls destined to meet again in the world, inspired by Platonic texts (*Symposium*) or of the substantial unity between lover and beloved; or exhorted a disinterested contemplation of the beautiful one, such as the invitation of the Zāhirite theological school to 'look upon the beardless youth and the woman of others' (something which was disapproved of by strict Islamic morals, which decree that in the presence of such people the eyes should be kept on the ground); or referred to supposed sayings of the Prophet such as 'Seek good in those of a handsome face', or 'Three things there are which give light to the eyes: to look upon the green of nature, gaze upon water, and look into a beautiful face'. This is either attribution of a preparatory function to human love, as in the Zāhirite doctrine that human love with the suffering it brings is an exercise which accustoms to obedience to God, or the theory of a relationship between God and human beauty, whence the idea that God shows himself in various forms which are 'veils' or 'curtains' hiding his beauty which, were it manifest, would consume the world. The foundation on which the Sufic myth of love is based, as it is found in Persian and Turkish poetry, is however a theory formulated mainly by the Arab mystic Ibn 'Arabī of Murcia (1165–1240). God created the world and, in particular, man so that He might contemplate Himself in His creation and enjoy this contemplation in the same way as did Narcissus. All earthly beauty is but the reflection of the Divine. What every lover in reality loves in the beloved is the beauty of God or, better, God loves Himself. So the theory of double love is outlined: 'real' love or love of God, and 'metaphoric' love, that is love for the beautiful in human form, 'witness' (*shāhid* with reference to the Koran LXXX. 3) of God which is only a bridge thrown across towards 'true' love. The lines of the ghazal, which allude to the mystic union, refer to such a function of love. This is the stage in which all duality between lover and beloved disappears. The lover loses the consciousness of his own individual ego and identifies himself with the cosmic I.

Not all the Sufis maintained that it was necessary to pass through the stage of metaphorical love, and many dedicated themselves only to the 'true' love. Fuzūlī is not among these.

O thou who dost advise me, deny me not comely youths! The 'metaphor' is the splendour of the sunlight of Truth! (CXIV. 6).

He dedicated his whole life to the practice of love:

I am a whirlwind which became giddy for the passion of love: wherever I've stopped, I've thrown my dust to the heavens (CXC. 6).

The ending of the divan is no less significant than the beginning. It is represented by two ghazals composed probably at the moment when the collection was being formed or at least put where they are intentionally.[6] The collection thereby acquires its own spiritual unity. At the outset Fuzūlī declares his own faith in love and then in thousands of lines he tells of his own amorous experiences. At the end, when he is already on the threshold of old age, he confesses that he has been entangled in the toils of sinful love. He has repented and decided to entrust his own salvation to the cult which is related directly to God and to the observation of the Law of Muhammad:

O mine eyes no longer look upon those bloodthirsty narcissi [the eyes of the beloved] *no longer darken my life with the sickness of love!*

O tears! abandon this bewilderment! No longer bar the way for those who are as stately as the cypress tree.
O heart! Thou hast given my heart to the winds with love!
No longer gaze upon every rosebud mouth and rose-petal cheek—Sigh no more!
O my soul! Look not upon the downy cheeks of the beloved!
Take care! Add not sin to sin!
O Fuzūlī! Leave the taste of wine and of the beloved—no longer make thyself a rebel to the court of God! (CCLXXXIV)

O heart! The very end of life hath come, hast thou not enough of the pleasures of the cheeks of the beloved?
Thy hair is grey, hast thou not enough of the passion [blackness] for the black locks of the friend? . . .
Thine ears have heard the sound of the bell announcing the departure from the garden of fate.
Why movest thou not, hast thou not enough of contemplating the rose of the face? . . .
Thy friends with difficulty have reached the stage of the right way.
Thou alone hast remained in error.
O Fuzūlī! Hast thou not enough of such shame? Say not that it is difficult to reach the desired goal, shall not perhaps he who grasps the folds of the Law of Ahmed the Chosen One [Muhammad] *arrive there?* (CCLXXXIX)

These lines bear eloquent witness to the fact that mystic love was none other than a literary tradition imposed on the poet, an ideal which lent a halo of spirituality to the expression of earthly love. According to a definition given by a famous Turkish writer of Herat, 'Alī Shēr Navā'ī, Fuzūlī is therefore one of the poets who mingle 'metaphoric' with 'true' love.[7]

In reality we do not know who was the object of Fuzūlī's love, since it was a rule not to mention explicitly the name of the loved one. We cannot even say whether it was a male or a female because in Turkish (as in Persian) there is no grammatical category of gender. However it may be supposed that it was youths rather than maidens or women. This may be supposed not so much on the grounds of what we know about the widespread practice of homosexual love in Persian and Turkish society (it seems originally to have been foreign to the Arabs), as on the grounds that the love of the mystics was preferably for the handsome youth. Love for women was considered as being more susceptible to the seduction of the senses. On the other hand some of Fuzūlī's lines speak of a 'Christian youth' (CXXI. 6) or of a 'son of a janissary' (CC. 1). Ghazals are dedicated to a youth riding a charger (XXXVII), another going to the public bath (CLXXXII), to a barber (XXXI), to a shoemaker (CCXLIV). Then it must be remembered that since the language of love had become the means of expression of all types of ideas, it cannot be excluded (in fact in many cases it is the most obvious interpretation) that the expressions of love are simply expressions of friendship and moreover of homage to the powerful who has been identified with the beautiful 'witness' of God.

The theme of the ghazals never departs from the circle of conventional motives which ambiguously lend themselves to interpretation both in the sense of 'true' love and 'metaphoric'—either as friendship or courtly honour. Not only are the themes conventional but the language also is basted together by means of commonplace sayings which the poet tries to enliven with conceits and complex figures of speech. The description of the loved one, for example, is just a list of metaphors rather than a description. His face, his teeth, his body are compared to the sun, to the rose, to pearls, to the cypress tree, etc. Fuzūlī does not limit himself to the statement of the metaphor but he often presents it by way of the rhetorical figure of aetiology, which consists of giving some graceful but fictitious reason for some fact or occurrence. In this way the beauty of the loved one exceeds all possible comparisons:

Do not imagine that what you can see on the earth is the shining of the sun [what has happened is that] *the revolving sky, on seeing* [the greater glory of] *my resplendent moon* [my beloved] *has flung its sun down to the earth* [in despair].

The wind consenteth not that the moist rose petal should rub its face in the dust of thy feet, if the dew doth not first wash his face [yüz] *one hundred* [yüz] *times* (CLVIII. 3).

The sun is in love with thy cheek, the tender rose petal with thy rubies [lips]. *Thou lackest not lovers. They come down from the sky and grow up from the earth* (CLII. 1).

Perhaps the breeze whispereth to the sea of thy teeth so that the rolling pearl within its shell may hear (X. 5).

Think not that it is the reflection of the cypress tree in the water. Having seen my gracefully moving cypress, the gardener hath uprooted his tree and thrown it into the water (XXXVI. 6).

The poet uses the same aetiological figure in a ghazal where the couplets all end with the echo rhyme 'the morning'. A secret meaning is given to the phenomena which accompany the rising of the sun:

I know not for love [mihr, also: sun] *of which moon weepeth the morning! It daily showeth to the world a hidden scar.*
The stars have set and the sun hath risen or else is the morning the slave of love and hath it strewn pearls of tears and drawn a sigh of blood?
Naturally the breath of the morning will raise the dead since at all times [or breath] *the morning repeateth the mention of thy rubies* [lips].
Perhaps the zephyr hath actually announced the arrival of a sun since the morning scattereth a thousand royal pearls for him.
The morning is a faithful lover. Every dawn reneweth his grief, and with sighs reawakeneth the sleeping people.
Morning is a painter who with his gilded pen draweth the cheek of the beloved on the face of heaven.
O Fuzūlī! There is no hope that the night of sorrow will end. They talk of the existence of morning only to comfort thee (LV).

The meaning of this ghazal is not exaggerated if we read God instead of the beloved, as is quite permissible in this type of poetry. The same thing may be said of the two following couplets.

Perhaps his goal is union with thee—Night and day the bewildered sky revolveth restlessly and untiringly.
The fresh breeze is linked by the chain of passion to thee. The ocean with parched lips thirsteth after the cup of union with thee (XXXII. 6).

Other metaphors connected with the portrayal of the sufferings of love are skilfully dealt with by the poet. By artistic devices he tried to establish a magic link between the beloved and the lover. The motif of the twin locks is for example elaborated thus:

My heart openeth on seeing thy locks so dishevelled. My tongue unfoldeth on seeing thy smiling rosebud [antithesis of open: closed] (LIII. 1).

Other very common motifs are the bosom set on fire by the sufferings of love or the smoke of burning sighs or the bloody tears:

On seeing thee riding about on horseback clad in a red robe, my [weeping] *eyes cause* [bloody/red] *fragments of my heart to float about in all directions upon* [the sea of] *my tears* (XXXVII. 3).

Incessantly [or drop by drop] *the pupils of my eyes drink blood for thy locks and thy beauty-spot. Thus it is usual for the men of the sea to get their sustenance from the land* [*qara* 'dry land' and 'black' referring to locks and to the beauty-spot] (LXXXVIII. 2).

Besides his use of various rhetorical devices Fuzūlī also adopts combinations of images to express the psychology of love:

Treat not the bleeding wound in my breast with balsam. Put not out the lamp that thou hast lit with thine own hand! (CCLXI. 1).

The morning breeze hath brought joyous news of a beauty rising like the sun. Alas! The time hath come for me to flicker out like a candle (XV. 5).

Open my breast and look upon the heart that suffereth for love!
Open the window and look upon the river rising in waves with every blast of wind! (LVIII. 5).

Is there wrong in the heart dragging body and soul toward the land of thy road? Twigs and straws are required when a bird builds its nest (LXXII. 2).

If in the desert of suffering the cypress of the whirlwind reareth its head over my tomb, O wave of the mirage, let not that cypress lack water! [reference to the love for a person as slender as a cypress] (XXIX. 4).

Finally, out of interest, I give some images which refer to typical institutions of the Ottoman Empire:

The sickness of our ailing heart found a remedy in thy village. Thou art an Agha—we are thy slaves, our tīmār [feudal fief] *is in thy village* (CXX. 1).

I have made the son of a janissary Sultan of the city of my heart.
It was like Egypt and I have made Joseph the Canaanite king [reference perhaps to the beloved's name Yūsuf] (CC. 1).

Draw not ever the sword of thy look to plunder the heart. Be not a sipāhī greedy of spoils in a land which is most humbly obedient! (CLXXIV. 2).

This last couplet is clearly satirical against the *sipāhī* corps, the feudal Ottoman cavalry.

The following ghazal dedicated to the pains of love shows a certain unity of inspiration. It is constructed entirely on the formula of the rhetorical question and embellished rhythmically by internal rhyme (except the first couplet) so that each couplet forms a quatrain.

My friend hath made me tired of life, will he not tire of being cruel?
My sighs have set fire to the heavens, will the candle of my desire not light?
My beloved distributeth medicine for the illnesses of all who are ailing for him. Why hath he no remedy for me? Thinketh he not that I am ill?
I was hiding my illness and they said, Reveal it to thy friend! Should I do so, I know not whether that infidel would believe me.
The night of separation [from my beloved] *burneth my soul. Mine eyes weep tears of blood. My sighs wake people up. Will not my fortune wake?*
A stream of blood floweth from mine eyes towards thy rose petal cheeks. O dear one! Now is the season of roses; will not this clear flowing water become muddy?
It was not I who turned to thee. Thou stolest my reason. Will not the unmindful fellow who blameth me be ashamed on seeing thee?
Fuzūlī, mad drunkard, is always despised by man. Ask him: Whatever passion is this? Will he never tire of this passion? (CCLXIV).

This ghazal is an example of Fuzūlī's easy style and meets the requirements that it should be 'easy to read and write'. This he considers essential to the type of composition which is mainly intended to be sung in order that it may become famous and widespread. This is stated in the prose preface to the divan. Elsewhere it is said that the ghazal must be enjoyed by all—be on the lips of those who love joy and merriment. Its contents must be pleasant and easy to understand. 'What is to be gained when the expression is abstruse and whoever listeneth is bored?'[8] Single lines, if not entire ghazals, based on this assumption are not rare. This effective fluency is one of the best poetic qualities of Fuzūlī and one of the main reasons for his success. In this connection, a couplet which has become famous may be quoted:

Pull not thy skirts waywardly back from those who have fallen at thy feet! Stand in fear lest those grasping hands should invoke Heaven! (LXXXV. 3).

One characteristic of Fuzūlī's divan is the accentuated idealization of love, in the sense of that which once was called 'Udhrite Arabic love (see Ch. III) and thus Sufic love. The concepts of the fatality of love, of absolute and complete dedication to the beloved, of total sacrifice to him, of pleasure in suffering, of love as liberation, are all concepts which keep recurring, some more, some less often in Persian and Turkish divans, but perhaps no one uses them so often and so intensely as does

Fuzūlī. These very concepts are at the basis of the poem *Leylā and Mejnūn*, which is our main object of interest.

My head reeled in passion in the valley of love even before this Rolling Dome [the sky] *began on its revolving way* (CXXII. 3).

Prepare the table of thy conscience like a mirror for the image of the beloved. Remember him alone and forget all that is in thy memory (XLV. 6).

Would that I with my broken heart might have a thousand lives to sacrifice to thee one by one! (XVII. 3).

Since I have fallen prey to love sickness I am free in fate. O Lord, inflict me more with the sickness of love! (XLII. 6).

More than other poets Fuzūlī insists on the denial of the physical pleasures of love. The concept constitutes the central point of the poem *Leylā and Mejnūn*. The lover does not yearn for the physical presence of the beloved; in fact he prefers distance, for he knows that material union is ephemeral:

What is desired of the beautiful is the union that satisfieth. The lover asketh merely to contemplate without possessing (CXXXVIII. 1).

Look no longer on me for the passion of the pleasure of union with the friend, because I have bartered the pleasure of union for the torment of separation (CXCVII).

O Fuzūlī, I have well observed the linking together of the causes in the Creation. There is no enjoyment without repentance like that of contemplation without possession (CLVI. 7).

It is obvious that the transient joy of 'metaphoric' love is ideally contrasted with the eternal beatitude of the mystic union.

The poet himself says that he intended that the quintessence of the divan should be the same as that of the story of *Leylā and Mejnūn*.

Listen to the woes of my heart. Turn not to the fable of Mejnūn, since this is the very meaning of the tale (XC. 4).

We are therefore not surprised at the numerous references to the mad Bedouin lover. Fuzūlī declares that he has taken his place or that he has surpassed him in love and madness.

The honour of love has without doubt been entrusted to me and to Mejnūn. We both bear the burden of this anguish, once he and now I (CCXVI. 2).

Fate entrusted me with the manners of love—and Mejnūn in spite of having run his utmost hath not yet reached me (XIII. 1).

Is this perhaps the whirlwind in the desert or is it the dust of Mejnūn, which has noted my arrival, upright in homage? (CLXXX. 5).

At other times he refers to motifs found in the poem, as for example the birds that nest on Mejnūn's head or the camel who takes Leylā to the last meeting with her lover (see Ch. V).

Think not that it is a bird's nest on bewildered Mejnūn's head. It is the whirlpool of the sea of madness which hath put thorns and straws together (CCXXX. 5; the same motif CXXXIII. 2).

The camel hath carried Leylā's palanquin to travel in the desert. O bell, warn Mejnūn of this! (CXXV).

Probably the ghazals in which there are references to attitudes of the idealization of love and to the legend of Mejnūn were written after the composition of the poem.

Two other themes that are closely linked with that of love in Persian and Turkish lyric poetry are widely represented in Fuzūlī's divan, without however showing deviations from the tradition. One of them is the Bacchic motive to which there is a reference in the introductory ghazal. Wine, which is a forbidden drink to strict Muslims, is sung of as the symbol of mystic love.

Come, let us lay our heads at the foot [ayaq, also cup] of the wine jar. One must bow to it. It is a high personage (XCIII. 3).

As a drunkard I have given up my soul. As a sign of honour the grape hath made a cupola and the pergola formed a hall [eyvān] over my tomb! (CLIV. 3).

In the following ghazal the exaltation of wine is linked with a brilliant description of the evening which might match the already translated description of the morning.

When the new moon becometh a key which openeth treasure houses, the night will let the cup of heaven count out jewels [paronomasia: *peymā* 'counting', *peymāne* 'cup'].

The amphora of heaven which hideth the spring water of the sun will let the stars drip out.
The azure vault of heaven will turn tulip purple in the dusk, like a crystal glass through which red wine sparkleth.
The cup-bearer of destiny will take round the cup of the new moon and will infuse the stars of the firmament with the intoxication produced by passion.
It is not surprising that like the dregs in the cup I seize the skirts of the wine; this philosopher's stone hath transformed so much earth into gold.
I too shall pour into the cup that life-giving liquor, from whose drops the tree of merry-making will grow, when the cup is passed round. O Fuzūlī! I'll sing of the wine, fire on the threshing floor of anguish, water of life to the wise (XXIII).

Often the theme of wine is associated with the theme of antinomianism, that is, the superiority of the practice of mystic love over the observance of the religious duties.

Without drinking wine the door of divine pardon openeth not, the old Zoroastrian sweareth [lit. drinketh oaths] *on this* (LXXVII. 3).

Drunkenness hath taken away from me the duty of prayer. God hath infused me with the intoxication of the rose-coloured wine cup (XIII. 2).

Far better than a thousand lessons which the master imparts in the college [medrese] *is that a handsome youth should offer a cup in a tavern* (CLXXIII. 6).

The condemnation of religious bigotry leads to the paradoxical reversal of values, by which, in the religion of love, disbelief is preferable to faith and the beloved is identified with God.

The preacher describeth Hell. O bigot, go to his sermon and see what Hell is! (CXXXI. 3).

God forbid that the chain of the lines of the Sacred Book should be an obstacle to me distracted by passion for thy beauty-spot! (CXLIX. 3).

It is not blasphemy to say that thy words are revelation inspired by God. While misbelief hath seized the world thou hast given news of faith (CLXV. 3).

It is my custom to prostrate myself whenever I see an idol. Think of me as an unbeliever or as a believer—this is my religion (CCVI. 1).

O angel figure, admired by all in astonishment: whosoever be man calleth thee not man but God (XXI. 1).

Another among the most common themes is that of contempt of worldly goods and earthly glory in the name of the so-called mystic 'poverty' (*faqr*, whence *faqīr*). The mystic in his own way is a sultan; as Fuzūlī says in the introductory ghazal, the kingdom of this world counts as nothing.

O thou who as sultan boastest that in the world there is none other than thee, know then that thou art an owl and the world ruins (XLIII. 6).

Seize the opportunity from the way of beggars in the kingdom of poverty. Forget the care for offices and the court of the Sultan! (XLV. 4).

Lastly, the venting of personal feelings takes up a large part of the divan, but it is always in the form of generic complaints:

No one hath pity on me [lit. burns for me] *except the fire of the heart. No one openeth the door, except the breeze* (CCLXXIII. 5).

Disgusted by my tears and sighs, people have gone away from me. Only waterspouts and whirlwinds are around me (LXII. 4).

The ghazal which pessimistically sums up the life of the poet in the field of love and elsewhere is famous! This is E. J. W. Gibb's translation:

Feres are heedless, spheres are ruthless, Fortune is inconstant quite;
Woes are many, friends not any, strong the foe, and weak my plight.
Past away hope's gracious shadow, passion's sun beats fierce and hot;
Lofty the degree of ruin, lowly is the rank of right.
Little power hath understanding, louder aye grows slander's voice,
Scant the ruth of fickle Fortune, daily worsens Love's despite.
I'm a stranger in this country, guile-beset is union's path;
I'm a wight of simple spirit, earth with faerie shows is dight.
Every slender figure's motions form a stream of sorrow's flood,
Every crescent-brow's a headline of the scroll that madness hight.
Learning's dignity's unstable as the leaf before the wind;
Fortune's workings are inverted, like the trees in water bright.
Sore desired the frontier, fraught with anguish lies the road of trial;
Yearned for is the station, all the path of proof beset with fright.
Like the harp's sweet voice, the longed-for beauty bides behind the veil;
Like the bubbles on the wine, reversed the beaker of delight.

Separation is my portion, dread the way to union's land;
Ah, I weet not where to turn me, none is here to guide aright.
Tears of cramoisie have seized on Fuzūlī's sallow cheek;
Lo, what shades the sphere cerulean maketh thereupon to light.[8b]

Up till now we have been considering the serious side of Fuzūlī's divan. There is another side, a humorous one which is represented however only by a few ghazals. This too had precedents in Persian and Turkish lyrics but perhaps no one before Fuzūlī had bestowed so much grace on the form. In the following ghazal, where the characteristic is the repetition in every couplet of the word 'fast', the poet succeeds in weaving in many humorous motives all on the theme of the ritual fast in the month of Ramadan (the antinomianism to which reference has been made should be kept in mind).

My full moon grown thin with fasting is so changed that for the closing festival it will but be a crescent.
The month [also the moon] of fasting hath made that sun fade away day by day. Think that the light of the sun passeth bit by bit to the moon.
This slimming by fasting hath perhaps changed my friend to a ghost, I know not. Otherwise that which I see is not my friend but a ghost?
If I were able to drink water (instead of wine!), I'd drink and dismiss fasting which before mine eyes wants my sun to set [read *içerdüm* with Tarlan's edn].
I would that the moon were eclipsed, that the sun should fall upon the earth in this period of fasting since my affectionate [mihr-bān, mihr: sun] *moon is annoyed by this month and days* [moon and sun].
Those wine-coloured rubies [lips of my beloved] *wish to drink my blood this night* [when after sunset, the Ramadan fast ends]. *They have been fasting* [all day] *and are presumably looking for some licit drink* [i.e. my blood—unlike wine, which is forbidden] *with which to break their fast.*
O Sun, remove the thought of food and drink from the fasters. Do good from morning to night, flaunt beauty.
O officer of the police [muhtasib], *dispense Fuzūlī from fasting. He is weak and cannot bear this burden* (CLXXI).

Another ghazal, also satiric in tone, is devoted to Ramadan. The holy month is shown in contrast to the paraphernalia of a Bacchanalian feast.

It is Ramadan. Beauty—Wine hath drawn its face behind the veil. The harp in mourning for wine hath let down her hair.
The musicians understood what was happening and took away the guitar. Bottle and pitcher removed themselves from the feast.

The law of the banquet hath been broken. Why do the harp and drum not join forces and rebel on the judge's doorstep?
The month of Ramadan, the gate of paradise must be opened. Is it just for the door of the tavern to be closed?
Let us recite the 'opening' Sura of the Koran so that the tavern will be opened; perhaps a closed door will open for us.
The sun of the cup riseth not in the month of Ramadan. Oh woe to us— what a dark day, O Lord!
While waiting for the rose-coloured wine and by continual watching for the Bayram moon our eyes will fail [lit. black water will fall over them].
It is Ramadan. Fuzūlī feareth to drink not for so many days and thus suddenly to become a bigot (CCXXXIX).

The terminology of a given environment is one of the components of such a trend of humour. In one ghazal, words from the art of the shoemaker appear, used in images referring to a handsome exponent of that art, as for example in the following couplet, which is the last:

He stretcheth at his feet like a boot, he who [for desperation in love] *rendeth his clothing: O Fuzūlī, look how disdainful he is!* (CCXLIV. 7).

Another ghazal which follows the same composition structure is dedicated to a handsome barber:

In the morning the sun drew his sword [or his razor] *across the sky* [or across the wheel] *and struck it on the stones* [or on the stone to sharpen it],
[So] *he showed himself to belong to that barber who resembles the moon.*
Time after time as a result of his razor's movement [shorn] *heads shine, in the same way as waves continually form bubbles in the water.*
If there were a head on every hair of my head, and if it should cut off all these like hair, I should not withdraw myself from his bleeding razor [also sword].
The mysteries of beauty are revealed by means of the essence [or metal] *of his razor since it pulleth back the veil of grace from the darkness* [or passion] *which covereth the head.*
Because of the anguish of my head [or caused by my head] *my body hath grown thin like a hair, since my head cometh between my body and his razor.*
It is fair that I should compare the Chinese gazelle to his swift razor since it scattereth pure musk in the desert of the curls [chīn; also China] *as it walketh by.*
I lose not hope that his razor might touch my ruffled locks, O Fuzūlī! for the clouds are full of flashing lightning! (XXXI).

Lastly, and this is the jewel of the genre, there is a ghazal which is dedicated to a handsome youth making for the public bath. It is a happy imitation of analogous ghazals composed previously by the Central Asian Turkish poet Lutfī and by the Persian Jāmī.

Early in the morning that graceful cypress tree, coy and with elegant gait, set out for the bath. The bath lit up with the radiance of his face.
His body could be seen at his open neck. He unrobed and showed the fullness of his new moon.
He wrapped his naked body in an indigo coloured apron. Imagine a shelled almond fallen among the violets.
The lips of the pool had the honour of kissing his foot. The eye of the glass window lit up on seeing his gentle face.
They thought his pearls of sweat [or aquavita] were for sale. Many put their hands to their purses [kīse: also 'massage glove'], *seized by vain hopes.*
The comb, as it loosened his locks, perfumed the air with musk. The razor, as it scattered his hair, coloured the ground with amber.
The bowl kissed his hand. Envy melted my liver. The water touched his members and jealousy took peace from my body.
He came out of the bath wrapped round with the curtain of my eyes, and quietly sat down in the corner of my eye [that is: I watched him furtively *or* out of the corner of my eye].
The pupils of mine eyes poured streams of water at his feet. Water must flow continually at the feet of the cypress trees.
O Fuzūlī! I shall offer my soul as money in payment of the bath. He who hath a cypress-like figure and silvery body doth not spend gold!
(CLXXXII).

A dozen verse compositions in stanza form, forty or so fragments of from 2–9 couplets, and more than seventy quatrains are added to the divan of ghazals.

One of these verse compositions is of a laudatory nature, rather like that of the qasidas of which we shall soon speak. The themes of the others are similar to those of the ghazals with a prevalence of moralizing and satire, as in these lines:

The sovereign who reigneth corrupting his people with gold and silver coins prepareth the army to conquer new lands.
Putting into action a thousand deeds of intrigue and evil he conquereth the land. This too is without trace of security and right. . . .
Let not sultans offer me their bounty in this world! The diadem of success (with God's assistance) in moderation on my head is sufficient for me.
Nothing in the world is important to me. Let it not be that in order to

support themselves the People of Eternity enslave themselves to the People of Dissolution (p. 496).

One verse composition is noteworthy because it is dedicated to a girl. This is the only open reference to a female in the divan. The following translation is by E. J. W. Gibb.

Roseate face, and shift of rosy hue, and trousers cramoisie:
Thou hast donned thy flaming garments, and hast made us fire to dree.
Paynim maiden, ne'er was born of seed of Adam one like thee;
Sun and moon in beauty's circle 'fore thy face undone would be.
Sure the shining moon's thy father, and the sun thy mother fair.[8c]

This circumstance should let us see that we should not exclude that the love of which some ghazals sing is addressed to women, even if the poet is always faithful to the conventional form used for youths.

Usually the divans of the Persian and Turkish poets are composed of ghazals and qasidas together. The latter are usually much longer compositions than the former and principally of a religious, or philosophic, and moreover encomiastic nature. Fuzūlī instead compiled a separate divan for his qasidas in Turkish, Arabic and Persian after he had already collected the ghazals. The reason for this singular procedure is given in the prose Preface to the qasidas[9]. He declares that while many qasidas had been lost, others had been hidden because it was not opportune (*na-munāsib*) for them to be known. He goes on:

Having wakened from the sleep of unawareness, I thought that it might be right to put together the remains of my writings which have been scattered and to collect those works that have been badly treated by fate so that saving them from the danger of being lost they might be known. Since they [the qasidas] *are a valuable kind of poetry it would be a pity if they were lost and did not bring pleasure to future generations* (p. 28).

Fuzūlī does not tell us the reasons for the concealing of some of the qasidas and of his successive repentance, but we may easily guess. It is not far from the truth to suppose that the clandestine qasidas were dedicated to important figures of the Safavid régime and were also those with a strong Shiite colouring. The decision to make them known was evidently taken long after the period of Safavid domination in Baghdad was over, when there were Ottoman governors like Ayās Pasha who were well disposed to the Shiites, and lastly after the passing of many years when the sentiment of Shiite piety had become very marked in Fuzūlī (see Ch. I). However, the qasidas which it can be presumed were not in circulation were for the most part in Persian.

There are (apart from the three in *Leylā and Mejnūn*) in all forty[10] Turkish qasidas. The first belongs to the type known as *tawhīd* inasmuch, as the Arabic word itself says, it develops the idea of God as the One and only Supreme Being. The poet, instead of plunging immediately into the theme as was usual, begins in the same way as in the pangegyrics with a preamble in which a flower garden is described. The *girīzgāh* or 'passage' from the preamble to the main body of the ode is unique. The flowers are accused of theological error and the nightingale of idolatry:

I saw the elegant ones of the field arguing strangely, all of them in astonishment following the path of error.
All of them claimed with perfection the way of salvation but, for all their argument, the claim was false.
The bud, believing that first principles were the rows of trees, maintained that it would be permissible to multiply the pre-existent causes.
The distorted nature of water reinforcing the continuous succession denied that the primal cause might be demonstrated.
The drunken narcissus, considering creation mere fantasy, in ignorance denied the reality of things.
The nightingale, a disbeliever by nature, prostrating himself before the rose, hopeth to find salvation in idolatry.
The zephyr, becoming aware of it, forbade the heresy. O lost hosts—follow the way of Salvation.
There is no lack of a master in this workshop. A powerful and a wise one is necessary for such a power.
The existence of every created thing indicates the cause, but for what purpose, since the blind cannot see?
All created things derive from that Pre-existing Being whose perfect essence does not accept annihilation (pp. 17–18).

Then the poet expresses the attributes of God and searches for signs of the Creator and His power in the Creation. As in typical works of this kind inspired by mysticism some lines are dedicated to Divine Love.

At the end, tried by fate and grown old, the poet makes his act of contrition in the invocation:

To him be conceded along the high road of love for Thee that he might continue to find approbation and be constant in the practice of faithfulness (p. 20).

This qasida of the *tauhīd* type is of ninety-two couplets. There are four qasidas of the *na't* type, i.e. in praise of Muhammad, and these are of about thirty couplets. Three of these are particularly artificial because each couplet ends with a particularly difficult echo-rhyme, respectively: *su* 'water', *khanjer* 'dagger', *sabā* 'breeze'. Here is a passage from the 'water' qasida which is one of Fuzūlī's famous compositions in which the Prophet's miraculous works are mentioned:

To refresh the splendour of the rose garden of prophecy, by his miracle the hard rock gushed forth water.
In the world his miracles have been like a boundless sea since water hath been poured upon thousands of fire temples of the unbelievers.
He biteth his finger in wonder who heareth of how he gave water from his fingers to the 'adherents' [ansār] on the day of difficulty.
If his friend drinketh serpent's poison it will be the water of life for him. If his enemy drinketh water it will certainly become serpent's poison.
From every drop he hath made a thousand seas of pity swell, when taking water with his hands to perform his ablutions he threw water on his rose-coloured face.
One life after another continually, the vagrant water runs hitting its head from stone to stone hoping to reach the dust touched by his feet (p. 24).

Only one qasida of the *menqibet* type, that is in praise of 'Alī, is included in the Turkish qasidas. It is composed of thirty-three couplets. The preamble states the idea that patience will find its reward. The themes in praise of 'Alī are the usual ones in religious poetry of this kind.

There is a twenty-eight-couplet qasida in which the appearance of the flowers is introduced to testify to God, to the Prophet, to 'Alī, to Fatima, and the twelve Imams. This concludes with an invocation to 'Alī. This qasida does not appear in all manuscripts. Where it does appear it is at the end of the qasidas, while its normal place would be after that mentioned above in praise of 'Alī. It is therefore probable that the composition was not included in the collection made by the poet.

Two qasidas addressed to Suleymān are characterized by their length. They are of respectively seventy and sixty-two couplets (an intermediate length between the qasidas addressed to God and those addressed to the Prophet or to 'Alī). The first opens in praise of Baghdad to which reference has already been made (Ch.I). The other is a piece of bravura composed with an echo-rhyme: *gül*, 'the rose'. Here is a passage:

The old Wheel [the sky] *hath impressed His* [Suleymān's] *sun* [or love for him] *on its head from past eternity, as those with the rose-petal cheek place a rose to decorate a turban.*

The rose would never suffer harm from the vicissitudes of time if it had received from Him the decree to flower for ever.
In the middle of the market of pleasure the rose would not find currency with her colour if she had not taken the design of His seal as a dīnār coin.
In order to be music at His feast the rose having taken a tambourine [dā'ire] *every morning learns the science of musical rounds* [edvār] *from the nightingale.*
The rose doth not wait idly. She is busy in the art of pulling her thorn [turning the spit] *in the kitchen of His generosity, to the smoke of which the hyacinth is a servant.*
The land which He conquereth (feth—to open) *is saved from the evils of disorder, for the rose necessarily leaves the thorn when it blossoms* [is opened].
In order to explain His nature to the irises, the rose every morning openeth a scroll from her bud in the rose garden.
Is it a dewdrop or hath the rose, opening its hand like a beggar, taken a royal pearl from the treasurer of His benevolence?
The rose leaveth not in ruins the workshop of the rosebush. It hath become an architect for it, standing on one leg.
In the time of His justice think not that it be dew. It is the rose, wishing to console him, who hath kept a silver coin in her bosom for the nightingale (pp. 39-40).

When speaking of the biography of the poet, we have already mentioned the qasidas written for various dignitaries. Many of the preambles have spring as a theme. Others are courtly in content, similar to the ghazals, or else they moralize. The preface to a qasida dedicated to Üveys Pasha is original in describing a ship by way of a riddle (*laghaz*):

Whatever is that fortunate winged bird, swift in flight which continually and strangely appears in new forms?
Its mouth is open but no voice cometh out. It hath no feet—but it goeth—it moveth with the soul (jân) [the wind] *but cannot be called animal* (jānver) (a total of fourteen couplets, p. 104).

There is a strange matching between the themes of the ghazal and epic narrative in the preamble to an ode to Ayās Pasha:

The image of thy [white] *face and of thy* [black] *dawn hath taken seat in mine eyes.*
The armies of Anatolia [white men: Turks] *and Syria* [black men: Arabs] *have united to move in conquest of Bahrein.*
The dust of thy court hath chosen my eyelashes on which graciously to appear.

The warriors of the House of Peace [Baghdad] *have occupied the bank of the river!*
Along the path of my love for thee my tears continually bubble forth.
The army must strike its tents when the departure hath been decided (p. 56).

The themes of the encomiastic parts of the qasidas are usual. This may be seen in the passage translated from the qasida in praise of Suleymān. There are some qasidas which are told in epic narrative, something which is rare in Ottoman compositions of this kind, and they are interesting for their historical content. The final lines usually give vent to personal feelings of a vague nature.

There is not much to be said about Fuzūlī's other writings in Turkish. The poem *Beng u bāde,* 'Nepenthe and Wine', a youthful work composed in the time of Shāh Ismā'īl is about eight hundred couplets in length and belongs to the genre of the dialogue poem which was current in Persian, and also in Turkish, literature. One of these dialogue poems had already been written about these two substances a century earlier by the Central Asiatic Turkish poet Yūsuf Amīrī. In Fuzūlī's poem the matter is treated more extensively and it is distinguishable by the insertion of two anecdotes. Nepenthe and Wine are shown as two sovereigns contending for supremacy (it was inadvisable to partake of these two intoxicating substances at the same time), boasting of their superiorities and supported by their respective followers: *'Araq* (aquavita), *Boza* (a kind of millet-wine), *Nebīz* (date-wine), Opium, etc. Wine is aggressive and impetuous while Nepenthe is calm. Boza, who is sent as a messenger by Wine to Nepenthe, goes over to the enemy. In a skirmish between the two parties Wine gets the worst, but having sworn to spare his adversary, he finds favour with God and wins. He pardons Nepenthe and brings back peace to the world. Nepenthe, however, dare not be seen when Wine is present. At the end, the poet asks pardon for having used the language given him by God to speak of Wine and Nepenthe instead of speaking of Him. He excuses himself by saying that his name is Fuzūlī and, as his name implies, he cannot but behave in this impertinent way (see Ch. I). The Soviet writer H. Araslī sees in this poem an allegorical representation of the struggle between Safavid and Ottoman and a satire of the court environment, but this does not seem very plausible.

The same scholar would detect the intention of social satire in another poem, consisting of about two hundred couplets and entitled *Söhbetü 'l-asmār,* 'Conversation of the Fruits'. Owing to the simplicity of the language, which leads one to think that the work was written for children, it has been doubted, perhaps mistakenly, that this work belongs to Fuzūlī. The various fruits (apple, pear, grapes, orange, date, almond, pistachio nut, fig, etc.) are introduced to sing their own praises and criticize the others. For example, the cherry boasts like this: *That day in which God put me into the world, he dressed me in a splendid coat. No gem is equal to my dress. No jewel is equal to my body. Sometimes I am the planet Venus, sometimes Jupiter, sometimes an angel, sometimes a fairy. Each of my branches is like a cypress tree. The beautiful ones long ardently for me* (ed. Baku, 1958. p. 269).

The plum replies:

O most despicable of our times! Water and seed for crows and ravens! For which excellence praisest thou thyself? With such defects, how boastest thou? Thou art none other than a drop of water—and the rest of thee bone. Whosoever eateth thee will suffer. If the gardner planteth thee, in the end he will lose much by it (Ib.).

Another of Fuzūlī's poetic works is the translation from Persian of forty quatrains which in turn are a translation in verse by Jāmī of forty sayings of the Prophet.[12]

In prose we have five of Fuzūlī's letters which are essays in an extremely artificial style. Four are not very long and addressed respectively to Ahmed, Sanjakbey of Mosul, to 'Alā'uddīn, Qadi of Baghdad, (on the birth of a son), to Ayās Pasha, governor of Baghdad, to a certain Bayezid Chelebi (who is unlikely to be the prince, son of Suleymān, because the letter is in too familiar a tone).

Another letter is far more interesting. It is about four pages long and addressed to the Ottoman *nishānjï* (Secretary of State). In this letter Fuzūlī complains because he has not received the pension allocated to him (see Ch. 1). The subtle irony used is most unusual in satiric writing of the time:

When in the most unpropitious circumstances and in the most feeble conditions I went into their presence [that is, the trustees of the Vaqf 'mortmain property'] *I saw a group of people rambling on, and in their reporting was no trace of ease or sign of sincerity. Their assembly was a net of deceits. Those present at their council* [recalled]: *'they are like herds, in fact further from the path'* [Koran, 7, 178]. *Their improper deeds were like files filing away the spirit. Their words full of reproof were like the waves of the flood of Noah. I gave them a greeting. They did not accept it, because it was not a bribe. I showed them the decree and they took no notice of it saying, 'It's useless!' ... I exclaimed 'O friends, what a mistaken way to behave* [khatā, also Cathay] *and what frowning* [chīn, also China]. *They answered 'This is our usual procedure!'* ... [The decree seemed to say]: *'My mercy as a king and my magnanimity as a Chosroes have appeared and I have put forth this edict of generosity. I order that forthwith he [Fuzūlī] may know that the level of his power and the rank of esteem are more despicable and lower than, of all beggars, moreover of beasts, of stones, of earth'* [Baku, II, 1958, pp. 302-304].

Lastly Fuzūlī is the author of *Ḥadīqatu 's-suʻadā'*, 'The Garden of the Blessed', a free translation in Turkish, with the addition of lines and information from other sources, of a vast prose work of the Persian Husayn Vāʻiz Kāshifī, devoted to the tragedy of Karbalā'. Perhaps this is the important work to which he makes reference in the Preface of the divan of Turkish ghazals, excusing himself because he cannot wait to write new ones:

While the hawk of my talent was wheeling over big prey, he could not waste time on small game (p. 7).

There is still no critical edition of the work and no full analysis which throws light upon the contribution of the Turkish writer. The style seems no less artificial than the original.

Only for the sake of completing the study shall I briefly mention the writings in Persian and Arabic, in which Fuzūlī's strength does not lie. His poetic works in Turkish and Persian are quantitatively equivalent and of approximately eight thousand couplets each. That Fuzūlī should have written so much verse in Persian is explainable when we consider that Mesopotamia in those days was part of the Persian cultural environment. The poet himself defines his native land as 'Iran'.[13] There are more than four hundred ghazals in Persian, which are therefore more numerous than those in Turkish. The themes are more or less the same but in general they are so banal that it would be useless to look for the stylistic refinements and the variety of attitude of the Turkish compositions. The qasidas are more numerous too—about fifty. One of them of an exceptional length, of one hundred and thirty-four couplets, is entitled *Anīsu 'l-qalb*, 'the companion of the heart'. It is an exhortation and was composed in imitation of similar works by the Persian poets Khāqānī, Khusrav of Delhi, Jāmī, whom Fuzūlī quotes as being his predecessors.

When Fuzūlī dedicates his own lines to Suleymān the Magnificent, he is not beneath them in the audacity of his arguments against unjust and cruel sovereigns—an audacity which is put forward in the form of advice:

O unjust governor, use not the saw to construct the throne from the tree which the peasant hath grown for thy use. . . . What wouldst thou do

with such a throne, which would depart like a boat on the water which the poor man poureth from the tips of the eyelashes? (Ed. Mazıoğlu, p. 21).
The poor man should kiss the chamberlain's mace for it keepeth him away from the disaster of being near the sultan (Ib.)
Thou who art unaware of the behaviour of sultans—think not that the sultan is generous and that the pay of his courtiers is generosity. Indispensable gifts cannot be called generosity, for the sultan is a criminal and his notables are tax-collectors.
That kind-hearted man who giveth to friends and enemies alike may be called generous without hypocrisy (Ib., p. 22).

The laudatory qasidas do not differ in structure and content from those in Turkish and require no particular comment. A notable place is occupied by those qasidas dedicated to 'Alī, to Hasan, to Husayn, and to the other Imāms. It is clear that Fuzūlī preferred Persian for his own religious poetry. These works are notable because they are among the first important attempts at religious Shiite poetry in Persian. The poet does not limit himself to praising the holy personages, making references of interest for the study of popular religiosity, but he also inserts lengthy accounts of episodes relating to them.

The qasida dedicated to his son, about which mention has been made (Ch. I), occupies a special position. This opens with an apologue about the fruit which when it has ripened is best picked from the plant. This beautiful work is worthy of translation.

There is an allegorical work of about twenty pages in prose, called variously: *Sihhat u Maraz* (Health and Sickness), *Husn u 'Ishq* (Beauty and Love), *Rūhnāma*, or *Safarnāma -i Ruh* (The Book of the Spirit or the Book of the Journey of the Spirit). The main character is Spirit (*Ruh*) who comes to live in the kingdom of Body and settles in the city of Heart. The first part is medical and tells about the various procedures which lead to health and to sickness. The second part by contrast is of a mystical nature. The story ends with the return of Spirit to higher realms and with the theory of mystical unity.

Rind u Zāhid, 'the drunkard and the pious man', is another prose work. The two main characters are father and son. It ends with the father's admission that the tavern is as worthy a place as the mosque. This conclusion obviously has a mystical meaning referring to the symbolic value of wine. In satirical passages the work deals with the characteristics of the various human occupations.

A *sāqī-nāme* in verse is dedicated to wine as a symbol of mystical intoxication. In this the instruments of the feast are reviewed.

Lastly, in Persian there are forty enigmas, which are each represented by a couplet.

Eleven qasidas have been preserved of Fuzūlī's poetic works in Arabic, which probably were much more numerous. (He refers to his *rajazs*, a particular type of composition.) The eleven surviving qasidas are not long. They are of a religious nature and have the characteristic of beginning with a long preamble of an erotic nature.

In Arabic there is also a kind of catechism, the *Matla' al-i'tiqād*. This, if not the *Hadīqatu as-su'adā'* is probably the important work to which we have said that Fuzūlī alludes. The author does not take a particular stand in theological matters. He conscientiously gives the opinions of the various sects. So, as far as the Caliphate is concerned, he first gives the Sunnite theory and then that of the Shiites. The Sunnites and the Shiites were left to decide for themselves whether the first or the last place was more important. One looks in vain for original points of view in this work.

CHAPTER THREE

THE LEGEND OF MAJNŪN

The story of Majnūn and Laylā (in Turkish Mejnūn and Leylā) has been and still is as famous in the Islamic East as Romeo and Juliet is in the West. Throughout the centuries it has been, more often than the latter work, the subject of literary elaboration and from time to time its character has been modified by the genius of other poets and the fashions of their times. Furthermore, for Arabs, Persians and Turks, Majnūn is not only the hero of a pathetic love story but is above all the symbol of love carried by passion to the bounds of madness—as the only reason for and interest in life—pure to the point that it is considered by the mystics as the love of God.

When Fuzūlī chose the story of Majnūn and Laylā as the subject of his poem, it had already acquired a definite form among the Arabs and it had been dealt with many times in poetic versions of Persian and Turkish authors. It is not however necessary to give details of all the versions existing prior to Fuzūlī's composition. It will be sufficient to note two essential stages: the formation of the legend in an Arab setting and the romantic version of it in a Persian setting which is the work of the famous poet Nizāmī of Ganja.

Majnūn is not a name, but a nickname which means 'the possessed of the djins', that is by the spirits who exist between the sky and earth according to primitive Arab animism, which was taken up by Islam, and thence the 'mad', 'the inspired'. In the Koran it says that Muhammad had to deal with adversaries who wished to consider him as belonging to this category. More than one ancient Arabic poet has been given this designation. Among them is Majnūn, whom tradition identifies with the poet Qays Ibn Mulawwah, who became 'mad' for the love of the beautiful Laylā, and who lived in the second half of the seventh century at the time of the Umayyad Caliphate. He lived among the Banū 'Āmir, a tribe which was spread over a wide area of the Najd—the central upland plain of the Arabian peninsula which is for the most part steppe, the remainder stretches of stony or sandy desert with rare scattered oases.

Learned Arabs in the eighth century had their doubts and modern scholars have shown their disbelief that a poet nicknamed Majnūn really lived among the Banū 'Āmir. However an Arabic scholar, the Russian I. Krachkovski, has maintained in a masterly article published in 1946 the thesis of the historical existence of Majnūn and of the substantial veracity of the information which tradition has passed on about him. This information seems to be reliable as it closely fits historical and geographical references. Since then, no voice has been raised in contradiction. We can here leave this problem aside—our interest being in the examination of how the legend arose around the figure of the mad lover and what form it assumed. I call it legend because the information which is given about him has on the whole a legendary tone and bears obvious signs of a stylization according to conventional motifs. These are analogous in the legends which have arisen around other famous poets of the same background and period.

In establishing the genesis of the legend of Majnūn, great assistance has been found in the collection of literary records in Arabic known under the name of *Kitāb al-Aghānī*, by Abūlfaraj al-Isfahānī (d. 356/967). In this there is a chapter of more than ninety printed pages dedicated to Laylā's lover. It is not a continuous biographical account but a collection of scores of various traditions which are partly repetitive or contradictory, in juxtaposition and interwoven with verses. Abūlfaraj carefully indicates his own sources. He uses both oral and written traditions, generally the former, and he distinguishes one case from another. When he gives his oral source he indicates not only his direct informant but also according to Arab custom all those who have passed on the information. Thanks to these clues it is possible to reconstruct how the information about Majnūn has been built up. The nucleus goes back to the eighth century and makes use of the testimony of famous learned men such as 'Awān ibn al-Hakam (d. 764), Ibn Da'b (d. 787), and others who lived at that time. The story of Majnūn must have been very much in fashion at the time of the caliphate of Hārūn ar-Rashīd (786–809) and in the years immediately following it, since at that time interest was taken in the story by other learned scholars such as Hishām Ibn al-Kaibī (d. 819), Abū 'Amr ah-Shaybānī (d. 820), Haytham ibn 'Adī (d. 821), al-Asma'ī (828), Ibn A'rabī (d.844), the first three of whom appear not only among the oral sources of Abūlfaraj but also among the written ones. The fashion is explainable by the general favour that romantic stories with a Bedouin background enjoyed at the time. As Krachkovski has observed, many of the stories are based on the verses.

During the ninth century the legend of Majnūn continued to arouse interest. Among other things there is mention of a monograph about him (*Akhbār Majnūn*) by the well-known historian az-Zubayr ibn Bakkār (d. 256/870). This work, like those others which spoke completely or in part of Majnūn, has been lost. The oldest source which we have which speaks of him is the *Kitāb ash-shi'r wa ash-shu'arā'*, by Ibn Qutayba, the well-known writer who died in Baghdad at the latest in 276/889. There one chapter contains some information of particular antiquity which later appears in Abūlfaraj but without indication of its source (except in one case where the indication agrees with that of Abūlfaraj). In this collection of biographies of the poets, this chapter is longer than those dedicated to other poets who were also famous lovers, such as Qays ibn Dharīh, 'Urwa ibn Hizām, Jamīl, and even than that dedicated to 'Umar ibn Abī Rabī'a, a star of primary importance in the firmament of Arabic poetry. The greater length does not necessarily indicate greater esteem on the part of the author for Majnūn (he does however note the 'delicacy' of his verses) but does undoubtedly indicate the exceptional vastness of the available material on Majnūn and therefore his popularity.

Krachkovski believes that the story of Majnūn and Laylā was finally drawn up and became known especially in the period of the Caliph al-Muqtadir (295/908–320/932). This outstanding Arabic scholar argues that at the time stories intended for evening wakes (*asmār*), and stories of fantasy (*khurāfāt*), were very much in fashion; that the booksellers (*warrāqūn*) edited books and invented adventures (*kadhabū*); and above all that Majnūn had been ignored by the poets who speak of famous poet-lovers and by early works of an anthological nature or literary history. Only then, in a well-known book of al-Washshā' (d. 325/936) on *bon ton* did Majnūn head the list of famous lovers, followed by Qays ibn Dharīh, Tauba, Kuthayyir, Jamīl and other famous poets, beginning thus what Krachkovski calls a 'victorious march' which continued from then on in Persian and Turkish literature. Apart from the evidence about the popularity of Majnūn, which passed unnoticed and indirectly can be deduced from Ibn Qutayba, the fact remains that in contrast with Krachkovski's theory not only was the legend of Majnūn contained *in nuce* in traditions which go back to the eighth century but it may also be considered to have been fully formed at the time of Hārūn ar-Rashīd, in all its essential parts and even in numerous details. To this period belong almost all the traditions which are gathered in the *Kitāb al-Aghānī* and no noteworthy addition appears between that age and the period of the composition of this famous Arabic literary collection. In order to accept Krachkovski's point of view we should suppose that the indications of the first sources in Abūlfaraj are false, a supposition which is legitimate but doubtful, or even if they were true, that the relevant information has undergone modification in the period which runs between the first and last informants. This is something which is not demonstrable and is in part contradicted by the data of Ibn Qutayba.

The literature dealing with Majnūn is not limited to the works of Ibn Qutayba and Abūlfaraj. Apart from the stories or quotations in verse which appear in anthologies, in writings on the psychology of love (first among others is *Kitāb az-zahra* of Muḥammad ibn Dāwūd, written about 890), or at any rate containing tales of famous lovers, or of mysticism (we shall return to this later), some monographs have been preserved. Among these there is one ascribed to Abū Bakr al-Wālibī who, according to more than one source of reference, lived towards the end of the eighth century.[1] This however, observes Krachkovski, seems to be rather a late rewriting which in part repeats and in part amplifies the information contained in the *Kitāb-al-aghānī* especially the poetic quotations.[2] Such writing and others of a similar nature[3] do not differ formally from the chapter on Majnūn in the *Kitāb al-aghānī*, because they are simply collections of information with more or fewer quotations from the poems. The literary elaboration of the legend of Majnūn in Arabic circles never went beyond this stage. Only in modern times has it been the object of a different treatment, in a play by the well-known Egyptian poet Aḥmad Shawqī.[4]

The abundant information which is contained in the *Kitāb ash-shi'r wa 'sh-shu'arā'* and the *Kitāb al-aghānī* about Majnūn is sufficient to give an idea of the development which the legend of Laylā's lover had at the hands of Nizāmī and Fuzūlī. It is therefore justifiable to deal only with the essential facts in these sources. I think that it will be pleasant to read some passages translated from ancient Arabic prose which are praiseworthy for their lively presentation and their vigorous simplicity of style.

Qays and Laylā meet in childhood. When they grow up their love becomes evident. According to the Bedouin code of honour this was an inconvenient circumstance, and the girl's father refuses the boy's father when he asks for the girl's hand in marriage for his son. Qays in desperation goes mad (other versions attribute the madness to other circumstances). His family, in the hope that he will recover, take him on a pilgrimage to the Kaaba. Here, Qays, who has by then become Majnūn, instead of asking God to cure him of his love, as his father wanted, implores that his love and affection for Laylā may increase and that he may never forget to mention her name. A historical personage intervenes in Majnūn's favour. This is Nawfal ibn Musāḥiq who was collector of the *sadaqa* tax in the territory of Medina and died in 87/706. He was also a great lover of poetry. He goes to collect the taxes of the Banū 'Āmir and there meets Majnūn. As he feels sorry for him he promises to intervene with Laylā's relatives. These however welcome him with sword in hand and swear that as long as they live Majnūn will never put foot in their dwellings. Nawfal tries to convince them. At the end he gives up, declaring that it is better to leave Majnūn to his fate than spill blood.

Various episodes deal with the meetings and exchanges of messages between Laylā and Majnūn, before and after the onset of Majnūn's madness, and before and after Laylā was given in marriage to one who is sometimes described as a Thaqafite and sometimes as a certain Ward. Among other things, Majnūn takes advantage of the absence of this man and of Laylā's father who have gone to Mecca, to visit his beloved by night. Majnūn's madness is thus described:

He lived on the edge of the camp, isolated, naked. He tore whatever was put on him, went into delirium and made signs on the ground. He played with earth and stones and did not answer when he was questioned. If they wanted to hear him speak or see him sane, they mentioned Laylā to him. (Aghānī, II.17.)

Or

He would wander with the wild beasts in the desert, eating only herbs and drinking only with the gazelles when they went to watering-places. He let the hair of his head and body grow and gazelles and wild beasts kept him company. (*ibid.* 22)

One tradition presents a pathetic picture:

He [Abū Miskīn] says: A young man broke away from us and reached the Maymūn well. There he beheld a group of people on one of those mountains, and he saw that among them they were holding a very tall fair-skinned, curly-haired, large-eyed youth—fairer than any one he had ever seen. But he was pale, emaciated and of a sickly colour. [The youth relates] I asked, 'What is he doing here? And why are you holding him tightly?' They said, 'Because of what he does to himself—since he hurts himself in such a way that even his enemy would have pity on him. He asked us to take him where he might feel the breeze of Najd and we have brought him here facing the land of Najd and perhaps the wind will blow upon him. We don't feel like letting him go free lest he should throw himself from the mountain. If you wish, you may go up to him and tell him that you come from Najd. He will ask for news of that land, and of his country and you'll tell him. I said 'I'll do it'. They said, 'Abū 'l-Mahdī! This man comes from Najd.' The young man sighed so deeply that I thought he would burst his liver. Then he began questioning me about every wadi and every place. I described them to him and he cried the most warm heartbreaking tears (*Kitāb ash-shi'r*, 360–361; *aghānī* II, 23).

The portrait of Laylā is just as pathetic.

One of the Banū Murra was travelling on business towards Syria and Hijaz. When he reached the outskirts of Taimā' and Sarah in the land of Najd, a tent appeared before him. As it was beginning to rain he went towards it and coughed. A woman then spoke to him and asked him to get off his horse. [The traveller relates] I got off. It was evening and large numbers of the camels and sheep together with the shepherds of those people were coming back. The woman said, 'Ask him where he comes from'. I answered 'From the region of Tihāma and Najd'. Then the woman said, 'O servant of Allah! Which part of Najd have you come through?' I answered, 'All of it'. And she said, 'With whom did you stay down there?' I said 'With the Banū 'Āmir'. She then sighed deeply and said 'With which of the Banū 'Āmir?' I answered, 'With the Banū Harīsh'. Then her tears began to flow and so she went on, 'Did you hear of a youth of theirs called Qays, nicknamed Majnūn?' I replied, 'Certainly, I stayed with his father. I went to see him and I saw him.' She said, 'And how was he?' I replied, 'He wanders about the desert, lives with the wild beasts. He reasons not and does not understand unless the name of Laylā is mentioned. Then he begins weeping and reciting verses which speak of her.' The woman raised the curtain that was between us and she appeared like the moon. She was more beautiful than anything my eyes had ever seen. She wept, sobbing so that, by Allah, her breast would seem to break. Then she wept until she fainted. When she recovered I asked her, 'Who are you, O handmaiden of Allah?' She answered, 'I am Laylā, the woman who brought doom to him, she who brought him not comfort'. Never did I see sorrow and affliction equal to that of hers for Majnūn nor even equal affection. (*Kitāb ash-shi'r*, 358–359; *Aghānī* 11, 86–87).

According to one tradition the death of Majnūn is so related:

They showed me a tent and I went towards it. There I met his father who was a very old man and his brothers who were already grown up. They had a lot of livestock and their well-being was evident. I asked them about Majnūn, and they all began to shed tears and cry. The old man said, 'By Allah, he was my favourite son. He fell in love with a woman of his tribe who, by Allah, would never have dreamt of one like him. When their feelings became evident her father opposed the marriage because the information [about their love] was already known and he gave her in marriage to another man. My son then lost his reason because of his burning love and passion for her. We shut him in and tied him up but he began to bite his tongue and his lips so much so that we feared that he would bite them off. When we saw this we set him free and now he lives in the desert with the wild beasts. Every day someone takes him his food and puts it down where he may see it. As soon as they go away he goes and eats it. When his clothes are worn out they take him others and put them in a place where he sees them and then go away. When he sees them he goes and throws away his old clothes and puts on the new ones.' I asked them for some indication of how to reach him. That day I went in search of him and did not see him until the afternoon. Then he was sitting on a heap of sand where he had traced some lines with his fingers. I went towards him without apprehension, but he was frightened of me just like a wild animal when it sees a man. By his side was a pile of stones. He picked up one. I went right up and sat beside him. He kept still a while as if he were frightened and ready to spring up. Since I remained sitting for a long time, he became calm and began to play with his fingers again. I looked at him and said, 'These lines of Qays b. Dharīh are beautiful'. He wept for a long time and then said, 'By Allah, I'm a better poet than he, with these lines of mine'. Then a gazelle came towards him and he jumped up to reach it. I went away, and went back the following morning but I did not find him. Then I went back along the road and told his family. They sent out the young man who usually took him his food and from him they learned that it had remained untouched. Majnūn had not been near it. I went back the third day and did not find him. I looked at the food and saw that it was still untouched. Then early in the morning his brothers, members of the household, and I went out to the place and we looked for him for a whole day and night and did not find him. When morning came we looked over the edge of a stony wadi. He was lying dead among the stones. They took him away and buried him. (*Kitāb ash-shi'r*, 361–363; *Aghānī*, II, 88–89).

This tradition goes back like the preceding one to 'Uthmān ibn 'Umāra, a person who really lived in the eighth century,[5] and is referred to by the famous al-Mas'ūdī (d. 956) as one of the most interesting love stories.[6]

The picture of the legendary figure of Majnūn would not be complete without reference to his poetry which is inserted in the anecdotes or handed down separately. Even if we admit the historical existence of Majnūn, grave doubts arise about the authenticity of these verses because of the uncertainty of attribution, evident in ancient sources, and on the evidence of ancient philologists. Ibn Qutaiba, after having defined Majnūn as a most prolific poet adds that many lines have been attributed to him because of their similarity to his and because of their delicacy. Al-Jāḥiz (d. 869) and Ibn Mu'tazz (d. 296/908) note that people do not fail to attribute to Majnūn every line in which Laylā's name appears. For us it will be sufficient to try to establish the circle of sentiments and images in which Majnūn's poetry moves, leaving aside the problem of authenticity. We shall however limit our field to the study of verses quoted in the *Kitāb ash-shi'r*, in the *Kitāb az-zahra* and in the *Kitāb al-Aghānī*, leaving aside the more copious but undoubtedly later evidence in al-Wālibī, and excluding lines of uncertain attribution.

Except for a few lines in which the poet announces that he has sacrificed a camel on the tomb of his father and other satirical lines against the family and husband of Laylā, the poetry of Majnūn is exclusively love poetry. It belongs to a type of Bedouin poetry which carries on a previous tradition with a marked idealistic tendency and is in opposition to a kind of urban poetry which finds its prototype in 'Umar ibn Abī Rabī'a, a Don Juan from Mecca who went from one adventure to another. The Bedouin poets are represented in the main by the famous triad: Qays ibn Dharīḥ, 'Urwa ibn Ḥizām, Jamīl al-'Udhrī, who dedicated the whole of their lives to one woman only, whom they dared not touch but remained far from her because of the adverse course of destiny, and perished 'killed by passion'. The love which they sang was commonly called 'Udhrite love from the name of the tribe of Banū 'Udhra, who were believed to be of Yemenite origin. This love brought them eternal fame (the Asras of Heine: *'welche sterben wenn sie lieben'*, and Rubinstein). Although he belonged to a North Arabian tribe, Majnūn claims to be a Yemenite as far as passion is concerned and thence ideally relates himself to the 'Udhrites.[7]

The motifs of Majnūn's poetry do not leave the range of conventions then reigning in that genre of poetry in which he wrote, as will be noted by those familiar with ancient Arabic poetry. However, I think that in some of the verses attributed to him there can be seen that mark of authentic poetic individuality. If this impression of mine were confirmed by an exhaustive study of the remains of the poetic works of Majnūn (which no one has yet undertaken), there would be proof of the historical existence of Majnūn and a criterion would be obtained for judging the genuineness or not of single lines.[8]

Majnūn's poems are dedicated only to Laylā, with one exception where he complains that a certain Karīma had preferred Munāzil, another poet, to him although he had prepared the meat of his camel for her. He presents Laylā's physical beauty but also her moral qualities:

Laylā the 'Āmirite rocks on the camel's back. She hath tied back those curly locks with a ribbon of silk.
When the comb moveth her tresses on high, it diffuseth the perfume of sweet basil and pink amber (Aghānī II, 81).

Shining white, of whiteness pure, like the moon in the middle of a frosty night . . .
Marked by beauty, envied, for beauty brings envy in its wake.
Her tears reveal the spendour of her pupils, so dark that antimony is superfluous.
A good girl who if one talks too much takes refuge under the protection of her modesty and if she speaks is brief and to the point (Ibid. 83).

The circumstances in which the love arose are reported thus:

I became attached to Laylā and she was still an innocent maiden, the swelling of whose breasts was not yet apparent to others of her age.
We were two children who took the animals out to pasture. Would that we had not grown till today and that those animals had not grown (Kitāb ash-shi'r, 356).

The strength of the love which binds the poet to this woman is vividly expressed:

It is as if my heart were caught in a bird's claws tightening on its prey, when Laylā is mentioned.
It is as if the corners of the earth were the band of a ring impressed on me, without leaving space either in length or in breadth (Aghānī, II, 83).

I treated my passion for Laylā with Laylā as a drunkard treats himself with wine.
Doth Laylā perhaps think that I love her not? Yes. [I swear it] 'By the ten days and by the even and by the uneven' (Koran LXXXIX, 2-3).

If I hear her name my heart bounds with joy, like a sparrow shaking the rain drops from its back (Kitāb az-zahra, 33).

Majnūn has nothing else to ask God for in this life but Laylā. He declares this in the following verses, which are related to the episode of the pilgrimage to the Kaaba:

The pilgrims wrapped in the ritual mantle by night would call upon Allah in Mecca, and would ask that their sins might be cancelled.
I shouted, 'O Lord! The first thing I ask for myself is Laylā then Thou shalt suffice for me!'
'If Laylā is given me, as long as I live, no servant shall turn to God in greater repentance than I' (Kitāb ash-shi'r, 361).

His love almost becomes religion:

Imagine that when I recite the ritual prayer, I turn my face to her, even if the place of prayer is behind me.
But this for me is not polytheism. The love for her is like choking which closes the throat, which the doctor cannot cure.
I pray but know not, when I recall her, whether I have prayed twice or eight times (rak'ats) *in the morning.*
I have not gone to her to be cured with a look; I look at her and I go away with my ailment (Kitāb az-Zahra, 28).

According to the 'Udhrite ideal, Majnūn's love is invincible and eternal:

They said, 'If thou wished thou couldst find consolation elsewhere'.
I replied, 'I wish it not'.
Love for her hath possessed my heart and even if restrained, it shall be eternal' (Ibid. 329).

Majnūn's love, like that of the 'Udhrites, was destined to remain unrequited.

O my heart, die in sadness, but fear not, for he who feareth among men will not be eternal.
Thou hast fallen in love with a maiden the possession of whom would be paradise. Look for a way leading to that which thou shalt [in reality] never find.
I love Najd and in the long nights despair of ever returning there.
O Thou! No Laylā, no Najd! Accept thine exile till the day of the Resurrection! (Ibid, 349).

It would be sweet and I should quench my thirst, if only I wished to, with the water another offereth, but I abstain.

All my passion is dedicated to her, though sure I am that only refusal will be my fate (Ibid. 361).

The theme 'love-death' beloved of the poets 'who have died of love', is naturally well represented in Majnūn.

I see that these relapses of love kill me; and yet at the beginning they were sufficient for me.
Desperation deals me mortal blows, but hope hath smiles which give me life again (Kitāb ash-shi'r, 358).

The memory of her hath worn away the flesh and then my bones, like a knife which carveth a piece of wood to make an arrow (Aghānī 11, 67).

In this respect Majnūn declares himself superior to the champions of 'Udhrite love:

I wonder that the story of 'Urwa the 'Udhrite is passed from tribe to tribe. 'Urwa died a peaceful death. I, instead die daily (Ibid. 84).

The allusions to madness brought on by love, which are not lacking in poets of the same tendency, are found also in Majnūn in keeping with what is outlined in the stories passed on about him.

She said: 'Why did you go mad?' I answered, 'Love is a worse illness than madness.'
He who loveth never recovers, while the madman raveth only from time to time (Ibid, 36).

In these lines we find the state of misery to which the poet knows he is reducing himself,

I think that the passion for her will lead me to a wilderness, without goods, without a family.
Without anyone to turn to with my last will and testament,
With only my horse and saddle as friends.
My love for her hath eclipsed all previous affections and taken a place which nothing before hath ever had (Ibid. 46).

The motive of erotic monomania and thought concentrated on a single object of love recurs persistently:

Unhappy is he who in the evening is robbed of his reason and goeth completely mad in the morning.

Abandoned by all friends except those who chide me and derided by those who once kept their distance.
On hearing Laylā's name I understand, and strength returns to my troubled mind.
They said, 'It's true that in him there is no ghost of djins or madness. These are only slanderous lies' (Kitāb ash-shi'r, 358).

I try to sleep but slumber cometh not, hoping that an image from thee will meet my fantasy.
I go away from meetings with the intention of speaking about thee to myself in secret and alone (Ibid. 364).

I came not to listen to other words if not about thee because other things do not interest me.
I stare at him who questioneth me so that he may think I understand, but my mind is with thee (Aghānī, II, 71).

Majnūn's love for Laylā is reflected in everything that bears a sign of her. He expresses this sentiment in lines which echo the already conventional themes of Arabic poetry. Having heard that one day Laylā had stopped on the two mountains of Nu'mān, he waits for the breeze to blow from them.

O twin mountains of Nu'mān! Let the zephyr blow free in order that its breath may reach me pure.
That I might find its freshness or it might cure that burning fever which consumeth my liver to the extreme (Kitāb az-zahra 221).

According to tradition he wandered aimless, unaware of where his steps were leading him, as far as Syria or the Yemen. He continually asked for Mount Taubād where as a boy together with Laylā he had led the animals to pasture. In these circumstances the following lines were allegedly composed.

My tears began to flow when I saw Taubād and it on seeing me exclaimed: 'God is great!' [that is, thou art here!]
I shed tears on recognizing it and it called me, shouting loudly.
I said, 'Around thee those people lived and I lived with them for a while.'
It answered, 'They went away and left the country to me. Whoever is left in one place by life's troubles?'
I cry for fear thou shouldst leave me tomorrow, once those two camps were one.
My weeping is a torrential downpour (Aghānī, II, 53).

Majnūn sees a fellow-sufferer in a cooing dove.

O dove of the woods, why dost thou cry? Art thou far from the one thou lovest? Or doth thy friend torment thee?
Is it passion and desire that force thee when the merry songster singeth midst the branches in the morning? (Ibid. 72).

So at the end he turns to a gazelle set free by a hunter who had caught it, noting in her the features of Laylā.

O likeness of Laylā! Fear not, for I today in my wild state am your friend.
O likeness of Laylā! If thou wouldst but stop for a while perhaps my heart would find relief from its sufferings.
She taketh flight since I have untied her bonds, but if thou wouldst hear the truth it is for Laylā that thou hast been set free! (Ibid. 82).

The picture we have from the translated lines imbued with pure and intense passion—and the examples could easily be multiplied—is very slightly clouded by some contrasting words where Majnūn expresses a selfish desire.

O my Lord! Make her love equal to mine, so that neither Laylā nor I have the advantage.
Otherwise make her hateful to me, her and her people. This would indeed be a gift from thee to me, O Lord of the Throne! (Kitāb az-zahra, 26).

Or else he makes mention of sensual pleasure, but always with delicacy.

My hands almost become damp on touching her and around them grow green leaves (Aghānī, II, 70).

His oath is more daring.

By the Lord of the Throne! I kissed her mouth eight times [that is to say, times innumerable] *(Ibid. 25).*

But it recurs in satiric lines against her husband who is defined as a 'dog' and therefore the canons of the poetry of ideal love were out of place.

Krachkovski has inquired why Majnūn has had the fortune to be placed in the front line of poet-lovers and held up as a model of mystic love. The reason for this he finds in the antagonism between the North and South Arabian tribes which profoundly influenced the history of the Arabic empire at the time of the Umayyads and the first Abbasids. The above-mentioned antagonism was extended also to the field of poetry. While the South Arabians were able to boast of the three leaders of the Platonic type of Arabic poetry, 'Urwa, Qays, and Jamīl, the North Arabians had for a long time no one to counterbalance these. At first they reacted with contempt, as would appear from the anecdote which has been recounted by the traditionalist 'Īsā ibn Da'b (d. 171/787), according to which one of the Banū 'Āmir, when asked if he knew the 'Āmirite Majnūn who 'died of love', replied that such an 'Āmirite certainly never existed because the Banū 'Āmir had 'too large a liver' for things like that, which instead were typical of the Yemenite (that is, the South Arabians) foolish people with small heads and not of the Nizārites (that is, the North Arabians). The North Arabian attitude was to change later and uphold Majnūn as their single representative of ideal love, a champion in opposition to the 'Udhrite poets. Another story told by Ibrāhīm ibn Sa'd az-Zuhrī, a contemporary of Hārūn ar-Rashīd, makes a 'Udhrite himself, when asked to say which were the more tender-hearted, the 'Udhrites or the 'Āmirites, reply: 'The 'Udhrites, but the 'Āmirites with their Majnūn will certainly be placed first'. This second anecdote, according to Krachkovski, has been expressly forged in 'Āmirite circles in order to raise Majnūn as a champion of an ideal of love which they had adopted as their own. To support this theory Krachkovski, besides the two anecdotes, adduces evidence which should be biased in favour of Majnūn and against of the 'Udhrite poets. Among this evidence are the lines concerning 'Urwa translated above, whose authenticity Krachkovski denies. Further on the Russian scholar sets forth the fact that verses of 'Udhrite poets were attributed to Majnūn. This theory has however not convinced another famous Arabic scholar, H. Ritter, who in a note to his German translation of Krachkovski's article published in 1955, expresses doubts about the theory that tribal boasting extended to the literary field. It is more likely that Majnūn's fortune is due not so much to extrinsic as to intrinsic factors of the legend and the poetry itself.

According to Ritter, there are elements in Majnūn's love which distinguish it from that of other 'Udhrite love poets and which contributed to its being selected as a model of mystic love. Above all, the 'total absorption of consciousness in the thought of the beloved, in such a way as to leave no room for other expressions of life', and the total immersion and sinking in sentiment, a state to which man willingly aspires but which, without destroying existence, can be achieved only by fantasy'. Another aspect would be the fact that in Majnūn the sentiment of love is detached from the real person of the beloved and becomes completely interiorized, for which his figure is especially apt to illustrate certain mystic states of the soul. 'Such spiritual attitudes could have contributed to the fortune of Majnūn only from the moment in which they were recognized and evaluated positively.' This would have happened at the latest in the second half of the ninth century, an age in which lived Shiblī who was the first to indicate Majnūn as a model for the mystics.

Besides such interior aspects of the figure of Majnūn (the second aspect which is implicit in the first seems to me to become evident not so much from the evidence of a narrative nature and from the verses as from mystic speculation, as we shall see shortly) I maintain that to the fortune of Laylā's lover some exterior traits of his traditional figure have contributed. These traits are precisely those of the 'love-distracted': pale face, emaciated body, unkempt hair, refusal of food and clothing, living only on plants, wandering aimlessly, avoiding human company, living with the wild animals. These are traits which are more or less common to Majnūn and to other famous 'mad lovers' created by the fantasy of poets, like the Yvain of Chrétien de Troyes, Rustaveli's Teriel (who however rather derives from the figure of Majnūn), and Ariosto's Orlando. Even these traits were later evaluated by the mystic and, as we shall see, were of use to Nizāmī in depicting Majnūn as an ascetic. These, and in general the typical madness of Majnūn—peaceful, calm and deep, in spite of some manifestations of an epileptic nature, and erotic monomania rather than madness—were elements which aided the imagination as much as the elements brought to light by Ritter, and were destined to react on sensitive minds. This wide human interest in the figure of Majnūn explains how it found favour both in the court of the Caliphs and also among the mystics.

In mystic circles the legend of Majnūn was interpreted and enriched in such a way as to require ulterior explanations. Mystic speculation insists in particular on the motifs of identity between the lover and the beloved and on the abstraction of the lover from the physical body of the beloved. These are the ideas expressed by Shiblī (274–334/861–945) in a sermon, 'O people! This Majnūn of the Banū 'Āmir! If one should ask him about Laylā he would say: "I am Laylā!" He for Laylā [spiritual] would abstain himself from Laylā [physical] in order to remain for ever in her presence. This made him abstract from every idea except Laylā and he saw everything only for Laylā.'⁹ And on another occasion: 'Like Majnūn of the Banū 'Āmir who when he beheld the wild animals said, "Laylā" and when he beheld the mountains said, "Laylā" and when he beheld men said, "Laylā". In fact, when he was asked his name and how he was, he replied, "Laylā".[10] The presumed saying of Majnūn, "I am Laylā" recalls the famous words, "I am the True [i.e. God]" of the Sufi Saint Mansūr al-Hallāj, a friend of Shiblī, who paid for his daring on the gallows.'[10]

In the first phase Majnūn's love remained only an example for the mystics. The ideas of Shiblī are taken up again for example by Ahmad Ghazzālī (d. 1126), a brother of the great theologian Muhammad, according to whom Majnūn paid no attention to Laylā when he saw her in front of him and said, 'Go away'. This was in order that the crudeness of her physical presence should not disturb the sublimity of his spiritual vision.[12]

Majnūn's love for Laylā was also seen as a preparation for Divine love. Earthly beauty is like a curtain which hides Divine beauty, whose brilliance could not be borne by the human eye. By practising earthly love, man prepares himself for the divine. According to the Persian mystic 'Aynulqudāt, executed at Hamadan in 1132, Providence wanted Majnūn to practise with the love of Laylā in order to dedicate him later to Divine Love, as if he were a steed destined for a king and first ridden by others until he was tamed and trained.[13]

We thus arrive at the concept of the identification of the spiritual Laylā with God (Chap. II), which is proclaimed by the famous Egyptian mystic poet 'Omar ibn al-Fārid (d. 1235) in the famous qasida in *tā'* rhyming.

The beauty of every beautiful man or woman is a loan of beauty from Her (Divinity). Qais of Lubna and all lovers of equal rank such as Laylā's Majnūn, or 'Azza's Kuthayyir were hopelessly taken by her.[14]

The outstanding success of Majnūn in mystic circles is reflected in the literary field of allegorical writings in which the legend has provided us with numerous new anecdotes. Thus in the poems of 'Attār (d. 1220) there are about twenty anecdotes which refer to Majnūn. Some refer to the identity of the two lovers. In the same way the figure of Majnūn appears more than once in the famous *Mathnavī* of Jalāluddin Rūmī (d. 672/1273).[15]

It is in writings of this type and not in romantic poems imitating Nizāmī that Majnūn first comes into Turkish literature, two centuries before Fuzūlī. In the free Turkish translation of the poem *Mantiqut-tā'ir*, by 'Attār, one of the earliest Turkish poets of Anatolia, Gülshehrī of Qïrshehir (previously called Gülshehir, d. 713/1313) introduces a story (*destān*) of Leylā and Mejnūn, composed of seventy-nine couplets.

Leylā sets out to look for Mejnūn and finds him lying in the desert daydreaming with thoughts of her. She asks how he is. Mejnūn does not recognize her, and pushes her away, affirming that two Leylās cannot exist and that he needs no Leylā other than the one which is within him,

What use to me is a mortal Leylā? I need a Leylā who will stay alive.
Behold, you see why I have broken with the world saying, 'Leylā, Leylā!'
I shall break with Leylā too and then only the Lord remains.
The true lover never seeks union.
His companion is separation and his friend imagination.[16]

Analogous concepts are expressed by his fellow countryman and near contemporary 'Āshīq Pasha (d. 1333) in a vast didactic work of mystic tone, the *Gharībnāme*. He tells how Leylā and Mejnūn met at school, how their secret leaked out and was known 'throughout Baghdad' and how at the end they were separated and Qais became Mejnūn. He concludes with the idea of the Divine narcissism. While Mejnūn's tongue was saying 'Leylā! Leylā!' the words came out 'Mevlā' (Lord) and the difficulties disappeared. Since God is the source of this love He, the absolute being, loves Himself. What Mejnūn saw was the reflection of the Lord (*Mevlā*) and to this love he gave his soul calling 'Leylā!'.[17]

CHAPTER FOUR

LAYLĀ AND MAJNŪN BY NIZĀMĪ

Majnūn's fame soon reached Persia where Arabic literature and culture had long enjoyed that pre-eminence acquired and maintained during the Arab conquest of the country and its conversion to Islam. The story of Laylā's mad lover must have been very popular for in 1188 a sovereign of Shirvan of Iranian lineage (in present-day Soviet Azerbaijan) Akhsatan I defined it as 'the king of books' and invited Nizāmī of Ganja, the greatest romantic Persian poet of the time, to put it into verse. Nizāmī, who had previously sung the Iranian saga of Chosroes and Shirin, at first hesitated, for the reasons which he explains (these lines are in part quoted in Persian by Fuzūlī).

If the hall of the fable is narrow, the discourse by dint of running back and forth will limp.
Neither gardens nor royal banquets nor wines nor lutes nor joys. Among the arid sands and rugged mountains discourse at the end becomes sorrowful (pp. 44–5).

He allowed himself to be convinced and the difficulty he encountered acted as a spur—'I began the discourse and my mind replied. I dug and the spring shot forth'. He thus created a poem of supreme artistic dignity which was destined to be imitated *ad infinitum*.

Here it is necessary to speak of Nizāmī's poem at greater length than is usual speaking of the antecedents of a work of art. This is because of the very special link between it and Fuzūlī's poem as we shall see when we examine this later. The following analysis of Nizāmī's poem is therefore necessarily broad because it is intended to make the comparison possible. It does not aim, however, at being a complete treatment of the poem and much less of the poetic world and style of Nizāmī in general.

The text which I am using is the critical edition published in Moscow in 1965. In it, large portions of the story are included which are considered spurious by the Persian editor Dastgirdī, whose opinion has been accepted by many other scholars although it is completely without a solid critical basis.[1] This is the story in brief.

A powerful Arab chief longs for the birth of an heir. At last a son is born and given the name of Qays. When he grows up and goes to school he meets the beautiful Laylā. Between the two, love develops, and before long it is quite evident and they are obliged to be patient. Qays cannot stand up to the test and gives signs of madness for which he is given the name Majnūn. He repeatedly goes up to Laylā's dwelling and once he succeeds in seeing her on the threshold of the tent. Then he goes back to wandering in the desert. His father asks for Laylā's hand in marriage for his son but the girl's family refuse, using as an excuse the madness of the young man. In order that he will recover from his illness he is taken to the Kaaba, where he begs God to increase his love. After this he escapes again into the desert. His father goes after him and brings him home, talks to him, and persuades him to remain at home, but only for a short while.

Laylā in the meantime is faithful to her love. She hears Majnūn's songs and replies by sending him notes imbued with tears. Once in springtime she goes out with her friends to the garden. She leaves the company and sits apart under a cypress to vent her feelings freely. On hearing a voice unexpectedly singing one of Majnūn's songs she bursts into tears. A friend, who has, unbeknown to her, been watching, tells her mother who, however, does not intervene. A youth, Ibn Salām, sees Laylā as she is going back from the garden and asks for her as his bride, but the request for the moment is not granted on the pretext that the girl is suffering from a passing malady.

Naufal, a young nobleman intervenes on Majnūn's behalf. His people and Laylā's meet twice. Naufal wins, but when faced with the decisive denial on the part of Laylā's father and not wishing to be a tyrant he abandons Majnūn to his destiny. The young man takes to wandering again. He pays to set free some gazelles and a young deer which have fallen into a hunter's net. He gives a message for his beloved to a crow. At last he takes the place of an old man led along in chains by an old woman, begging for alms, and pretends to be a prisoner asking for an offering to set him free. Thus Majnūn goes from house to house and succeeds in seeing Laylā for a moment or two. He breaks his chains and flees again into the desert.

Ibn Salām finally obtains Laylā's hand, but he is disappointed. The young woman violently rejects him and swears she will never be his. The bridegroom accepts the situation and is content only with the sight of her, and it is not long before he discovers her feelings for

Majnūn. Majnūn is informed of the wedding by a friend who in great pity reveals how Laylā has remained faithful to him. Majnūn in a message given to the wind confirms his own love for Laylā.

The death of Majnūn's father after a last meeting with his son, begins a series of sad events. Majnūn visits his tomb and waters it with his tears. His uncle Salīm who often comes to visit him tells him that his mother wants to see him. After a talk with her son, his mother dies too and is bitterly mourned. Laylā tries to console him by sending him a message. A meeting requested by Laylā is arranged between the two lovers in a palm grove. Majnūn recites a poem while Laylā, chastely hidden ten steps away, listens. A young Baghdad poet who is also in love, Salām, goes to see Majnūn to collect his poetry and stays some time with him. Majnūn finds a sheet of paper on which are written his name and Laylā's and he rubs out hers. When he is asked the reason for this he answers that his name includes that of his beloved, in the same way that the skin of a fruit covers the pulp.

Ibn Salām dies as a result of overeating. The news is taken to Majnūn by a certain Zayd whose love for his cousin Zaynab is contrasted. Laylā observes her widow's mourning for two years according to Arab custom, and then finally goes back to her father's household. Free at last she sends Zayd to call Majnūn. The two of them meet in Laylā's room and chastely embrace. Then Majnūn flies away asserting that he is carrying Laylā within him. Laylā, who is distraught because of the state of her friend, falls ill and dies. Majnūn dies on the tomb of his beloved. Zayd in a dream sees the two lovers blessed in paradise.

We do not know what the direct source or sources of Nizāmī's work were. It is clear that he repeats the general outline of the Arabic sources, to which we referred in the preceding chapter. A more precise comparison, which would be out of place here, would show that he also followed them in particular details. Nizāmī only vaguely mentions as a source a 'noble' (*dihqān*), 'an eloquent native of Fārs' and 'the expert narrator of Baghdad'. It cannot be excluded (and his knowledge of Arabic was certainly sufficient) that he made direct use of Abūlfaraj (to whom the two expressions just quoted might well refer, because he was born in Fārs and lived in Baghdad, if it were not for the difficulty of the word *dihqān*, which really indicates a gentleman of Iranian extraction and not an Arab which in fact he was). It is more probable however that he had in mind the text of al-Wālibī of which many copies are preserved in Persia, some with interlinear Persian translation. Thus Nizāmī probably found his themes, absent in Abūlfaraj, of Majnūn's talk with his father, of the old man in chains, of the exchange of letters between the lovers, of Laylā's death, and that of Majnūn on her tomb. The Persian poet probably elaborated the story of al-Wālibī, adding from some other source dependent on this, selecting, arranging and developing. In this last respect we do not know whether to attribute to Nizāmī or to some unknown source the themes which are absent in Abūlfaraj and in al-Wālibī, such as that, common in folklore, of Qais being the long-awaited heir; or that of the two lovers meeting at school, a theme which is in keeping with the life of the urban bourgeoisie who had reached prosperity in the Seljukian period (it has already been seen in Gülshehrī and we do not know whether he took it from Nizāmī or from a source which he shared with him); or again the theme of Naufal's struggle adapted to suit the Persian epic; or finally the story of Zayd and Zaynab which doubles the theme of Laylā and Majnūn. The episode of the two names is similar to one of the many anecdotes which, as has been seen, were circulating about Majnūn in mystic circles.[2]

Whatever may be Nizāmī's direct source or sources it is certain that he achieved an original work in giving the story a coherent development. His merit does not consist so much in this as in having gone into the matter psychologically. Deep psychological analysis is one of the chief characteristics of Nizāmī's art and is that which distinguishes him and raises him above the level of the other romantic Persian poets. The pathetic figures faintly outlined in the pages of Ibn Qutayba and of Abūlfaraj are changed into real people who each lives out his own drama.

Above all, in Majnūn Nizāmī put what he had inherited from Arab sources, the trinomial—love, madness, and poetry—as the essential components of a character. The external signs of madness are the same: lack of interest in food and clothing, extreme thinness, wandering and avoidance of men, friendship with the beasts, obstinate silence and discourse only of Laylā, but no epileptic fury against self. His poetry is moving. It is carefully collected and diffuse. The lines which Nizāmī puts into Majnūn's mouth are not attributed to him by Arab tradition but are lines which are entirely created by the Persian poet. They are the expression of the deep madness of the youth and of his love, which are one and the same thing.

Majnūn's love as it is conceived and represented by Nizāmī is of a complex nature. Three aspects of different origin can be distinguished. They, however, alternately interpenetrate and integrate, and thus contribute to the harmony of the poem. They appear as so many phases through which the soul of the character must pass. As the preceding phases foreshadow later expressions so the successive phases do not deny the preceding, but rather set them off in a new light.

A first aspect of Majnūn's love is not dissimilar to 'Udhrite love, a love composed of absolute and perpetual dedication, which sublimates itself with chastity and exalts suffering. This same love we find in the lines of Majnūn, but it is not from these lines which Nizāmī's inspiration comes but rather from a poetic convention transmitted from Arab literature to Persian.

Majnūn's love is not a flame which suddenly spreads, but is a sentiment to which he is predisposed, which he had sucked in with his mother's milk and which was destined to last throughout his life.

Love for thee cannot be removed from the heart; this mystery cannot ever be revealed to anyone.
This mystery came into my body with my mother's milk and it will go out again with my soul (p. 145).
I feed on love; if love dies, I die too. My nature hath been brought up on love; my destiny must only be love (p. 150).

Love which is not eternal is a toy of youthful lechery.
Love is that which doth not diminish, which goeth back not one step as long as it lasteth.
This love is not amusing fantasy destined to disappear for ever (p. 146).

True love despises the pleasures of the senses. To Salām who observes:

This flame which is the reboiling of the affections cometh from the fire of youth.
When youth departeth from man that ball of fire cooleth down (p. 432)

Majnūn indignantly replies:

I am His majesty the Emperor of Love. I have not been ashamed of lust.
I became immune to the lechery provoked by terrestrial flatterings by means of a bath of purity.
I have freed myself from the impurity of my lust. I have destroyed the market of the passions (p. 433).

And he affirms:

Love which is separated from chastity is not love but passionate lechery.
Love is a mirror of light. Lechery doth not enter in the reckoning of love (p. 504).

Sorrow is the inseparable companion of love:

O thou! Pain and suffering for thee are the peace of the heart, balsam and a wound of the heart! (p. 123).

Suffering allows a state of grace to be reached:

I am free from the slavery of time. Pain enjoys me, I enjoy pain.
My bosom thirsteth and I am immersed in water; I am blind and companion of the sun! (p. 410–11).

While recalling the concepts of chastity and pain there is an indication of the concept of liberty in the lines translated above. They really belong to the second phase where love is seen as a liberating force. This concept of love sinks its roots in Nizāmī's religiosity which is shot through with asceticism. Indeed, in *Laylā and Majnūn* one sees a pessimistic vision of life expressed principally in the poet's long reflections and comments on the death of the main characters. Here statements on the world, like the following, occur:

This is the temple of demons, not a place of election. Rise up! It is in the path of the wave.
Alas! Thy cypress is in a field whose water is salt and whose grasses are swords (p. 306).
As long as they pull thee not from this Well, they'll let thy rope down and down (p. 309).
Every morning when from these graceful Arches [the sky] *fire falleth on the threshing floor of the world,*
Every evening when from this Jar dirtied with earth smoke riseth towards the amphora of heaven,
It teacheth thee that this is a temple of fire wrapped in smoke (p. 464–5).
The little Chest [the earth] *which goeth round the Arches* [the sky] *is immersed in the blood of the just* (p. 517).
Peace cometh only with death:
To whoever liveth in this Village [the World] *peace of heart is forbidden.*
In the man [mard] *who took away the soul from this Castle* [the World] *it is this that is dead* [murd] *and not he in it* (p. 305).
Man hath but little choice, he hurrieth on to death.
Before Destiny [gardūn] *breaketh the bridge beneath thee, make thy steed jump off* (p. 550).

Besides this conception is placed that of a cruel and inexorable destiny on which we shall dwell later.

It is indeed true that Majnūn's flight from human society is motivated by the events, by fear of persecution from Laylā's relatives and by madness, but it is also an escape from the world which results in the madman's appearance as an ascetic. This change seems to be brought about by the exhortation which his father makes in his last talk with him, which corresponds to the motto of the mystics, 'Die before dying'.

If thou wouldst not suffer when death arriveth, measure the strength of death.
He will save his soul from the claws of death who is already dead before death (p. 294).

The ascetic figure of Majnūn is externally realized in his friendship with the beasts (this victory over wild animals is a typical theme of the process of initiation) and with his feeding himself on resins and herbs, and his interior self on meditation on death:

He threw the order of the world from his hand and took hold of its disorder.
Aware of death's bitterness he provided himself with means for the journey (p. 438).

Majnūn's talks with his uncle Salīm and with his friends Salām and Zayd, appear to be useless accessories, but they do help to outline clearly the ascetic figure of Majnūn.

Against this background is placed the instrumental conception of love as a means for disentanglement from the world and from self. This conception is hinted at in verses already quoted and in others:

That suffering which gave him a diploma, liberated him from slavery to himself (p. 157).
Even if I am bound to thee, O fairy offspring! yet I am freer [āzādtaram] *than the free cypress tree* (p. 415).

Majnūn's condition as an ascetic is made clear in the chapter dealing with his 'greatness':

He held back his hand from instinct, the beloved was but a pretext on the way.
Until, if desire had assailed him like a brigand, he would have had a place in which to deceive the world (pp. 438–9).

And once more in the talk with Zayd:

One who hath fallen victim of grief in this place of transition. How cometh he out of the Well without a rope?
This rope is formed of the locks of the heartbreakers and yet they are in the hands of others. . . .

Whenever shall I adore the idols of others having first smashed mine own? If I push the camel towards the idol I free myself from mine idols (pp. 452–3).

Escaping from the world and from himself, the lover carries out the annihilation of his own personality and the substitution for it of the personality of the beloved, which is the last lap in Majnūn's spiritual journey. There is no doubt that the ideas of the identity of the lovers and the interiorization of the object of love are derived by Nizāmī from mystic speculation on Majnūn's love begun by Shiblī (see Ch. III). In Nizāmī however we have not an explicit assumption of Majnūn's love as a model for love for God, and not even the transfer of the matter into a symbolic sphere, in which the beloved is identified with God and love becomes a way of absorption of the individual ego into the cosmic 'I'. Majnūn's experience as expounded by the poet of Ganja touches on a theme dear to the Sufis but remains within the bounds of the psychology of the character.

The point of departure is the erotic monomania of Majnūn which is found again in Arab sources, that is the complete abstraction of the conscience of Majnūn in the thought of Laylā:

Should one disregard the name of Laylā he had pleasure in no other word. Whoever failed to open their discourse with this word was not listened to and had no reply (p. 122).

The concept is rendered evident in the parable of the two names written on the sheet and thence repeated many times, for example:

Whoever am I? And what is my name? How do they recognize me if not as thy shadow?
I reckon myself as nothing for I come from nothing and remain nothing (p. 495).

It is also made quite clear that the true entity of the beloved is the spititual reality of her, and not the physical, and this is of no benefit to the lover:

Since the love for thee is fixed in me, what is the use of thy image [sūrat]? (p. 374).
Since the love for thee appeared it is well that thy face should disappear (p. 375).

All such enunciations find their logical conclusion in the episode of the final meeting between the two lovers, which is the crest of the wave followed by Majnūn in his spiritual evolution. Faced with Laylā's offers of love, and having proclaimed his own creed, he, like a new St Alexis (but the circumstances and motives of the deed are both different), flies away thinking that he has become Laylā.

To talk of being I or being you is out of place here. In our faith there is no duality (p. 497).
Here I am. The other is but a beautiful portrait. Here you are. The other is dust.
No. No. I'm wrong. There is one house, for the confusion of Duality hath disappeared.
We are in harmony together in the same way as the bass and treble are.
When the harp [chang] is taken up by the palm [chang], it singeth not if not with bass and treble (p. 498).

Mistaking himself for the beloved, he took her to the Market [the World] instead of to himself.

That entity Majnūn blew away the leaves from him, and that which was left of his breath became Laylā (pp. 502–3).

The psychology of the character is probably more complex than appears from the preceding abstract scheme which was perhaps sufficient to outline the concepts of the Nizāmīan philosophy of love. It is insufficient however to give a complete and concrete idea of the poetic figure of Majnūn, which goes beyond the author's intention of merely making of his hero, as he does, a champion of asceticism.

As a matter of fact, Majnūn is a highly dramatic figure in the first place because of the paradoxical situation in which the young man finds himself. His love cannot be requited, just because of its intensity bordering on madness. Secondly we have Majnūn's attitude when faced with destiny. He pathetically explains his desperation at his lot in the adieu which he makes to his companions at the moment when he sets out for the desert pursued by Laylā's people:

I would that a wind [bād] would blow down upon me and make me disappear [ba-bād dādī].
Or that a violent thunderbolt would descend and destroy house and clothing.
Is there no one who will bring fire and draw smoke from me and tear out my soul?
No one who will thrust me into the crocodile's jaws so that the world may be rid of my shame? . . .

Relatives are like thorns because of my nature; my friends are ashamed of my name (p. 140).

When he meets his father in the desert he regrets the fact that he is not free to have his own will:

Thou knowest it. I lean not on myself and so cannot choose.
I am bound in stocks and these are of iron. What is the point of looking for a remedy. This is my destiny [qismat] (p. 168).

He is a victim of the inevitable force of destiny from which nothing in the world escapes:

I am not alone in being wronged. Perhaps there is an eye [dīda] *which hath not seen* [dīda] *a hundred similar cases?*
The shadow falleth not of its own into the well. The moon did not reach the zenith by itself.
There is nothing from the massive bulk of the elephant to the ant's wing which is not exposed to that force (Ibid.).

He is saddened by his condition:

Bad luck [baxt] *pursueth me. Who can wipe away his own misfortune?*
If there were a way of acting along this path, I should be the sun or moon. . . .
I, poor wretch, live not with a gay heart but whoever hath such a thing?
I close my lips to smiles as I would to lightning. If I should smile I fear I should burn (p. 169).

He therefore denounces the iron-like fatality of destiny expressed in terms like *qismat* and *baxt*, one Arabic, the other Persian, which like the Greek *moira* indicate the destiny assigned to each one of us. But it is clear, even if the poet does not explicitly say so, that this destiny is willed by Providence. This is evident not so much from the words of Majnūn already referred to, by which he accepts his destiny of love, as from the fact that at the Kaaba he asks God that he may be faithful to his destiny of love and the sorrow which it will bring with it.

They tell me to leave love alone. This is not the way of expertness. O Lord, for the lordliness of Thy lordliness and for the perfection of Sovereignty! Make me carry love to those extreme bounds that it remain even if I should not. Give me light from the fount of love. Take not this bistre from my sight. . . .
Even if I burn like a taper suffering for her so that my days may never be without pain for her (pp. 150–2).

Majnūn, himself, one sleepless night, at the sight of the majestic firmament, denies the pagan belief in the virtues of the stars and implores God to change the course of events which are against him. The following day a loving message arrives from Laylā and is taken as a sign of Divine grace.

One can see a contrast between the sentiments of Majnūn and the ideal forms of love to which he leans and finally reaches. In fact the Majnūn whom Nizāmī represents is a lover who knows all the impulses, the anxieties, the contradictions of passion before he is the ascetic lover proposed by the poet to the reader as a model. He addresses passionate appeals to his beloved, radiates with joy when Naufal promises him that Laylā shall be his, while in the course of the battles undertaken on his behalf he takes the side of his adversary. He reproves Laylā for not having kept her word and forgives her because of her beauty. He declares that he is unworthy of her. He regrets that Ibn Salām marries her and trembles with jealousy. He yearns for tender meetings, runs gaily dressed in his finest to the last meeting and then stands motionless while Laylā caresses him. Then he complains that he is finished:

While I flew like a hawk I saw no trace of the partridge.
Today the hawk hath its wings clipt and the partridge riseth in flight
(pp. 495–6).

Besides, Majnūn shows tender sentiments of filial piety. For a moment he hesitates and almost accepts his father's advice in order to please him. Then he weeps warm tears at his death and regrets having disappointed his hopes. And so he weeps bitterly over the death of his mother, too.

The character of Laylā is psychologically less complex. From the beginning to the end of the poem she is animated by a tender passionate love. She too has her drama which is the drama of the Muslim woman, slave of the will of others and obliged to conceal her own feelings and disguise her own sorrows. She gives in to the will of her family and marries Ibn Salām, but finds sufficient spirit to refuse to give herself to him. This she does in an outburst of rebellion and she does not care whether her husband discovers her secret. Thus she does not avoid but rather looks for the company of her beloved, and plans to meet him, although, respecting the rules of honour, she keeps her distance. After her husband's death, when at last she is free, she wastes no time. At their last meeting she alone is active. She languidly caresses her beloved and in such a way concludes the meeting. She makes no comment on Majnūn's refusal. Perhaps she does not understand the reason, perhaps she blames his madness. The poet does not explain; he shows us only that she dies of grief, consuming herself with compassion for her beloved.

Majnūn's parents and Laylā's are also characters depicted dramatically. Majnūn's father is a noble sorrowing figure. At the end of his days ('old age, weakness and dejection guided him on his way towards death'), in vain he sadly and pessimistically asks his son to return to reason. He begs him to act (*'ishva*) though he himself maintains that it is useless. He fears that a stranger will inherit the goods destined for his son who will arrive too late. Then there will be nothing to do but weep upon his tomb. He then bids him a moving farewell:

Place thy hands around my neck. Rise up. Weep tears on my heart.
Till I with this water complete the ablutions for the Journey, till, rocked in the cradle of the Journey, the dream taketh me pleasantly away. . . .
None the less I am not extraneous to what affects you, I die and suffer for you (p. 304).

The appeal which Majnūn's mother makes for him to come home is pathetic:

Animals and birds stay away from their nests till evening.
But at the first signs of nightfall each bird returns to its nest (p. 386).

Laylā's father is portrayed in chiaroscuro. Wounded, aged, and desperate, hated by his own family, he proudly and firmly invites Naufal to take his daughter and give her to the lowest of the servants, burn her alive, throw her in a well, pierce her through with a sword. He will say nothing but he will never accept the idea of giving her to a madman. He himself would rather cut off her head and give her body to the dogs to devour. The same man speaking later to his daughter boasts of having acted with cunning.

Laylā's mother is an undecided person. When she learns of her daughter's love she does not know what to do. If she encouraged her, then she would be pushing her towards a madman. If she begged her to be patient, she would see her consumed in grief.

Naufal is a man of a generous impulsive nature. At first he wants to help Majnūn, but, when faced with the difficulties it involves, he hesitates and suspends the struggle. He is victorious but allows himself to be moved to pity by Laylā's father. And so, moved by humanity and moderation, he gives up his plan. Ibn Salām appears as a weak character. He easily adapts himself to the conditions imposed by Laylā, though he suffers as a result of them. His end is almost comical. He falls ill, gets better, but does not keep to his diet, and dies. Less characterization is shown in the others, such as the uncle Salīm or the poet Salām. Two anonymous characters are notable for their symbolic value: a negro riding a camel who passes 'swift as a serpent' taking Majnūn the news of Laylā's marriage; and a knight 'all shining with light' who instead takes him a long message from her.

It is necessary to stop a moment and examine Nizāmī's style of composition and his verbal style, because they have characteristics in part inherited from tradition and in part the original creation of the poet of Ganja.

The introduction is remarkable for its exceptional length (almost eight hundred couplets out of a total of 4,000), intended perhaps to compensate for the relative brevity of the narrative part. We find the usual elements, praises to God and the Prophet (with a description of his ascension) and praises of the sovereign Akhsatan (repeated at the end of the poem). Related to, but extrinsic to the main argument, there is only the usual chapter about the circumstances of the composition of the work. For the rest there are personal ventings of the author and vague considerations of a philosophic or moralistic nature. The introduction ends with a series of invocations to the cup-bearer which precede each exhortative theme: The cup-bearer and wine have symbolic values as can be noted from the first invocation:

I am one who adoreth wine: where is the cup-bearer that should put the cup of wine into my hand?
That wine which is a liquid as clear as my tears is permissible in the religion of lovers.
I'll take wine in the hope that this torn heart will open (p. 86).

The various steps in the narrative development are generally marked by fixed formulae. The typical initial formula is the reference to a previous narrator, whose individuality remains vague, so that a slightly fairy-tale atmosphere results. Except for the 'noble born in Fars' or the 'narrator of Baghdad', the rest of the formulae mentioned are of this type:

He who hath laid out his garden placeth this brand upon the leg of the discourse (p. 191).
He who tuneth the organ of his orchestra so harmonizeth his voice (p. 232).

Other repeated formulae are brief descriptions of the sun rising or of the coming of night. These are notes which cover an imaginary period of time, as imaginary as the character in the previous formula. Sometimes the mere repetition of a word serves to link the formula with what goes before or what comes after.

When that traveller Night high above the Well bought a handsome youth as fair as Joseph, like the moon,
The firmament-Egypt swarmed like the Nile crowded with the sellers of eyes [the stars].
That one [Majnūn] *with transfixed eyes* [mīl kashīda] *mile after mile* [mīl bar mīl] *wandered like the Nile* [Nīl] *his clothes dyed indigo* [nīl] (p. 244).

The dawn when the azure sphere decorated its blue in yellow.
The smile of that yellow rose [the sun] *turned the horizon into the colour of a red rose.*
Majnūn as a rose blown by the autumn. . . . (p. 245).

When the night with the pendant of pearls filled the ear and the chin of Time.
That pearl [Laylā] *shed like the Pleiades rivers of pearls from her eyes towards the constellation of the Virgin.*
It was she [alone] *and the night and pain and sorrow* . . . (p. 476).

Series of epithets are used in two cases as initial formulae. One series refers to Majnūn:

The sovereign of the throne of the dawn-risers, the warrior of the army of tear-spreaders,
The hidden walker on the pathway of tenderness, the enchained in the street of the game of love,
The organ of the Baghdad singers, the customer of the groan-dealers,
The drummer of the screetch of the iron hub, the priest of the church of lamentation (and so on for another four couplets; p. 121).

In the second case the series which lasts for eight couplets refers to Laylā (pp. 174–5).

As an element of composition we find a series of couplets constructed on the Majnūn-Laylā antithesis:

Majnūn is within waves of blood. What is Laylā's state?
Majnūn consumeth his inmost soul. Whose witty conversation doth Laylā enjoy?
Majnūn is pierced through with arrows of thorns. In what flattery doth Laylā slumber?

Majnūn moaneth with a thousand cries. What entertainment doth Laylā propose?
Majnūn possesseth nothing but pain and sores. Which garden and spring doth Laylā enjoy?
Majnūn girdeth on the belt of supplication. To whose cheeks doth Laylā smile openly?
Majnūn's heart is lost because of the separation. With what excuse doth Laylā remain unperturbed? (p. 189).

Nizāmī does not withdraw from but, in fact, participates with diligence in the tradition which had already been affirmed by Firdausi according to which the poet was to mingle the useful with the sweet. Thus the poem is strewn with judgments and more or less lengthy moral considerations. For example, we have observations on insolence, on a good name, on love, etc. He even inserts three apologues. The main intrusions are however on the vanity of life, in keeping with the teaching which the poet intends to impart with his work. These are placed as a comment on the death of the father of Majnūn (forty-four couplets), of his mother (twenty-one couplets), of Ibn Salām (fourteen couplets), of Laylā (thirty-one couplets), and of Majnūn (forty-four couplets). In general these are commonplace and even his poetic art fails to vivify them.

The descriptions, isolated pieces of bravura, real and proper clichés of a conventional nature, have a place apart, like the moral sermons. There are two symmetrical descriptions of spring and autumn respectively towards the beginning and towards the end of the story. One introduces Laylā's visit to the garden (at the height of its beauty), the other her illness and death. They insert the human story in a cosmic symbolism and give the poem an imaginary unity. The effect seems to be that which the poet desired, since it is not imaginable that it is just by chance that the same procedure occurs again in a later poem, although in the reverse situation of winter to summer.[3] Two other descriptions are dedicated to the two fights which Naufal undertook. The longer, one of the longest Nizāmīan descriptions, describes a starry night and is a *tour de force* which goes on for fifty-seven couplets and is, as has been said, a solemn prelude to Majnūn's denial of the power of the astral forces and of his affirmation of his faith in God.

In these descriptions the relation between man and nature is symbolic and while it is merely extrinsic there is recourse to metaphoric procedure. A more intimate relationship of an affective nature is found instead when the characters look for relief in nature from the pains of love. After having described spring, the poet imagines that Laylā goes to the garden to humiliate the flowers with her own beauty, but at once changes his mind, and, using the rhetorical figure of epanorthosis, he attributes to her instead the intention of confiding in the nightingale and listening for signs of her beloved in the breeze. Majnūn sees the likeness of Laylā in the gazelle and in the little deer he sets free, and imagines that the deer suffers like him by being separated from his companion, or that the crow is black because it is a victim of 'black' fortune. Again, he asks the planet Venus to bring him perfume from his beloved and the planet Jupiter to bring a sign of her. We have seen similar attitudes, which are commonplaces in Arabic poetry, in Majnūn's verses. (Here however the crow is a cursed bird as it represents the bird of separation; see Ch. III.)

The narrative parts are relatively little developed. This certainly depends on the thinness of the plot but also on the fact that the poet is interested, more than in the adventures of the characters, in the motives of their souls. In order to represent these better he adopts more suitable forms, such as dialogues, monologues, and intermezzi such as the songs of Majnūn. If the poet intervenes directly it is to inform the reader of the character's exterior attitude. He describes what is interior only in the chapter which is dedicated to the greatness of Majnūn. The extension of direct speech, to which above all the presentation of temperaments, sentiments, and ideas is entrusted, gives the poem the aspect of being a dramatic work. The two lovers exchange letters from a distance (as happens on the other hand in the Arabic sources). The exchange of letters has perhaps a direct source in the poem *Vīs and Rāmīn* of Fakhruddīn Gurgānī (d. about 1074). As Petrarch did to the waters of the Rhône, so Majnūn entrusts his messages to the breeze, that same breeze which in the tale of Ibn Qutayba he greedily breathes in because it comes from Najd, where Laylā lives. He also entrusts messages to a little deer and to a crow with which he has found he has feelings of sympathy in common.

Nizāmī's verbal style is characterized by the intense use of imagery. Direct metaphor is particularly frequent. We can see in the preceding translations expressions like 'yellow rose' to indicate the sun, or 'eye-sellers' the stars, or symbolic expressions to indicate the world: 'well', 'bridge', 'village', 'little chest', etc. The genitive construction with the function of a comparison is as frequent. It is usually used to render the abstract concrete, often with daring images, as for example in the lines already translated the expressions 'the hall' (p. 85), or the 'leg' (p. 104) of the discourse, 'ear and chin of time' or again 'sword' of carefreeness. (Love came and emptied the house lifting the sword of carefreeness, p. 116.) Such images (in the rhetorical terminology called *istiʿāra-yi musarrakha*) are justified by complementary elements, e.g. the discourse that comes and goes, the pearls that embellish time

(p. 105), the house emptied *manu militari*. In such cases, as is the rule with the coupling of images, the law of formal similarity is observed, that is that the images must belong to a given field. An evident example of images thus connected is in the representation translated above of the starry night, where all the images are inspired by the Koran episode of Joseph: the well, the crowded market where Joseph was sold, Egypt, the Nile.

A procedure which recurs, one might say, at every step is the use of the images in a kind of counterpoint. The poet, after having announced a concept or represented a situation, takes it up again in the form of related images (sometimes concepts and situations are simply outlined or merely implied). The relationship between these terms in the sphere of fantasy is that of substitution for the real terms with the intention of enlivening the discourse and making it more convincing, thanks to the magic of visual imagination. Often the image evoked on its evidence has a didactic value which gives place to some winged saying:

They tried to be patient to cover naked love. But what is the use of patience in love? One cannot whitewash the sun with clay (p. 117).

I shall add some further examples to those already translated. The desire of Qays's father to have a son is thus explained:

He was most desirous that the hand of fortune should take a branch from his tree.
That is, that when the trunk of the cypress should dry out then another trunk should grow from that trunk.
In order that when it landed in the field a pheasant will see a cypress where the cypress tree stood.
As it does not see the trunk of the old cypress it stoppeth in the shade of the new one (p. 106).

Majnūn's father asks for Laylā's hand in marriage for his son:

I ask with affection and bond thy daughter for my son.
Given that this son of the sands, with parched bosom, hath set his eye on thy fountain,
Every fountain which hath fresh water, when the thirsty drinketh he tasteth with his soul (p. 132).

As can be seen, the images, instead of being in the form of comparisons, are suggested by a kind of parallelism, without an explicit term of transfer, at times, as in the two preceding examples, in the guise of logical explanations.

The image triumphs in the descriptions. The reader sees nature come to life under his eyes as if by a magic touch. Almost every element of the description acquires a life of its own, it moves; it reacts. The procedure may be better seen in the following couplet:

The water lily, because of the pink-coloured sun, without fighting hath thrown the shield in the water (p. 183).

The shield which the water lily throws away like a warrior, as the sign of surrender under the attack of the rays of the sun, is obviously the plant's own leaf. The broad circular leaf suggests the image of the shield; and this, linked with the further image—not expressed, but left to the reader's intuition—of the 'attacking' rays of the sun, leads to the final image of the waterlily 'surrendering'. One finds a fictional relationship set up and substituting for the real one between the two elements of nature, the plant and the sun when transported to a sphere of fantasy. The scene which results from this procedure is nothing more than the rhetorical figure of aetiology, and is analogous only in appearance, because of its personification of nature, as a product of mythical thought. In reality the entities which are personified do not come fully to life but remain closed within the limits of the image. Even the dynamism which the Western reader might be induced to see in the same scene is only apparent. The movement is only fictitious and the only reality on which the poet's fantasy lingers is the motionless leaves of the waterlily on the water.

Again the insistence on certain words is characteristic of Nizāmīan usage. A good example can be found in the repetitions of the word 'pearl' and 'cypress' in the lines already quoted.

Besides aetiology, Nizāmī makes considerable use of other rhetorical expedients, such as paranomasia (with regard to this note, especially the Persian words indicated in brackets in some of the above translations).

Of the numerous Persian parallels to the poem of Nizāmī, it is sufficient for our purposes to speak of only two. One is the work of Jāmī the last great poet of classical Persian literature (d. 1492; the poem dates from 1484); the other is by his grandson, Hātifī (d. 927/1520–21; date of the poem is unknown). These writers both lived at Herat, in what is today Afghanistan.

As for Jāmī, in connection with Fuzūlī's poem, it is of interest only to point out that he was first among the Persians to give the story of the two Bedouin lovers a mystic meaning. He does not, however, elaborate the theme allegorically, but only states his interpretation in a few lines which follow Majnūn's death in which as an explanation of the young man's refusal of Laylā it is said that he was seduced by 'metaphorical' beauty; that his inebriation did not come from the 'cup', that is Laylā, but from the 'wine' contained in her, that is Divine love; that under the name of Laylā he understood another name, the name of God.

More attention must be given to the outlines of Hātifī's poem because of the wide use Fuzūlī makes of it. Regarding Qays's childhood, this adds one episode of the boy crying and comforting himself in the lap of a beautiful woman, and mentions the rite of circumcision. When Laylā leaves school there is a talk between mother and daughter. Majnūn's father goes in search of his son who has left home before, and not after, having asked for Laylā's hand. Majnūn's arm begins to bleed because at the same time a blood-letter has incised Laylā's vein (the episode is to be found in the *Mathnavī* of Jalāluddīn Rūmī).[4] Majnūn's father goes to an expert in love matters but his suggestions have no effect. At the same time as the request for Laylā's hand, Majnūn showed that he was completely mad by clasping a dog to his breast in front of Laylā's house (this episode too is found in the *Mathnavī*).[5] For the pilgrimage to the Kaaba is substituted a visit to an ascetic whom Majnūn begs to pray that his love may increase. The son of Ibn Salām (and not Ibn Salām) marries Laylā. She violently rejects him and the irritated young man repudiates her. In the meantime an old woman has informed Majnūn of Laylā's wedding, and letters are exchanged between the two. Then Hātifī speaks of Majnūn's friendship with the animals and his moaning at night. The young man goes to visit Laylā. A custodian who intervenes by uplifting his sword finds that his arm is paralysed. The episode of Naufal, which has been postponed to this point, ends differently from the Nizāmī version. After Naufal has won, he falls in love with Laylā and in order to get rid of Majnūn he prepares poison which he himself drinks by mistake and dies. Majnūn, instead of freeing a gazelle, buys a cypress which was to have been burnt. Laylā, when on a journey, lets go the reins of her camel which carries her off the road to a place where Majnūn is waiting. At first the two do not recognize each other. Majnūn faints. Laylā takes his head in her lap and when he comes to his senses she begs him to unite with her for ever. Majnūn refuses because he does not want the girl to lose her honour. He takes her back home and goes away moaning. Laylā dies. Majnūn dies too but not on his beloved's tomb. A caravan coming from Hijaz buries him.

In as much as the interest in the poem of Nizāmī is directed internally, so in that of Hātifī it is external. Hātifī is interested rather in the adventurous plot which he treats with grace and with a polished tendency to realism. Composed to satisfy unsophisticated tastes, the work must have been very popular as can be seen from the numerous copies which have been preserved and from the fact that it was kept in mind by other Persian and Turkish authors of poems parallel to that of Nizāmī.

CHAPTER FIVE

FUZŪLĪ'S LEYLĀ AND MEJNŪN

Many Turkish poets prior to Fuzūlī were inspired by Nizāmī's Laylā and Mejnūn. The most ancient appears to be Shāhidī, a courtier of Jem, brother and rival of Bāyezīd II, who completed his poem of over six thousand couplets, in AH 883 (AD 1478–9). Even before Jāmī (see Chap. IV), he gives a mystic interpretation to the story with frequent allusions to, among other things, 'metaphoric' love and 'true' love and the appearance of the 'mystery of the Lord' on Leylā's cheeks. The last meeting between the two lovers takes place in terms which are very similar to those used by Gülshehrī (Ch. IV). We know at least six other poems by Ottoman writers prior to that of Fuzūlī. Hamdī, a poet of a certain fame, is among these writers. A poem on the same subject moreover was written by 'Alī Shēr Navā'ī, the greatest Turkish poet of Central Asia, around 1484 (after that of Jāmī), and another in 1524 by Haqīrī, a Turkish poet from Tabrīz. None of these poems offers a mystic interpretation. The most recent, apart from Nizāmī and some of his imitators, mainly follow Hātifī.

None of these authors seems to have had any knowledge of their Turkish predecessors. This goes for Fuzūlī too. In the introduction, he declares in fact that he has begun the work encouraged by cultured Ottoman friends who begged him to be the first to put the story of the celebrated lovers into Turkish verse. Evidently the Turkish poems of *Leylā and Mejnūn*, even the works of such famous poets as Hamdi and Navā'ī, which already existed but of which apparently there were few copies in circulation (in fact, of some only one copy is known), were not known in Baghdad. Fuzūlī knew the divan of Navā'ī and was influenced by it as it was better known everywhere than the poet's romantic poems.

Fuzūlī's poem (in Ch. I we have seen the circumstances in which it was written), like innumerable other Persian and Turkish poems, is a reply (*jevāb*) to Nizāmī's poem. The 'reply' was a typical practice quite widespread in Persian and Turkish literature. The poets used to compose poems which had as a rule the same metre, the same subject, and the same style as the poems of writers whom they admired and desired to emulate. In the same circumstances, in other literatures where the concept of originality is more greatly felt, continuations, or works with similar themes, are more customary. Now the relationship between the 'reply' and the work to which this is addressed is obviously not the same as that between the work of art and its sources or between the original and an imitation. For the author of a 'reply', keeping close to the original was not a shortcoming; rather he felt that the nearer he kept to it the more successful he was. Rather than supplying new themes and moods they aimed at supplying variations on the same themes and moods. The result is, in our case, that on superficial examination Fuzūlī's poem may seem but a very slightly different repetition of the Nizāmīan poem. Only a careful comparison from which identities and differences clearly result can lead to an exact judgment.

Fuzūlī's poem like that of Nizāmī is composed in *hezej* metre, which goes $--\cup/\cup-\cup-/\cup--$. The unit of composition is the couplet formed of two lines which rhyme. From the sample that follows (the first six couplets of the narrative part) it can be seen that the words derived from Persian (or from Arabic through Persian) indicated in italics (to some, Turkish suffixes are added) come to about eighty per cent of the total. Samples from any other parts of the poem give a similar result. Only in these non-Turkish words do long vowels exist 'by nature' (in a Turkish word a vowel can count as long only 'by position', i.e. by appearing in a closed syllable); a vowel long by nature appearing in a closed syllable gives rise (unless the closing consonant is *n*) to a supplementary short syllable (–∪). In the lines that follow there are some cases of *imāle* licence which permits a Turkish vowel in an open syllable to be considered long.

Dihqān-i hadīqa-i hikāyet
*Mā'nī chemen*ine *gül* tikende
Qïlmïsh bu *revish*de *nüktedān*lïgh
Kim *khayl*-i *'Arab*da bir *jevānmerd*
Mūstejmi'-i *jümle-i fezā'il*
*Emr*ine *'Arab mutī' ü münqād*
(474–479)

Sarrāf-i jevāhir-i rivāyet
*Söz rishte*sine *güher* chekende
*Gül-rīz*lik ü *güher-feshān*lïgh
Jem'iyyet ü [1] *'izz ü jāh* ile *ferd*
Bulmïshdï *riyāset-i qabā'il*
Geh *Basra maqāmī* gāh *Baghdād*

The peasant of the garden of stories, the jeweller of the gems of tradition,
In planting roses in the meadow of ideas, in threading jewels on the thread of discourse,

In this way he subtly expressed himself, so hath he scattered roses and strewn gems.
Among the Arab cavaliers a generous man was unique in his following, honour and dignity.
He who within himself had united all virtues, had had command of the tribes.
The Arabs were obedient unto him and followed his orders. At times he stayed in Basra, at times in Baghdad.

Fuzūlī's language is therefore extremely Persianized. He not only uses a large number of Persian words but also Persian constructions such as the *izāfet* represented by the vowel 'i', which unites genitive nouns and links adjectives to substantives. (The first couplet would sound the same in Persian.) It is also mainly of a literary type, since only a small part of the Persian borrowings which appear therein were in use in the spoken language. Today the poem could not be read by a Turk in Turkey or in Azerbaijan without the help of a dictionary. At that time those characteristics were an advantage, because the Arab and Persian words which exhibited short and long vowels were adaptable to a versification of this very quantitative type. Furthermore they were an advantage because Persian was the common denominator of all Turkish literary circles. This made Fuzūlī's poem easily understood by cultured people not only in Baghdad but also in Anatolia, in Azerbaijan, and in Central Asia. The Turkish words were not an obstacle to general comprehension. They were few and these few were all or almost all in common use in the regions mentioned. In particular Fuzūlī's Turkish is not far from Ottoman Turkish. There are few phonetic and morphological differences and these are of little importance as far as understanding the text is concerned, e.g. *men* instead of *ben* ('I'), the gerundive form *-ende*, the accusative with the ending *-ni*, which however occurs only sporadically and was common in Central Asian Turkish.

Fuzūlī does not differ from his predecessors in his plot. They all based their work on that of Nizāmī, but they integrated or modified it on the basis of Persian 'replies' to the same. Those nearer to Fuzūlī's time used Hātifī's poem as a basis. This use of Hātifī is explainable not only because his poem was the last word on the matter in Persian literature, but also because it must have been very popular at the time (Ch. IV). Thus Fuzūlī makes use of both Nizāmī and Hātifī. While he mentions Nizāmī and gives his judgment on the subject of the poem, quoting some lines in Persian for this purpose, he does not mention Hātifī, contrary to what was required and to what his forerunners had mostly done.

On the whole Fuzūlī strips the plot of episodes contained in Nizāmī or Hātifī which were not indispensable for its development. When choosing between the two sources he does not proceed mechanically but with intelligence and artistic sensibility.

At first it would seem that he only proposes to rewrite Hātifī's poem. He follows it in fact almost word for word, reducing rather than amplifying, from the beginning to the episode of the request for Leylā's hand. However, a meeting between Leylā and Mejnūn in the springtime takes the place of the episodes where Mejnūn visits Leylā pretending to be blind and a beggar. The Turkish poet also leaves out the episodes of the blood-letter and of the expert in love matters, the motif of Mejnūn embracing the dog during the request for marriage. The point at which Fuzūlī leaves Hātifī in order to model himself directly on Nizāmī is where the former substitutes the episode of the pilgrimage of Mejnūn to the Kaaba with that of the visit to the ascetic, an unjustifiable and unhappy innovation. This means that an element which, in Nizāmī, is essential to the religious atmosphere of the poem, is lost.

Thus Fuzūlī keeps to Nizāmī from the episode of the pilgrimage to the end of the poem. In comparison with Nizāmī's poem Hātifī had introduced some innovations into this part. For example, Leylā is repudiated by her husband Naufal who tries to poison Mejnūn. There is no mention of the death of Mejnūn's father either, and to Fuzūlī this must have seemed odd and inopportune—so much so that he continued to follow Nizāmī's version. He does return to Hātifī but only occasionally and with wise discernment. From him he draws some of the details for the episode of the marriage of Leylā with Ibn Selām, of which we shall speak later. He also takes up again the episode of the visit of Mejnūn as a blind man to Leylā, and that of the blood-letter. These he had previously left out in order to insert them in more opportune places, one after the visit of Mejnūn as a prisoner in chains to Leylā, the other at the end of the last talk which the young man had with his father. Here the strength of Mejnūn's love is well demonstrated. Finally Fuzūlī takes the circumstances of the last meeting between Mejnūn and Leylā from Hātifī for reasons which we shall see later on.

In that part of the poem where Fuzūlī follows Nizāmī he obviously omits the meeting of Mejnūn with his father after the visit to the Kaaba which he had already, following Hātifī, placed before the visit. In this way he lets us understand why Mejnūn is with his father and not in the desert at the moment when he sets out on the pilgrimage. He also omits a whole series of episodes (absent also in Hātifī), the visits to Mejnūn of his uncle Salīm, Mejnūn's talk to his mother, the meeting of Leylā and Mejnūn in the palm grove, the visit of the poet Salām of Baghdad to Mejnūn, and the contrasted love of Zayd and Zaynab.

All things considered we note that Fuzūlī adds nothing of his own to the plot, with the exception of the springtime meeting of Mejnūn and Leylā towards the beginning. Even this episode does not seem original. Although it is inserted in the part taken from Hātifī, it would seem to be inspired by Nizāmī and precisely by the Nizāmīan episode to which it corresponds in the plot—Mejnūn sees Leylā on the threshold of the tent (a characteristic scheme of antithesis is repeated, as we shall see later). In the following scene of Mejnūn's desperation some of the lines seem reminiscent of Nizāmī:

He gropeth with his hand and rendeth his shirt; this corpse needeth not a shroud (Nizāmī p. 136).

With repugnance he tore off his shirt, the martyr of grief was ashamed of his shroud (Fuzūlī 863).

In ragged clothes, head uncovered, prostrate on the street of shame (Nizāmī p. 137).

I have dyed myself with the colour of shame and burned on the fire of passion (Fuzūlī 868).

The ampulla of wine I was holding fell and the glass broke. When the pieces of broken glass spread over my path, the wave happened to pass and carried away the glass, so that whoever should come to me should not cut their feet on the glass (Nizāmī p. 141).

Let not sparks fall from me on thee; since thou hast not received good, thou shalt not receive evil (Fuzūlī 871).

Both poets express the concept that Mejnūn does not want his friends to be hurt because of him.

Chase me not from this land; I myself am on horseback ready to flee (Nizāmī p. 161).

I am a bird. I fly from the nest; the idea of a house is not congenial to me (Fuzūlī 873).

In the episodes taken from Nizāmī, Fuzūlī modifies some details. So Mejnūn in chains takes the place not of a prisoner of war but of a murderer who must pay the price for the blood he has shed. The news of Leylā's marriage to Ibn Selām is taken to Mejnūn by Zeyd and not by a negro. Mejnūn talks to the night instead of to the planets Venus and Mars, to Mercury and to Jupiter. The scene where he sets the gazelle free follows the pilgrimage to the Kaaba, instead of the episode of Nevfel, and is accompanied no longer by the scene of Mejnūn with the deer and the crow but by the single scene of Mejnūn liberating a dove and entrusting it with a message for Leylā. The detail of the dove which builds its nest in Mejnūn's hair is found in Jāmī's poem. Since there is no other evidence that Fuzūlī used this, it is to be supposed that the detail itself is either a theme which he and Jāmī derive from a common source or an invention of Fuzūlī himself. An analogous theme occurs in lines of his divan (see Ch. II).

If we pass from the examination of the plot to that of the whole meaning of the work and the artistic realization of it, we shall see that Fuzūlī has his own conception of unity and his own interests, which in part agree and in part disagree with those of his sources. Fuzūlī, more than his predecessors, the Turk Shāhidī and the Persian Jāmī, places the mystic interpretation of the story in the foreground. So much so that his own work becomes an allegoric poem in which Leylā is the symbol of earthly beauty, which is destined to disappear when the soul of Mejnūn matures his love for Divine Beauty, that is for God himself. The transition from the ascetic theory of love of Nizāmī to the mystic one of Fuzūlī is a consequence of the great diffusion of the theory of the manifestation of the Divine Beauty in the human, and of 'metaphoric' love as a state preliminary to 'true' love in the period between the two writers. We have already spoken about this theory (in Ch. II); its most brilliant and popular exponent was Jāmī, not long before Fuzūlī. This conceptual evolution affords the explanation of the transformation performed by Fuzūlī of the romantic poem in imitation of Nizāmī into an allegoric poem. However an interpretation in the allegoric sense of the story of Mejnūn had already been given in the mystic literature both in prose and verse, even by Turkish writers such as the already mentioned Gülshehrī and 'Āshïq Pasha. Such an interpretation had already been accepted in the genre of the romantic poem by Shāhidī and Jāmī. Fuzūlī's giving his poem an allegoric structure does not indicate that he had been influenced by these two poets. It is quite unimaginable in the first case and improbable in the second. He in fact did not know the poem of Shāhidī and nothing makes us think that he knew that of Jāmī. (The common motive of the bird that built its nest on Mejnūn's head is not a deciding factor.) As Shāhidī had accepted the allegoric element independently of Jāmī, being anterior to him, so it is to be supposed that Fuzūlī did after Jāmī. He however goes further than the other two in giving to this element a literary value. If there was an influence of the mystic doctrines of Jāmī on Fuzūlī, it happened presumably not through the *Laylā and Majnūn* of the bard of Herat but through other writings of his of which Fuzūlī must have been aware (among others he translated a pamphlet of Jāmī's—not however on a mystic subject; see Ch. II). The influence of Jāmī on Fuzūlī is however a subject which still awaits special research.

The allegorical value of the poem is declared by Fuzūlī in the prose Preface I give here a literal translation, according to Baku edition, p. 11. (A free elegant translation below, p. 120):

My God! Then when the Leylā of the mystery of the truth retaineth that it is necessary to appear from the pavilion of Unity and with manifestation of her beauty adorneth the space of Form.
And then when the spirit of Mejnūn while wandering stunned in the Desert of Unawareness, seeing that splendour of beauty, loseth control of the reins of will.
If the tie of the Superior Fathers [the celestial spheres] *and the bond of the Inferior Mothers* [the four elements], *ignorant of that soul restoring savour and that gladdening joy, with deceit which appeareth like a sermon and with trickery which appeareth like advice want to move the chain of the breaking of the pact of union and procure the pretext for the dissolving of the way of connection,*
The hope is that this fact causeth not that, that Laylā ornament of the world be late in lifting the corporal veil,
Nor that this event make necessary that, that Mejnūn the wanderer of the world should fail to reject the representation of lust.

The same concepts are expressed in three quatrains (*rubā'ī*) about which we are not clear if they were meant to precede the prose Preface or the beginning of the poem itself.[2] The poet turning to God declares that he is about to deal with a religious mystery (the beloved's curls are in the phraseology of mystic poetry images of the impenetrable Divine mysteries). As he affirms that he speaks by the mouth of Mejnūn, he makes it evident that he desires to live the experience of the mad lover personally:

O Thou, the intoxication of whose beauty reacteth on love; Thou who constructed with love the building of the Created; Thou who twisteth in curls the locks of Leylā; Thou who putteth [them] *the chain around Mejnūn's neck!*

If I while searching for Reality set out along the way of the metaphor, if with the pretext of the fable I expose the mystery, if I undertake to describe Thee through Leylā, if I beg by the mouth of Mejnūn, kindly transform the night of my hope into day, make my fortune shine, and grant me success. Let my words cheer up the heart, as Leylā, make my verses as burning as those of Mejnūn (ed. Onan, p. 1).

The internal law of the poem and its characteristics are therefore to be looked for in the allegorical meaning. First it should be made clear how Fuzūlī's concept of life differs from that of Nizāmī. The *Laylā and Majnūn* of Nizāmī is permeated by a pessimistic vision of the world; Fuzūlī's poem is not.

This does not mean that Fuzūlī does not denounce—and several times—the fallacies of the world. Also through his characters he despises the adverse course of destiny. But these are fleeting attitudes and are contrasted with a different conception. Fuzūlī values the world (*dünyā*) positively, as a place of trial and pleasant sojourn:

What is the world and its accessories? Life in the world is but the thought of death.
Nevertheless I do not say that it is bad: it is a place of trial.
God knoweth that this pleasant residence hath given such peace to the heart,
That I have forgotten my ancient abode and I believed this world was my motherland and here I have settled.
Now it is difficult to leave it for another abode (vv. 76–79).

He actually takes up the defence of the world in one passage which is a typical example of *'mughāyara'*,[3] that is a paradoxical affirmation which would be said to be opposed to the opinion of Nizāmī.

The world is a heart-ravishing beauty but beware of judging her unfaithful.
Although thou art distracted with love for her, she surpasseth thee in searching for thee.
Thou searchest for her in ignorance, she is thy friend in knowledge.
For all the time that thou art her guest thou art blessed in pleasures and amusements.
When thou choosest to leave, when thou settest out towards God, she useth thy dust as eye-shadow, she will be thy guardian until the day of Resurrection.
For thee she consumeth herself; she conserveth and handeth thee over to Eternity.
Whosoever understandeth this subtle concept will not be contrary to the turning of the firmament.
Neither will he find torment in life nor avoid death (2162–2170).

Alongside the world Fuzūlī values positively 'the wheel of the firmament' (*charkh-i felek*), that is the fortune of the stars. Nizāmī only implicitly recognizes its subordination to Divine will and thus its providential worth. Fuzūlī is quite explicit on the matter and gives the impression of being polemical. In the introduction to the poem he affirms:

O thou without sight who looketh not at wisdom, ignorant of the contingencies of time,
Stay not there to blame the Wheel for being unfaithful and that its work is always cruelty and tyranny.
Explain to me what the Wheel hath done and what tyranny hath appeared? What possession of thine hath it taken from thy hand? From what position hath it thrown thee down? . . .
It hath lit the taper of thy hope, hath made every desire of thine easy.
It hath made thee a man from nothing. It hath gathered up means so that thou mightst enjoy it.
Thus hath the Wheel turned for thee. Say! What hast thou done for it?
At all times thou hast called it unfaithful, thou recitest a thousand prayers so that it may turn.
Since it hath been so affectionate to thee, repay not good with ill. (145–155).

At the end of the poem Fuzūlī returns to the subject. He scolds fortune (*felek*) for protecting the unworthy and for persecuting the worthy such as Mejnūn and himself. Fortune in its turn protests in self-defence:

O thou who art ignorant of how things stand, O incapable one who criticizeth all the acts of wisdom,
I go round in conformity with order: the cruelty I bestow is fidelity according to wisdom (3054–3055).

Fuzūlī differs from Nizāmī in making his centre of interest not so much the victory over the world as the passage from 'metaphoric' to 'true' love.

While the aspects of the love of Mejnūn which are represented by Nizāmī appear to be substantially the same in Fuzūlī, yet they are given different proportions and colour by the Turkish poet in accordance with his different formulation of the poem. (No change is observable as far as the other two elements of the Nizāmīan triad, madness and poetry are concerned.)

Mejnūn is from birth aware of the sorrow (*gham*) engrained in the existence in this world. This sorrow is not the total of all the sorrows of life, but rather an abstract cosmic sorrow, a concept absent in Nizāmī, which is particularly elaborated by mystic speculation. Grief of the soul far from the Divine presence is inevitable.[4] This is the meaning of Qays weeping when he opens his eyes to the light. These lines have no corresponding passage in Hātifī.

From the moment in which he fell into this dust-receptacle aware of his state, he began to groan.
Recalling that eve he wept tears and moaned.
This was because existence is a net of pain. The fatherland is Nothing.
(508–510).

The infant almost assumes the pose of the redeemer of sorrowing humanity:

With his cry he seems to say: O cruel world!
I have understood that the sorrow thou bringest is our lot and that not one of us is able to bear it.
I have come to be a companion to grief. Forward! Put my wretched self to the test!
Wherever grief is, linger not. Gather it and put it within my sad heart.
Give me the perfection to bear grief. Empty the world of sorrow. (512–515).

Because of his vocation for sorrow Mejnūn appears from the very beginning in the clothing of a 'saint'. It is not however that of the ascetic saint who mortifies himself and fights against his passions but of the saint who sublimates himself with infinite suffering.

The concept of love as liberating one from sorrow, rather than from the world, appears at the beginning of Fuzūlī's poem instead of being gradually introduced as in Nizāmī.

O love! I have come a pilgrim into this world and wander through the valley of sorrow. . . .
In this banquet where the wine is blood and the cup-bearer a ruthless butcher,
Pass me wine that I may become intoxicated and stunned and forget myself for ever,
That I might not know that I have come to this earth nor what fortune is.
That the world should become nothing in my eyes, that I should not notice the entanglement of this thread (519–525).

Mejnūn has an innate disposition to love which was within him even before he sucked it in with his mother's milk. While Hātifī explains the scene of Qays, a child appearing in the lap of a beautiful woman, with the phrase 'He would have become famous for love of an idol', Fuzūlī concludes, 'it is love that bowed to beauty'. Then the concept of sorrow returns, but accompanied by that of love and inseparable from it, as an instrument of freedom.

The soul was lost when sorrow for thee [Leylā] *came. I have freed myself of the worry of perishing.*
The taste of sorrow hath shown me eternal pleasure and perpetual gladness (775–776).

Mejnūn is aware of his destiny and accepts it willingly, not only at the moment of his birth but at all times. Nizāmī (and after him Hātifī, whom Fuzūlī follows in this part) in the first talk that Mejnūn has with his father after his madness, puts only words of discomfort for the inevitability of destiny into the young man's mouth. Fuzūlī on the contrary insists on the concept of the providentiality of love and sorrow and of voluntary acceptance of them in so far as they are part of the divine plan.

That day when within the matrix the pen of Power undertook the ornament of the form of my creation.
It filled my mind with passion and tied melancholy to my feet.
From head to foot love for my friend filled every vein and the skin of my body.
It gave my heart as property and my soul as a trust foundation to cruelty.
I transgress not this decree, I cannot dispose of that property and foundation (996–1000).

This determination inspires Mejnūn's prayer at the Kaaba which is expressed in words which are almost identical to those of Nizāmī.

Make the building of love for ever permanent within me, as sound as the foundations of the Kaaba.
Infuse within my heart grief for love sickness, at every instant, at all times, in every moment (1113–1114).

In speaking of Mejnūn's love Fuzūlī does not insist on the idea of chastity. This is not the side of Mejnūn's personality which the Turkish poet puts in evidence as much as the mystic impulse which makes him a saint. According to an innovation of Fuzūlī, Mejnūn's prayers provoke the initial failure of Nevfel's weapons for he is an adept of the

Truth (*ehl-i Haq*), a seer (*sāhib-nazar*), whose prayers are accepted by God and are efficacious. Later Ibn Selām dies of love-sickness, but also because he is the target of the sigh-arrow of Mejnūn (2434).

Mejnūn is however still in the state of 'metaphoric' love. The crisis in his soul, as in Nizāmī, seems to originate from his last meeting with his father, but is differently motivated. Fuzūlī faithfully follows the reasonings which Nizāmī attributes to the father but then he suddenly innovates. The old man criticizes Leylā with an attack which might seem ungenerous, but which in reality derives from the intention of the poet to show the inconsistency and fallacy of metaphoric love.

The fortunate hawk whose prey thou art every moment flieth from hand to hand.
Now it obeyeth Neufel's orders, now it is the companion of the soul of Ibn Selām.
Thou art so entangled in disadventure, thou art like the lamp at the banquet of others (2082–2084).

The subject is concluded in fact with the exhortation:

Be ashamed of this philandering, of this melting of the soul without profit.
Given that this worldly life doth not last, suppose that the beloved became thy friend,
Unite not with her since thou knowest that thou must part from her.
Abandon this foolish behaviour, remember God, name no others but Him.
He is indeed the place to which the soul will return. End the discourse with Him for He is the conclusion (2085–2089).

Naturally the father does not speak in terms of mystic love, but rather in terms of terrestrial wisdom. The mystic way with the annihilation of the individual 'I' in the cosmic 'I' is, however, at once suggested by the 'Sultan of Love' (*'ishq shehriyārī*) symbol of God, which recalls the young man who was on the point of giving in to his father's advice.

O thou whose existence in the world belongeth to me. What hast thou of thine in thy body or soul?
Put not forward claims on the soul since that is mine. Abandon the body which is my dwelling.
Abandon thy ego, separate thyself from body and soul! Forfeit thy existence. Know that thou art with thy entity! (2108–2110).

The episodes of the blood-letter and of the two images are parables to illustrate this concept. The minor importance which Fuzūlī attributes to the process of Mejnūn's detachment from the world may explain the absence in the poem of the conversations of the young man with Zayd, Salīm and Salām, in which Nizāmī goes deeply into the ascetic side of his personality.

The last meeting between the two lovers, as in Nizāmī and Hātifī, is the culminating moment. Fuzūlī takes the themes from both sources but he elaborates them in his own way. He repeats the lines of Nizāmī about the unity of the lover and beloved almost identically but while the Persian poet concentrates his thought exclusively on the annihilation of Mejnūn's 'I', Fuzūlī counterbalances this theme with Mejnūn's refusal of the corporeal Leylā. We have seen this theme before in various writers, the last being the Turkish Gülshehrī, 'Āshïq Pasha and Shāhidī.

What appeareth in me is thee, I exist not. That which exists is thee. . . .
If I am I, who art thou, O friend. If thou art thou, who am I, unhappy one?
Being full of thee along the path of Unity it would not be convenient
That I should search for thy sign externally, that I consider an extraneous abode as thine (2703, 2705–2707).

In Mejnūn's last words the theme dear to Nizāmī, that of Mejnūn's purity, mingles with that of Hātifī about Mejnūn's concern for the young woman's good name. This last theme is not only seen by Fuzūlī from the point of view of Bedouin morality but is also confused with the mystic motives of the veiled divinity and of the lover who throws aside both honour and intellect.

It seems to me, however, that, from the aesthetic point of view, the expression of the emotion in Mejnūn's heart seems to prevail over such themes. This is suggested to the poet by his human sensitiveness. The young man does not end his conversation abruptly with a dry refusal of the terrestrial Leylā, and take no further interest in her destiny, but he continues to address affectionate and reverent words to her which allow tender sentiments to continue to flow between the two.

If thou hast compassion, O fairy-faced idol, it would be sufficient as an act of compassion,
That thou remain for ever behind a curtain, that thou accustom thyself to remaining hidden.
That thou show not thy beauty to others by going around like the sun every day.
Thy way of conduct is evidence of my manner.
I am dust on the path of love. All would have it that I am pure.

Have pity on me, O faithful idol! See to it that the wagging tongues of slander have nothing to say!
Having adopted the way and the conduct of love, I've forgotten the path of honour.
Leave thou not hold of the hem of intellect, keep thy honour from all detriment (2718–2725).

After the conversation is over the poet intervenes directly to describe Mejnūn not only as an ascetic, which he is only in Niẓāmī, but also as a mystic saint.

His abode was the flourishing city of Nearness to God, it was dutiful for souls to pay him honour....
Under the guise of wild animals angels had come to accompany this human being....
His pure body became light without the contamination of food and drink. Having reached the purity of behaviour he had seen Truth through the Metaphor (2788, 2790, 2796–2797).

He is in short 'the perfect being' (*zāt-i kāmil*, 2807), that is, the mystic who has reached the last goal in the journey towards God.

In so far as the aspect of saintliness prevails, so the figure of Mejnūn loses its drama. And in truth from this aspect Fuzūlī's Mejnūn is but a pale reflection of that of Niẓāmī. The Turkish poet repeats with little originality a large part of the various attitudes which Niẓāmī attributes to the young man. A comparison on this point with the Niẓāmīan version is therefore superfluous. There is however an element which is worthy of note in Fuzūlī which does not appear in Niẓāmī, apart of course from the higher lyrical tone, about which we shall speak shortly. This, in singular contrast with the elevated spiritual atmosphere of the poem, is the tendency of Fuzūlī to good-natured realism which at times comes close to humour. This tendency is obviously connected to a similar tendency in Hātifī. It can be demonstrated, however, that in Fuzūlī it is not a simple reflection of the Persian poet, but on the contrary corresponds to an authentic poetical disposition in him. Fuzūlī does not only repeat themes of this kind introduced in Hātifī but he develops and creates his own. One example relating to Mejnūn (we shall notice later others relating to Leylā) is this: a bare hint of Hātifī referring to Qays's childhood (he was going to see her on the pretext of asking: Is this slate yours or mine?) is elaborated by Fuzūlī with a whole series of neat and original evocations of the miniature world of children.

Fuzūlī differs from Niẓāmī by being inspired by a typical motive of lyrical love, the desire to die by the hand of the beloved. While Nizāmī gives no explanation of the strange behaviour of Majnūn during the fights fought for him by Naufal, Fuzūlī justifies the desires of the youth that the adversary should win. If these were granted he would become a prisoner and either would live beside Leylā if accepted by her or would die happily by her hand. The same motif occurs in another innovation of Fuzūlī's, that is Mejnūn's jealousy for Ibn Selām's death as a broken-hearted victim of love. Previously Ibn Selām had been reproved by the poet for having renounced Leylā for fear of being killed.

Where Fuzūlī seems to be at his most original is in the manner in which he deals with the character of Leylā. He gives it a prominence which is undoubtedly greater than that which it has in Nizāmī. He not only renders it lyrically, as he does for Mejnūn, but, either following Hātifī or of his own initiative, he expresses the girl's sentiments of love, joy, and sadness according to the tendency which we have already mentioned. He catches her in moments of naïve artfulness more suitable to a girl in everyday life than to a heroine. In Hātifī, when Leylā is scolded by her mother for flirting with the young man, she replies:

O my lady, tell me what be love? Who is loved and who loveth?
Perhaps love is a spring flower or the name of a village in some country
Or is love something we eat? For the love of God tell me well.
I have never heard this word. It is a word which is not often heard by people (f.92).

Fuzūlī not only welcomes this suggestion:

Thou sayest words that I know not, I understand not their meaning.
Thou sayest beloved, lover, I am an innocent simple-minded maiden.
I know not the meaning of this discourse. Tell me how shall I not feel disturbed?
No one hath ever mentioned love, now I hear the name from thee.
In the name of God, Mother! What doth love mean? Unveil this occult mystery (684–689).

He now continues in the same ironic tone:

I go not to school of mine own free will. There is nothing that I do without thy permission.
Thou sayest to me: Go to school. And thou too tellest me: Take care, go not.
Which word must I believe? How may I trust thee?

On the other hand I adapt not myself willingly to this oppression, to being displayed like a candle at a meeting.
Mixing with strangers, suffering fixed in one place
Without being able to look, passing the time in boredom.
The master never leaveth in peace, now reading now reciting.
God knows if it were my intention to go. Do children perhaps like school?
(690–697).

Later on Leylā, surrounded by her friends who are telling her stories in order to amuse her, pretends to have hurt herself so that she may cry, forgets make-up, clothes, needle and silk and invents a game which allows her to stay alone in the country.

Let's fold the delicate skirts to our waists, let's pick gay flowers.
And whoever collects the most shall be among the most proficient of these idols (1357–1358).

For the maiden the hour of her marriage to Ibn Selām is drawing near. The scene of the dressing of the bride is taken from Hātifī. The realistic notes this time point to a soul in distress:

The hairdresser combed her locks and prepared her beauty-spots to accentuate her beauty with ornament.
With sighs and incessant tears she smudged the beauty-spot, ruffled her locks (1723–1724).

The symbolic value of the character appears for the first time when the maiden implores Fortune not to separate her from her predestined lover.

I am his and he is mine from Eternity. Keep this lock unscathed.
O Wheel! When this bond was sealed, perhaps thou didst not even exist.
Forward! Renounce tyranny and cruelty! Look, God is present. Be generous (1738–1740).

The motif of cunning returns again. Fuzūlī does not take Leylā's violent refusal of her husband from Nizāmī (followed by Hātifī). He rather attributes a strategy to the girl. A jealous goblin with raised sword would kill her and her gloom if he approached her (the theme of the goblin with the sword drawn is perhaps inspired by Sa'dī, for whom the menaced one is Majnūn).[5] Again Leylā disguises her grief cunningly by pretending to be homesick for her father, for her mother, for her friends; or to be annoyed with the dressmaker who has sewn her dress badly (1975–1978).

I have the impression that Fuzūlī gave up the idea of Leylā's rebellion to her husband and substituted another motif, because the serious offence seemed contrary not so much to the psychology of the character as to his particular conception of the submissive position of women. The behaviour which he attributes to the girl makes one think of a severe and puritanical attitude even if on the other hand her behaviour itself is sufficiently justified by the halo of purity—almost of saintliness—which emanates from the symbolic value of the character.

Fuzūlī differs from Nizāmī in that Leylā after her marriage does not reveal her feelings to her husband and above all does not dare to invite Mejnūn to a meeting however chaste. After her husband's death and her return to her father's house, instead of giving free vent to her feelings and joy and sending for Mejnūn without wasting time, she keeps up the pretence of mourning for the death of Ibn Selām. She has not the courage to take a decision and gives herself up to God:

If I have rent the robe of patience, the road of Thy judgment seemeth dangerous.
If I should yield my heart, grief and affliction would be beyond my power of resistance.
Should I abandon honour in showing myself a friend to Mejnūn?
I fear that my chastity should come out of it trampled underfoot and that the situation is not in keeping with the Decree.
If instead in this passion I should maintain my honour and the Palace of the Union remain preserved,
I fear that the smoke of Mejnūn's sighs change the colour of my state.
The sighs of the sincere are efficacious. It is dangerous not to keep watch.
This and that; in my weakness I know not what advice to follow
(2519–2526).

The dilemma is resolved not at the level of the female heart but at the symbolic one. Leylā is only a store for her beauty. She will have to keep it intact until the end which is imminent arrives. (The hint at Mejnūn's magic power is a forewarning of death.)

O Lord! Help me so that this deposit may be guarded until the day of Resurrection.
So that in the moment when I approach the Nearness I may go with high head and a pure face (2534–2535).

It is not Leylā who attracts Mejnūn to her, not does she direct her own steps in his direction but it is the camel guided from on High who leads her as she invokes the presence of the beloved. In the different conception of the character may be sought the reason for which Fuzūlī abondoned the Nizāmīan version of the last meeting and chose that of Hātifī, although he inserted it in a very different psychological and spiritual context.

At the last meeting, Leylā, still with continual allusions to the allegorical sphere, expresses herself in touchingly human accents. She proudly exalts the beauty and merits of the beloved. Full of emotion and joy in recognizing him, she tenderly offers her own love and at the end she is sorrowfully surprised at his aversion. These are the most beautiful pages of the poem, for the expression of the moving drama. Fuzūlī's inspiration is original even when following the versions in part of Hātifī and in part of Nizāmī. The motif of reserve occurs again in the last words which Mejnūn addresses to Leylā. It is useless to say that in Fuzūlī there are no traces of the passionate caresses which Nizāmī's Laylā bestows on Majnūn during their last meeting.

The last to speak is not Mejnūn, as in Nizāmī and Hātifī, but Leylā. Reflecting sadly on all the care which once she dedicated to her own beauty to please her beloved, she (and here the symbolic value is prevalent) accepts the destiny which awaits her:

Until when will the dust of form cloud up the mirror of my essence?
It is time that the mirror should shine, that the Essence throw aside the attributes. . . .
That I cover the body with a robe of Nothing and spread over my face the veil of annihilation (2757–2758, 2762).

The death of the girl thus finds a justification at the allegorical rather than at the human level, as it did in Nizāmī. The human side reappears however. For she has remained immaculate; the terrestrial Leylā will unite with her lover blessed in Paradise. This even more than in Nizāmī is a yielding to the motif of the happy ending.

In Fuzūlī the secondary characters are at a lower moral level than in Nizāmī. Mejnūn's father, following Hātifī, gives his son some precepts of common morality at the first meeting and then he deceives him by saying that Leylā is waiting at home. At the second meeting, Fuzūlī follows Nizāmī, apart from the innovation already indicated, which in itself is psychologically on a lower level. Fuzūlī also adds the admonition which fits his philosophy of life better than that of Nizāmī, that is the concept that the world is a workshop in which each has his task allotted to him. Leylā's mother gives a rather shallow little sermon on good behaviour, on the lines of Hātifī. Leylā's father does not address Nevfel as, in Nizāmī, in a proud speech but simply offers him his daughter. Later he is defined briefly as 'of a black heart, benefactor of the despicable, an ignorant old man' (2026). Nevfel gives up the idea of taking advantage of his victory. This victory had been obtained by him as a result of his vows when he was not able to win, and because of Mejnūn's invocations. Notwithstanding this, Fuzūlī puts the same magnanimous words into his mouth as did Nizāmī. Ibn Selām cuts a better figure than he does in Nizāmī. At first he is almost held in ridicule for the fear which the goblin inculcates and for the credulity with which he allows himself to be tricked by Zeyd, who tells him that the messages he passes between Mejnūn and Leylā are amulets. He, however, redeems himself by dying not from overeating but from the torment of unrequited love. Zeyd substitutes the two symbolic messengers which we have seen in Nizāmī.

Fuzūlī's plan of composition reflects that of Nizāmī with only slight but significant differences. The construction of the introduction is in part original. The prose Preface and the three quatrains placed at the beginning are both elements which are unusual in the romantic poems. They are connected, as we have seen, to a particular meaning which the poet wishes to give to his work. The obligatory parts (in praise of God, of the Prophet, and of the Sultan, on the motive of the composition of the work) are connected as in Nizāmī with philosophical and personal considerations. These have already been referred to, and, with the addition of the qasidas, offer with their different metre a break in the rhythm of the *mesnevī*. After the qasida in praise of Muhammad, the chapters which follow (including the praises of Suleymān and the motive of the composition of the work) are introduced by invocations to the cupbearer (*sāqī*). The lines after the first invocation may be considered as corresponding to the *sāqī-nāmā* of Nizāmī, while the succeeding invocations represent introductory formulae, which are taken up, as we shall see, in the course of the poem. The songs in praise of the governor Üveys are on the other hand introduced by an invocation to the pen (cf. chap. II). The final part is original with the trial of Fortune, which ends in the exaltation of Poetry.

In narration too, Fuzūlī uses introductory formulae analogous to those of Nizāmī. He repeats Nizāmī's reference to the 'noble native of Fars' (1223), but for the rest he too uses vague references like the lines quoted above as a sample from the text. In some cases Fuzūlī's adaptation of the formula to the subject introduced is notable. In the following example the formula and the subject have a warrior-like tone:

The sword of the warrior of the tale so dipped in the blood of this battle (1454).

and in this a mournful tenor:

Those who gather roses in the meadow of suffering, those who give bad news in the world, in writing the book of grief, have thus exposed it (2923–2924).

A similar procedure may be noted in one of the introductory formulae of a descriptive nature which also precedes a warlike subject:

When the warrior of Anatolia [the sun], *his sword drawn, subdued the people of Syria, the victory went to the* [white] *Turkish army; the* [black] *Arab army was defeated* (1576).

Another formula of the same kind introduces the episode of Leylā on the camel:

When the moon-Leylā, crossing the firmament, suddenly lost the night-caravan, the sun like Leylā rising alone, placed a yellow litter on the camel (2568–2569).

Only in this case do we notice in Fuzūlī the typical Nizāmīan type of verbal link (in the preceding verse the word 'moon' occurs). Another introductory formula adopted by Fuzūlī—which even if it does not occur in the *Laylā and Majnūn* of Nizāmī occurs in other poems of the same Nizāmī and also in his imitators—is the invocation of the cup-bearer.

O cupbearer, bring that pure wine, for the account of sorrows has reached the requisite degree.
Sorrow is the enemy of the unfortunate soul. Delay not, drive it away for it is misfortune (1022–1023).

Since the wine poured out by the cup-bearer is the symbol of mystical experience, the repeated formula keeps the reader aware of the higher meaning of the story.

Fuzūlī's epithets are not so brilliant as Nizāmī's and they are not connected in long series. None the less they reflect a certain inventive power. Mejnūn is said to be for example 'emperor of the kingdom of love', 'moon of the apogee of misadventure and suffering' (2128), and 'rare Hūmā (mythical bird) of the zenith of reverence' (2344). Leylā on the other hand is 'springtime in the meadow of fidelity, field of tulips of the love-sick grief' (1224), 'shell of the pearls of sorrow' (1225) and 'cypress with the jasmine-scented breast, plunderer of the goods of patience and tranquillity, empress of the kingdom of beauty, moonlight in the night of mirth and peace' (2411–2412).

Fuzūlī also uses series of contrasts as an element of composition. Here is how he deals with the above-quoted passage from Nizāmī (pp. 77–8). The inversion is an innovation:

Though great is Leylā's grief it does not equal sad Mejnūn's sorrow.
Leylā's hand is offended by the needle, swords do not offend Mejnūn.
The touch of silk mortifies Leylā, Mejnūn finds pleasure in chains.
Leylā seeks to diminish her sorrow, Mejnūn continually increases his.
Mejnūn is a captive of sorrow. To whom doth Leylā give consolation?
The torture of fever holdeth Mejnūn. For whom is Leylā a doctor?
O my Lord!
Mejnūn is a prisoner in Leyla's net. Toward whom doth she incline (1409–1415).

Fuzūlī regularly repeats the descriptive clichés introduced by Nizāmī: the beauty of Leylā (565–580); another similar one which he adds for Mejnūn (584–594); the garden in spring (1321–1339); Nevfel's fights (1514–1525, 1570–1573); the starry night (2240–2279); the garden in autumn (2823–2834). It is worth noting that Fuzūlī's descriptions are shorter, several very much so. This may arise from the smaller dimensions of the Turkish poem in comparison with the Persian one, but also because of Fuzūlī's lesser interest in developing such parts as are principally of an ornamental nature. Fuzūlī seems to prefer small scenes after the manner of Hātifī to the great frescoes of Nizāmī. Nizāmī condenses the image of Laylā coming back from the garden into two couplets:

The roses were tied in a bunch to the top of the cypress [Laylā], *she had ruined the market of julep and roses. The two curly locks interwoven and intertwined in a chain* (p. 191).

This is extended in Fuzūlī with new details:

In order to camouflage the blood streaming from her eyes, she wore a tunic and dress of a rose tint.
So that it should be similar to the smoke of sighs, on her head she wore a violet scarf.
So that the sound of lamentation might be trodden under foot, bracelets tinkled at her ankles.

So that the tears should not be noticed on her face, she wore strings of pearls on her cheeks.
On her graceful head she had put handkerchiefs, she had tied her skirts to her waist (1422–1426).

The scene of maidens amusing themselves is an invention of Fuzūlī's:

A host of chaste maidens accompanied her with graceful gait, lifted the veil of propriety from their faces, took away the curtain of bashfulness,
Whoever knew a game or a trick showed it off without fault;
Sometimes they sang songs, uniting their voices with that of the nightingale.
Sometimes the sweet patterns they wove in dancing made the box-tree ashamed (1345–1349).

In another connection we have already mentioned the scene of Leylā's wedding toilet; we can now add that of the wedding procession.

Idols with rose-pink faces came together, each bearing a candle.
Five hundred idols with rose-pink faces and sweet lips prepared the ceremony of mirth.
A hundred fragments of moon, with rosebud mouths, sprinkled rose-water on the path.
A hundred rose-pink cheeks carrying censers of sweet aloes perfumed the air with amber.
A hundred faces like the moon united their voices to that of the orchestra.
A hundred inebriated narcissi carried round the cups, offering the rose-coloured cup to the friends.
A hundred trays of gold on the heads of a hundred roses were destined to be scattered around (1779–1715).

Little everyday dialogue scenes rendered with liveliness and naturalness of speech, almost mimes, are taken from Hātifī. Examples of this are the talk between Leylā and her mother already mentioned, and the scene where Mejnūn's father asks for Leylā's hand for his son. This is almost folkloristic in tone. Into the mouths of those who are trying to comfort the weeping young woman and are ignorant of the real motive of her tears, Fuzūlī places words which are exactly the opposite of those used by Hātifī on the eve of Leylā's marriage, but they are inspired by the same spirit of realism.

They tell her:

Thou who art as sweet as jasmin. Thou who art accustomed to mother and father.

Now that thou art taking leave of them thou shalt see how cruel absence is. No one will forbid thee to cry.
Many people suffer from this separation, but, since this is the habit of people, exaggerate not in grieving.
Girls remain not for ever in the house of their father. They tie not always their affection to their mother.
It is necessary that thou shouldst drink the wine of forgetfulness and forget thy father and mother (1761–1766).

Like Nizāmī, Fuzūlī does not forget to ornament the poem with pearls of a didactic nature. However, he indulges much less than Nizāmī in digressions which interrupt the thread of the discourse. Intrusiveness on the part of the Turkish poet is short and rare. The longest intrusion (twenty-two couplets) is dedicated to the Sanctity of Mejnūn (2786–2808). In general the moral or philosophical considerations of Nizāmī are banalized in Hātifī; thus in Fuzūlī we have the example of what happened to Nizāmī's words referring to the desire of Qays's father to have a son:

He was not aware that in that delay was hidden good. . . . The end of the skein of the unknown is hidden; many locks if thou shouldst consider well have keys (p. 107).

With these words the poet alludes to the sad fate which awaited the baby, which had better never have been born. Hātifī takes up this Nizāmīan concept again, adding his own lines on the uninspired idea that it is better not to have children than to have bad children. Fuzūlī describes this idea at length without preserving any trace of Nizāmī (288–294).

The long disquisitions which Nizāmī introduces on the occasion of the death of the principal characters are limited to a few lines by Fuzūlī. In order to expound his own philosophy the Turkish poet makes his starting point mainly in the invocations to the cupbearer the function of which as introductory formulae we have already seen.

Fuzūlī pushes the use of direct speech much further than does Nizāmī. A quantitative comparison is here significant. The parts in direct speech occupy about one sixth of Nizāmī's poem and about one half of Fuzūlī's (excluding in both cases the introductory and final parts). But the difference between Nizāmī and Fuzūlī is not only quantitative. Fuzūlī in fact gives particular importance to the development of monologues of a lyrical type following two lines, one of them in common with Nizāmī, the other his own. The first is that of prayer to God or lamentations over destiny, but above all of speeches to animals and things. The few examples of this in Nizāmī are multiplied in Fuzūlī. Mejnūn turns to the Kaaba (1103–1120), to the mountain (1149–1157), to the gazelle (1175–1184), to the dove (1199–1210), to the chain (1624–1628), to the planet Mercury (2284–2289), to the planet Mars (2292–2296), to tears (2951–2956). Leylā addresses the candle (1245–1265), the moth (1268–1280), the moon (1288–1296), the zephyr (1305–1315), the cloud (1361–1369), the night and the morning (2497–2511), the camel (2549–2558), the garden (2840–2844). The object of some of these is to entrust messages for the beloved to the animal or object. In general, the person tries to establish a relationship of sympathy with the thing which he is addressing, attributing to it sentiments of love. This relationship is introduced by rhetoric and therefore the speeches often show traces of artifice. Besides this they do not fail to produce the impression of mannered pathos. For example, Mejnūn's speeches to the mountain and to tears seem to me not entirely devoid of poetic effect. If we imagine the poet balancing himself in a mystic sphere where the idea of love dominates as a cosmic force, the process, no matter how artificial and mannered, finds a proper aesthetic justification. The use of speeches of this kind by Fuzūlī has precedents in Arabic literature. Offhand it would be difficult to indicate another Persian or Turkish romantic poet who makes such frequent use of speeches of this type.

The other method followed by Fuzūlī is the insertion of compositions such as the ghazal (altogether 24) and the murabba' (2) which, being in a metre different from that of the rest of the poem, have the effect of breaking the monotony of the repetition of the same rhythm. They also bring about a variation in tone and style which is particularly suitable for the expression of the sentiments of the characters.

Examples of such a procedure in Persian and Turkish romantic poems prior to Fuzūlī are numerous. Among others, it is used by Shāhidī, who wrote the first 'reply' which we know in Turkish to Nizāmī's poem. It seems obvious that Fuzūlī was influenced by the fact that the poem had a poet as a chief character. It is natural that Mejnūn should sing in lyrical solos and that by reflection so does Leylā, so much so that in the Arabic version some verses are attributed to her.

I have mentioned the differences in style. In fact, the lyrical passages, more than the rest of the poem, are similar to the ghazals of the divan whose style I have previously tried to illustrate with the typical thematical variations and characteristic motifs of the mystic-erotic lyric. The author even uses his *makhlas* (poetic name). Thus it happens that the poet mixes his concepts and attitudes which are properly mystical, such as the ideas of poverty (*faqr*) and of annihilation (*fenā*), of reproach (*melāmet*) and of misbelief (*kufr*), or else the argument against 'the intellect' (*'aql*) and the bigot (*zāhid*). Obviously such mixtures may produce discordances. On the whole the poet succeeds admirably in adapting the lyrical parts to the varying situations, especially towards the end of the poem when the allegorical meaning is revealed and the mystic terminology used in the lyrical tradition is thus justified.

Whoever reads Fuzūlī's poems in translation will hardly be able to form an adequate idea of his verbal style. No matter how well translations are done they can never, from this point of view, offer a true mirror to the original. The reader remembering what was said about Nizāmī's style will note that we are faced with the same stylistic tradition. There are, however, differences between the poets. Nizāmī's pomp contrasts with his subject. The poet himself was aware of this. He knew that the sad story was unsuitable for his aesthetic ideas. Fuzūlī's style is relatively simpler and therefore more suitable to the subject.

Fuzūlī's metaphors are generally less audacious than Nizāmī's and tend to be too common. Fuzūlī too makes wide use of the genitive construction in the function of comparison. Some examples taken from only twenty couplets are: 'the door of mercy', 'the candle of intention', 'the chest of hope', 'the design of desire', 'the offshoot of the garden of intent', 'the rose of the garden of generosity', 'the net of suffering', 'the valley of suffering' (500–520).

These, all worked in the same pattern, are sufficient to give an idea of his repertoire. In Nizāmī, for example, metaphors are used vividly and with panache, but in Fuzūlī become a purely mechanical process. There is a passage based on Hātifī which is significant in this case. Fuzūlī gives all his images according to forms of letters of the alphabet.

O Alif, fall from thy upright position. Be ashamed of thy tall figure. Thou braggest of thy desire for her person. She hath gone away. How strange that thou shouldst remain upright.
O Nūn, since the eyelashes of the beloved are hidden, take care that thou remain not exposed to the look.
O Mīm, since her mouth hath disappeared, Nothing should suit even thee (751–754).

The poet likes the scheme so much that he employs it again with other letters, but once more with the lineaments of the beloved as the other term of comparison (950–951).

Fuzūlī, though less frequently than Nizāmī, comments on the concepts or situations, or introduces them directly in the key of images.

In general he is less original in his choice of image and makes use of commonplaces:

Leylā was obliged to remain at home, the royal pearl returneth to the shell.
The star remaineth fixed in the constellation, the gem was prisoner of the chest.
The ruby was imprisoned in the bosom of stone, the rose-water was held in the narrow flask (703–705).

Mejnūn's father asks for the hand of Leylā for his son (the analogous situation has been seen in Nizāmī; see above):

Now I desire that this rare pearl be placed on the plate of the balance to weigh against the ruby.
So that the ruby and pearl may be matched and I may form a substance which cheers the heart.
To many mines as a pick I have turned, from many I have asked news of rubies.
Although in each mine there are many rubies, there is none worthy.
I have heard that thou hast a ruby worthy of my pearl.
Please satisfy me, be generous! Honour my pearl with thy ruby (1044–1049).

Mejnūn explains to Nevfel how every attempt to obtain Leylā has failed and concludes with the aphorism:

Much gold was wasted on the ground but the philosopher's stone was never found. . . .
Know that antimony increaseth the light, but what is the use if the eyes are blind? (1477, 1479).

Fuzūlī's scenes are more crowded and complicated than those of Nizāmī in the descriptive clichés, but for this very reason they are less convincing. Fuzūlī too uses the magic wand of aetiology quite ably and at times with pathetic tones. In the description of spring, the cloud splits the head of the bud with stones of hail, and on opening the bud itself medicates its own wound with cotton wool, that is, with white down (1326–1327).

In the description of autumn, the violent rain beats the garden with darts, and the wind with its icy breath turns the water into ice, and it forges a breastplate in defence (2831–2833).

This emotional use of aetiology, which in Nizāmī has usually only a decorative function, is most convincing in the speeches which offer a precise interpretation of nature from the emotional point of view. One example among many is the speech Mejnūn makes to the mountain: the pebbles which roll down its folds are stones with which the mountain smites its breast (a conventional indication of grief); the water which gurgles from the spring are tears falling from its eyes (1153).

The use of imagery by Fuzūlī is particularly elaborate in the representation of the sentiments, where the language is similar to that of lyrics. He subtly combines conventional images, succeeding, for example, in expressing satisfactorily the vain suffering of Leylā:

She sighed but to what avail? That breeze could not open the bud of her heart. She wept tears, but to what end? The tree of intent did not spring up (707–708).

Or else with analogous combinations her joy in finally meeting her beloved:

It seemeth that the rain of tears hath been efficacious for a tender shoot hath appeared in our (my) rosebed.
Evidently the fire of sighs burneth for it hath lit the lamp for the night of our (my) separation (1642–1643).

The play sometimes becomes subtle, even remaining within the range of the conventional repertoire. While in the verses quoted above, we have metaphors: 'tears' = fertilizing water; 'sigh' = wind or fire, which pass naturally into the other series: 'tree' = intention; rose-shoot = Mejnūn; 'bud' = heart; 'lamp' = night of separation, in the following example an artifice is used to connect the images. This is the ambiguity implicit in the word *perīshān*, which first of all evidently refers to Leylā's hair as 'dishevelled' and then to Mejnūn's state as 'deranged'.

I go towards the fountain with the pretext of taking a bath.
There alone, my body bare, I loosen my hair, I look in the mirror and see thy state just as it is (1980–1982).

In the verses immediately following, the images of the breeze-arm and of the zephyr-lips are arranged according to the rhetorical figure of *leff ü neshr*, a kind of parallelism.

My neck is not laden with other necklaces. On my rubies [lips] no other discourse runs. My neck asks the breeze for thy arm. My rubies asks the zephyr for thy lips (1983–1984).

We may also note the double meanings of *havā*—'breeze' and 'passion', *sormaq*—'ask' and 'suck by kissing'.

Another example of the artificial figuration is the episode of Mejnūn going to Leylā disguised as a blind man. The episode is taken from Hātifī, and Fuzūlī adds the motive of the bandaged eyes represented as two malefactors, guilty of having looked upon Leylā and ready for their punishment.

Hyperboles which would have delighted a seventeenth-century poet go hand in hand with rhetorical artifices.

He was a cloud of disasters, the rain his tears, the lightning his sighs. His rain and lightning from the body and from the soul were at such a sign that
If a flash of light had reached the seas, or a drop of water had fallen in the deserts,
The seas would have become deserts and the deserts would have become seas (902–905).

With other rhetorical expedients Fuzūlī is on the whole not so lavish as Nizāmī. The repetition of the same word is rare in Fuzūlī but so frequent in Nizāmī that it constitutes a characteristic of his style. We have an example in the repetition of the words *rose* and *pearl* in the lines translated above (p. 77).

Fuzūlī uses not only Persian homophones for his ambiguities but also homophones which have different meanings in Persian and Turkish, sometimes with expressive efficacy. An example of the first case is:

Say not that I should stay far from men [merdüm]; *the pupils* [merdüm] *are within the eyes* [or one cannot help seeing men] (615).

An example of the second case is found in Mejnūn's speech to the mountain:

Thou art a suitable companion for me. The lover is always with the wound [dāgh in Persian] *or with the mountain* [dagh in Turkish] (1152)
or in the line:
He is not a stranger [yad in Turkish] *for thee. Remember* [eyle yād: yād Persian] *thy son. See that the enemy hath not to rejoice* (2034).

If we wish to condense the difference between Nizāmī's and Fuzūlī's poems into a few words, we should say that in the first a sense of the pessimism of life prevails, in the second we have a supernatural experience. In the first the austere representation of human affections dominates, while in the second there is good-natured realism. The first shows signs of a greater power of fantasy and the second of greater sensitivity and lyrical tension. The first is more complex, the second more linear. The first is involved often to the point of being obscure, the second more simple and more flowing. The first is more original, the second more conventional and stylized, but not without a certain graciousness. The respective merits have allowed Niẓāmī's poem to remain for centuries as the unreachable model for the height and the dignity of its art, and that of Fuzūlī has overshadowed all its predecessors in the Turkish world which are for the most part modest and insignificant adaptations of the traditional story, and has remained unsurpassed and widely and constantly popular.

PART II

LEYLĀ AND MEJNŪN BY FUZŪLĪ

translated by
SOFI HURI

TRANSLATOR'S NOTE

To Mejnūn's love, to the love that passeth all human understanding, do I dedicate this work.

The story of Leylā and Mejnūn is one of the oldest and most popular themes of Arabic, Persian and Turkish folklore. It is to be found too in other Eastern folklores. There are few folk-songs or love stories where Leylā and Mejnūn do not find a mention. So that the love story of Leylā and Mejnūn has passed through the ages as the type of idealized love and is, in our modern times, still the symbol of true and sublime love.

Like many an Oriental, the translator has been acquainted with the story from childhood, has listened to Mejnūn's poems as they were read aloud on long winter evenings when relatives and friends gathered together. They would sit around the fire in our home, and song after song was sung in unison led by my father who was gifted with one of the most beautiful voices that ever fell on human ear. Theirs was the gift of story-telling too—those grand people. At times some of those stories from the olden days come back to me so vividly that I go back in imagination to those golden childhood days, and am, once more, the little girl close to her father's knee listening with all ears to the wonderful stories related by the elders of that small community.

I had the good fortune to be born into a happy family, as daughter of a person for whom I can find no name! I do not know whether to call him saint, priest or man! For he was a priest of the Arabo-Orthodox church, a deeply religious sage, a real minister of his people and a friend to all peoples. He was of the saints, who have trodden this earth throughout the ages, and it is because of them that this dreary world has become a happier place in which to live; a man, whom one may call 'a man of the world' in his understanding, tolerance, charity and loving nature.

To him, my father Khouri Boutros Roumi, I am indebted for all that I am and ever shall be.

Under his care my happy childhood passed, as he in person laid the foundation of my education, teaching me to read Arabic and Turkish, supplying me with books and newspapers (in those days not as plentiful as they are today).

The time came when as a grown woman, sundered from the belovéd home folks, with a family of my own to support, I was to tread the thorny paths of life drinking deep of the bitter and the sweet. The experiences of life strengthened in me the innate religious belief and developed my mystical nature. I sought to study the lives and writings of mystics of all creeds finding nourishment and strength for my soul.

My favourites among the Islamic mystics were Mawlana Djalal Al-Din Rumi, Yunus Emre, Niyazi Mısrî and Fuzūlī[1] who served to open before my heart's eye a vast spiritual horizon, and widened the sphere of my own thought and outlook. My heart was filled with their melodies of divine love.

It was during a period of great distress when the Second World War was raging, and my family was in a war-stricken land—it was then that Fuzūlī became for me a great source of consolation. The suggestion by a close friend that I give myself to the translation of Leylā and Mejnūn left me wide-eyed. I had something like the feeling of Fuzūlī himself, when his friends challenged him to write this same tale of Leylā and Mejnūn. The very suggestion, however, had inflamed within my soul a desire for the enterprise, and so I eagerly brought out my book and plunged headlong into the depths of Leylā and Mejnūn reading and re-reading it, studying and trying to grasp all the meanings that the poet would communicate to me.

There are a variety of versions of the story of Leylā and Mejnūn. One legend has it that the handsome young Kays Bin Amer (later Mejnūn) riding his most beautiful she-camel, was passing by the home of a woman of his tribe where a number of young and intellectual ladies were gathered, now discussing matters that interested them, now reciting poems extempore, as was the custom among the Arabs of those times. The hostess called to him to stop and invited him to join the party. The group of women were delighted with the young poet as he stood talking to them, when suddenly his eyes fell on Leylā's beauty. Thereupon he forgot all else, and stood before her spellbound. He had no ears to hear what the others were saying as they tried to attract his attention. When finally he felt that he must say something, he looked at her and asked, 'Do you have anything to eat?' Leylā in her turn gave him a piercing look as she answered as if in a dream, 'No, sir!'

Kays smiled at Leylā pleasantly, then went to his she-camel and stabbed her with his dagger and prepared a feast in her honour, and that was the beginning of the sad episode.

Another legend is that both Mejnūn and Leylā as little children tended the herds and used to drive them to pasture on Jebel Nubad.[2] When the companionship of childhood developed into love, Leylā was subjected to the tribal rules and her freedom was restricted. So when Kays was cut off from her and could not hope to see her any more, he lost his mind. His people sought to arrange a marriage between him and Leylā, but Leylā's people refused to give Leylā in marriage, for according to the customs of the time, when a love affair between a lad and a girl is known, it would be a disgrace for the family of the girl to consent to such a marriage. So Leylā was given in marriage to a person who met her on her journey to Mekka. For, according to another legend, Leylā herself was love-sick and her people sought to cure her by taking her to the sacred sanctuary.

The events within the story and the sad ending are more or less common to all the legends, despite the variants in narrative, order and colour. But in all of them, the stress is laid upon ideal love.

Although the theme has been taken up by many, in Arabic, Persian and Turkish, it is Fuzūlī who has glorified the story and created a monument to ideal human love, soaring to the heights of the sublime, and eventually losing itself in the mystical.

Fuzūlī is conscious that while love is one of the most sublime feelings of human nature, faith is the greatest need and nourishment of the human soul. Fuzūlī's faith becomes more brilliant when we see it combined with the great gift of poetry. Fuzūlī loves his God passionately, and combines this with human love in a narrative of divine inspiration. To Fuzūlī, the light-streaming curls of the beloved are reflected in Divine love, and the light-radiating rosy cheeks glisten therein.

The flowers that grew in Fuzūlī's garden of faith were not only those of the Sharia,[3] but also of the Tarika.[4] Fuzūlī's faith was not based on a blind belief; but one that was the outcome of seeking, knowledge and thought. It is probable that Fuzūlī, drew great inspiration, from the company of a circle of intellectuals and sages, adept in mystical matters, who gathered together—women among them—in the perfect freedom of the atmosphere of a Bektashi Dergâh, and drank deep of divine love, poetic art and faith.

The saints of old, used to place fire and cotton[5] side by side in a little box and send it to sceptics. Neither the fire in these boxes would go out nor the cotton would catch fire. Likewise, in these gatherings where men and women were side by side, the souls were enraptured, while the minds kept their serenity. In those places man was inspired with the love of God. Men were taught not to search for God in heaven, but to find him in their own hearts. Human love was considered the beginning of a deeper emotion that led to God. And such love surely could not be wrong!

This beginning of one of Fuzūlī's most beautiful prayers is sufficient to give us an idea of his faith: 'Oh Lord! Cause the light of Thy grace to be my guide! Show me not that path that will not lead me to Thee!'

Fuzūlī's flame burns in the heart of Mejnūn and makes one feel that Fuzūlī himself is telling his own life-story and singing his own love song.

In a suffering world when human beings could find happiness only by giving themselves to Love and to God, Fuzūlī, had put his faith in these two powers which he tied closely together: Love, was the way leading to and causing one to reach God. While God had engraved His own beauty on the bodies and eyes of earthly beauties. Fuzūlī felt the sweetest of pains as he left himself exposed to the arrows of love cast by the belovéd.

In the story, Mejnūn, is taken to the Kaaba to find a cure for his love-affliction and is ordered by his father to pray for relief. Here again we see Fuzūlī speaking through the lips of Mejnūn and praying that his affliction may be increased and multiplied.

When Mejnūn finds himself before the Kaaba, he goes into an indescribable rapture, and imagines the Kaaba as an incarnate lover. Then giving utterance to his feelings, he says: 'Love's blessing has become visible in thee; and has caused thee to become the Kıble of all tribes', and then begins his prayer in which love and faith are melted in one crucible:

> For pain of Love's affliction is my prayer
> O, Lord, that ne'er a breath
> I draw that grieving sorrow does not share,
> Let love but die with death.
>
> Let not my dignity to worthlessness
> Sink, 'neath the pain above:
> That she charge not a false forgetfulness,
> Or blame for faithless love.
>
> Bestow upon my Idol greater charms
> With every wind that blows;
> And let me still clasp sorrow in my arms,
> As still her beauty grows.
>
> Without her let my body weakly sink
> That merest zephyr slight
> May waft me to her, making airy link
> And change to day my night.

This intense mystical love was the secret of Fuzūlī's mature character and places him among the immortals. Fuzūlī found such joy in this mystical love that while another might have found life intolerable, he was glad to go on living, so as to partake still deeper of his inner nature, he was as humble as the poorest.

'The valley of unity, is in essence the abode of love. And in that place the sovereign and the poor cannot be discriminated', he said.

Fuzūlī, possessing this great wealth of faith and love was rich in humility as well. Although he felt like a sovereign in the wealth of his inner nature, he was as humble as the poorest.

Fuzūlī has been a continuous source of inspiration to me during the years in which I exerted myself trying to do justice to him in translating his work for the English speaking reader. But translation is always a poor substitute for the original, and if this translation can convey a little of the real spirit of Fuzūlī, I shall feel greatly rewarded.

I should like to acknowledge, with deep gratitude, the late Professor Sydney Balister's help in correcting the manuscript and for the suggestions he made which served to improve the text. I am grateful to Dr Abdülkadir T. Kafadar, and also to the late Kilisli Rıfat Bey, the distinguished teacher of Arabic, for reading with me the entire original text; to the late well-known poet, Huseyin Rıfat Bey, for his help with the Persian passages in the text; to the late Dr John Kingsley Birge, scholar and Orientalist, and to Mr F. Lyman MacCallum, translator of the Mevlüd of Suleyman Chelebi; to Dr Andreas Tietze and Dr Howard Reed, and to Professor Fahir Iz, for their interest in reading over the manuscript and giving encouraging comment. Last, but not least, I would express my indebtedness and gratitude to the late Hasan Ali Yücel for his enthusiasm and for his invaluable help in introducing this work to the publishers.

SOFI HURI

Texts used by the Translator

Master Text:
Külliyatı Divanı Fuzūlī, printed and published by Ahter Matbaası, date: Shevval 3, 1308 H.

Reference Texts:
Külliyatı Divanı Fuzuli, printed and published by Tasviri Efkâr Matbaası, date: Zilkaade 1286 H.
Külliyatı Divanı Fuzuli, printed and published by Mektebi Sanayi Matbaası, date: Safer 17, 1291 H.
Divanı Fuzuli, printed and published in Tabriz, date: 1267 H.
Külliyatı Fuzuli, with an introduction by Köprülüzade M. Fuad, date: 1342/1924, Istanbul.
Leylâ ve Mecnun, by Necmeddin Halil Onan, printed and published by Devlet Matbaası, 1956.
Divan Mecnun Leyli, by Mahmud Kamel Ferid, Cairo.

PREFACE

[NOTE: The actual narrative begins on page 149. The earlier part, which consists of a prose Preface and verse preliminary is the usual introduction customary to classical Oriental literature.]

O, Lord God, when under the mighty urge of becoming manifest, Leylā was brought forth from the mystery of the Truth of Privacy to adorn the world with her excessive beauty; and when, in that wilderness of mental sleep that is called Unawareness, Mejnūn's bewildered Soul saw the full splendour of that beauty and, dazzled and entranced, let the reins of his self-control fall from his hands; then, had not the higher forces of the seven tiers of heaven, and those lower bonds, the four earthly elements, not worked together with exhortation and trickery to enforce a separation and a breaking of the Chains of Connection that should have united these two, there would have been no reason to fear that the uncovering of the earthly veil would have caused any distress to Leylā, the ornament of the universe, nor that the pre-ordained banishment of worldliness from the soul of Mejnūn, the world wanderer, would have occasioned any blame. And if the eloquent excellencies of those whose sole anxiety is clarity of speech, acting under the pretence of the legendary, of true love and eternal beauty, by connecting one with the other, the jewels of mystery on the chain of manifestation, thus tearing aside the covering of the invisible, it is to be hoped that with the favour of the goodness of Thy assistance the required degree of attainment, the perfection of its manifestation may be reached. Then should Leylā become the especial object of their highest fancies, while Mejnūn should become the purpose of their complete sincerity; each being free from that denigrating reviling of the ignorant, and the humiliation of the stupid whose o'erleaping attacks fail before the high seriousness of great poetry, and whose limitations and defects of speech, whose anxiety to establish Leylā as worthy but of censure and whose denial of the qualities of Mejnūn is void of effect. And if this passionate lover, Fuzūlī, lacking issue and insignificant though he be, humbly begs to enter on the road of men of reality, and desires to enter into the company of men who are versed in subtleties, although he commands the scantiest knowledge, and has an extreme lack of eloquence, it is because he purposes to force the treasure house of Leylā's beauty and repair the ruin of Mejnūn's love. It will be only with an extreme of care and watchfulness that the labour of the pen and the loftiness of the style may hope to be successful and thus make acceptable the world shaking story of Leylā and the divine affliction of Mejnūn.

THE LOVE STORY OF LEYLĀ AND MEJNŪN

IN THE NAME OF GOD THE ALL-COMPASSIONATE, THE MOST MERCIFUL![6]

O thou, Whose beauty holds a joy
Affecting love; Who didst employ
Great Love in building of the mighty world,
Gave Leylā's locks to massive tangles curled,
And set them, iron chains, round Mejnūn's neck:

And O, that now my sentences I deck
With fine conceit, and still escape the wreck
Of Truth distorted, pouring forth my heart
Upon excuse of using feeble art
To tell a tale: here now I speak Thy praise
By Leylā's reason, and my voice upraise
In Mejnūn's language, setting forth my plea.

Be kind, and swiftly turn the night I see
Into a day of hope; achievement free
Be mine: illuminate my line
Till, like to Leylā, brightly it may shine,
While still maintaining Mejnūn's fire divine.

I

Herein is set forth Praise and Supplication to the Lord of Glory to supply Man's Wants; and a Thanksgiving and a Prayer for the excusing of Faults.

All praise to thee, the Great Bestower of kindnesses;
To the Owner of Mercies let thanks be rendered!

For He, from Time's beginning knows no change,
And still remains Eternal at the end.

His words were spread abroad through all His deeds,
From long duration is His honour great.
Praise be to God! The Great! The Excellent!
Alone He stands, no match nor equal known.
He numbers and ordains each single hair;
He strings the jewels on the thread of life:
The critic He, of all the jewels of Truth,
Disclosing still all fine and hidden things.
Yea, He discloses whatsoe'er is hid,
And what is evident securely hides.
He is the Architect of the House of Existence;
In the meadows of vision 'tis He who satiates.
O, Lord, be Thou my help for I am troubled,
Bewildered am I, miserable and humble.
No skill is mine save in unskilfulness,
Not mine the knowledge of its bounteous gift.
Here, headlong fallen in a strange estate
Whereof both start and ending is obscure,
This occupation as a rocky hill
Fast bars my way, an ocean full of fear.
Without Thy help, divinely showered on me,
Without the leading of Thy kindly Grace,
Though wishing still to gather mid the rocks
The ruby, from the seas the pearl;
Without Thy help, though yet desire were keen,
The keenness of desire were nothing worth.
Bring then enlightenment to glad my heart
The light of understanding give my mind,
That bright the mirror of my heart may shine
And gladness reach the tablets of my thought
Fill now the fields of my prosperity
The kindness of Thy Prophet send as rain,
That I may find the key to ope the door
That I may find the goal of my desire.

II

Herein is contained the Firman of the Rose Garden of the Worship of the True God, and the First Fruits of the Garden of Praise.

O Thou, the mention of Whose Name is the joy of all who love Thee;
Thy Name is the Key that unfastens the doors of hope:

O Thou, Whose Name is the Charm, the Treasure of all gifts,
Thou art the hidden Treasure and this world is thy Charm.
O Thou, the Giver of Liberality, and its very existence to the Universe
How necessary is confession of Thy Person!
O Thou, the Regulator of the Great Chain of Existence,
O Thou, Sustainer of the rabble and of the great,
O Thou, Unveiler of the Great Unknown,
The Defender and the Keeper of order in the world,
Who art the Master of the figures and the lines of space,
The Calculator of the mighty mountains,
The Mine where lie the jewels of necessity and possibility;
O Thou, the Founder of all creation,
Who givest to all the power of sight,
Whose veil is the great curtain of the world,
Who hast no covering save Thee, Thyself:
O Thou, the Secret of Whose Being stands revealed in clarity,
Outside of Whom none other has existence,
O Thou, by Whose Bounty the seven roses of the earth are blessed,
And the nine rose gardens of heaven, gay with bloom;
O Thou, Who givest life in death and death in life,
Whose Existence neither breath nor whisper can deny;
O Thou, the seer of all the veiled invisible,
Thy Thought is the rose of the spring of knowledge.
O Thou, from Whom the universe draws its generosity and its bounty,
From Thee comes the honour of existence to the peoples of the world.
O Thou, Whose pleasure is sought by all the world
While yet the world is filled with the bounty of Thy generosity:
O God, Illuminator of the wick of the candle of Eternity,
The Light of Eternity's great beginning,
To Whom no peer, no equal is assigned;
Who knowest the secrets of the beginning and the end of Time:
O Thou, both God and Creator, adorning the universe,
Whose works know only praise as judgement:
O excellent and perfect Sage, Thy works we humbly praise,
Tho' knowing still how vain to praise Thy works.
In the beginning of time, when nothing was created,
'Now let it be!' Thy word, and forth creation sprang:
Thou wert the Judge of each obscure condition,
The cycle of the years and months, their motion learned of Thee.
Of Thee came shape and thought of every man of Adam's generation,
Each action of his mind in every movement of his time, of Thee drew
    inspiration.
I think no more of things:

My thoughts in every breath, in every moment of my life, are but of
    Thee.
But yet, without things made manifest by Thee
How wouldst Thou choose to manifest Thyself?
Eternal, Uncreated, is Thy Essence:
How then can comprehension come to minds of men?
The more we wonder, trying to reach understanding of Thee, the more
    aɪe we bewildered,
And in this very bewilderment we find proof of Thy Unity.
No understanding may be allowed of the Personality and the Essence
    of God:
It is enough for man to know that he may not know Thee.
In that far time when Thou madest firm this building of the world,
Then Thou madest the designs of the world's order,
And verily the order was good:
Thou gavest it its perfect embellishment,
Every necessity Thou gavest it: naught was left to yearn for.
Thus from perfect preparation came forth Perfection
And still, in its faultless perfection the world holds much of what is
    great and small.
In all is revealed Thy mystery, though it may be revealed by none:
For how could things have awareness of Thee
When all power and all duration is to God alone?

III

*Herein is a jewel from the Ocean of Prayer, and a Gem from the Mine
of Supplication.*

> O Lord, now let Thy graciousness shine forth
> On me, now wretched in humility:
> Thy Throne of Grace is all my trust and hope.
> From merest clay was fashioned out a man
> To house a soul, and worthy of a mind.
> The soul is but the earth beneath Thy throne
> Of graciousness, the mind a traveller
> Upon the road that is Thy path of grace,
> While I, within the garden of the soul
> Am but a thorn, the mirror of my mind
> Is dusted o'er. Yet why this tale of self?
> Now swift obliterate me from my sight!
> In that far day when I no being held,
> From far off, hidden state, to tread the world

Was I called forth. Thou gavest me a soul,
Bestowed on me a living, pulsing heart,
Till, capable of understanding all
Within the world, I stood a man complete.
Had Fate not thus close limned me as a man,
What image on the canvas had been drawn?[7]
But now, created in the shape of God,
Existence made acceptable to Thee,
A hundred thanks I make, nor contradict
Thee, O my Maker, though I stand confessed
Of sin, I still sweet justice understand.
Not numbered I among the heedless crowd
Who in the interval of life upraise
A barrier to all belief and faith,
That all belief should slowly fade away
While seeking still for evidence of Thee
And of Thy Unity. And yet unsettled still
And restless is my seeking after Thee.
I make request, though humbly, full of shame,
'Tis pity that the straight and direct path
I have not trod, nor reached a stopping place:
Yet everywhere, in word, in deed in field,
I saw Thee, and pursued Thee, thinking thus
To find a union with Thee in the world.
Then came imagination to confound
My first ideal with a crooked shape
That turned to nothing hope within my mind:
And thinking thus to find Thee, still I failed.
For guidance now I search within my mind
And learn the mind leads but to error's path.
For how would human mind enquiry make
In all its blindness? Whither should it lead?
Yet, shouldst Thou, in Thy graciousness ordain
Thy Guidance as my one companion dear,
That all the hardness of my path be eased,
See now my great ambition: grant success
According to Thy Will, while yet I hold
Firm both to perseverance and desire.
Within Thy knowledge my belief is clear:
From Thee comes all dear desire of Thee.
For what, indeed, is all this dreary world
And life itself but fear of ghastly death?
But still I say this may not be a lie,

And death the goal of every ordeal tried.
O God, that this heart captivating goal
Could give such calmness to a troubled heart
That I forget my old accustomed place
Long though to be my home, and find afresh
A mansion for my soul. How difficult to leave
A place beloved for other yet unknown!
But here revolves my thought: the restfulness
Of every aching heart must rest in this;
No other may there be, no place of ease
Is found within the temples of the world.
Although this world is Thine, beyond it lies
That other world that is the Seat of God,
Where, soul at peace, the heart's desire is won.
Believing always, I have known Thy Word
To be unique: I know that all Thy Will
To make perfected men Thy servants true,
For though within the world they may attain
Degree of great perfection, there remains
Prosperity of union still to seek
Beyond the portals of that other world.
Thus comes the duty to resolve a course
Towards the *apex*[8] of perfection,
Nor vainly to eschew the pointed road,
For that which leads to Thee is surely good.
When first the first day's light spilled o'er the world
Thy Grace was known: when now the last day comes
Withdraw not all Thy healing grace, O Lord!
When near my life the dear soft breezes reach
Of union close to Thee, when last my soul
Sets forth in hope to reach Thy effluence,
Let not that instant see Thy kindness wane:
Then set me free, no captive still to self,
Nor let me reach Thy door with mind and soul
Distraught and all dishevelled: let no saint
With me see dire humiliation come:
Let none be mournful at my near approach.
Thus, when at last I leave this prison house
And start on absolution's stony path,
They may not, fretting, full of sore complaint,
Desert me, making protest at Thy Throne.
Let not my coming inauspicious be;
Let no lamenting be my welcome then.

IV

Herein is set forth a Poem in Praise of God, the All-glorious.

All praise, O Great Designer,
Creator of souls,
Lover of man,
Maker of all things,
God of all creatures,
Lord of all worlds.
All praise, Inventor of the works of power,
Constructor of the human body,
Designer of its clay and water,
Great Holder of the elements of Nature:
O desert Wind of Mightiness, effecting as the fires of hell,
O Cloud of Mercy, satiating the highest Paradise:
Thy Power is a garden wherein the lovely lotus is but a weed:
Thy Wisdom a candle round which Gabriel is but a moth.
The sky itself, and all the revolving heavens of the universe become
    but a candle to light Thy portico:
The whole world is but a single page in the Great Book of Thy works.
The attainment of Thy Benignity: in this alone is refuge found:
The cord of hope tied to Thy benevolent mercy is alone the means of
    approach to Thee.
At the Gate of Thy Reverence and Honour all may find their desire:
In Thy Goodness and Benevolence the gleaner, man, finds treasure.
With Thy blessing each dustmote is a thing of loveliness:
Each drop of water, touched by Thee, becomes a precious pearl.
Thou art the Great Giver of all Abundancy:
Thy royal bounty knows not of discrimination among religions of the
    world, nor the blasphemies of life:
The keenest mind of the creature, man, fails in comprehension of Thee:
Still closed to all intelligence is understanding of Thy Unity,
And he who claims a measure of understanding knows well his know-
    ledge halts at fault and limps.
He to whom the City of Thy Protection is a fortress
Sees no affliction in Time's adversity.
Hope lives for all: the sinner in his sin, the hermit in his cell, the soul
    disgraced: they ask for help
And may attain Thy Court.
Thou art the manifestation of love to the lover and the beloved;
Thou givest sorrow of desire to those that love.
The sorrow of Mejnūn, sad with the passion of love,

That came from Thee:
The beauty of Leylā was born in the beam of Thy beauty,
O King! The requirement of Thy wisdom has wakened the huri and the Garden of Paradise,
By these are they pledged to obedience.
Fuzūlī follows the path of obedience,
As in his power he may:
Nor with greed demands the garden of the huri,
The desires of carnal self,
Fuzūlī has surrendered self:
He desires but Thy Will.

V

Herein is set forth an Argument to prove the Self Existence of God, wherein may be found a useful Proof for the Endurance of Others.

> Abundancy of blessing comes of God,
> And he o'er whom it flows must have the power
> Of seeing clear, investigating deep
> Unto the root of all Creation's Cause.
> Such are the blessèd ones who clearly see
> The fount from which all hidden treasure springs,
> And thus the answer seek, and, seeking, know
> Just why the spheres revolve in manner strange,
> And why the earth stands firm. What rule prevails?
> Who gave the body all its many forms?
> Why did the fire still need its living light?
> Though each creation clearly has its cause,
> I wonder still: Who then is manifest
> In this and that? If *kef*[9] and *nun*[10] conjoined
> In accents of command brought forth the world,
> It still is left to wonder by what chance
> These two themselves were made, and how brought forth.
> 'Tis not for naught this workshop of the world,
> Nor vainly does Time's endless wheel revolve—
> Let not the charm of all this precious world
> With all its great Design still stand denied
> Of Great Designer: let not this Gate sublime
> Stand wrapped in beauty, knowing not Thy name.
> Think but on this, observe Divinity,
> And ponder if Creation was by art.

Each clear perception plainly manifests
A clear dependence, every part on each.
If this, O, Lord, is meant to be Thy goal,
Then here is shown the source of all: if not,
If in extinction is the Absolute,
In that extinction may a God be proved.
If knowledge rest in Thy ability
Then understanding comes that in the world
Though all are mortal, yet mortality
Still proves an immortality beyond
The mere endurance of an age. Indeed,
All being, all Creation, is but one:
Existence still in singleness is housed,
And rests in One alone: all others known
Or seen, are but reflections pale
Of Him the Absolute: that other world
That world wherein we think the spirit rules,
Is where, in non-existence, being dwells.
Thus men, unknowing, blind them with deceit
In thinking after life is nothingness.
No value has the body's earthly state.
God is its mirror, and the mighty world
Its dust, and therefore, potent mind,
In good contentment, be content with this.
With God's great Attributes remain at peace,
Nor seek, with drear conceit, to find
Some knowledge of the Essence of a God.
None lives who knows a way to part the veil,
Rest sure of this, nor try to pierce the screen.
Could human wit this secret comprehend,
The Prophet, in his wisdom, born of power
Would not have laid commandment, saying thus:
'O Lord, we could not know Thee if we would.'
'Tis therefore that the creatures of the world
Are deep submerged in wild bewilderment,
Thus pointing all the differences clear
That 'twixt Creator and created rest.
Each string that God has placed within the world,
And clearly shown, has yet its hidden end,
For mark, should but the God-made creature learn
The secret of the God Who gave him life,
Then, in despite of order and restraint,
Another world he might, in spleen, create

More near to his desires. God's wisdom, thus
Is clear and perfect, keeping absolute
And hidden still the symbol's hidden sense.
This knowledge universally is known,
That God's great secret is from every eye
Still secret: in the world it stays unknown.
The sign we see: the sign still unresolved.

VI

Herein is a Confession of Ignorance, and a Confession that One has gone too far in Sin.

O, sightless one, on wisdom looking not,
Of life's conditions all too unaware,
No more, with tongue of censure, use the word
'Disloyal' of Fortune, swearing that her wheel
Gives naught but cruelty and endless pain.
Now tell, ungarbled, what has Fortune done?
What cruelty has sprung from out the wheel?
What hadst in hand that Fortune basely raped?
From what high rank has Fortune cast thee down?
The sun, the moon, and their rotation sure
And all their light and shadow Fortune gave:
It caused the candle of thy hope to shine
And made successful every passing wish.
From nothing Fortune made thee as a man,
And gave abundancy of happiness.
All this has Fortune giv'n: for thy past
Now answer for the gifts thou hadst in store.
Yet still the word 'disloyal' from thy lips
Springs forth, with curses, calling for a change.
How like a friend has Fortune favoured thee:
Be not an ingrate giving ill for good.
O Soul, the sup of ignorance was thine
And deeply hast thou drunk, forgetting all
Thy love of country, people, place and name.
Who made thee tread this narrow wretched road?
How came thy fall to all the traps and snares
That in this world abound? That other world
Of non-existence, sent thee forth to claim
The honour of existence, and bestowed

The wisdom drawn of God, and on thy road
Gave sense and mind to be companion.
When thus thy entry to the world was near,
And thou its mart unstable 'gan to walk,
Some profit of thy capital was due,
For profit is but pleasure due to God.
But now, a bankrupt, empty of thy stock,
Bewildered and oppressed, with empty hands,
Estate all ruined, fall'n to low degree,
If to thy starting place thou mad'st return
What hope is possible to find respect?
Disgraced and miserable, sore ashamed
Should this behaviour make thee of thyself.
Be undismayed by all ambition's grief,
Strive not to hoard, as do the wretched ants:
Heap not the heavy torments of the grave:
Take not within thy hand the limpid wine
Lest life's great whirlpool seize thee and engulf.
Seek not deception in the hashish green,
For hemp but rusts the mirror of thy faith.
Let not amusement still vibrate thy breast
As music thrills the hollow *tambourine*,[11]
Nor like the *flute*[12] whose notes fast rise and fall
Still follow every fancy's fond desire.
Come, hold thee to the road of law, of faith;
Forget the faults that sinned against the law.
Seek steadfastly to find attainment true
With God, and to this end now dedicate
Thyself anew to all the Prophet's words.

VII

Herein is a Page from the Book of the Attributes of One whose Name is the Headstone of the List of the Prophets (Mohammed), and a Leaf from the sweet Rose-garden of the Pure.

O Thou, King of the Throne of *Laulaka*[13]
But for Thee, but for Thee, verily the spheres would not have been created.
The skies have become the very dust of the road,
Thy rank in its greatness has reached to heaven's throne.
O Thou, Great Writer of the Book of Meanings,
The Builder of the City of Religion and its Science,

King of Kings, on the throne of the apostles,
Designer of all the rules of justice:
O Thou, Who ascendeth to heaven and caresseth the Throne,
Who hast gladdened all earth with Thy kindness,
'Tis Thou who wilt keep the great Book on the Day of Judgement
Among the glorious company of the prophets, Thine is the first name.
    Yea, first and last of the prophets art Thou,
Great Founder of the Holy Faith,
Causer of the descent of the Qur'an from God:
Thou alone art King; all other men Thy sheep,
Thy subjects.
Thou art the bright candle in the holy chamber of God,
The mansion where Gabriel inhabits.
'Twas Thou who brought the Name of God to man,
And gave it currency:
'Twas Thou who earned esteem for all God's law.
O Thou, the true *compass*[14] for all Believers
Dear Treasure of the Jewel of Intercession:
The dust of thy feet is the very crown of the Throne,
Thy mind the candle of the *Night of Power*.[15]
Great Intermediary in the universe
For order,
Chief Vizir to all who walk and have being,
Alone thou knowest the Attributes of God;
'Tis thou alone can read the universe.
O Thou, for whose sake man first was created,
Before thee, in Adam, are prostrated all angels.
Yasin[16] makes manifest, *Taha*,[17] the rose garden of thy person was sent
    to manifest thee and all thy qualities.
O Thou, teacher in the school of knowledge,
Judge in the City of the Laws of Faith,
Thy gate is made the meeting place of all the prophets:
To thee the heavens kneel, and thee they magnify.
Thou hast brought enlightenment to all,
And set fixed bounds to good and evil.
Injunctions and prohibitions and all their conditions hast thou made
    known to man.
Thou hast given us knowledge of God: without thee had we stayed
    in ignorance.
Thou hast led the wanderer into the path of truth,
And held the hand of succour to the fallen.
The world entire has heard thy words of counsel:
Nothing hast thou left undone.

But we, poor mortals, lacking thy felicity,
Still fail to make thy way our daily habit:
Neglectful in obedience to thee,
In service to thee still own we many faults.
Such shame is ours, deep rooted in our guiltiness,
Yet hope is ever ours that thy abundant kindness
May make our fearful hearts at last to leap for joy,
That, at the last, the refuge of the perverse and ignorant
Thou mayest be.
With thee as intercessor
Why do we grieve for Sins?
Were mine obedience absolute
Its manifestation would still find intercession.
Thou art the King,
The refuge of all of this kingdom.
Each age saw the coming of a prophet,
Each epoch the light of an apostle
To adorn the way of creation and lighten it with the candle of thy
    countenance
For thus to brighten the road of life
Is the custom and the manner of a king.
In the sleep of nothingness, when the world was yet in Chaos,
It dreamed of thee,
And dreaming, decked itself withal a crown of light,
That, a king, brought from out the womb of emptiness,
Restless desire remained.
Interpretation then was sought of God,
And God, all Manifest leaned down from Heaven's Gate and whispered
    news of thee.
Thus first was heard glad tidings of great joy
Of thy benevolence:
Thus first was heard the warnings of the joy
Thy happiness has brought:
Thus first was born the world's great expectation
Of thy arrival, at the very time
That Adam first appeared.
The world endured still seeking, searching, wanting
To find thee in each epoch, every age
As step by step it saw the prophets all ascend
The *Mi'raj*[18] one by one
No shadow should accompany thy grace,
For, slender as a sapling, o'er the world, O Moon,
Thy shadow gives a joy beyond compare.

VIII

Herein are set forth Lines in Honour of the Night of Miraj and the Anecdote of the Rise of the Sun in the Sky (The Prophet).

O, pure one, mighty prophet of the Lord,
When first the dear benevolence sublime
Of thy existence poured upon the world,
Then were the heav'ns themselves with envy mad
To See the earth all happy in thy smile.
The angels gazed upon thy countenance
The heavens stooped for kissing of thy feet,
While such confusion reigned that far and wide
They prayed with fervent passion unto God.
In God's good time an answer was vouchsafed:
Came Gabriel and brought the Firman clear,
That thou, O Cypress in the garden fair
Of skill and knowledge, King of mountain *Tur*,[19]
Supreme in state and honour, gracious be
And still enhance the mighty Night of Power.[20]
Come, make thy sun cast shadow o'er the sky:
Come, let the Miraj be sublime of rank:
Lift up the cover of the mighty world:
Observe the dwelling place of him who knows
Nor space nor place, deep in the empty void.
The angels, yearn, desiring of thy grace,
The heavens themselves cry out for union:
The planets in the sky's pavilion
Have ope'd in expectation thousand eyes.
How grand that moment when, in happy state,
On *Burak*[21] mounted, all aglow with faith,
Thy fortune carried thee to heaven's gate!
Then, o'er the elements that make this world,
Until the holy stairs of three and three
Thou reachedst, finding there the portico
The upper chamber that is heav'n itself.
Then humbly bowed the moon and paid respect
Caressing e'en the shoes upon thy steed,
Receiving from thy smile the living rays
Of light that tell of faith and life restored.
Then Mercury, in homage, bowed him low,
And wrote, declaring: 'Now I am thy slave!'
While stately Venus smiled with glowing pride

And held great orgy in her many halls.
While yet the sun, when once his eyes beheld
Thy grace and stature and thy mighty face,
Desire for other comradeship forswore,
And thus example rare of solitude
Set forth for Christ to learn.
'Twas in thy sword that *Behrem*[22] found the key
And learned the lessons of the art of war,
While Jupiter,[23] of Fortune favoured high
Found joy in all thy sweet benevolence.
Great Saturn's gloomy night was turned to day,
Thou wert the candle in his mighty halls.
Thy seed of love was sowed in every field,
'Twas thou that coloured all the satin sky
And gave it new and ceremonial rites.
Thou hast adorned thy tablet of decrees
That shows the path that leads to God Himself:
The throne above and the mighty sky
Their bright illumination owe to thee.
But Gabriel first and then thy steed Burak
Were left, while thou in unity
And steadfast singleness of constant mind
All close to God remained. For through the veil
Where all is private thou alone wert found,
Where none attained, attainment thou didst find.
Thou wert ambassador to mighty God
Presenting our petitions and requests.
And, kindly still, from God thou broughtest us
Good tidings of the joys that are to be.
Thus, born of grace of God came thy success
And thus thy words for ever will endure.
'Twas God that gave the key that would unlock
The treasure house of knowledge, while the hope
Of blessing and of mercy came from thee.
And thus, with wealth beyond the ocean's pearls
Returning from thy journey, still thy couch
Was warm as was the dust of heaven's road.
How greater comfort, where more goodness find
Than such a journey in an instant passed,
With such effect enduring for all time!
Such great beneficence upon thee fell
While yet the world remained all ignorant.
'Twas thou who didst inform the questing wise

'Twas thou made manifest the hidden power:
The doors of grace and kindness didst thou ope:
Thou saw'st the needs of all, according help
Each in his own degree.
      Since then thy grace
Is measured out for all the world to share,
Be gracious: leave me not alone bereft.
For I, Fuzūlī, scant of fortune, pale
Of misery, and deep in anguish fall'n,
In deep humiliation, full of sin,
Infirm of judgement, lacking purpose too,
Need now thy help, which, if thou shouldst withhold,
Then woe untold will take me to my grave.
O thou, the light upon the darkest road,
The guide upon the slender narrow way,
Let all thy kindness guide my feeble steps
Send but a glance as my companion true.
Then, freed, with all defilement swept away
All joyous may I tread thy path of truth,
And this my garden, bright with glowing bloom
May be of thee and all thy host approved.

IX

Herein is set forth a Prayer in praise of the Prophet Mohammed (Peace be upon Him!)

Mine of all loyalty, source of all kindness,
Fountain of gifts, collector of loveliness,
Chosen of all as the bringer of tidings,
Chosen by God to tell of His blessings,
Judgement of God fall on thee for thy goodness,
'Twas thou God selected for glory and kindness.
Who hoped still for kindness was not disappointed,
Who followed thy path, never lost, ever guided.
Thou helpest all those who from trouble would flee,
Thy shelter, a cave whence all sorrows go free.
Great Jesus who drew all his power from on high
Thy rank and position has never been nigh:
Great Moses attained all his faith on the mount,

The Miraj in heaven is thy magic fount.
Thus thou with the heavens, while Moses with earth
Each reached to his greatness: how different their worth!
That day 'twas Thy water extinguished the fire
That *Nimrod*[24] had built to be *Khalil's*[25] dread pyre.
How sadly unfaithful to follow a law
But thine own canonical road without flaw.
Adherence to others leads sadly astray,
In thee, thee alone, can we tread the right way.
While yet all the faiths of the world are diverse
Each fighting the other: none better; none worse,
The thread of the line of the prophets will stay
Fast tied to thy teaching: to thee do we pray.
Anbiya the prophets are named in our tongue.
Didst thou find thy place all the prophets among
Like *elif*, the first and the last letter now
The first and the last of the prophets art thou.
God in his greatness makes every decree
Accord with thy wisdom still valuing thee.
Thy person so like the sun giving light
Makes thousands of lands and religions seem bright.
The one goal of being is thou, thou alone,
All others are parasites, living unknown.
The Padishah thou, king of sovereignty too,
The Lord of Dominion, like beggars the few
Who question thy grace, while the archangel's broom
Is the tip of his wing, making roses to bloom
As he sweeps all the dust from the road of thy march,
The heaven's great vault is thy triumphant arch—
On the great Day of Judgement, all those sick with sin
May hope for a draft of cool sherbet to win
All made of the honey that still sweetly flows
From thy intercession, ere Judgement Day close.
O Prophet, whose friends still perfume all the air,
Ebubekir, Ali Osman and Omer[26]
Whose loyalty, kindness and justice are known:
Thy law from these four noble pillars is flown.
Mustafa, be merciful, kindness show still
To this poor Fuzūlī, who prays thee for skill:
Bestow on him greatness, bequeath poet's fire
That thus he may reach to his heart's one desire.

X

Herein is a Declaration of Powerlessness and a Statement of Lack of Strength.

    O Saki, now adorn the company
    Be generous now, and circulate the cup,
    And with a single draft refresh the mind.
    Be gracious, Saki, let thy kindness flow.
    Alone, within the vasty halls of grief,
    All, all alone, with neither love nor friend,
    I dwell, bereft, in deepest solitude.
    All those I knew have faded far away,
    While order has forsaken all my words.
    'Tis thou and I alone remain conjoined.
    Come, therefore, let the orgy be increased:
    Give now the cup that I may deeply drink
    And, haply, while my verses I recite,
    Thou wilt in kindliness incline thine ear.
    How wretched are these days when all about
    The fire of poetry no market finds:
    How low in sad esteem, are verses fall'n,
    That all blaspheme to hear the rhyméd word!
    So sadly am I fall'n, low in fame
    That though in suffering I spent my soul,
    And poured my very life blood in my lines,
    Or strung red rubies on a thousand threads,
    Or planted thousand gardens with the rose
    Of poetry, not one would deign to glance
    Upon a line I wrote. My splendid rose
    A thorn, in vulgar spite would be miscalled,
    And all my rubies rare be termed base rock.
    Yet 'tis a fallacy that fair Bagdad
    With all its fertile soil no nurture gives
    To poet's art and poem's linkéd word.
    Though sadly this confession must be made
    That not a land, not Hindustan itself,
    Nor Sham,[27] nor Shirvan, current value give
    To verses magic. Did a muse exist
    Then surely would his treasure public be,
    For never cavern deep enough was found
    To hide the sun or cool the poet's fire.
    Deep hidden in the mine the stone may rest,

But, soon or late, its rays enrich the world,
And though the times seem sadly indisposed
And seem determined that the light be hid,
Yet am I bold to challenge custom here—
In this, perchance I prove myself apart
From those of kin and generation, too—
And waiting seek to circulate anew
The currency of verse. If perchance
Sad poetry is sick, its medicine
Will I provide to cure it of its ill:
A seeker I, to heal a damaged art—
With God's great help, I pray I may not fail.

XI

Herein is set forth a Mesnevi: a plaintive Poem to Saki.[28]

Come! Help me, Saki, in distress I groan;
My feet are tied to grief: I sadly moan.

The wine cup holds the medicine for grief:
'Tis wine alone that makes its ills seem brief:

Whate'er of mercy thou bestow'st on me
Think not that unrewarded it will be.

The pearly shell am I, thou April's cloud;
Give now thy wine, and take my treasure proud.

The blackest earth am I, thou art the sun;
Take now the jewel, o'er me thy liquour run.

Be my companion, hear my plaint, be friend
To me, so strange, with sorrows without end.

In days long dead, the poets in their pride
Had friendships all congenial, all well tried,

As, one by one, they entered in the world
And, honour crowned, passed on, their pages curled.

The time was ripe, each epoch brought a name
That lived esteemed and honoured, died in fame.

To each was granted a protector proud,
A King, who merit to their word allowed.

The Turks, the Arabs, yea the Persians, too,
All from their poets inspiration drew.

Harun the Caliph, famed both far and wide,
Made happy *Ebi-Nüvas*[29] in his pride.

The King of Shirvan brought Nizāmī joy,
While Kirami rejoiced in his employ.

In Korasan, the King of Kings himself
In Nevai's verses found a joyous wealth.

All cast their glance o'er all the jewelled word
And gave their treasure for the treasure heard.

But now no more of eloquence remains,
No more fall poets' lines as summer rains.

Beneath the cloak the poets hide the head
And, knowing their condition, wish them dead.

'Twas thus that, hoping still that verse might live
And little recking who reward might give

On me the duty fell to hold the gate
And save from utter ruin the estate

Of poets' rhyméd word, the pearls to string
In magic order and a song to sing.

Necessity this duty clear ordained,
No hope of comfort left, despair remained.

For all my oath an emblem now became
To fan with verses all the poet's flame.

But since against the crowd I choose to go,
They think me frail of judgement, insults throw

On every word that painfully I scribe.
From all comes forth a bitter diatribe.

For jealousy and all the envious spite
Of malice, brings reproach for honour bright.

The hope remains that this annoyance sore
May yet be changed, and poets as of yore

May scatter verses for the people's hand
In words of beauty they will understand.

As when the rose was fresh, the grass new sprung,
That every zephyr scattered flowers among,

Then gems were honoured; now the stick and thorn
I, cursed of Fortune, gather every morn.

In that far happy time, the feast was held
When wine was pure; its novelty impelled

Both wine and verse to be their nourishment.
Now lees and grief are left: in banishment

Have verses fled. Yet will I drink the lees,
Transmuting them, in hope that they may please.

XII

Herein is set forth an Address to the Saki of the Drinking Party concerning the Wine Cup.

O Saki, be kind, let the wine cup go round,
Nor let it remain still unfilled on the ground.
Accord not time disproportionate zest
Pass round thy goblet; no more let it rest.
The fine silver flagon take firm in thy hand
And in the gold cup pour the wine of the land,
And let all thy kindness descend upon me
And from all my loneliness let me be free.
Much work must be done in this workshop, the world,
No helper but thee sees my banner unfurled.
Be thou my companion, nor think it a shame,
Nor follow the world, making hatred thy aim.
If lacking in knowledge of me, my estate,

And all the dark fount of my life's wretched fate,
To learn of my skill make demand of the wine,
And ask of this fierce burning heart that is mine.
Thy help now affording, may God make thee bless'd
And help thee as now helpest thou the oppress'd.
For know I am Moses, the poet of words,
For whom all the bowls of the wizards are shards.
Magician whose origin Babylon gave
E'en *Harut*[30] himself, lying deep in his cave,
From me could his artistry learn to improve,
And haply from tortures his body remove.
The word and its meaning, intelligence fine
Has mastered, and now all its virtue divine
Is tuned to my purpose, now music is known.
My falcon soars high, never drops like a stone.
And now the *gazel*[31] is my aim and desire
And constancy still gives it passionate fire.
At times with the *mesnevi's*[32] coupleted lines
I find that my muse in its fancy inclines,
And then in the sea of the mesnevi fine
I seek the bright pearls that in radiance shine.

'Tis thus in each language, where men of the art
Love science and beauty with passionate heart,
I am a craftsman of arts manifold
Drawing souls evermore, their delights to be told.
'Tis thus I desire a rich market to find
That each may therein find his wishes enshrined.

XIII

Herein are set forth Lines for the Mortification of the Flesh and the Subduing of the Passions: herein also is an Introduction to the Praise of the Padishah of the Age.

What was this rosy coloured cup of wine
That wrought so great a change upon my soul,
O Saki, that beneath its influence,
My words are dust and all of no avail?
Vexation to my mind came from the cup,
Vexation causing all my change of heart,
That now I know not where I be, and find

A grave impossibility of thought.
And find no utt'rance worthy of its words.
If still within my speech be quality
Then sure, full rich and prosp'rous had I grown,
Full worthy of all honour and respect,
And meet to bow before a sov'reign's court;
Acceptable before the seat of state
Of that great padishah, the king himself:
Nay, worthy to attend the King of Kings,
And still the *Shahinshah*[33] respect would pay.
But still the Padishah, whose eyes are fixed
On all the high, the whole world at his feet,
Protector of the Faith, the refuge sure
For all of Islam, Mecca sings his praise,
Medina knows him, lightning of revenge,
Protector of the right, dread foe to wrong;
O great Sultan, thine alone is the gift
Of justice, and to every man of art,
The Turk and Arab, and the Persian too,
Sure hope of refuge and the shelter sure
Who, like the ocean, in each stroke of time
Bestows the hope of favours yet to come,
Who gives the pearl to all those near at hand,
And sends the cloud refreshing those afar,
Who makes his pearl the light of all the world,
And moistens thirsty lips with water pure;
Like Fortune's wheel, his kindness manifests
And prodigally spreads his treasure round
Like all the sun when in munificence
It scatters pile on pile its golden coin.
Great Suleyman, the emblem of the line
That first in Osman brightened all the world,
The breaker of the petty lords of war,
Remains apart in purity and faith
That should his *tugra*[34] slip his hand, and fall,
The earth would boast a treasure and a prize.
If in the sky, the bird of paradise
Flies in the orbit of his mighty glance,
With added brilliance then, the shining bird
Would even cast a shadow on the sun.
Or should his spear of steel assault the east,
The sparks of fire would scatter o'er the sky
And make the sun for shame to hide his head.

Or should the west be wounded with his sword,
As crimson as the dawn the blood would flow
And flood the sphere.
                    I gazed towards the wheel
Of slowly turning Fortune, read aright
The tablet of the moon, saw shining bright
The great inscription on the tablet fair
And breathed a poem on the waiting air.

XIV

Herein is a Poem in Honour of the Padishah of Islam.

O Padishah, so perfect, so compact
In all thy parts that the subtlest mind of all
Still fails in comprehension, still remains
In sad bewilderment, with never a word
To name thee, most unmatched of all mankind!
Thy honoured person is a pearl unique,
Chief prize in Fortune's casket full of jewels;
Thy soul is bright with wisdom, while the world
Is all thy garden, fair beneath thy feet.
Thy rule is as a winding, spiral stair
That reaches still from heights to greater heights.
Beside thee God is ever standing nigh,
While on thy other side stands subject man.
Thy worth, thy stature in this puny world
Is greater than *Mukarnas*,[35] in its pride,
That scrapes the vault of heaven's mystic blue.
O, Suleyman, just-hearted Padishah,
Born as thou art to greatest victories,
Whoever still neglects thy Firman, he
Is branded irreligious, faithless, cursed.
Shouldst thou, O Sov'reign, purpose to possess
The world and all its lands and people too,
Iran would be thy seat, or far *Turan*.
The ocean, in its greatness, fails to reach
The greatness of thy great munificence,
It sees thy great nobility, and heaves
Its breast in envy, shaking in its rage
The very fabric of the world itself.

Thy slightest gift is like the ocean wide
Immense beyond assessing, as a mine
Unknown and bottomless, thy people find
Thy noble generosity of soul.
In thee came God to walk the mighty earth
And bless mankind: in thee obedience
And bounty show the attributes of God.
Thy court is like to Solomon the Great
Of ancient times, where genie take the place
Of subject, and the fairies all unseen,
Still operate the Firman's just decree.
A mighty cloud is all thy armed host
Whence rises sound that scares the thunderclap:
While swords, keen edged and sharply piercing, come
From all the grievous hailstones of the storm.
Thy steed outstretched in gallop o'er the plain
In speed excels the swiftly shooting star;
Thy army moves with slowly moving breast
As wave inexorable on summer seas.
When to war thy mind is set to march
The sky becomes thy carriage and the void
Of heaven is thy slender running board.
Warm is the sunshine of thy steady smile.
Thy people wax in wealth and in content,
Intoxicated by their love of thee,
That all their locks, dishevelled, disarranged,
In dear disorder know not of the comb.
Thy beauty is a sun of brilliance
Wherein thy people joy each passing hour;
None weep, for none have cause to make lament,
'Tis but the candle now drops idle tears.
While thou, the son of Osman; on the throne
Of Osman, keepest thy estate, no change
No fear of change, for justice and the cause
Of righteousness in thy soul enthroned.
Beneath thy gaze corruption flies afar,
And honour worships Suleyman the Great,
Who found success and gained the victory
That gave his people bounty as of God.
For Suleyman, Fuzūlī offers prayers
In hope that still prosperity and name
And God's dear blessing ever be his lot,
For, as the Padishah protects the Faith,

As all repent who once his word denied,
O God, in kindness grant a simple prayer,
That he, the King of Kings, may ever reign,
Nor pass the Portals, leaving us alone.

MESNEVI

O Lord, may he win all his battles of state,
In his person the building of justice stand straight.

So worthy is he of the crown and the throne
'Neath the shade of his justice none stands now alone.

XV

Herein are set forth Lines in Praise of the exalted Personage of the Prosperous Bey.

Unruly pen, still ever on the watch
The time has come to scatter all thy pearls.
Yet I am weak, my subject difficult.
Be not unheedful, help my failing hand,
Show now thy generosity of soul,
And move thyself and let the lines be writ.
Show now thy skill, this name of mine lift high:
Now write in anguish: I will reap the joy.
O pen, the date palm of the orchard fair,
The key to all the treasury of gems!
'Tis with endeavour that the jewel be found,
Yet think not understanding is withheld
From man, nor think the market scant and dull,
With never purchaser to buy our goods.
Is not the Prince, the general of the time,
Our Sultan *Uwais*,[36] patron great enough?
An ocean is his generosity,
His kindness deep as is the deepest mine.
His attributes are justice, mercy sweet,
And thus earns honour and esteem of all.
The people name him soul of all the world.
See now, how knowledge, valour, breeding too
As with an honoured garment fold him round:

The very harp his praises sweetly sounds
As still with practised hand he plucks the strings.
The wind no more distracts his candle's flame,
The moth, unsinged goes free of every hurt.
His word, soft spoken, earns obedience
The moment it is whispered on the air.
In manner valorous, in practice skilled,
A sun before the world he stands revealed.
His fame is talked of in the land of Rum,
While distant Arabs all extol his name.
Should any seek his generosity,
With kindness all impatience is suppressed—
None need to ask a favour, none may ope
New doors to reach his generosity.
The *emaret*,[37] his guest house, rests secure
On justice, valour, knowledge, kindliness.
O thou, to friends so kind, to foes so dread
Who movest like the falcon in its grace,
A nest is now prepared to give thee joy,
A home eternal decked as paradise,
Approaching near the fabulous *Irem*.[38]
Rest here in peace until Eternity,
And in this garden fleet the merry hours.
This work I offer, faulty though it be,
Is yet sufficient to enhance a name,
While I, in eulogy, thy praises sing
As *Selman*[39] sang the praises of Uwais.
For this my purpose, that eternally
Thy name before the world in high esteem
Be held: this garden green endure
And keep our names as verdant as its leaves.

LEYLĀ AND MEJNŪN

I

Herein is set forth the Origin of this Book and the Reasons for the undertaking of so much Trouble.

O, Saki, hear my call!
Come, take my hand, and lead me o'er
The perilous road whereon I am embarked!
Thou art my friend, so close and dear to me;
Who else, but Thou, canst help me in my need?
Deep in confusion have I fall'n headlong . . .
Bring me my cup, o'erbrimm'd with flowing wine.

It chanced one day, surrounded by my friends,
The wine cup pass'd.
My years, of autumn's hue.
Fell from me one by one, and Life, as Spring,
Ran hot within my veins. Too bold I grew,
For, flushed with music, song and fresh *meze*,[40]
My cup was raised and emptied without end.
And still, within my soul, my spirit grew
And burgeoned with an added mirth,
Till all seemed verdant as the lusty spring,
And I its restless, singing, nightingale.
The orgy mounted high, restraint was gone,
The thousand barriers to inner thought
The moment had o'erthrown.

Among the fluent throng of chatterers
Was many an exquisite from far off *Rum*[41]
(To quote from *Rum* is always to assert
That such is such, no room for doubt or smile.
A people they that, versed in every art
And every subtlety, do lightly play
With words and phrases, coining forth a thought
That shines and glistens with an added fire.)
Now these, my friends, would point their lucent talk

With Sheyhi's subtleties, Ahmedi's wit,
With Bursa's famed Jelali, he who writ
Of Leylā and unhappy starr'd Mejnūn,
As he of Azerbaijan, Nizāmī.

And here they sprang a trap, for in my cups
Full eloquent, I claimed the gift of verse,
Not thinking of the pit before my feet.
And thus, to prove my measures—as the Bull
Is set before the boastful archer's gaze
That he may prove his aim—they softly spoke:

> 'O thou, great weigher of the mystic word,
> Use then thy craft to tell that Turks may read.
> Of Mejnūn's saddened end, of Leylā's love.
> This legend oft in Persian has been told:
> By Turks well known, in Turkish yet unwrit.
> Come, vivify for us this deathless love!
> Come, let us hear this tale in numbers told!'

Now what a test was here, for Leylā's tale
Is long calamity and endless pain,
And passion without end, in metres short,
Yet full of sighs and long laments of grief.
The tale is born of sorrow, ends in pain:
Is rarely coloured with the hue of joy,
Nor is the melody of joy supreme
In all its many moods.
How stern a reprimand to idle thought
This luckless love! One saddens at the thought.

Why, pause a moment! Here a famous tale
Lies waiting, yet in years unnumbered, few—
How few the fingers of a hand may tell—
Have dared its secrets to set forth.
The greatest of the great confess despair,
As Nizāmī, who ends confessing thus:
> 'Speech comes of joy and sweet coquettish airs[42]
> And thus arises need of instrument[43]
> A vast and mighty scope mere words demand
> That those of skill their genius may portray;
> While here, in barren desert, torrid, dry,
> What sweet well water springs to quicken words?'

Think for a while: the Master thus complains!

What justice may he claim
Who sends the lesson back to pupil hands?
I know 'tis tyranny and grief o'er grief
But, like a thunderbolt, the challenge fell,
And naught is left but frankly to express
Apology for daring, patiently
To journey forth through this afflicted land
And tell the tale so rudely claimed of me.

But friends I need, and where is friendship found?
Why, he who knows both pain and sorrow mix'd
Who understands contentment and dismay,
He is the friend I choose: no man of mirth
Shall go with me: and for a steed
No horse nor saddled beast, but sharpened quill
And time-defying ink: for sustenance
Good words and phrases join'd, recounting all.

Then come! No help is in delay!
We travel post, and, Fortune, loyal still,
And fellow traveller on the weary road,
Remain till all is told!

II

Herein is found the Prologue to the History of Grief: herein is the Great Seal of the Firman of Love.

As bright flowers spring 'neath the gardener's hand,
As jewels are gathered throughout the land
By the craftsman who strings them into beads,
As roses of thought when occasion needs
Spring from the thinker's deepest thought
And, one by one, into pearls are wrought,
So now let the words of the Gardener fall
From the Garden of Speech in a tale to enthrall.[44]

'Tis said that the Arabs, those far off and near,
Were ruled long ago by a Prince without fear,
Young, bold and virtuous, never a peer.
Through all his broad lands for his people he strove
And into one thread many families wove.

The Arabs, both near and afar, when they heard
Of his justice, with one accord followed his word.
No fainéant he, in a turreted moat,
O'er his lands far and wide he would wander and note
Where worth called for praise, where viciousness sprang:
Now Basra, now Baghdad acclaimed him and sang
Of his justice, his greatness, his all-seeing eye
That saw as a friend, as a father would try
To people a desert, bring Paradise nigh.

Mid the greatest of gifts that the world can bestow,
The loveliest rose that the garden can grow,
Is an heir to one's loins, a son of one's flesh;
With this all possessions are closed in a mesh
Of fine spun security: failing this gift,
Broad lands and fine palaces slip through the rift
In the one perfect round of a dutiful life.

This Prince of our story had many a wife,
But never a son to inherit his name,
In whom he would live after death, with his fame
Untarnished. A child is the life of the soul,
And, lacking a child, no ruler is whole.

Yet, be it remembered, a chieftain's own son
Has a troublesome task ere his race it be run.
For people are captious and critical, too,
And eagerly watch what the new chief will do.
Be his conduct unthinking, his actions unjust,
His character weakly, ungoverned his lust,
Not only his parents will shrink in disgust,
His people will murmur and crawl in the dust.

Our Chief knew the duty he owed to his State;
Took many a beauty to bed as his mate;
Great vows did he offer at every tomb,
Beseeching and praying to find yet a womb
That would furnish a son to inherit his name
And carry his glory and water his fame.

Came the day when his sighings and groanings could end,
When God gave him mercy, God showed him a Friend,
And the Reed Pen of Destiny slowly inscribed

The face, form and features yet close circumscribed
As the bud of the sapling, the close tiny sheath
Of the tightly held bud that will furnish the leaf.
The months hurried past till the ninth one was sped,
And a new moon arose from the proud mother's bed.
The universe shone and great paens of praise
Surrounded the infant.
                       A great many days
The father and mother, much joy in their breasts
Did spend in rejoicing and emptying chests
Full of treasure and riches, that all might rejoice
And sing hymns of praise with full throated voice.
For perfect in childhood, on that happy morn,
Like Jesus himself, our small hero was born.

But soon as he entered this world dry and drear
He cried full and loud for his sorrows were near;
He knew, without telling, that sorrow and grief
Would both be his portion, or ere, like a leaf
He fell, old and wearied, and maddened in death.
Of his end did he think in that moment of birth,
With tears from that moment he watered the earth.

And, indeed, what is life in this world but a net?
No escape has been found by philosopher yet.
Once tangled in life, the feet tread the way
Of stony distress every sorrowful day.
Though mute and unspeaking, our infant began
From his cradle a griefsong. Its sad burden ran:

> 'O sad, sad, world,
> Wherein is grief so great that none may bear
> Its heavy load, now seek with jealous care
> To make me mate of all thy ills unfurled,
> Thy every hurt and spite.
> Neglect no dark, reveal no ray of light,
> Bend all thy great disasters on my head.
> Let this, my entrance in thy mansion wide
> Be signal for these grievous ills, beside
> Which ills of all who live or lived must face.
> See suffering in my perfection paid.
> Pour sorrows on my soul till I be dead,
> Let life be spent a captive unto grief.

No pleasure send, for pleasure's reign is brief.
Fill now my cup intoxicate, that I
May drink, and drinking, while I live or die,
May know the world is naught, uncaring still
To know if life or death brings greater ill.

Now born a roamer in thy gloomy vale
Of sorrow, no escaping may avail;
Let me, through suff'ring, banish sorrow's pain.
Keep still in dignity my purpose plain.
Fill now my cup with bitter wine of blood,
Let Saki, executioner, now flood
This orgy of disaster with my tears.
Neglect no evil, world, suppress no fears.'

The aged nurse then cleansed him of his blood
And washed him with the tears from out her eyes:
The milk she gave him poured from out her heart.
The tribes and nations near, rejoiced and laughed,
His parents cried that Qays should be his name.
With heart out-poured, and more than nurse's care
The tender child embarked upon his voyage;
But though no care was lost, no art forgot
That might have comforted a puling babe,
No comfort could he find, but, night and day,
Wept and bewailed the fate that gave him life.
No pleasure took he in his pampered state;
With daily repetition hurt his limbs,
And sobbed himself into uneasy sleep.
Whene'er he sucked it seemed that angry blood
Not milk was coursing down his tiny throat;
The very nipples seemed like arrowheads.
In short, no guile deceived nor gave him rest:
No guile throughout his life could daze his wits.

One day, while walking on the public road
Whereon his nurse sought out a cure for grief,
It chanced that from a house that fringed the path
A beauty—Moon's own peer—ran forth and stood
And gazed full on Qays, and straightway fell
Into a state confused and pitying.
She took him in her arms and, at her touch
The child forgot to murmur, felt at ease;
Forgot to cry and moan; at last was still.

His hand in hers entwined, called forth a charm
That passed no sooner was her hand withdrawn.
At this the nurse, from wisdom ages stored
Within her wrinkled soul, solution found,
And let this Moon companion all his days.
When forth she shone and bathed him with her rays
He straight forgot his mother and his nurse,
And cared for naught but her, his new-found friend.

'Twas love of Beauty that in Qays now stirred
And brought this swift surrender when it came.
This state is known to all, for is't not said
That Beauty is the Amulet of Love?
But here befell a contradiction strange,
That Love which, ere he died, should cause him woe
Untold and unforeseen, should start its course
By giving peace and happiness and calm;
Should sweetly take him by the hand and lead
Him forth at last to deserts of despair.

As day by day into the years he grew,
The teaching of the philologue and nurse
Worked on to build upon foundations firm
The perfect edifice, and day by day
Perfection was attained: the crescent moon
Waxed imperceptible—at last was full.
And then, as days succeeded with their gifts
Of chaliced cups and constant loyalty,
He ended as a drunkard, dazed and still
Within the silken trap of perfect love.

Now came the day when ten full years had passed,
And circumcision rite the custom claimed.
From far around the joyous father called
All friends and potentates, all worth and fame
And honour; all around came nigh
To celebrate the custom of the land.
Great was the feasting, mighty were the sums
Of gold and silver freely scattered forth,
That many marvelled lest the gen'rous host
Should rue the day and into poverty

Should sadly fall before his life was run.
For truly such a feast was never seen
The wine cup never looked with empty gaze
On orgy such as this save at the feast
Of *Jamshyd*[45] when he celebrated wine.

The way of *Sunnet*[46] and of childhood passed,
The Circumcision Feast now left behind,
A new road opened clear and learning's book
Its early pages spread, as off to school
Our infant loitered with a manly stride
To drink of knowledge and to gain the arts
That to his station and his pride were due.

III

Herein is recounted the Structure of the Building of Misfortune, and the Antecedents to the Pain and Affliction that follow.

Gay was our child with his constant companion
With angel-like beauties he passed all his time.
In rows sat the pupils, all facing the teacher,
The first one of girls, the second of boys.
Together were gathered these nymphs in their glory
And soon became friends. No surprise is in this,
The market of love with occasion grows brisker
For languishing maids can enchant with their eyes.
And how can a lad bid his spirit be patient
When amorous glances and coquettish airs
Surround him and tease him and quicken his manhood?
Were patience his portion, what word could he say?

Among all the girls was one bright as a fairy,
Who aimed all her glances directly at Qays.
So beautiful she, with her ways and her graces,
That many an elder, forgetful of vows,
Might find all his virtue caught up in her curls.
Calamitous chain for the neck was the garland
Of ringleted locks that fell down in a cloud:
Affliction for lovers was spelled by her eyebrows,
As lovely as twins, and, as twins, forming one.
Each eyelash that curved from her lids was an arrow
That pierced to heart and that stirred all the blood:

Her eyes from their shelter poured forth fiery glances
That, piercing the soul, spread the fever of love.
Her brow, like an ocean, far spread and smooth rolling
Like the ocean had many a peril in check.
The black of her eyes shamed collyrium's darkness
And made it a captive in chains to her mole.
Her cheeks flushing red, paled her rouge to a whiteness,
No rouge ever sullied their delicate blush.
Should her eyes lose their pupils, no blindness would follow,
Her mole would become a black pupil of sight.[47]
Her teeth, pearly white, from between her lips' redness
Gleamed forth as bright pearls in the heart of a rose:
When the doors of her speech were full opened, one fancied
The dead must spring forth from their mouldering tombs.
From her round dimpled chin her neck curved to her bosom;
Her stature and form were creation divine.
The falcon itself, a bird sacred to kingship,
Unhooded, can gaze in the eye of the sun,
But the eyes of this child, with their antelope softness,
Could flash forth a look that the falcon outshone.
Her motion was graceful, her words sugared honey,
No act but had grace, every movement a joy—
But why count her beauties? Put all in a sentence:
The whole world itself, in a passion of terror
Clung fast to her hair, as she went on her way.
Belovéd of all the world was this maiden.
Qays looked and he perished, for Leylā her name.
As he with a sorrowful passion of yearning
With sighs fed the fire that her beauty awoke,
So she in a thousand sweet joys lost her reason
For him without whom she knew living was death.
She saw how the world gave its ultimate wonder,
She saw how he held all her world in his hands.

IV

Herein is set forth the Attributes and Characteristics of Mejnūn, and the Affliction of the One who sorrowed.

A beauty with a stately figure, cypress statured, like a rose,
Rosy cheeked and sweet as jasmine, as a statue in repose;
Sweet his lips, the source of speaking, bring to life the thoughts that
    charm.

His graceful carriage and his motion, joy to him, to others harm.
To tell his attributes o'er simply many words would endless flow,
To count his kindness, sing his praises, needs more than may Fuzūlī know.
Like the narcissus enchanting, gleaming forth to tell of love.
So his eyes gleam forth entrancing, 'neath the *noon*[48] high arched above.
The tulip, dewy in the morning, with its curling fall, the *lam*,[49]
Mirrors forth his curling ringlets, nature's splendid epigram.

No words can tell with shadowed justice of the secrets of his mouth,
How describe his many charms, mystery's chain'd link uncurl?
To sing his beauties is to warble sweetly sad of sorrow's joy.
His mouth the fount where murmured ever subtle words of coquetry.
His face, full round, a smiling morn, outshone by far the Queen of Night:
The dust from off his feet may darken more than painted *huris'* eyes.
To make an end, to reach conclusion, when her beauty he beheld,
Had he gazed upon his mirror, then himself, not her had loved,
And Leylā, fairest of the fairest, had not stirred his heart at all.

But these two, tall, fair as jasmine, straight and slender as a dart
Were bound and tied, the one to other, firmly fast by loving art.
Drinking deep the wing of pleasure, drinking deeply of desire,
Drowned in unity of sadness, all engulfed in passion's fire.
Were Qays addressed with posing riddle, Leylā's treble answered clear;
Were Leylā questioned, Qays would answer in a voice that knew no fear.
They learned loyalty of purpose, abnegation born of love
When Leylā cast her books beside her, Qays became her textbook dear.
When Qays essayed the art of writing, Leylā's brow was his design
O'er their writing, o'er their reading, artistry to love lent aid;
A thousand sweet disputes were born and ended in a thousand charms.
Disputes were friendship's sweet advances, arguments but fed their love.

And so these two, long happy days together spent their childhood hours.
Two things are sure; love ne'er is secret: he who loves may have no rest.
The sign of love's sweet fire is noted when the gossips[50] first begin
Calamity of love is beauty; sorrows strengthen love's cement.

And thus they came in rapid stages, plainly marked and fully known,
With reason trodden down, forgotten, when they found the voice alone
But a faulty instrument to carry tone and overtone.
Then the eye and then the eyebrow slow usurped the place of speech:
Question gained reply from eyebrow, brow and eye played each to each.

Yet all talk with eye and eyebrow would not still suspicious tongue,
People live within the eye and from the eye the truth will flow.
Then the next sweet stage they entered; learn'd the value of neglect,
Learned the joy that came pretending each had wanted in respect.
Like the Men of Melamet, of Dervishes the strictest sect,
Courting public reprobation by a public abstinence
From the outward forms of duty, yet with inner continence.
Yet the guiles devised by Leylā did not 'scape Mejnūn's quick eye,
Neither did Mejnūn's devices leave the eye of Leylā dry.

Now o'er mirror of their pleasure grievously vexation fell:
Now lest all should know their secret, care took caution as a guide,
Finding clear pretext of reason ere they talked upon their way,
Waiting till the moment offered through the weary livelong day.
Qays would thus forget his lesson, say to Leylā: 'O, my friend,
Learning brings me deep depression, hear my lesson till its end.
For exceeding mine thy knowledge, let me of thy wisdom share,
Let me read my lesson to thee, listen thou with every care.'
Then, while on his slate he scribbled, many faults would Leylā find,
While he timed his artless questions so that, peeping, quite unkind,
Leylā's rosebud lips were parted in a smile that warmed his heart,
Smiling undeceivéd ever, understanding all his art.
Skilled he grew to prompt her sallies, to provoke her into song—
For song it was to hear her saying: 'This is right', and 'That is wrong'.
Then again, when in a circle, all the children meekly ranged
Chanted o'er the barren lesson, he and Leylā soft exchanged
Whispered sweetings 'neath the droning of the lessons idly conned,
Each to other went their phrases, never travelling beyond.
When, at last, the day was ended, Qays would find his books forgot;
Hide his books and seem in anguish, misty eyed, face flushing hot:
Stop her on the homeward path, ask if she had seen his books,
And, on this excuse, a moment stop and feast him on her looks.
And on his copybook he'd scribble 'lam' and 'ye'[51] repeatedly:
'These', he said, 'must be my lesson: these my task unendingly.'

V

Herein is related how Leylā's Mother reproached her, and How the Springtime of her Meeting with her Belovéd turned to Autumn.

Thus pondering dolefully, Qays the unfortunate
Passed many hours, many sorrowful days.
No pleasure is found where Lover the importunate

Seeks for precautions and secretive ways.
Secrecy cannot exist where affection
On two loving heads its soft finger-tips lays;
Hypocrisy leads but to lovers' dejection—
Ignominy pressed on the shoulders of Qays.

From tongue to tongue the tale went forth
That Qays and Leylā, both,
Were gall'n in love: her mother's wrath
Did tax her with her troth.
The mother's face became inflamed,
It shone as liquid fire,
As Leylā, utterly unshamed
Withstood her mother's ire.

'Thou bold and saucy shameless one, what naughty tale is this?
What wicked secrets do I hear censorious neighbours hiss?
These wicked tongues will blacken fast the proudest maiden's name,
And once thy name is gossipp'd o'er, 'twill never be the same
Thou like a tender rose-leaf art, and like a petal sweet
Art bruised and damaged with a look, then crushed beneath the feet
Of him who loved. But what avail this censure harsh of mine?
Enough of censure; Listen, now, and in thy heart entwine
These simple words that wanton's fate shall ne'er be fate of mine.

Charge not thy dignity serene with crazed and maddened mirth,
Nor cheapen all your many charms. Be proud, girl, know your worth.
Look not at every face you meet as if therein to find
Thine own reflection. Never flow like water unconfined.
Though wine gives gladness to the brain as upward yet it mounts,
It climbs so quickly, falls as fast; its height but little counts.
Shameless and cold, the mirror shows a bold and brazen face:
Be not thou, like *Narcissus*,[52] so saucy-eyed. Thy place
All maskéd from the eye should be, in quiet seclusion hid,
That all should call thee precious, child. Go not to all that bid.
Though like the candle giving light, seek not each idle breath.
Lest, like the wind upon the flame, words blow with icy death.
Seek not, with colours gay, to be a doll for all ye meet,
Nor look abroad with eager gaze like windows on the street.
Be not the wine cup passed around from hand to hand in glee,
But be like cunning music, set all steady, in one key.
Be not the shadow that the sun moves on from place to place,
Stand not nor sit with anyone, nor yet unveil thy face.

Be simple thou; let others tricksters seek to fascinate,
Let not sad deception woo thee from thy strictly maiden state.
The gossips say thou art in love, and with a stranger's comely face:
Whence cometh this desire for love? Go child, and know thy place.
A boy may fall in love full oft and drink his pleasures deep,
But little suits it for a maiden thus to hold herself so cheap.
O thou, my eye's clear shining light, shame not our honour so,
For honour's bloom is quickly spoiled by all the winds that blow.
Our name is good, it stands secure with all both high and low,
Let not thy conduct start a spring from which reproach may flow.
Thou knowest well that were I soft and idle in my care,
Nor sought to stop thy foolishness, thy father would not spare
Thy modesty, but in his rage, forgetting childhood's state,
Would punishment severe inflict, would grievously berate.
Come, leave thy school, and playmates fond, and teachers so revered,
Thy parents both thy teachers are, to see this scandal cleared.
Talk not henceforth of penman's art, nor read a musty tome,
Observe my word, embroider here, and keep thee fast at home.
Seek not thy friends: companionship with them from now must go,
Seek thou thy doll, my little one. Come, take thy needle, sew,
And make this house thy dwelling place. Be proud, accept its joys,
And, like the *Unca*,[53] live apart. Be happy with thy toys.
And living thus, unseen, thy name will earn respect of all,
No more be tossed from mouth to mouth as boys may toss a ball.
Remember, child, that they who hide their daughter from the eyes
Of all the questing, greedy throng, enhance by far the prize,
And gain respect, esteem and awe. Come, now, this realize.

VI

Herein is related how Leylā answered her Mother by Denial, and how by forsaking the Realm of Companionship, she entered into the Palace of Troubles.

Now Leylā, hearing this reproach
Concluded in her heart
That evil Fate did thus encroach
To play an evil part,
And Destiny, to her unkind,
Had entered in the game
To force her love from out her mind,
To quench her burning flame.

The happy days of sweet content
And union were sped,
And separation's dull lament
To absent love was wed.
No word she knew, no cure could find,
Nor think, nor scheme, nor plan,
But, weeping, to deny unkind
Reproaches she began.

'O mother, in whose shelt'ring arm
I passed my infant days,
O, life's companion, safe from harm
Thou guardest all my ways,
Thou usedst words I do not know,
And cannot understand:
I know not whence these questions flow,
Their meaning 'scapes my hand.

'Of love and lover is thy rage,
Belovéd, too, I hear;
But how can I be of an age
To know their meaning clear?
A simple minded, faithful child
Am I, thou knowest how—
What knowledge I, of passion wild,
Or love that maidens vow?

None spoke to me of love till now;
I hear its name from thee.
With bended knee I ask thee how
Its beauties I may see.
For God's sake guide me this new way,
Be my instructor here,
And teach me, 'gainst the coming day,
This secret that I fear.

'Twas not my wish to go to school.
I nothing contrary
Or said or did against thy rule,
Of school obligatory,
Days past thou saidst: "To school, my girl!"
And now 'tis "Stay at home!"
Speak, mother, for my brain's awhirl,
My senses far do roam.

I know not how to take thy speech,
It points now North, now South;
I cannot safe conclusion reach
From this thy changing mouth.
But this thy chiding is not fit:
Think not that yet I be
A brief Mosque candle, dimly lit [54]
Exposed for all to see.

By sorrow tied in darkened room,
Among the lowly born,
Oppresséd by a heavy gloom,
By eyes my veiling torn:
While still the teacher drones along
And struggles to impart
The arts of reading, writing, song,
And wearies every heart—
Why, who could find a joy in this?
In sunshine or in rain?
This matter from thy mind dismiss!
Give me no further pain!'

Now when the mother heard these words a doubt grew in her mind
That she had spoke too hastily, with words that were unkind.
'Twas clear, she thought, her lovely moon as yet had nothing learned
Of passion's flame, of sorrow's joy, or flames of love that burned.
Relief brought comfort to her breast, brought ease unto her mind,
Nor dreamt that Leylā, kept at home, was thinking thoughts unkind.
Now she, a pearl within its shell, a jewel in its chest,
In one sweet current turned her thoughts, while all around her pressed
The stony walls that shut her in as tightly as a flask
Encloses scented rose-water, and no relief could ask.
Her heart, once hopeful, was depressed, with grief her life was dark,
With endless sighs she fanned to flame her sorrow's lonely spark.
But idle breath will never ope the bud of passion's flower,
And all the tears of all the eyes of lovers make a shower
Too slight to feed the thirsty palm for yet a single hour.
Just as the hair that curled and fell upon her shoulders bare
So curled her spirit in its pain; it writhed in deep despair.
Her eye was dulled, her body sick, her face with grief was drawn
No mate, no sympathizing friend, could comfort her forlorn.
Her heart just like a painted gauze, [55] revolving with the lamp,
A twirling flame was now become, with sorrow's every stamp.

Imagination fired her heart, but sorrow damped the flame,
And grieving all the day she knew no joy would be the same
As that sweet joy she once had known, and thus to pass the time
A long involved *gazel* she sang, with many a cunning rhyme.

VII

Herein is set forth the Ode or Gazel sung by Leylā in her distress.

  A cruel Fate now drags apart
    To live in lonely grief
  The fondness of a loving heart
    That loved a moment brief.
  Were Fate a sentient, living thing,
    Or bred to fear its victim's sighs,
      Then, with a fear that passed all fears of man
      Or woman sad,
  Would Fate, a-tremble, dread the curse I sing:
    My sighs, spark-clad,
    Outpouring fast make Fate in flames to rise—
  Yet flames my heart more fierce with sighs to fan.

  My grief, though secret, grew apace,
    And killed my soul so gay:
  Now ended ere half run my race
    Like summer gone with May.
  My flushing cheeks were unaware
    What cause I had to sorrow deep,
      Each breath as tortured, twisted sigh escapes
      Its prison breast:
  'Twas thus when first my lungs drew living air.
    Till all's at rest
    This House of Grief may no more safely keep
      Its treasures where its every wall wide gapes.

  What need express in dismal tones
    A secret all must know?
  For, as I cry, the very stones
    With pity are aglow.
  My garments rent, in tatters torn
    Make evident my state,
    Yet think not that my love's dear seal shall leave

        My aching soul
Nor that of love I'm left alone, forlorn,
        Alone, not whole:
No image in my weeping eye is born
        Within my heart he lives while yet I grieve.

O wind, that blowest freely, by thy art
Bring tidings sweet of him I yearn to see.
'Tis thou alone Fuzūlī, know'st my heart,
'Tis thou, alone of poets, know'st the ill
That is my portion: choose what words ye will,
But with thy verses set my spirit free.

VIII

Herein is concluded the first Part of the Story of Leylā and Mejnūn, wherein the Poet comments on the sad condition of these unhappy Lovers.

    O Saki, hear me yet, and bring the cup
    Full brimmed with wine, to drink and to forget
    The cares that mar the world. Ope now thy heart
    To pity for grief of this my tale,
    Now just begun; drain forth my heart's dear blood.
    With cruelty of care my breast is pierced.
    Come, bring me wine, for I would deeply drink,
    And numb my mind, till, heedless of the wheel
    Of slow revolving Fate inexorable,
    I know not of its torture or its pains.
    'Tis clear that, blindly thus revolving Fate
    No constancy nor value may acclaim.
    Were this revolving world, thus rudely flung
    In Time's eternal round; to work for good,
    And bring sweet union to lovers twain,
    Or fire and water magically join,
    Why then, these two, on whom our pity flows,
    Could hope for reason for their captive state.

    But O, what danger and what pain is found
    In Friendship, when, with separation dread,
    Friend loses friend. The Gardener of Speech
    So loves his words, so decorates his land,
    That Qays becomes the cypress of the field,
    Full nurtured by affliction and by pain.

IX

Herein are set forth the Mesnevi, or Couplets, which tell of Mejnūn's Distress.

1. Now every morn Mejnūn went forth to school
   Where, freed of care, he mastered every rule.

2. With studied ease he followed all the lines
   Of Leylā: never book marked love's confines.

3. His heart with pleasure sang when'er the day
   He, like the sun, pursued his constant way.

4. At school a happiness he looked to find
   The happiness of love, not yet unkind.

5. When passed the day that Leylā cameth not
   The sun was darkened, tho' its rays were hot.

6. All sunless sped the day, and school, as night,
   Fell dark and gloomy, darkened, without light.

7. He guessed that Fortune's cunning trickster hand
   Had turned from him the pleasure he had planned.

8. The jealous gossips, so the thought was born,
   Upon her petalled rose had cast a thorn.

9. With grief at heart and sorrow in his mind
   He railed at Fortune, calling it unkind.

10. 'What evil have I done? What left undone,
    To kill my soul by banishing the sun?

11. 'What sin mine, that now, in sad eclipse,
    Thou dashest wine of pleasure from my lips?

12. 'Thy favourite once was I, and happy, glad,
    Beneath my idol's look in pleasure clad.

13. 'O Fortune! Now thy wheel to torture turns,
    And now the graces of content it spurns.

14. 'Didst thou then fear that with a single sigh
    That from my burning heart should reach the sky,

15. 'I might thy heaven into ashes turn,
    And teach thee how these separations burn?

16. 'Were this achieved, then Separation's pain
    Thou, too, might'st know.
                              But, teacher, turn again,
17. 'Nor think alone that dreary grief is mine:
    The grief that tears my heart is also thine.

18. 'O, *elif*,[56] straight, unbending as a rod,
    Be shamed, and fall, to moulder 'neath the sod.

19. 'Still now thy boastful voice, seek not her height,
    For she is gone! Why standest thou upright?

20. O, *noon*,[57] thou joy on beauty's eyebrow set,
    Go, hide thyself! Seek not my soul to fret.

21. 'O, *mim*,[58] thy crooked shape no purpose holds
    Now Destiny her smiling mouth withholds.

22. 'Corrosion seize *thee, inkstand*,[59] may thy heart
    Rust in thy bosom. Feel its angry smart!

23. 'Turn now thy ink that tender love expressed,
    To pale and sickly water in thy breast.

24. 'And thou, O pen, as blots thy sorrow prove,
    All restless, kissing not the hand of love,

25. Yet still cry on, pretend no day were here—
    There is no day if Leylā be not near.

26. And as for thee, O hard and ashen slate,
    Talk of her hand and blackly grave thy fate.'

27. The days moved on and still to school he went
    But passed his days in blackest discontent.

28. From morn till eve his lamentations deep
    Disturbed instruction, and at night no sleep

29. Its solace brought to ease his weary mind:
    Always to Leylā were his words inclined.

30. 'O, thou, the joy of heart, the light of eye,
    Now, lacking thee, afar all light does fly.

31. 'Thy sweet companionship is sadly changed,
    Give but a reason why thy soul has ranged?

32. 'Why thus intoxicate my giddy mind?
    Why, making me a captive, be unkind?

33. 'If all thy purpose was to fling me out,
    Why give me darkness and tormenting doubt?

34. 'My heart the flame of parting hourly sears,
    My eyes are wet with longing's bitter tears.

35. 'My heart, aflame, glows like the morning bright,
    An angry dawn, with crimson clouds alight.

36. 'My tears, a mighty ocean without shore
    Well up, each asking more and more.

37. 'No friend I seek, thy friendship to replace:
    Alone, take thou the image from my face.

38. 'Remove it, lest upon my heart, a crown
    It burns, or else among my tears should drown.

39. 'With heady wine of longing I am drunk,
    And deep in pain's bewilderment am sunk.

40. 'Let not these pains accompany my day
    Lest grieving deep, my secret I betray.

41. 'A drunkard fully masters not his will,
    No heed can have bewilderment of ill.

42. 'My soul is lost upon this road of pain
    I ne'er shall feel afraid of death again.

43. 'One gift I have: this grief for thee has taught
    A gladness that was joy with passion fraught.

44. 'At times I wonder: what if Death should come?
    No soul is left to seize; pain were its only sum.

45. 'A candle am I, burning in the night
    Of pain and suff'ring, stirr'd by breezes light.

46. 'Yet though my heart in torment forces tears
    And, 'gainst my head, grief's fiery sword appears,

47. 'This agony of pain I would not yield,
    But, suff'ring all, make suffering my shield,

48. 'And keep these days of misery's deep despair
    When restlessly I wander, full of care.

49. 'Should Destiny the Book of Life indite
    'Gainst thee these days of suffering, or write

50. 'The record of my life, I'd scorn the page
    And tear the note to fragments in my rage.

51. 'They say the sun translates dark time to day:
    Resolve this subtlety, all ye who may.

52. 'The day whereon my sun declines to shine
    I cannot call a day, however fine

53. 'The skies above. Alas, that there is none
    To whom in pity is my sorrow known.

54. 'With every thought my grief grows mountain high,
    Each gusty sigh brings fiercer flames more nigh.'

55. His mind then on his early meetings bent,
    Upon this poem all his forces spent.

X

Herein is set forth the Poem composed by Mejnūn as he sorrowed in his Loneliness.

> How sweet were the moments I spent as a friend
> And intimate partner of Love!
> Feasting on pleasures I thought would ne'er end
> How gleefully then did the slow days unbend,
> How gladly the roses blew!
> My life, a glad springtime, before Autumn's hue
> Fell dread, like a bolt from above.
> But now comes the night time, for love, it has sped,
> And hidden far out of my sight.
> My fault, if a fault, is a memory dead.
> Unaware of my fault is my head.
> Yet though sweet lament
> Reaching up to the dome of the sky's arching tent
> No grieving turns wrong into right.
> Tho' wilful my tears, yet the all-avid throng
> On my sorrow shall ne'er feast its eye.
> Attached to the Book of my Life as a song,
> Was a preface of joy, then along
> Came Fate with its ghastly knife.
> Fuzūlī! 'Twas written that never my life
> Be twain with that bright Moon on high.

XI

Herein are set forth the Couplets that mark the end of the First Stage of Mejnūn's unhappy Story.

> Thus Qays pined, lonely and sad,
> While quickly abroad spread the news of his state:
> The world thought it shameful, and renamed the lad
> From Qays unto Mejnūn, with Sorrow as mate.

XII

Herein is set forth the Manner in which Mejnūn encountered Leyla, and how, from this Meeting, the Crescent of his Love waxed to a Full Moon.

> The world's bright candle, early Spring, came new
> And brought the bounteous gift of life restored,
> And spread afar its veil of pearly blue,
> And urged the nightingale to trill its song;

Spread far the limped wine of morning dew,
And filled the open'd tulip's crimson cup;
Inflamed the rose that in the garden blew
Agleam with torquise and the ruby's glow

His friends about Mejnūn now crowded thick
And urged a change of life, well knowing he was sick.
'Mejnūn, come, look around and see the rose,
That in the springtime now so gaily blows.
Now is the time when hope is born anew.
Come! Gather now thy friends! Thou hast a few!

No cloud art thou; rain not these salty tears:
Thou art no torrent; moan not; banish fears!
Let not the rose's thorn thy bosom rend,
Nor for a pillow to the earth descend.
Come out to fields and woods, where grows the vine,
With all thy friends, come, sing and quaff the wine!
Come with thy friends, a-seeking out new ways;
Leave grief behind with winter's chilly days.

'Come, seek the vineyard where the age-long art
May banish grief. Take heed lest others smart.
Thou art the cypress of the age, the rose;
Wed not thyself to sorrow's grief: seek those
Of joyous soul, for care is body's woe,
And constant grief distils a poison slow.
Remember too, the rose of thy desire
May yet come forth. Feed not despair's dull fire.
Come! Walk abroad, for these glad days of spring
May unsuspected joys and pleasure bring.'

Now Mejnūn slowly rose and took his way
Across the hills and through the valleys gay,
But ne'er a lightsome song could pass his lips,
But lamentations deep at love's eclipse.
He told his secret to the spreading trees,
Imploring all the tulips of the leas
To tell his love in Leylā's pearly ear
If e'er it chanced that Leylā should be near.
The timid violet his secret heard,
That she in Leylā's ear could pass the word.
He pressed the tulip's petals to his eyes

And kissed its feet with lover's heavy sighs.
Upon the narcissus he sadly gazed
Remembering the eyes of love amazed—
The nightingales, full throated in the brake
Were told his secret, ordered then to make
A song of all his sorrow, while his love
He sang to every silver throated dove.
With each new flower he saw a heavy sigh
Burst forth to join the yeasty clouds on high.

One day it chanced, for Fate was still unkind,
(Though seeming fair to those of simple mind)
That in his path the broken Mejnūn saw
His love, still peerless, lovely without flaw.
Before him Leylā and her maidens passed
And o'er the rose and tulip shadow cast.
For pitched within a meadow was her tent;
Her presence safe within, refulgence sent,
And cast a halo o'er the favour'd spot—
A rose within a rosebud, wilting not.

The candle that lights an assemblage is Leylā,
Mejnūn the heat of a fierce burning fire.
The huri that roams over Paradise, Leylā,
Mejnūn the King of the Land of Desire.
Unique in all ages and beauty is Leylā,
For Mejnūn the poets still pluck at the lyre.
The saping of Sorrow's green Meadow is Leylā,
Mejnūn ever faithful her love to inspire.
The Moon in the sky ruling heaven is Leylā,
Mejnūn but the sport of the evil below.
The chief in the line of the beauties is Leylā,
Mejnūn keeps the gate whence all sorrows do flow.
Sweetly entrancing, enticing is Leylā,
Mejnūn but the fountain where tears ever grow.
Desirous of beauty and happiness, Leylā,
Mejnūn unto *Melâmet* ever inclines.
The pearl in the mother of pearl, this is Leylā,
Mejnūn in the pride of her radiance shines.
Perfection of beauty and modesty, Leylā,
Mejnūn for her lovesomeness ever repines.
Desiring and yearning to see him was Leylā,
Mejnūn in desire for her sadly reclines.

Now these two tall and slender creatures, graceful as the jasmine flower,
Bosom friends grew each with other, firmer with each passing hour.
Tempered steel struck hard on granite as they came each face to face,
Self control and will both vanished in this fiery meeting place.

Two strings on a single *saz*,⁶⁰ they played a moaning melody,
The market of their passions ardent gave a mournful prosody.
The one gazed sweetly at the other, found a joy all unconfined,
The other looked and found a beauty, knew that love his soul entwined.
In Mejnūn reason had no basis, no foundation could be found,
Sanity departed from him, all his senses fled the ground.
Unable for an instant's briefness on her face to fix his eyes,
At her feet (a living shadow) fell, nor had the power to rise.
And Leylā, too, felt all her senses reel and swoon in dizzy rout,
Could not see him for an instant: love had put her candles out.
Down she fell of all bewilder'd, till her maidens o'er her face
Sweet rose scented essence sprinkled, while she slow returned from space.

'O brightst Moon, this sure is madness,'
Thus they told her in distress,
'Should thy father learn the sadness
That thy swooning here doth show,
That familiar with a stranger;
Or that he thy love doth know—
Full of harm were this, and danger
On our heads will sorrow press.

'Nothing good thy course presages,
Unworthy is this conduct bold,
Learn the wisdom of the ages,
Heed the lessons taught of old.'

Then bringing forth the carpet of the tent
They took the girl, still dazed, but obstinate,
To her own zodiac: eclipsed the Moon,
Lest that her father or her mother guess
The shame that she had heaped upon their name.
Nor of the dragon countered in their path,
Nor of their treasure's sickness spoke a word.

Now Mejnūn, raining blood from out his eyes
Was soon recovered from his sad collapse,
His tears alone refreshing, sought the place
Where Leylā looked upon him face to face.

But not a soul was there to meet his gaze.
The dry and arid earth stretched lonely round.
'Twas clear, he thought, that, having driv'n him mad
The youth who loved her, having scorched his soul,
She had withdrawn and left him to his fate.

He rent his garments, one by one, and moaned
Aloud his sorrow; changing thus his state,
Put off the vestments of a moral man,
Becoming mad and clothed in bloody tears.
About his head, as ringéd *reed pen*,[61] wound
A jet black turban, but the fiery sighs
Exhaled beneath its rim, fast burned it off
And left behind but dreary, blackened ash.
In self disgust he tore away his shirt
Ashamed to be a martyr in a shroud.
This trouble seeker cast his sandals off
That were but fetters to the feet of love.
And then to his companions, all amazed
And standing round, he made apology.

'My love's sweet attack like a torrent did flow,
My friends and companions, this truth ye must know.
'Tis time that we part for my dangerous state
Unfits any living to stay as my mate.
I burn in a torment of passion intense
Take heed lest I scorch ye and shrivel your sense.
No doubt can exist that this fire in my heart
Can send forth keen arrows with death poison'd dart.
O friends and companions, approach not my pyre,
Nor share my affliction: burn not with my fire.
No good have ye gained from my company sad,
Take heed that no evil from me turns ye mad,
For love crossed my path and made my life dark,
And left of my own free will never a spark.
A wandering bird am I, flown from the nest,
From home and the love of home, gone without rest
Or tranquillity, always to roam,
Alone without friendship, and now without home.'

'Should my father address ye, and ask of my state,
Or question the sorrow that dwells at my gate,
Explain with decorum my woeful estate,
Explain all my Destiny, blackened by Fate,'

'O Father, my Father, thou sad, broken Chief,
Complain not, nor mourn for thy fatherhood brief.
Nor idly and peevishly marvel what care
Has descended on Mejnūn to make him despair.
I knew not the cares of the world, or their worth,
Confusion of heaven, disorder of earth.

'In those far happy days when I knew not of cares,
When hours of sweet youth with dear innocence shares,
So happy in ignorance lingered my days,
No dreams had of Beauty, or Love's tearful ways.

I perish: my prayer is that thou should'st live long,
And hope my successor to greet with a song.
Forgive and excuse, Father dear, what has chanced,
'Tis sickness in me that has left me entranc'd.
With faithful endeavour all effort I made
To turn me to thee and to dwell in thy shade.
Yet every endeavour was futile and vain
Each started in sorrow and ended in pain.
My garment the thorn of affliction still caught
Still flooding my path came the tears I ne'er sought.'

Then, painfully, with cunning rhymes enwrought,
He sent this poem to his father's court.

'Twas thou, thou alone, gave me being and life,
'Twas thou madest obstacles; pledg'd me to strife.
Thy blessings were sorrows, no hope in my breast
Sprang high that thy autumn of days would be blessed.

XIII

Herein is set forth the Poem sent by Mejnūn to his Father.

When I saw the vast meadows of love, I abandoned all soundness of mind
That is sent by the gods up above, of all their sweet gifts most unkind.
Seek not now to look on my face, alone let me stay with disgrace,
Blame not, o advisor of youth, good excuse can be found for my place.
Seek not to prevent if my collar is rent,
No garment of shame my dress:

The desert's hot sand I now understand
Is the home where I hide my distress.
No slave of the dark from now on, for, hark!
A seeker am I after light,
To sickness of mind should my thoughts be inclin'd
The choice never mine for my plight.

Affliction in love, and the care of my love, I ne'er will surrender: my needs
Encompass not Paradise, ascetic soul, or huris that dance o'er the meads.
Observe my delight in her ringleted curls, the curve of her brow gives me pleasure,
With China's great Emperor, Fağfur,[62] I vie, or Chosroes,[63] rejoicing at leisure.
The aim of all life is to make a great name: mine shall last till the mountains dissolve:
Fuzūlī! Rejoice! I am famous, but mad! To be mad, drunk with love my resolve.

XIV

Herein are set forth the Attributes of Mejnūn's Madness, and the Quality of the Passion of the Valley of Love.

Skilled master of the arts of love,
His testament now made, Mejnūn
Set forth to roam his weary way
O'er deserts waterless and strewn
With desolation, leaving friends
And social intercourse to end.

And caring nothing of the road
Now like the lithe gazelle he fled
The stones of hills and valleys, too,
Were quickly changed to ruby red,
His head on every stone he beat
And made it smoke with bleeding heat.

Each stage his journey counted o'er
His tears made running streams abound;
His tears were rain, his heavy sighs
The lightning flashing all around.

From one to other passed these two,
The lightning's heat, the tears' wet dew,

That, had the lightning reach'd the sea
The sea a desert dry had grown:
Or had the tears the desert known
A mighty ocean all would see.
His maddened cry filled all the world,
The very birds and beasts that heard
In chorus joined and passed the word
To heaven's gate where Chaos whirled.

XV

Herein is related how Mejnūn's Father learned of his Condition and found Him in the Desert of Affliction.

The sad Narrator from his store these lines
As shining gems fast scattered on the ground,
And all the grieving friends that stood around
A farewell bade, and turned to the confines
Where yet the old Chief sat, to him unfurled
The story of his son's distress, how whirled
His mind in madness, sick with Love's disease;
How neither friend nor father could give ease.

Now when the sage this dismal story heard,
He grew, as his sad son, disconsolate;
Bewailed his doom, then violently spurred
Across the desert, while in yeasty spate
His tears gushed forth, as earnestly he sought
The love crazed youth, unknowing if in aught
He knew, or did, or said, could comfort find,
Or words to ease Mejnūn's distresséd mind.

Afar he roamed, examining each place
But quite invisible had Mejnūn grown;
Till, last, he turned a hill, and there some trace
Of Mejnūn's passing on the rocks was shown.
And there, within a corner, broken, dazed,
Uncaring, and with sorrow all amazed,
Was Mejnūn, lying in his broken state,
Alone, with Misery his only Mate.

His rose red cheek had turned to saffron hue,
His breast was torn, his graceful figure bent
From stately *elif* into *dal*[64] askew,
Thin as a pen, fit subject for lament:
The mirror of his soul, his face, begrimed
With dust, no poet ever rhymed.
His friend the ant, the snake his comrade near,
His resting place the earth, sharp thorns his bier.

So many gaping windows could be seen
Where thorns had pierced his flesh with bitter dart,
That when his father looked, his sorrow keen
Dried up his words and blistered o'er his heart,
As in bewilderment he gazed: his eye
For tears too dry, his throat too tight to sigh.
Some time he stood, then, tearing off his dress
These piteous words to Mejnūn did address:

'O, nightingale within this desert harsh,
Why turnest thou this desert to a marsh?
Make known thy secret and recount thy pain.
Say who has ta'en thy manhood. Think again.
Tell all thy sorrow and explain thy grief,
Then, haply knowing, we may find relief.
Say who has brought this darkness to thy life.
Why thus unsettled? Wherefore comes this strife?
Explain the reason for his bitter woe,
And why in sorrow thou art fallen low?
If in the sea thy bright desire's sweet pearl
Lies hid, thy father tell: or heaven hurl
Thy destined candle to the hidden land
That lies beyond the sun, why, this my hand
And this my body, with a father's zeal
Would strive and seek for thee, my son, to heal.'

Mejnūn, unrecognizing answered: 'Life
Is speech and wisdom skilled. Know then, this strife
Wherein I am encountered knows thee not.
Seek not to meddle in my dismal lot.
Take thy absurdities and foolish boast
Away from me. Thou knowest not the host

Of sorrows crowding fast my life to end.
Go from me! Neither father thou, nor friend.
Or, should'st thou stay, 'tis but of Leylā dear
Thy tongue should speak, for only that I hear.'

The old Chief said: 'Thy father dear am I,
The Stone of all Reproaches hard that lie
As Melâmet upon my shattered head—
But thou art fire, fierce flaming, hot and red.'

Mejnūn replied: 'Say, what are parents dear?
All, all save Leylā, is but legend clear.'

Now when the father saw that from his son
All show of sweet obedience had fled,
And knew that of his words of counsel, none
Could reach the mind whence reason far had sped,
To trick the crazied Mejnūn he essayed,
And said: 'But come! Thy Leylā calls! The maid
Thou callest Leylā stays with us as guest:
Thy ruby waits at home to give thee rest.'

Now when he heard the spell of Leylā's name
And learned her lodgement in his father's home,
He ceased lamenting and with heart aflame
Sprang up, assured he need no further roam.
'Command, my father,' said he quickly. 'Lo,
Unto the *Kaaba* let us fleetly go.'
And thus the sage and his Moon crazéd lad
Came sick and mournful to their dwelling sad;
But in the youth no thought of father stayed,
Or mother dear, for Leylā was his maid.

But once at home, his father straight essayed
To teach with sound advice, and mother counsel made.

XVI

Herein is related how Mejnūn's Mother gave Advice, and how she garnered the Thorns of Regret from the Garden of Reproaches.

'O, thou, my soul's comfort, the light of my eyes,
My only and choicest son,
In thine ancestry the fame of Arabia lies,
Rank, honour and valour, hard won.

Of kings take thy counsel through every day,
Make ritual of valour thy life:
Yet should a curved eyebrow yet hold thee in play,
Why, who would oppose thee with strife?

Remove from thy heart all those eyelashes black,
Seek rather the arrow of fame:
See how that the full-figured spear never lack
Its blood: blood and tears are the same.

Ecstatic the joy born of locks of bright hair—
Dal curls in a lovelier space.
If the heart be entranced by an eyebrow so fair
Come, seek it in *noon's* charming face.

For thou art the cypress, be not so oppressed:
A free man, no captive, no thrall:
For thou art the ruby; no stone ever dressed
By the sun's changing rays as they fall.

Be purposeful, constant, and ne'er till time stops,
Be pleased with a whim in thy head;
For whims of the mind and the quickly gone dew drops
Are, lacking foundation, soon dead.

No basis secure can be found for the fiction
Of love: only ruin it spells;
For love gives the head the pale candle's affliction,
Its burning its own death foretells.

The candle sinks slowly; falls into disaster,
Consumed by its own fiery heat
Surrender to fancy but hastens the faster
A strife that must end in defeat.

Pass not thy ripe manhood with wine and its pleasure,
From chaste self control gather aid;
For wine and a maid leave but little of leisure,
Their penalty soon must be paid.

Can the drunkard have sense, or idolator worship,
Or poet believe in his lies?
No beauty or virtue is found in this kingship—
And he who believes in it dies.

Seek thou for perfection, nor waste thine endeavour
In wandering far and unknown;
For thou art our sapling, in thee our hopes ever
Are fix'd, now to manhood full grown.

Let not this thy conduct call forth sad reproaches
To trample rough-shod on our fame:
Thy name and our fame flatters each who approaches—
This honour reflects from our name.

Tribes more than a thousand are here in our land
Each tribe many beauties arrayed—
Let each after each sweetly offer her hand.
Thus honour and duty were paid.

Thus of stature so graceful, jessamine breasted,
For marriage we'll find thee a pearl:
And ramming the day when from grief thou art rested
We'll wed thee a beautiful girl.

And riches we'll give thee beyond all thy spending,
(Consider my counsels with care)
Forsake thou this path of deep grief never ending,
And cause not thy parents despair,

By cutting our stem so that thy generation
Shall spell out the end of our race.
Come, heed our advice, most belov'd of our nation,
Let sorrow be gone from thy face,
Remembering ever the stern condemnation
The poet set forth in its place.

XVII

Herein is set forth the Ode of the Master referred to by the Mother of Mejnūn.

    Give not thy heart to grief or gloom,
    Nor sink in Love's despair;
    For Love's calamity is doom,
    The world knows this. Beware!
    For grief, though born of passion deep
    Still causes heavy loss—
    Then seek not Love: thy manhood keep,
    Forswear the worthless dross.

    Each eyebrow stabs as dagger fierce;
    Each lock makes poisoned darts
    That seeks thy very soul to pierce,
    And from each lovely look there parts
    Ill past all counting o'er;
    A torment and a heavy fate
    Brings jaundiced pallor sore
    To Love's bedraggled state.

    I know the torment born of Love,
    For lovers sigh and moan,
    They ask no solace from above,
    They seek to be alone.
    Talk not of eyes as black as ink;
    Avoid the pupils' glance.
    Though black the eyes, 'tis blood they drink,
    And keep thee in a trance.

    And even should Fuzūlī claim
    A loyalty and joy,
    And, counting o'er his beauties, name
    The words he would employ,
    Be not deceived, for ever he
    Is caught the more he tries
    To scape the net, and further, see,
    All poet's words are lies.

XVIII

Herein is related how Mejnān refused to take the Advice of his Parents, and how his Father's Grief could not find a Cure for his Sadness.

Mejnūn who hearkened to these words
That fell from off his parents' honoured lips,
Until their close, a careful answer gave;
Beginning thus:
                'O, parents, most revered,
My fount of life, esteemed beyond compare,
How well I know that wrongful are my deeds!
How well I know the justice of your words!
This shame unshameful, by the world bestowed,
Brings forth black sighs of sorrow, while my face
A dismal, grim humiliation shows.
No lesson new is this ye read to me.
Now rather tell me what to say or do.
In this my sorrow is no choice nor will;
No longer in my hands I hold the reins
That guide the will: my mind is sicklied o'er
With Love's consuming rage, my heart perplex'd
With whirling in the heady dance of love.
But what care I if poets laugh at Love?
Enfeebled in the mind, Love dominant
Perplex'd the heart, the Idol beautiful,
Love's dear affliction, soul and body holds—
The world is nothing lacking my belov'd.
And, loving thus, how can the thought of self
Be in my heart? And who can find in me
Aught of myself? Can any change their fate?
Bethink thee, if I laughed and joyed the day
Would I thus pine in grief and sad despair?
Would not the sick apply the remedy
To ease their hurt, if remedy there were?
Would beggars revel in their beggard state
If, with a jump, thy might attain a throne?

The Destiny, close stationed at my gate
The day I saw the light, implacable,
Yet stays, and writes upon his endless page
Grief after sorrow as each grief draws near.

'Tis vain to seek reform; as well to try
To turn the rose to thorn, the thorn to rose,
For all things have their state and nature true—
Seek not to understand what ne'er was known.

Think! Can the rivers run to mountain tops!
Or can the flaming fire refuse to burn?
That day when Providence took up the pen
The mirror of my life to write and drew
My picture, ere created, that day was writ
My brain all charged with passion should become.
Those written words ordained that feet, enchained
With love, should cripple me, that veins and body all
Should burn from head to foot with Love's desire.
'Tis Providence that orders forth my heart
To misery, and tortures all my soul.
On me, unanswering, comes the planned decree,
That never act of mine can cast aside.

Can pain eternal ever yield to cure?
Can everlasting love decline to death?
I proudly stand, the candle in the hall
Of Separation, well content to burn
A tribute to the love within my heart;
And he who'd try this saddened joy to tear
From out my soul, be never friend to me,
But rather foe who seeks my overthrow.

The candle's brightest essence is the flame
And burning serves its purpose to fulfil,
And he who seeks to dim its burning out
Desires no more, no less than shameful death.
Name not as friendship this thine enmity
That seeks to cure the tumult in my soul
Deep drowned in love's great yearning, ocean wide,
Deep drowned in pining for the Idol dear.

'Tis only she can ease my grieving heart,
'Tis only she can bring repose of soul;
Seek not to cure with other beauties' charms—
One Fair alone can bring me remedy.
Discourse no more of other lovely maids,
Nor say that my affliction comes of them;
Blaspheme no more in saying they are fair
As Leylā, for the world holds not her peer.

Think ye, that when the nightingale in May
Is grieving for the rose, his sorrow deep
The tulip will assuage? No Khusrev[65] I
That Shirin[66] or Sikker[67] can give me peace.
I, as a dervish, on a single path
Pursue my way unchanging, as a star
Pursues its way through heav'n's dome on high.'

Thus spoke Mejnūn, then, to confirm his oath,
Set forth an ode that re-affirmed his troth.

XIX

Herein is set forth the Ode composed by Mejnūn, in which he re-affirmed his Unchangeability.

O, what a task ye doctors find
Who seek to part the body from the mind!
But still the doctors try
To seek a cure
For those who sadly sigh
And torment of a passion still endure
Beseiged with Love's sweet tragedy unkind.

Name not as lover he who wails
The cruelty of Fortune, for the scales
Fall not from eyes
Of Love's inebriates;
He sees no skies
Above, nor here creates
Distinction when his love his soul impales.

No lover roaming far in Love's domain
Can separate the City from the Plain;
For Love's sweet wilderness
No diff'rence shows
To City's noisiness.
The lover knows
Nor Town nor Desert, being never sane.
When once the dear belovéd of the soul
Find union with the soul, the chains unroll
That bind the flesh:
Such union brings
Love's rapture fresh
While loudly yet it sings—
Soul is from Body as is Pole from Pole.

His enemies say Fuzūlī dwells apart
The Friend of Love, for Love fills all his heart:
Though all they say
And every word they write
Be calumny, yet they
In this are right—
Fuzūlī always plays a lover's part—

XX

Herein is related how Mejnūn's Father sought Leylā in Marriage for his Son, and how the Father of Leylā would have none of it while Mejnūn remained uncured of his Madness.

Now Saki, bring the clear and limpid wine,
For now has come the requisite degree
Of passion fierce and Love's dear rapture fine:
Bring now the wine and set the victim free.
For thus the Poet, culling gems of words
From out the market of Mejnūn's mad mind
Had shown his father that of all his herds
And wealth and riches, never would he find
That comfort that would soothe his scattered wits
Till Leylā sat beside him. Thus the Chief
To Mejnūn's madness bound himself, as fits
The father of a son sunk deep in grief.

To win for Mejnūn Leylā's precious hand
His heart firm set and hope about him wrapped,
He journeyed to the *Kaaba* of Desire
And Leylā's father, not to be entrapped
In show of less civility, nor tire
His guest with hasty comfort, gathered too,
The greatest of his land, and journeyed forth
To greet the coming party. Well he knew
That honour must be met with honour's worth.

With welcome many times repeated o'er,
With hopes that happy auspices attend
Their visit, and that blessings pour
Upon them, they attained their journey's end.
A cypress tree in stature, tall and grand
He stood before them. They erect and straight

As candles sat, while near at hand
Refreshment waiteth—many a cunning plate
Of roasted meat, the lamb and tender kid—
It seemed that *Aries*[68] and *Capricorn*
Had left their places in the sky to bid
A welcome to the guests so travel worn.
(How strange it is to say these furnished trays
Were like the sky's plann'd zodiac on high;
As if the trav'llers thought, all in a maze,
That these conceits should fall from out the sky!)
Then, courtesy observed, the ancient Chief
Restored in body, still distressed in mind,
Set fort his errand, told of all the grief
His son endureth with soul to Love entwin'd.
'O, thou, thyself the Father of a Host
Of Tribes, the Fount, the Spring, the Corner-post—
My race and lineage thou knowest well,
Effective is my power with all who dwell
Within a thousand homes: my fame is spread
Many a thousand tribes. By all 'tis said
That much and freely to them all I give.
Within my friendship many peoples live.
My enmity is fierce: I spread it not;
No man am I of ruthless anger hot.
The leading name mine of all the days
Whereof men write—all join to sing my praise,
Know also that, beside my lineage old
Possessions have I, more a hundred fold
Than I can count. But still the brightest gem
That God has granted for my diadem
Is he for whom I seek a valued pearl
To balance with a ruby: boy and girl.
In many mines that richest treasure yield
I've dug, exploring; roamed a vasty field.
In every mine a precious stone is hid,
But not the ruby that my mind may rid
Of need for seeking. But a breath I hear
That thou, within thy tent, a ruby clear
Hast strictly kept, that well may match my pearl.
And thus I ask thee, in the dizzy whirl
Of all that comes and goes, by gracious now,
Respecting pearl and ruby, thinking how
The one to other joined, may, each to each,

Protection give, as cypress boughs o'er-reach
The blowing rose, and give it needed shade.
So should a youth protect a lovely maid.
Be not unmindful, comprehend my word,
A good affair is this, be not deterred,
And ask of me whate'er thou wilt in change.
O'er all thy great desires thy mind may range
Should treasure be thine aim, thy ruby's worth
Shall draw such treasures as may hide the earth;
If jewels bright thy goal, then jewels I'll send
To fill thy treasure chests without an end.'

To this address the father answered slow
As well befitted parent of the gem
That had no peer, the jasmine breasted dove,
The hidden treasure, guarded with the care
That comes when dragons guard the secret door:

'O, wise and gentle friend, who, like myself,
Art captive to a child loved more than pelf,
Full welcome art thou, bringing pleasure deep
To him who speaks, and yet in dust must creep.
'Tis hard to answer, yet response is due
To what thou sayest: let my words be few.
Much honour is enshrined in thy speech;
'Twixt thee and me were honour each to each.
Yet hear me now and take not deep offence
They say that Mejnūn is bereft of sense:
The people ill bespeak him, call him mad.
No marriage this to make my daughter glad.
'Tis not for me to sing my daughter's praise,
But 'tis my child, and will be all her days.
A daughter is the pupil of the eye,
Full helpless, hurt by all the motes that fly.
This cannot be: 'twere more than all unkind
A maddened giant and fairy child to bind
In marriage. Talk not thus my worthy friend.
Be silent on this matter. Let it end.
'Tis ruin needs thy madman, why expend
On madmen all thy treasure? Seek a cure
For this thy son, then shall my word endure,
That Mejnūn, healed of all his mad disease
Shall wed with Leylā for his sick heart's ease.'

XXI

Herein is set forth the Disappointment of the Father of Mejnūn, and his Attempt to find elsewhere a Cure for his Son's Madness.

Now Mejnūn's father, when he heard the words
Spoke by the sire of Leylā, sadly turned
And bent his steps towards his honoured home
Where reputation and respect had dwelt,
To where his son, with wits all turned awry
Awaited him, and thus with piteous words
Spoke sad and slow:
              'O victim sad,
In whom a cruel fire so fiercely burns,
Be not dismayed, for all can be composed
With wisdom, and the prize may yet be won.
Leylā is thine with one condition set,
And that, that thou regain thy healthy state,
Stand forth to all as one full sound of mind,
Accepting sound advice from them that know.'
Mejnūn replied:
              'O thou, so perfect made,
Replete of knowledge, can the mad be wise?
Can wits so scattered formally regain
Control of sense? In this my sad decline
I nothing chose. Had reason any voice
That could be heard, then daily would I show
High breeding, sweet accomplishment of race,
And stand secure in dignity and rank.
Had reason any value there were need
Of none of these, thy medicines or charms;
And even now, with all my mind distraught,
Think not with healing liquors to assuage
My troubled state. With conduct still unchanged
I give the answer that I gave before.
A man of wisdom thou, find thou the means
To spread dissimulation in the path
Of my desire, that never Leylā's name
Shall pass my lips, and I be wise anew
Restored to health, and thou again be free.'

The broken parent sought with cunning zeal
A cure to find o'er many distant lands.

Where e'er a doctor's fame was noised abroad
The father sat, a patient nightingale
Within his garden, telling of the need,
All pleading, for a cure to save his son.
A thousand skilled physicians tried in vain
To find a cooling sherbet, every tomb
That sheltered in its shade a holy man
Or prophet, place of pilgrimage became,
And in the dust that gathered at its gate
The saddened father deep oblation made,
And offered prayers, bestowing many gifts,
And vowing many more he yet would give
If only could his son be safe restored
And healed. Yet of a thousand great
And skilful sages, of a thousand charms
And many magic amulets of hope,
No healing came. Indeed what cure is found
To remedy an illness sent of God?

At last, when all had failed, the people said:
'O, sage, a single chance there still remains.
The Kaaba Stone awaits, and it may be
That God will smile upon a pilgrim mad,
That circles round the *Harem*,⁶⁹ magic tomb.
Let Mejnūn go submissive, postulant,
And rest his head appealing on that stone.
Who knows but what a miracle may come,
And even that black heart may pity know.

XXII

Herein is related how the unfortunate Mejnūn went to Kaaba, and how, with prayer, his Affliction grew.

The sage took heed his counsel to adopt,
And for his son a *trav'lling chair*⁷⁰ prepared.
Then took him by the hand and led him forth
To start the lonely journey to Harem.
And thus he spoke:
                'Hear now my words, my son,
Thou seeker after trouble through the world.
Before the Kaaba press thy tearful face,

Respect the customs sacred in this spot,
And pray with all sincerity of heart
That God perchance thy supplication grant
And send a cure to ease thy battered mind.
This is the spot, so honoured in our creed
Where prayers are mostly welcomed, where the ear
Of God inclines and sweet salvation grants.'

Mejnūn was siezed in whirl of ardent joy
And heady pleasure, and without a thought
Of hiding that which in his breast gave pain
He uttered deeply from his bleeding heart
A cry that reach'd afar to Heaven's Gate,
And told his secret to the Holy Stone.

'O, thou, Whose lofty Ceiling scrapes the sky,
Thou *Mihrab*[71] of the great and of the high,
O, Thou, the *Kible*,[72] pointing out the way
To those of worth and honour come to pray:
Thou Fragrant Mole upon the earth's sweet face,
Whose Cloth of Loyalty in prideful place
Hangs for the Faithful, of the selfsame blend
Black as the rug of lover dear, or friend;
O, Thou, the Rose Tree of *Siyadet's*[73] bud,
The Chest of *Saadet's*[74] Treasure, mingle blood
With me a fellow suff'rer, tho' Thy Place
Ne'er changes. I alone roam wide in space.
Thou strik'st a Grim Black Stone upon Thy Breast,
Thou sheddest tears like *Zemzem*,[75] never rest
May dry Thy weary eyes, Thy garments black
Contain Thy Passion, though Thy Heart should crack.
Thou hast achieved the Bounteous Gift of all,
The Gift of Love that made Thee *Kible* tall
Of all the nations. Fit companion I
To know whom Thou in love hast set on high.
For sake of this, Thy pure and lovely Shrine,
Make now to spring within this heart of mine,
With firm foundation, like Thy Kaaba strong,
The edifice of Love: its joy and song.
Distil Love's sorrows for my grieving heart,
Each moment, every breath I draw, let art
Increase my ardour that my love may grow
And growing thus may greater pleasure know.

Wherever in the world Thou findest pain,
To that sweet pain my aching heart enchain,
And banish from me every show of sense,
And closely bind me to a love intense.
For Leylā let me burn in fiercest fire,
That Thou in her I see is my desire.
And let my heart, innured to every grief
And loneliness, enjoy a moment brief
Where, 'scaping all the cruelty of man
Establishment I make where never ran
Man's inhumanity: with beast and bird
I'll sing my days in misery unheard.'
So spoke the pilgrim at the Kaaba Stone,
And sought an answer to his fervent prayer
Unheedful of Calamity's excess
He made an ode his feeling to express.

XXIII

Herein is set forth the Ode or Prayer recited by Mejnūn at the Kaaba Stone.

> For pain of Love's affliction is my prayer
> O, Lord, that ne'er a breath
> I draw that grieving sorrow does not share,
> Let Love but die with death.
>
> An addict to affliction's gnawing pain
> Make me, Thy suppliant;
> Let not Thy bounty fail, as desert rain,
> Let not Thy Grace be scant.
>
> While life endures take not my freedom dear
> To choose the road of tears;
> Affliction seek me always: I am near.
> I seek affliction's fears.
>
> Let not my dignity to worthlessness
> Sink 'neath the pain above:
> That she charge not a false forgetfulness,
> Or blame for faithless love.

Bestow upon my Idol greater charms
With every wind that blows;
And let me still clasp sorrow in my arms,
As still her beauty grows.

For where am I, and where my going back
To honour and to praise?
The joys of poverty no more I lack—
Make these my ending days.

Without her let my body weakly sink
That merest zephyr slight
May waft me to her, making airy link
And change to day my night.

And like Fuzūlī, with a joy and pride
Of love, increase my share.
O, Lord, leave not Mejnūn to Mejnūn tied.
Hear, mighty God, my prayer.

XXIV

Herein is related the Manner in which Mejnūn left the Kaaba, and of his taking of the Road to the Wilderness.

As one by one the heavy words were spoke,
His father knew that God would surely grant
The madman's prayer, that grief would surely grow
About his head: that yet the gossips' tongues
Would wag incontinent; that never peace
Would come to ease his son.
      In deep distress
He wept and moaned, then with reluctance sad,
All hope of cure abandoned, sat him down
In grieved bewilderment, while all alone
Mejnūn went forth to tread his thorny path
O'er all the deserts of despair, the street
Of love to vainly seek. The tears his guide
He took by day, by night the fiery flame
Of sighs, like burning candles, lit the road.
And thus, now stopping sad, now marching on,
He went, still murmuring the name he loved.

XXV

Herein is set forth Mejnūn's Encounter with the Mountain, and his Discourse with the flowing Fountain.

Now fast o'er the stones of the desert sped Mejnūn,
And, lo! A great mountain stood barring his way,
A garment befitting its majesty wearing,
Near reaching the heavens and clouding the day.
Its roof watched the spheres as they rolled in their courses,
Its belt was of rubies hid deep in a mine;
Its countenance gracious, its garment all splendid
Agleam with the brightest of jewels did shine.
The sea, while it prayed to it, flattered to wavelets
Its angry great breakers, and hoped for increase:
While the dry arid desert hoped to have keeping
Of all the sweet fountains that flowed bringing peace.
The father and mother of stream and of ocean
Was this mighty mountain, described in the brief
But clear spoken words in God's Book called the Koran,
When God said: 'Of all things, mountains are chief.'
Now Mejnūn beheld with amazed admiration
This mountain so mighty and tuned him a song,
And the mountain itself heard, and swelled its own praises
With echoes that rolled all the valleys along.

And now came conceit that Mejnūn and the mountain
Were merged into one, and Mejnūn as a friend
Accepted the mountain, and gave thanks a hundred
To God Who had sent him a friend ere his end.
'Now here, in this world full of dust', chanted Mejnūn,
'I find me a friend who will list to my tale.
O thou, lonely mountain, so chaste in aloofness,
See how these afflictions my sad heart impale.
Familiar thou with the pain of my burning,
('Tis well, mighty friend: Heaven's blessings enjoy!)
Thou knowest, for deep in thy heart is a yearning
That gives thee the friendship of love saddened souls.
A fitting companion and friend, mighty mountain
And here on thy slopes let all lovers remain:
Thou beatest thy breast with thy stones, and a fountain
Of tears thy affliction pours over thy breast.
What fate has befall'n that, drunk in this fashion,

A captive thou art, with thy foot tied to pain;
Thy breast overcharg'd with the blood of thy passion?
What rose is it now that blooms red in your garden?
What beauty has turned thy dear breast to a stream?
What cypress-tall grace withholds yet her pardon,
And leaves thee to mourn, weeping sad, in disgrace?
Now come, let us weep o'er our sorrows together
And join our two voices as one for a space.'

Thus mountain and man made a great lamentation
And loudly set forth their distress and their pain,
Then slowly Mejnūn sought to ease separation,
Took the dust laden pathway that led to his love.

XXVI

Herein is set forth Mejnūn's Speech with the Gazelle, and his Discourse in the Chapter of Love.

It chanced a hunter set a snare
To catch the fleet gazelle,
As Mejnūn passed his vacant stare
Upon the victim fell.
The fleet gazelle's black velvet eyes
Were filled with bloody tears,
Feet tied, neck bent, its groaning sighs
Fell sharp on Mejnūn's ears.
And he, compassion's saddened slave,
Felt pity in his heart,
And, tearful, sought around to save
The beast from hunter's dart.

'O Hunter, show thy mercy now
For this poor, dumb gazelle.
See now its fears and tell me how
Compassion may not dwell
Within thy soul: no sacrifice
Of this, thy captured prey,
Will save thy soul, nor yet suffice
To sanctify the day.
O, Hunter, cruel things are ill;
Blood ever seeks for blood:
Grant me this life and do not kill
This beast. Let thou the flood

Of sympathy flow sweetly now
And save it from the flame
Of cruelty's fierce fire, that thou
And it be bless'd the same.'

The hunter swiftly made reply:
' 'Tis much to ask of me.
Would'st thou my wife and children die?
They will, should'st this go free.
Nay, from my shoulders take my head,
If yet make delay.
My children wait and must be fed,
They have not eat today.'

Now every leaf that clothed the tree
Wherein his spirit dwelt,
Mejnūn took off and, standing free,
Before the captive knelt;
Set loose the cord that held it fast,
And whispered in its ear
That danger and distress were passed:
No need remain for fear.
The velvet cheek he then caressed
And, weeping eye to eye,
Sweet words of pity he addressed
The weeping eye to dry.

'Thou roamer o'er a desert place
In battle fierce and strong,
Whose body holds a slender grace
Result of lineage long;
Thy easy step adorns the earth,
Thy beauty, like the rose,
Is sweet and delicate, thy worth
The arid desert knows.
Among the rivers of the plain
Thou art the freshest plant;
The joy where jasmine blooms again
Thy beauty may supplant.
One boon alone is all I ask,
For I am frail and weak,
To lead me o'er the plain thy task.
Be thou the guide I seek.
As guide and as companion, too,

Accompany me, yet
Fear not my human form, nor rue
This day on which we met.
Go not, like these my falling tears
Down dropping from my eyes:
Withhold not now thy feet: thy fears
From nothing do arise.
Make thou my eye thy halting place
But be not unaware
That at the end our resting place
May be in chilly air.
My eye with pupil dark may be
Thy dwelling place, my tears
Thy water sweet, thy herbage free
My lashes, whence there peers
The saddened eye that sees in thee
A sad remembrance dear
Of that dear Idol that I see
With constant vision clear.
Make easy all my weary grief,
In thee let Leylā's eyes
Gleam forth awhile in sorrow brief.
Come, ease my weary sighs,
And bring to me a sweet relief.
From thee let solace rise.'
The swift gazelle now lost its fear
Of dread humanity[76]
And followed a companion dear
Mejnūn's insanity.
And as through all the wilderness
They journeyed every day
Gazelles came flocking numberless
To 'company their way.

XXVII

Herein is related the Manner in which Mejnūn explained his Condition to the Pigeon, and requested her to obtain for him that which was in his Mind.

It chanced a halting place was reached
Where, wretched and distraught
A pigeon languished in a cage,
Its life with danger fraught.

Each window of the trap a door
It gazed through in its grief,
A thousand sorrows smote the air,
It mourned its freedom brief.

Mejnūn beheld and straight his heart
With pity cried aloud;
His tears welled up in boiling blood,
In grief he cried aloud

And begged the hunter to be kind,
And set the pigeon free,
But still the hunter heeded not,
He said: 'Look thou at me!

'I am a simple man, and poor,
To poverty the slave.
Should I release this pigeon, then
For food my folk would crave.

'What profit then, to free the bird
If children hungry stay—
Come, understand, the bird goes free
If thou for food wilt pay.

But let compassion fall on me
Or e'er a tiny bird
Thy pity holds; nor take the food
From me, a hungry herd.'

Now on his arm a lovely pearl[77]
As eye of *Kevser*[78] clear
Was hung with bright transparency,
And Mejnūn held it dear.

He gave the pearl and took the bird,
Upon it succour shed,
And bathed its feet from bloodshot eyes,
So every claw was red.

And opened wide his yearning heart
And, as he strode along
He told the pigeon all his pain
In this his woeful song:

'O, thou, dear bird with speedy wings
That o'er the heavens fly,
The fast and bosom friend of all
Of proven loyalty;

The indigo's deep, dusky hue
Becomes this robe of thine,
O saddened bird that takes the grief
Of *Melâmet* for wine;

This grief so clearly manifest
By crying 'fore thy face,
Makes captive thou to mourning dread,
Fast 'prison'd in thy place.

O, wanderer through all the world
Of love thy soul dost know;
Flee not from one within whose breast
Love's sorrows proudly grow.

An instant stay, and, patient, hear
Executor of pain,
O trustee of my treasury,
The grief I tell again.

Within my hair make thou a nest,
And should'st thou seek for grain,
My tears shall flow to feed thy soul
As flowers are fed by rain.

A messenger I hear thee called—
Now take a message sweet
To her who holds my heart in thrall.
Fly fast! My goddess meet!

See all my suffering and my pain
In beauty of her cheek;
A message take, an answer bring—
Fly quickly, love to seek!

Billah![79] The threshold of her street
Shall stop thee short, while round
Her house, a Kaaba, let thy wings
Cast shadows on the ground[80]

Remember me, and merit seek,
All praise and honour thine:
Grant me the merit of thy tour
To greet my love divine.

Upon the dust before her door
Alight and ask for grain,
And make pretence until her smiles
Are showered on thee like rain.

While thou hast power, be not ashamed
To carry far from here
These kisses, so may Leylā tread
On them and make them dear.'

So much he spoke, the tiny bird
Felt near to humankind,
And safely in his matted hair
Its tiny nest entwined

All day his guard, when evening fell
She slept within his hair:
All beasts became obedient,
They knew him good and fair.

The animals that roamed around
Submitted to his word:
Of birds and beasts of all degree
He gathered soon a herd

And thus Mejnūn, the mighty Shah
Of all affliction Sad,
Of bird and beast an army made—
'Tis clear that he was mad.

For people gave he ne'er a thought;
His image in a stream
Disturbed his mind, for as he looked
A stranger did it seem.

The smoke of fiery sighs sent forth
To heaven did ascend;
His very shadow came to hate
And would not take as friend.

XXVIII

Herein are set forth the Details of Leylā's Condition, and an Account of the Manner and Behaviour appropriate to Love and the Beloved.

    Full deeply of the draughts of heady wine
    O, Saki, have I drunk, and sadly need
    A sweet corrective: see my sorry state,
    My sad captivity, and with one cup
    Extend thy help and take me by the hand.
    Since this great banquet of emotions rare
    Is of thy making, pass the cup in turn
    That all may drink, the rich no less than poor.
    Alone to Mejnūn hold thou not the wine
    Of passion, Leylā waits.
                      The Eloquent
    Who from the Garden sweet of tender Words
    Culls forth these roses, planted firm the Box[81]
    That all might see what ills befell the Spring
    Of Loyalty's Fair Meadow; how the fire
    Of Love's Affliction burned the Tulip up.

    Full firm and steadfast in her loyalty
    Was Leylā, pearly mother of the gems of grief,
    And like a treasure in a fortress housed,
    Was self imprisoned by advices sad.
    No joy was there, no cheering comradeship,
    Indifferent to father, mother, friends.
    And still, as moths about the candle flame
    Flutter and go, and come and flutter more,
    So at her side there gathered from afar
    Sweet girls in Beauty's image at her side,
    To rouse her saddened heart to newer zest,
    Her nature sweet to rouse from gloomy care.

    A thousand tales with new ten thousand words
    Would they recount, recalling to the mind
    Far off, forgotten legend, spinning forth
    A fresher tale from ancient history.
    But Leylā sought no comfort, shared no joy,
    All happiness abandoned: would essay
    To wound a limb and of its angry hurt
    Would find excuse to justify her tears.

And yet, though wound was seen, its pain well known,
None saw with Leylā's eyes, nor felt with Leylā's soul.

Should it befall that maid with *rastık* brush
Should ring her eyes with eyebrows dusky dark,
She felt the mirror of her soul, the face,
All rusted with corrosion's gnawing pain.
Or if in indigo a handsome mole
They painted on her cheek (a mighty charm
In Beauty's armoury), then she, in haste,
The lovely blemish with a napkin damp
Would banish from her face. Now never red
With henna stained her hands, but angry tears
Of brightest blood dripped from each finger tip.
No more she joyed in needle or in silk,
But every day poured forth in flooding spate
The tears that drowned the lashes of her eyes,
And, of the tears, an envious ornament,
A pallid jewelled necklace, sadly strung,
She wore as other girls may gaily wear
The brightest stones upon a silken thread.
Indeed, in madness she surpasséd that
Of maddened Mejnūn who for Leylā called;
And when at dusk her maidens left her side
She took her candle to the corner drear
And told the candle of her grieving heart:
Made manifest the pain within her soul.

XXIX

Herein is set forth Leylā's Conversation with the Candle and the Manner of her Asking for the Remedy for the Pain in her Heart.

O, thou, with eyes securely tied, whose heart is branded sore,
Who, ages passed, as now, the crown of blackened mourning wore,
Whose foot is constant in one place: come, let us, thou and I
Be one in soul, make manifest the reason thou dost cry.
What trouble makes thee slender, then; and so distress'd and pale,
Say why this burning head to foot, the garb of sorrow's wail?
Say why the blackness of thy heart escapes as sooty smoke
Sad sufferer of calamity, whose tears thy passion choke?
Of what sort is thy origin, that this hot, burning flame

Is water sweet that gives thee life, explain this eye of shame
That weeps about thy burning heart, reveal the secret clue
That followed will unveil thy heart, and all thy secret rue.
O, early riser, tell me now, what is thy magic sweet
That gives to water potency to swell thy passion's heat?
Tho' vexed I be, and sadly torn, yet leave me not alone,
Neglect me not for in my heart, I, too, a sorrow own.
I, too, like thee, in loyalty, am sorrow's slave, but stay,
Thy sorrow troubles thee at night; mine burns both night and day.
The lightest wind disturbs thy poise and bends thee to its will,
A grievous pain, but how much less than all my monstrous ill!
Thy habit 'tis to drip thy tears for all the world to see,
To tell the sorrow of thy heart with naught of secrecy
Where e'er the crowds are thronging, and from thy saddened breast
Thy tongue gives out the loyalty that in thy breast should rest.
But I am firmly anchored in the land of sorrow deep,
And like the flute a treasure that the air may safely keep.
No comrade mine, no chance found friend: I would not willing be
To tell my secret though my head should fall upon my knee.
I thought to tell my anguish deep to thee, O fickle flame,
But now no firmness stays in thee! Why, then, invoke thy name?
No satisfaction could I bring! Bethink thee how a sigh
That breathes the secret from my heart would make thee melt and die!
To one alone have I disclosed what in my heart abides
And that friend, Love, now left behind, that now no longer rides
Along the lonely road with me, but treads the mountain high
And ranges o'er the stony ways, all scorched beneath the sky.
I will not this discuss with thee, O, Candle, lest thou flee
Far, far away and disappear, for clearly do I see
Thou hast no tongue for language dear, sweet comfort to accord,
Nor yet a soul, whose holy words could solace sweet afford.

XXX

Herein is related how Leylā disclosed her Secret to the Moth and how she made Supplication to it.

    And now to the moth she plighted her troth,
    And told of her deep despair:
    'O, Bird of True Love, heaven sent from above,
    Perplex'd beyond earthly care,

'Tis thou alone who to one love ever true
Holds fast to the only way;
So perfect in passion art thou in thy fashion
That turns the dim night into day.

'Thou givest thy life for a moment of strife
That brings thee a glimpse of thy love:
The night and the day, two worlds wilt thou pay
O perfect exponent of love.
For a union kind in a passion refin'd
Whose dear consummation is death,
Yet, knowing thy fate, in thy true lover state
Never fearest its fiery breath.

Though in my belief I call thee the chief
Of the age on the highway of love,
'Tis hard to believe that we equally grieve
Yearning both for the soul that we love.
Thou flyest around, never touching the ground
Quite drunken with love, it is clear
What difference lies twixt thy love-forlorn sighs
And my closely fettered grief here.

The idlers say that with thee every day
Love dwells a most honoured guest,
While *Karin*[82] from me not a moment goes free
Separation is home in my breast.
Thou givest thy life after quick fiery strife
To a single all-conquering flame,
After swiftly born spark there cometh the dark,
From self immolation thy fame.

But could I secure many souls to endure
What I suffer in my soul alone,
Each soul every day should grieve every way
That I grieve in this soul of my own.
My own firm belief that no hidden grief
Still lurks in thy fast whirling flight
But if thou would'st claim hidden grief, then the same
As evidence bring into light.

I still see thy eye, never wet, ever dry;
Dear sorrow would cause thee to weep.
Thy blood never ranges nor temperature changes,
Thy passion seems ever asleep

Where now thy endurance and sad perseverance
In suffering torment and pain?
The love that thou claimest thou surely defamest
If love never drive thee insane!'

Now Leylā saw that succour from the moth
With all its insincerities of love
Was not within her fate, she slowly prayed
For help and succour to the Great Unknown,
And steadfast in her passion's angry hurt
When came the midnight hour and all around
Were gathered in the fountain of repose,
When midnight dews fell soft on meadow's eyes
And fed their thirsty lids, when all the light
Had fled before the dark approach of night,
And all creation fell to restfulness,
When all, both friend and stranger, sought the couch
Of deep oblivion, she only, she
The sufferer, all open-eyed remained
Unsleeping and dismayed.
                        And then she rose
This Moon of Beauty, pledged to sorrow's pain,
And 'scaped the house, and o'er the desert fled,
While wretched moans came forth from wretched breast,
And outcry raised on high, to where, serene,
That lesser moon that marches o'er the sky
Throughout the darkened hours, her bitter anguish heard,
And listened while the secret of her heart
In gushing torrent poured.

XXXI

Herein is related the Manner in which Leylā disputed with the Moon, and the Manner in which she burned like the Sun with the Fire of Longing.

Curved as the foot of a maid,
Bright ray of light for the eye,
Showing thyself unafraid,
Though lost, far away in the sky,
All hidden, as him I adore,
At times, with a shamelessness dear
Unveils the grief at my door
And shows my sorrow more near.

Changeability clear is a proof
That Love in thy heart is a sun
Whose absence, remaining aloof
Recks not of the ills it has done.
O, thou, knowing torment divine
Of Love, giving grief, giving pain,
Now see what a torture is mine,
With tears down-falling as rain.
Look thou on the flame of my sigh
And send me a remedy sweet
While searching the world from on high
Seek ever my lover to meet.
Roam far over every land,
Illuminate mountain and plain,
Take my King and my Hope by the hand
That yet I may see him again.

Tell all thou hast seen of me here,
Tell him how suffers my heart;
Explain to him all of my fear,
How I mourn him, now lonely, apart.
Tell him I sorrowed till morn
Chased the shadows away from the sky,
Beset with confusion forlorn
Till a nightingale roused him to try[83]
The first early note of his song
And joined my melodious chant
With lamenting and sorrowing long
That threatened my song to supplant.

'O the yeast that should leaven all life[84]
Is neglected and brought to an end;
Life's shadow is gone, though its strife
Reach'd the sun, it could not be a friend.
The Gateway of Fortune must close
For the task of expression is hard.
'Tis time to awake from repose
The strangers whose slumbers are marr'd.

Bright star in the heavens am I
Of longing and sorrow composed,
A poor, feeble candle, I try
Within a dead palace repos'd,

To light Separation's despair,
To turn the dread night into day.
The daytime a prison I share
With the cold clammy dead turn'd to clay,
At night comes deliverance grand—
Yet for lovers no light may abound.
The day and the night close at hand
Conspire to enchain me to ground.'

XXXII

Herein is related the Manner in which Leylā revealed her Love to the Zephyr, and how Hope came to dispel her Gloom.

The soft blowing zephyr now heard her complaint,
Spoken clearly with never restraint:
'O, sweet morning zephyr, I bid thee beware,
While strangers are yet unaware,
Stay but for a moment to breathe in the ear
Of my Padishah when thou art near,
The praise of the beggar he tired of before
He had tasted the fruits of her store.
Look closely and see whom he takes as a friend,
Now his first passion draws to its end.
Breathe softly the question: "Does Leylā still hold
The place that she cherished of old?
With whom does his heart sweet companionship find,
Now to Leylā he proves him unkind?
And tell him, O Zephyr, the King of all Kings,
No reproaches the sad Leylā sings.
Tell him never to grieve that an earlier mate
Is thrown off from the heart of the great.
When first seen I bloomed as the fresh, joyous Spring
With a sweetness that still I can sing.
A slave now to sorrow and grief, what avail
The Springtime that Autumn makes pale?
In the net of affliction a captive, I try
My sad, weary eyelids to dry,
But let him not feel any duty is owed
Where once was affection bestowed.
If time has brought changes, what use to bewail
Or lament now the leaves are all pale?
He still is the suitor of burgeoning Spring,

While Autumn's decay do I sing.
Yet still do I hope in my misery low
That remembrance sweet may yet grow
In the heart of my Prince, for he surely must know
My love for him ever will flow.'
And thus from the evening until the grey morn
Of a new day sadly was born,
The sweet jasmine breasted, forlorn as a star
Kept watch, sleep banished afar.
The passionate sighs of her weary lament
Endured till the night time was spent;
With the coming of day, like a melody veil'd,
On a sad single note she bewailed.
And through all the days and the desolate night
Sick at heart, sadly mourning her plight
She dreaded the night that followed the morn,
And day that of darkness was born.

XXXIII

Herein is related the Manner in which Leylā went to roam the Rose Garden in the Spring time and how she attained her Wish.

There came the day when world adorning Spring
On Winter's heels came bringing restfulness
And comfort to the world and people both.
The rust of winter in the greying skies
Was quite erased by the hand of time
And all about the world the lovely blue
Of winter's parting coloured every day.
The oft repeated charm of magic night
Infused a fragrance in the coming morn;
The richest violet of the night's dark vault
Set free the limpid pearls of silver dew
To fall as sweet caresses on the rose.
Now came the heady perfume of *abir*[85]
To vie with what the roses freely gave.
O'er all the desert, born on gentle breeze,
The dusty smell of musk was ever near.

The clouds now rained their tiny stones of hail
That broke the swelling buds and gave them birth,
And thus renewed the sponge of Nature's wound.

Now vegetation burgeoned, paying tribute
Of musk unto the rose, and paying tax
Of all its greenness with the joyful colours
Of turquoise, ruby and the rose itself,
All gathered up in manifold abundance
Adorned the day and scented all the air.
The bud now understood the sign, and winking
Its wrinkled face, burst forth in hundred hues
The mysteries of all a thousand roses:
The elements, fire, water, air and earth,
And all which in their virtues were united
Received the gift of time that all might see
How bounteous was Nature in her blessing
Upon the happy world.
                      The petals flying free
Through all the air of handsome, stately iris,
On many plants their passing shadows shed,
And where they fell, a lively, gushing brooklet
Of sweetest water flowed, whose magic spell
Had giv'n to steel itself a lively vigour
And made it leap as dagger's springing tongue.
And thus o'er hill and vale the lusty Spring
Such sweet embellishment so freely gave
As made the earth look like the very sky
Until the sun itself, the gleaming eye
Of all the universe, whose steady gaze
Has seen all secrets, yet was made to doubt
As down it sank to earth at close of day,
If truly to the earth it slow declined,
And not on heaven's glory rose anew.

Now everywhere the orgy high was held
While every garden held its lovely rose,
Each corner was a pleasance, every spot
A brimming beaker full of glory held.
Now Leylā's mother saw that, spite the spring
That banished Winter's pallor, Leylā yet
Was pale of cheek and wan with sickly hue,
And neither for the rose nor cypress green
Had show of inclination. Dull of eye
She saw a thousand buds burst forth in life,
Yet on her face no faintest petal bloomed.
And as the plants all scattered forth their flowers

A thousandfold, the mother freely spent
For every flower a coin from out her store
To match with glowing maid each glowing flower.
Away she sent her Idol from the house
Far o'er the fields to roam and catch the hue
Of freedom's laughter, knowing naught of grief
And care, while joying for a space
The merriment of grace and happiness.
Thus to the rose her own sweet Spring she gave
And watched her forth with many maidens chaste
With graceful swinging hips, high lifted head
Unveiled, yet modesty affronting not,
All thoughts of shame and bashfulness aside.
And each put all she knew to common stock
Of play or song or dance, the nightingale
In sweet contentment joined their chorus long
And knew full well his solo was surpassed.
Their skill in dancing, weaving patterns sweet
Made yet the moulded boxtree in his shame
And lack of grace, though graceful, hide his head.

But Leylā stayed apart, showed no desire
To join the happy game or weaving dance.
For her alone, the heady joys of spring
Had brought increase of sorrow and the ache
Of separation, longing still to see
The face that stayed the Idol of her soul.
Awhile she stayed, impatient to be gone,
And in a corner mourn, herself alone,
Nor ringed around with all the happy throng
Who, in their very presence, unaware,
Affliction piled on grief: her weary heart
A small deceitfulness began to weave
To trick them into leaving her at peace.

'My friends, more graceful than the cypress tree,
Why, like the cypress, steady in one place,
Are ye content to stay, when, all around,
Are joys unknown and beauties yet unseen?
At home, with opportunity behind,
'Tis sure we shall regret our narrow choice.
Come, lift your skirts, and fold them to your waists,
And scatter round, exploring all about,

And gather all the many coloured flowers
That bow so freshly here: and she who brings
The greatest number when our play be o'er
Shall be distinguished as the Queen of all.'

These words they heard, and then to every side
Ran off in glee as sparks fly all around
When fire is scattered, yet a kindled fire
Remained in Leylā's soul as, all alone,
She sorely grieved and scattered from her eyes
Sweet pearls of tears, as rain clouds scatter rain.

XXXIV

Herein is set forth the Manner in which Leylā pleaded with the Clouds and disclosed her Secret in the Chapter of her Love.

And now to the Cloud she began an address:
'Come, hear now the sorrows that on my heart press.
My confidant thou, heaving down from the sky
Thine own stormy sorrows to mix with my sigh.
Think not, because heaven is reach'd by thy head
That thou by the chief of all sorrows art led.
Spend not all thy thunder, thy lightning and rain
Nor talk not to me of the days of thy pain.
Releasing thy cry when the morning is born
With the flame of thy sighs from thy breast rudely torn;
Nay, rather, when tears of distress softly flow
In all thy humility come down below
Where I, with the ache of a sorrowful heart
Can furnish thee water to make thy tears start.
O, Cloud, hear my words: when thy water is short
No more with indignity let it be bought
Of the Ocean's jealously hoarded store,
But take the sad tears that my red eyelids pour.
Far more can I give thee than ever thy need,
The balance, unused, to the great ocean speed.
O Cloud, be loyal; my need of thee is sore.
Go, find my Idol! Help me I implore!
Find thou the rose face that I ne'er may see,
And sorrowfully give him this greeting from me.
With sorrowful weeping say Love is held dear
My greatly loved Idol no more to be near.

And say to him gently: 'O, sad heart's desire,
A sad heart awaits the dear warmth of thy fire.
Come, see the pale cheek and the blood reddened eyes,
How heavy on me the sad sorrow now lies!
No more may the soul all the sad burden bear;
The colour of life is no longer seen clear—
O soul of my soul, brightest light of my eye,
For granting compassion the time is now nigh.
I knew not that Love and Affliction were twain
Nor yet that in Love was embedded such pain.
On the highway of Love to be manly thy claim,
And naming thy partner, spoke only my name.
And now, quite deserted, all sick, full of woe,
My partner, affliction wherever I go.
All trouble, all care Leylā took in her joy,
Thy duty lay clear: not to make her thy toy.
With thy claim to be just, and thy boast, without fear,
Say, now, O Deserter, what justice is here?
If low as the dust that thy sandles o'erturn'd
'Tis for thee that I sink, tho' by thee I am spurned.

O, newly born Moon, what cost if thy rays
Fall here on the dust and lighten my days?
Or the rain of thy union, soft, limpid pearl,
Should water my bushes, its leaves to unfurl?
Yet be not bewildered by wine's muddy dregs
Forget not thy comrade, this loyal one begs.
Congenial thou in thy loyalty strong,
Like me thou art worthy, adoring so long.
Come, now, let not friendship fall into decline,
The shade of disloyalty never will shine.
They say a great lover of beauty thou art,
Is this, then, for lovers, the recognized part?
Each man should be perfect, fulfilling his task.
Can lovers be negligent? Well you may ask.
No rest may he have, every moment must roam
In the district of love, knowing never a home.
Thy path seems apart from this difficult way,
If, haply, thy love is another; then say.
If I had a freedom as great as is thine
For just but an instant, no sorrow were mine.
If it be Leylā, sweet comfort of mind
Should bide for a little. Be not so unkind,

If my neck were not chained by my close braided hair
Nor my anklet a fetter that bound me to care;
If only the world could pronounce my sad name
Without every second increasing my shame;
Why, then, Mighty God, my sole wish it would be
With thee, mighty love-light, not parted from thee,
While life may endure, every shadow to flee.
But yet, what availeth to pray, when my chains
Fast bind neck and foot. Yet my heart still complains
And I, to set forth all my grief and despair
Compose now a poem to breathe to the air.'

XXXV

Herein is set forth the Poem that Leylā composed in order to explain her Condition.

Since I became a captive in the filmy net of love
Full deeply have I sorrowed:
And since I learned the weary pain that comes of knowing love,
What deep affliction borrowed!

Ah! Speech has vanished from my tongue, no motion do I Know
In sad distress lamenting
A painted fresco am I to the treasure house below
That knows not of repenting.

No power is mine to tell in words the grief that eats my heart,
Yet silence holds no relish:
So sad am I that I and love are many leagues apart—
How absence holds dear anguish!

The spearhead of my vigilance has reach'd to such degree
My friends are all mid strangers;
A stranger I to Love am now—what sad extremity
With sweet enfolding dangers!

I cannot say again that now I love the lovely rose,
My hurt is past all healing;
For since the day I told thee that, O Flower, my sweet repose
Is gone: my pride is kneeling.

Gone heart and body, patience too, my senses all are fled,
One prayer is yet implicit;
That, God be thanked, with burden light, my journey may be sped
To seek the ocean's limit.

Fuzūlī! I am lost, unknowing what or where this place,
Quite unaware of being:
Bewildered by the image and the form of Beauty's face,
That I'm for ever seeing.

XXXVI

Herein is set forth the Manner of Leylā's Weeping in the Confinement of her Grief, and Mejnūn's Bewilderment in the Valley of Love.

Now as the Moon wept, grieving for the Sun,
A youthful voice fell soft upon her ear
And chanted Mejnūn's poem on the Breeze
And Leylā all its subtle meaning guessed.

'Think not that a lesser than Leylā is Mejnūn,
While whispering pleasures of Love:
Should any pretend that to Mejnūn an equal
In Leylā is found, heed it not.
And though great affliction is fallen on Leylā
Mejnūn grieves a hundredfold more:
The hand of dear Leylā is hurt by a needle;
While Mejnūn is pierced with a sword.
The soft touch of silk can mortify Leylā,
Mejnūn finds his pleasure in chains.
Mejnūn is the one who is captive to grieving—
For whom then is Leylā oppress'd?
The torture of fever sits fast upon Mejnūn—
For whom then is Leylā the leech?
Mejnūn is the captive 'neath Leylā's round tent roof—
To whom now does Leylā incline?'

As Leylā to this melody gave ear
She straight forgot to sing her dismal song,
And knew that all her upward flying sparks
Of passion, yet were cold, bereft of flame.

For clearly was it shown unhappy Mejnūn
Of sorrows, grief and sad affliction pale,
Had emptied all the storehouse Fate had treasured,
And left but scattered grains for Leylā's share.

XXXVII

Herein is related the Manner in which Leylā became Captive to Ibni Salam, and how, deprived of Love, she became chained to a Stranger.

And thus did the Maker of Speech
Erect him a mansion so clear,
And Leylā, unable to reach
Consolation, saddened by fear,
Her excursion brought to an end,
Homeward directed her way,
Alone and with never a friend
To comfort her sorrowful day.

Now richest adornment she wore:
Each trinket o secret concealed.
Blood red streamed her eyelids so sore.
But her blouse and her *shalvar*[86] revealed
But themselves, and covered her tears:
Mid the smoke of the sighs of her pain
A violent kerchief appears
In colour the smoke yet again.

The voices of meaning were hid
By the anklets' noisy lament;
To hide all the tears that unbid
Coursed her cheeks in a sad sacrament
A legion of pearls were displayed
That hid the distress on her cheek—
(She hoped that with all these arrayed
That none would her privacy seek)

All over her exquisite head
She scattered a thousand flowers,
Her skirts to her slim waist she led,
No longer they fell in soft showers.
Her candle never bereft

Of the moth, to the flame ever near,
And gathered what tears there were left
In a necklace of pearls without peer.
Thus the Moon in her sorrow arrayed
(O, God, be exalted and praised)
Walked in sorrow yet all undismayed
While prayers unto heaven she raised.

Now there was among the Arabs of that age, in good repute,
A youth of great nobility, no maiden yet could suit.
Intelligence was his to spare
And beauties languished everywhere
His manner was auspicious and his character sweet.
Considered by the nobles in the courts wherein the mighty meet
Of greatest estimation, God Himself was pleased to greet
His happy entry into life
An open road with never strife,
Ibni Salam named by Fortune and endowed with happy days.
Of eminent good fortune, calling forth all happy praise,
At heart a sweet tranquillity, enjoying happy plays,
All mounted on a jet black steed,
With falcon perch'd to fly at need,
The hunter's path had taken as he carolled happy lays.

And as he rode along the hunter's path
He met the Idol. Gave her but a glance—
One single glance, yet straight his heart and soul
Were burned to ash as quicksilver in fire.
At once he left the hunt, returning home,
All power melted by the maiden's eyes,
And then the customs, slowly built of old
By greybeards' cunning and experience long,
He cast aside, and sought with cunning skill
The master wizard of his people, then,
(Who when he spoke with words both soft and kind,
Could melt the heart of every hardened stone,
And make it change its nature, growing soft)
Sent forth the greybeard to demand the hand
Of Leylā, promising that all his store
Of wealth and riches at her feet to lay
If but this wish, the dearest of his heart
Were granted; holding not his life itself
From Leylā's service were she but his wife.

Now Leylā's parents, knowing what he gave
Full gladly closed his offer, thought their child
An offering to Venus well bestowed,
And knew the Sun well worthy of their Moon.

The news reached Ibni Salam, gave him joy
Its sea o'erflowed, his fortune mounted high.
He opened wide the storehouse of his wealth
And gems and money scattered all about
In happy joy at what was yet in store.

And thus he, cypress graceful, tall and straight,
The soul of freedom, gladly was enchained.

XXXVIII

Herein is set forth the Beginning of Nevfel's Intercourse with Mejnūn, and the Manner of his liking for Him.

O, Saki, yet again does grief intend
To wound the anguished soul, so fill my cup
Brimful, that wine all sorrows may assuage.
All friendless have I stayed, and weak of will.
What woe is mine without thy helping hand!
Be thou my refuge, thou my only hope
As friendless, in complete bewilderment,
I stand dismayed: give not in empty words
A promise that fulfilment ne'er may see.
More noble 'tis, with all endeavour keen
Thy promise to fulfil—But come, my tale must on!

In this confusion, dipping deep his sword
In blood, the champion great must now stand forth,
A man that tasted joy, well born of fame,
Whose blade had solved the turmoil of the field
Full many times and much of honour earned.
Nevfel his name, who much of love had seen,
And much of hatred, too, had borne the yoke
Of pain and pleasure both.
                        It chanced, one day
That in his hearing Mejnūn's verse was read
And brought much pleasure in its simple style

And fiery passion flowing into words.
He asked about the writer.
                    'Mighty Shah',
They gave him answer, 'Love has turned his mind,
Amazed he stays, bewildered by a Moon
Who smiles not on his state, and company
He keeps with beasts that roam the stony plain
And boasts his proud disgrace o'er all the land.'

Now Nevfel thought to look on Mejnūn's face,
And, taking friends, across the desert sped,
Till, in a corner, wretched and alone,
He found Mejnūn in sad dismay arrayed.
The beasts and birds flocked thickly all around
As, in a fortress, deep in gloom he sat.
But Nevfel, wielding straight his sword of fame
Dispelled the band that battened on distress.
As off they slunk, at healthy rage,
The loyal Nevfel reached his goal—Mejnūn—
And showing great nobility of soul,
With gentleness and kindness 'gan to speak.

'O, sad, afflicted man, what dreadful fate
Brings this affliction to thy gloomy head?
What treasures now are thrown to heedless waste
Amid the ruins of thy saddened state?
Bethink thee now what bird or savage beast
May know thy station, or thy rank respect?
Seek thou thine own to grant thee thy desire;
Mankind alone can understand thy fire.
If still of rapture and of ecstasy
Thou art a man, seek not among the wild
For consolation that it may not give,
But rather of the Bird of Paradise
Beseech Good-luck, or from the Dragon grim
Ask and receive thy treasure so desired.
Grieve not forlorn: this comfort clasp thee tight,
And know that as thy grief oppresses me,
Thy love again will come and give thee joy.
Should gold be needed to achieve the end
We wish, then quickly let us here unload
Of gold our richest store: or if it chance
Our blood be called, we'll seek the battlefield

And let the field be deeply drowned in blood.
While thou thy pillage seekest, let us join
Companions twain, each one to other bound.
Now I am thine, thy love again may shine
Within thine arms in ecstasy divine.

XXXIX

Herein is related the Manner in which Mejnūn entrusted the Troubles of his Heart to Nevfel and how he explained the whole of his Story.

'O thou, unique in solemn faithfulness,'
Said Mejnūn, 'know that cure for my distress
Full many friends, but all in vain, have striv'n;
And many sacred charms have counted o'er.
But every charm my cunning fiend withstood.
Upon the ground in alchemy was spread
More gold than would suffice a miser's greed,
Yet alchemy held no divinity
To cure me of my sorrow and distress.
What value to apply the *rastık*[87] black
To eyes that, lacking sight, are always blind?
'Tis kind to proffer thy compassion sweet,
But wherefore waste thy strength on luckless me?
For faith of self for self no more abides
My one desire, so difficult to grant.
Do all thou wilt, all endeavour sweet—
A grievous disappointment thy reward.
No friend my love. Who finds an enemy?
All friendless thou, as I without my love.
An evil Luck dogs every footstep still,
The blessings thou conferr'st are curses all.
Now hearken to this song my composing,
And thou shalt hear how Fortune still forsakes me.'

XL

Herein is set forth the Ode recited by Mejnūn to Nevfel.

If aught of loyalty or faithfulness
I asked, in expectation to receive,
I met unkindness and disloyalty

Unfriendly friends came quickly to deceive:
Where e'er I sought within this world disloyal,
All those I told my grief and wish'd a cure,
Owned greater grief than grief that I endure,
And suffered more disloyalty than I.
None could disperse the sorrows of my heart:
The joy of hypocrites brought no relief.
Whene'er I tightly clasped their flowing dress
They turned away and left me to my grief:
If still I thought the mirror would impart,
As mirrors should, a strict fidelity,
I saw, amazed, that just the contrary,
Of what hoped my sorrows would impress.

I boldly stepped within the door of Hope
And straight bewilderment did seize my hand:
I took a steady hold on skill's tight rope
And there before me did a dragon stand
A hundred times did Fortune show the star
Of all my gloomy fate, a hundred times
I looked at it, now near and now afar,
Each time I looked I saw that it was black.
Blame not, Fuzūlī, that I turn my back
From hundred cares and solace seek in rhymes.

XLI

Herein is set forth the Manner in which Nevfel gave Mejnūn Hopefulness, and how, with friendly Words he won his Pleasure.

'O, well instructed, perfect as thou art
In thy behaviour,' Nevfel said, 'think not
Too lightly of the help I bring, nor yet
Remain in ignorance of what I am.
Of power and zeal I have an equal share,
And that no miser's share, praise be to God.
Seek thou that Love may be thy chosen friend:
When Love is made a friend the end is sure.'

These words so timely gladdened Mejnūn's heart
He courage gained and doff'd his grim attire

And 'customed robes of sorrowful lament;
Shook all the angry dust from out his hair,
And dressed his torn and broken finger nails.
Then gave his body ornament of dress
And on his head a comely turban wound.
Nevfel stayed not his promise to augment,
And, with a mind to one sole purpose bent,
(And that to help Mejnūn, his new found friend)
He took the musky reed pen in his hand
And wrote a letter swift to Leylā's clan.

'Greetings,' he wrote, 'O, Tribe of high degree!
Treat not the friend who writes as stranger still,
But rather, with a deep concern, attend
And ponder well the cause in which I write.
Oblige a friend by giving Leylā now
As life's companion to Mejnūn, my friend,
For, just as she in Beauty's Garden grows
The choicest Tulip, know that Mejnūn now
The loveliest Rose, will make a fitting mate.
Though she, thy Leylā, like the Box Tree green
Surpasses all in beauty, know that he
Like pomegranate ripe upon the bough
Is fit companion to the box tree rare.
As she is meet for him, so he for her.
O, men of purpose, wherefore torment bring
A soul now burning with a fiery breath?
Be kindly then, and gold and treasure chests
And pearls unnumbered shall your portion count;
But know, besides, that, should ye cause delay
Or wantonly this good work set aside,
Then look to see the stinging thrust of spears,
And hear the angry din of clanging swords.'

This letter, reaching Leylā's clan, and read,
And all its meaning known, called forth reply:

'Know that for madness we possess no cure.
Know that for madmen we have no desire.
Pride not thyself on treasure chests and pearls.
Our pearl, for us enough, with us stays fast.
Boast not, with swelling words, thy mighty sword.
Know that we, too, have swords, and know their use.'

XLII

Herein is related the Manner in which Nevfel fought with Leylā's Clan, and how, winning Victory in this Fight, he determined to make Peace.

When Nevfel heard this answer, he abandoned youthful charms,
He put aside the wine cup, and gathered endless arms;
While cruel and savage swordsmen, each one athirst for blood,
With trumpets gaily sounding, and flags a waving flood,
Came flocking to the standard that Leylā's clansmen raised,
And, after days of idleness, the God of Battles praised.
No sense of shame withheld them, all gentleness was lost,
To tumult of the battle every kindliness was toss'd.
On both sides battle raged and fighting fierce began
As in the dawn the bloody sun its morning sky upran,
And banished all the planets and scattered far its rays,
And shattered all the darkness, and thinn'd the morning haze.
Like chessmen on a chequer board the two great armies stood,
Each one abreast the other, tried to make their standing good.
Each moment angry spears drank blood, while arrows ended life,
The spear and arrow symbols were, and reason for this strife.
The spear, so slim and stately, was the Idol's stature clear;
The arrow was the heart beguiling Love now drawing near.
The sword's long bitter tongue of bitter censure swiftly told
The end of all existence, leaving bodies growing cold.
The very eye of armour plate poured down a rain of blood
And weeping o'er the people, sorrowed deeply in a flood.
The heavy mace swung here and there, on all sides bringing death
To breastplate sheltered soldier and robbing him of breath.
Calamitous the battle grew, a rain of sorrows poured
From thunder and the lightning of arrow and the sword:
While mace and spear showed passage through the shield of armoured
    steel.
For sword and mace are weapons that may make the strongest reel.

Mejnūn as a spectator had drawn him to one side,
Standing fearless as a banner in an open field untried
By all the battle's clamour, all ashamed and deep dismay'd:
For his own side flew the banner: for the other side he prayed.
While Nevfel's troops around him for a victory cried clear,
Mejnūn could not withhold a prayer for Leylā's clansmen dear.
And thus arose the paradox, that, while his soldiers brave
Were helping him by killing foes, his foes he wished to save.

As every friend fell at his feet a thanksgiving he spoke,
For every enemy that fell his tears in torrent broke.
Should he be winnowed out from life a dagger would he wield
And strike his own brave fighters dead before he left the field.
One spoke to him:
              'Unfortunate, what riddle do I see?
Thou prayest for their victory; that we should turn and flee?
We tread our souls beneath our feet, we fight and die for thee,
Yet thou, a madman, seek'st to leave with them the victory.
What madness this? How lacking sense? How short of dignity
The mind that prays for friend to lose, that loves the enemy?'
Mejnūn replied:
           'A zealot, I, in Love's consuming flame,
And hopeful to attain the love of her I may not name.
And since the force opposed to us is fighting for my love
I may not hope our arms should win a victory from above.
Occasion soon I may have to find a union
With Love and Victory conjoined in sweet communion.
My life, my soul, is always her's acceptable or not,
Or killed or made a captive to her, each may be my lot
The battle now unfolding finds me steady in my place
To be, if yet she wills it, captive bound before her face.
So strange a circumstance affects me, makes me call a stranger friend
And a friend to name a stranger: strange results does madness send
Though mad, I know should Love draw forth a sword to take my life
For me alternative is none: I'd yield me without strife.
Yet think not that I have regret, or that—live in pain
To think that I may give my life, and giving, Love attain.'

The questioner heard answer Mejnūn gave to what was said,
And knew that in the madman's brain strange excellence was bred.
While the battle raged increasingly, around excitement grew
That Nevfel's army beaten was, now everybody knew.
From morn till eve the fighting raged, the stars began to shine
With night's oncoming, Nevfel thought: 'No victory is mine!'
As swift the Night's outriders took possession of the sky
The sky became a host of stars, and those who were to die
Had time to breathe a moment while, encamped full face to face,
The living yet uneasy slept in each uneasy place.

Now Nevfel opened all his heart and put a question clear
To all his comrades, bidding them to answer without fear.
'Interpret now, if yet ye may, this sad position found,

That I, the greatest of the day, am slowly losing ground.
The sky's great Sun of Battle, I; none owns a sharper sword,
None fights a keener battle with an interest unflawed.
Yet zealous strength and fighting skill but little now avails:
It seems that now, spite all attempts, the mighty Nevfel fails.
'Tis sure that God has willed it so: no other reason rests,
Unless the prayers of righteousness by heaven now are blessed.'

The soldiers said:
      'O mighty king, thou speak'st in ignorance
Of what thy friend Mejnūn has prayed in maddened arrogance.
For, while we fight on his behalf and lose our wretched lives,
He stands apart and prays to God for these our enemies.
We thought to win him his desire, he joins him with the foe—
Small comfort this that brings defeat, but this thou now must know.'

When Nevfel heard these words his bright enthusiasm fled.
He knew that Mejnūn was of God divinely favouréd.
Full well he knew that Mejnūn's prayer would reach to God on high;
That noble wishes, nobly asked, brought sweet felicity.
He knew besides that never yet had power of battle tried,
That force of arms had never yet brought love to lover's side.
Now fears began to throng his mind, he felt that omens bad
Presaged defeat when side by side the sane fought with the mad.
No more he felt that justice and the faith to friendship due,
And swore that if a victory came with the morning dew
He'd straitly chase from memory the name of Leylā dear,
And leaving all his wilfulness, go home with conscience clear.

XLIII

Herein is related the Manner in which Nevfel fought a second Battle, and how, despite his Victory, he failed to carry out his Promise.

When the Warrior, the Sun, his mighty battle sword unsheathed,
The Night, aghast, fled far afield, so deeply was it grieved.
The Turks, the Day's bright army, gained a mighty victory,
The Arabs, forces of the Night, were sunk in misery.
According to the custom now the two great armies fell
In line of battle steadily: none could the issue tell.
The champions took sword in hand while head from shoulder dropped,
And blood was shed as never more the soul in body stopped.
Sharp arrows opened windows in the body of the soul,

Which, lacking now a residence, flew off through every hole.
Intelligence now tasted of affliction in the head
And, losing now its mansion, swift to other houses fled.
Within the plated armour now the bitter spear was fast
As tight as buds on rose trees, ere a summer day has passed.
To come to a conclusion, put the matter in a line
On Nevfel in this second battle victory did shine.
The enemy now offered him submission, bending low,
And offered sweet humility, all standing in a row.
And Leylā's father came uncovered, weeping bitter tears
From bloody eyes, and thus to Nevfel set forth all his fears.
'O, King of Kings,' he murmured humbly, 'mighty King so just and wise,
If now, that pearl my Leylā, is the guerdon thou dost prize,
Then neither have I word nor daring to withstand thy proffered hand
Yet forget not ancient custom followed long in this our land.
Leylā's hand in solemn promise is bestowed upon a man
Full of worth and estimation, and a member of this clan.
Shame it were, O mighty Prince to bring confusion to the face
Of as lovely pearl as Leylā, if a second takes his place.
Promised is she, bond concluded, thus for ever is she tied—
'Twere deep disgrace the ancient custom rudely thus to set aside.
Throw not before the drifting winds the lovely petals of our rose:
Throw not our honour in the ditch that but dishonour knows.'
'O, Prince,' said Nevfel, 'choicest flower sprung forth from noble breed,
Affront to justice or to conscience stays not in my creed.
A loyal and a generous heart, to both I make my claim,
Munificence, a valued jewel, I treasure with my name.
No practice mine to deal in deeds of wrongful cruelty;
The scales of justice do I hold in perfect equity.
This last adventure brings me shame, I little thought to feel
The heartache of a cruelty affliction cannot heal.
No thought was in my mind that in this battle I acquire
For self unneeded riches—such was never my desire.
A medicine I sought for one whom Love has driven mad,
A true elixir, that no more he mourn a passion sad.
But now I see that out of strife no value may he claim,
As sick he was, so sick he is, and will remain the same.
And in repentance now I stand for error in my mind
And all thy cruel hardships, and hopeful yet to find
That God will grant forgiveness, for I seek not of thy wealth,
Nor any of thy household—may it rest secure in health!
So go, without a care to plough the furrows on thy brow
And know no evil reached thee. Thou hast my solemn vow.'

Thus spoke Nevfel, and straight prepared, before the close of day,
To journey from the battleground and homeward take his way.
Mejnūn now rained objections, and in accents torn by grief
Set fort in talk censorious the actions of the Chief.

'How futile are thy words, O Chief! How insincere thy vow!
And seeing thy behaviour how will men respect thee now?
What value have thy promises, what boots the silver coin
When vows so gravely spoken with fulfilment never join?
Thy Shadow, O Protector, from a great and mighty strength
The sunset of success achieved, makes weaker with its length.'

His friends did much to honour him, they sought with loving care
To find him his reward so he their happiness could share.
'Come, let us find a love,' they said, 'a yet more lovely pearl
Think not the task so difficult; we soon will find a girl.'
But consolation languished, Mejnūn no slightest heed
Would give this sweet encouragement. He knew his only need.
'Tis true that never yet did chain of sweet desire submit
To be enchained in second hopes, and thus defeat admit.
Again he rent his garments, grieving loudly as a child,
And sorrowing in loneliness, went off into the wild.

XLIV

Herein is related the Manner in which Mejnūn got himself chained, and how, on this Pretext, he went to Leylā's Side.

> Now as he travelled on the barren moor
> Accompanied by gathered herds of beasts,
> A sad greybeard slowly came in sight
> As sad companion to a slave enchained.
> Mejnūn observed the slave and straight his heart
> O'erflowed with pity and he gently asked
> The greybeard for an explanation clear.
>
> 'What crime or sin, O Father, may these chains
> And this forlorn expression expiate?'
>
> 'No sin,' replied the old man, laying bare
> His secret, 'for these fetters bind a friend
> And not an enemy.
>   'My years are full,

My heart is weary grown with endless work
For ever fettered to the daily needs
Of wife and children crying still for bread.
And yet, though poor, with poverty oppressed,
My comrade here is in a worser state.
Homeless and vagrant, wandering abroad,
He nothing owns, and only seeks for food.
See, now, we plan to earn our daily bread
With cunning trick and yet more cunning tale,
And thus the children may their stomachs fill
And eat the earnings of our quaint deceit.

'This man in chains to murder has confess'd
And thus remains a captive by my side.
Indemnity for blood guilt is my due—
Now understand the craft by which we live!
Abroad he goes, and begging far and wide
Seeks still to find untied his knotted chain:
And grain by grain we share whate'er we earn
One half for me, an equal share for him.'

Mejnūn replied:
              'O, Greybeard, see thy fault!
Thy chain should bind the crazy not the sane.
Come, let me wear these grievous, heavy chains,
And lawfully bind me while he goes free.
And, as thy shadow, ever at thy side,
Let me solicit alms from all who come.
Whate'er I gain from folk benificent,
Take all, nor waste a tender thought on me.
My purpose is, that I, in wretchedness
May roam like Jupiter, from home to home
And haply chance to see my Venus bright
Within the shadow of a sheltered house.'

The greybeard in his mind this offer weighed,
And gladly gave acceptance to the plan,
Set free the slave from all his massive chains
And fastened Mejnūn as a fugitive.
And Mejnūn tuned his voice to fit the chains,
Set forth the law for maddened frenzied fools,
And weeping, thus expressed himself in song.

XLV

Herein is set forth the Manner in which Mejnūn expressed his Grief in Chains, and declared the Chain of his Suffering.

'Thou Chain, the greatest Dragon of the Storehouse of all woe,
Thou art the Clue that followed through wilt show the way to go.
Thou hast a thousand gaping mouths; each mouth expresses pain,
Whene'er the slightest tremor comes, each mouth cries out again.
From head to foot thy body is composed of weeping holes
That bring to light thy secret: as the weary day unrolls
Thou waitest for a passing glimpse. Should Love pass ever near
O Chain, thou hast a thousand eyes through which to see her clear.'

This chanson ended, Mejnūn and the man
Who held him chained moved on, and soon the clan
Of Leylā's people gladdened Mejnūn's sight
And Mejnūn knew that Fortune held them tight.
With Mejnūn's halter in his aged hand
The aged man at each house took his stand.
And last, before the house where Leylā dwelled
Stood Mejnūn while his heart with passion welled.
And he, a fettered captive, all amazed
Before the wineshop sank, completely dazed.
No power was left to hold in check a sigh,
And Leylā, hearing it, knew Love was nigh,
And, sighing too, she tore aside the veil
And, for the poor, oppresséd one, a gale
Of tears streamed forth as she beheld him, weak
Invisible and sick, yet come to seek
His Love. No longer straight and tall he stood,
But, as an eyebrow, curved in servitude,
While from his eyes down fell in surging race
The bitter tears upon his fallen face.
His body, too, in sorrow with his soul,
In grief self-evident, no more was whole.
And now the Queen of every Sweetness found,
Revealed her face in story so renowned
Before them, while her troubled heart disclosed
Her secret in a song she now composed.

XLVI

Herein is set forth the Song composed by Leylā in which she set forth the Troubles of her Heart.

Love must had compassion on our weeping and our grieving
That he set his foot today in the cottage of our sorrow,
That this reward our falling tears are blessèd in achieving
This shoot that springs upon the rose today and not tomorrow.

Full well we know, for as the fire of passion'd sighing born
Becomes the smoky flame, the torch of Separation's Night,
If only we could claim that here a nightmare dream were born,
If but the weeping eye could sleep, not weep till day is bright!

This we behold must be a ghost, or else an Idol plain,
Unthinkable that Love should come so nigh without a fear.
Come, Heart and Soul! 'Tis true, and Love our guest will now remain,
Expend our treasures, riches all, the joyous day to mark.

The aim of Beauty and its purpose is to kill us, to destroy!
Fuzūlī! Come and help us to surrender dear of life,
Giving Life to sacred Beauty, turning Soul into a toy
That satisfied with toying, playing, lives for ever without strife.

XLVII

Herein is set forth the Manner in which Mejnūn met Leylā, and how he took Advantage of his Opportunity to make manifest his hidden Secret.

> The eye of Mejnūn, fallen on his Queen
> At once the secret of his heart laid bare.
> All sighing did he mourn his bitter lot
> And prayed, as suitor, justice from his Queen.
>
> 'O greatly prized and highly valued maid,
> Uncover where my guilt lies all concealed.
> In what remotest detail have I left
> Thy firman unfulfilled, what traffic base
> Have I concocted with thine enemies?
> This sad disfavour of wicked spite
> Of my detractors, bearing idle tales
> All false and fraudulent. Believer true
> Am I, and now upon thy threshold dear

I stand demanding who the instrument
And schemer of this malice and despite?
Far, far away, bemused, with broken heart
Far off I keep me from the very dust
That lies about thy porch; tormented still,
My only friend my sorrows: loneliness
The sole companion to my wretched life,
With never friend nor lover in the wild.
And even thou, my only heart's desire,
Thou grievest not me, nor wond'ring ask:
"Where, now, in lonely sorrow dwells my love?"
'Tis strange to find thee thus unmindful still.
Full sure thy anger is betokened here.'

It well may be that, innocent of guilt,
I yet remain a sinner: other cause
Or reason for this heavy misery
I cannot find, and yet, upon the ground
The chain about my neck, I bend my head,
Bismillah chanting, 'In the Name of God!'
And if excuse be none, acceptance find
And swift obedience to thy decree.
But be not vexed, my angel, nor despise
What here I bring. Stab thou with lashes sharp,
Or of the curléd lock a dagger make:
Stab if thou wilt, or hang me till I die,
Do as thou wilt, but let annoyance fade
From off thy lovely face, and gladden me
Nor leave me blushing in an angry shame.
Know, too, that if a reason should be sought
For all my blame, know that indifference
And thy unmindfulness brings speedy death.
O, thou, of tulip cheek and fragrant hair,
Thou treasure house of every beauty known
Or dreamed of, always am I tightly bound
By every curling lock that sweetly hangs
Upon thy lovely neck, and maddened thus,
I seek and cherish all my fetters dear,
And keep my foot for ever chained to grief.
Aloft, above all others do I soar
In madness of an all-consuming love,
And find that loss becomes my dearest gain.
Hear, now! My constant passion prompts a song!

XLVIII

Herein is set forth the Song chanted by Mejnūn at this Juncture.

See now how the Infidel weeps
To behold us thus disarrayed:
See, too, how the blasphemy creeps
From the lock of thy hair, lovely maid,
Till all our religion is torn,
And faithless we rest all forlorn.
How madly impossible now
To look on thy beautiful face:
When tears fill the eyes, tell me how
We may look the Beauty's sad face?
With weeping our eyes become blind,
They seek thee but never may find.

Give not all thy torture today,
Hoard some of it yet in thy store:
Thy sweet prodigality stay
Lest thy granary closes its door.
With covetous hand still supply
Dear torment and sweet cruelty.

So close to us sorrow abides
Close held with never respite,
That he who near us resides
And joyously lives with delight
Encount'ring all our despair
Departs from us heavy with care.

Each link in our wearisome chain
Has a tongue to cry our despair,
And tell without ending our pain
To the softly compassionate air.
Its accents so harshly reveal
That pain that all lovers must feel.

The grief of laborious days
Fuzūlī, is cruel on us now;
In feebleness voices are raised
With complaint to the King, yet allow
This tale of our sorrows, nor seek
To dry the sad tear laden cheek.

XLIX

Herein is set forth the Action of Mejnūn at the Completion of his Song.

>   For brief a moment Mejnūn sadly cried
>   His sorrow in brief words before the King,
>   Then snapping into fragments all his chain
>   Went forth again to lonely solitude.
>   His broken figure and his tearful eye
>   Disgraced and mad with passion's ecstasy
>   Yet fearless in the valour of his love
>   Drew as a spectacle the children near
>   And those far off, to follow in his steps
>   And while some laughed to see him woebegone
>   Some others, wiser, mourned his saddened state.

L

Herein is related the Manner in which Mejnūn, feigning Blindness, saw the Beauty of his Love, and how he caused the Eye of his Hope to attain the desired Collyrium, the Doctor who opens the Blind Eye.

>   Again, another day, a pretext found
>   This pretext maker, binding tight his eyes,
>   And saying: 'I am blind to all the world,
>   Unconscious how it moves or what it is.'
>   A dismal exhibition thus he made
>   Of weakness sad and hopeless poverty,
>   And as a vagrant passed from door to door
>   Beseeching alms of rest and nourishment.
>   And thus the vagabond to Leylā's house,
>   (The house wherein his Love was all enshrined),
>   Stood fast and raised aloud his piteous voice
>   So she, within the fortress of her room
>   Heard and came forth, well knowing whose the voice
>   That supplication made. As forth she came,
>   Bestowing double alms of Charity
>   And *Zekat*,[88] sweet forgiveness for all sins,
>   There, neath the bandage, Mejnūn's secret eye
>   Beheld the sun and opened all his heart.

'O, thou, whose blackened mole and darkened eye
Fulfils the longing of my heart and soul,
If eyes are blinded they have well deserved
The penalty, for on the vasty seas
Of great calamity, the greatest threat
Are they to every fond security.
Should they for ever keep their vision clear
Their salty torrents would engulf the world.
That eye which gazes on thy face unveiled
Disgraces thee to self and all around.
This knowledge have I gained, that 'tis the eye
That is thy foe, and now the eye is dead,
Self-sacrificed, self-slaughtered at the shrine.
Approve the offering that now I bring,
Entwined and bound and carried in my head,
To lay in solemn homage at thy feet.

'O, thou, whose glinting eye is honey sweet,
Whose tongue darts forth, a keenly burnished sword,
Pronounce a verdict: Guilt or Innocence?

'When first I stood within thy mighty courts
O, Huri, the dear light of eyes was all
I held as capital, since then the art
Of trafficking with grief I strangely learned.
'Twas grief that taught me how to commerce clear,
And, God be thanked, no loss has come my way
In this new trade. My stock was scant and small,
Yet have I sold it for a mighty price.
That I might see thee, lovely, yet again
The light of these my eyes, before thy feet
I now lay down before thee in the dust.

'O, Mighty King, regard this beggar here.
Make no display of strangeness with thy friend,
For, in the blooming of the Soul
The sweet and tender sapling of my grief
Was planted by thy hands, and thou the seed
Of sad affliction, thou alone did'st plant
In this my frame: now both are fully grown
All watered by my downward falling tears,
And warmèd by the hunger of my heart.
Come, therefore, visit now thy garden fair,
And see the riches thou hast made it yield.'

Thus spoke Mejnūn, and then, bewildered still,
Departed for the desert and the hill.

LI

Herein is set forth the Desire of Ibni Salam for Leylā, and the Manner in which the Dawn of his Hope proved to be but a False Dawn.

Now, Saki, give tranquillity of soul,
Be gracious, animate the lifeless core.
Give wine in plenty, pass the brimming cup
That all may taste of joy: let sorrow come
When joy and constancy are sped. Then ask
Why sad sweet sorrows follow hard on joy
This sorry business of this sickened world
No value holds; the wheel, unstable, turns
While Fortune offers now a treasure house
Of pain and suff'ring piled mountain high
To one so bless'd, and then unfairly deals
A pack of troubles to his neighbour near.
See, now, O, Saki, how the sapling wild
First born of water, now to fire gives birth!
'Tis Destiny that orders every day
And if her blind ordaining chance to fit
The suitor's needs then happiness may come.

Short time elapsed ere Ibnı Salam learned
The prize was unfulfilled for which he yearned.
He sent abroad his messengers to find
The greatest of his land in name and kind,
And wealth unbounded for the *Nikâh*[89] sent
And all, nay, more than all he promised, spent.
Iran and Egypt, *Hicaz*, famed of old,
Sent forth a thousand horses shod in gold:
A thousand handsome youths and lovely lads
Embellished all in silk and fine brocades:
A thousand camel cows with rosy skin
And softest fur that all might revel in,
A thousand loads of candied sweetmeats bore,
While from the treasure came forth a store
Of ambergris, and musk a thousand trays
And sparkling jewels that blinded every gaze.
With unalloyéd gold and abir sweet

The contract of the marriage to greet,
And thus each requisite was gladly sent
The dower fixed: each party was content.

Few moments passed ere Leylā heard the tale
And o'er her blooming Spring fell Autumn pale.
Her eyes were filled with dust of heavy grief,
The sapling of her wish shed every leaf.
A backward turn took all that she desired;
She felt her fortune by Misfortune hired;
That she, desirous of the blushing rose
Was given but a thorn: desiring those
Bright beams of Love's dear light, was burned with fire
That of the light was born. Her keen desire
Turned all her wedding feast to mourning drear,
And mourning spread to wedding quarters near.
For, when the women came to dress her hair
And thus with bright adornment swell her share
Of beauty rare, the child her maid did shock,
And smudged the mole and ravelled up the lock.
From off her crescent eyebrow *rastık* fled,
The *surme* from her eyes in tears was shed.
The comb forbidden now her hair to deck;
Her very gems lay heavy on her neck.
The mirror wept, confronted with her sigh;
No inky line would crescent eyebrow try.
The henna found no hand to kiss her foot,
Her walking made the dismal, drumming *ut*
Vibrate in accents low, while flushing face
Burned off the milky lotion from its place.
The sweetest perfume seemed a vulgar smell,
She feared no thorn from out of slander's well.
She, like the rose tree, tore her clothes apart,
And sighed and moaned with sadly breaking heart.

'O, Fortune, now observe my sad estate,
Was this the boon I asked of thee but late?
My faith was placed on thy revolving wheel,
I hoped that thou would'st all my sorrows heal.
Make no mistake, the love for which I prayed
Is not the love for which I am arrayed.
Think'st thou 'twas this I asked with anxious care?
That this I prayed for with a heart laid bare?
The one I love on Loyalty's page is graved,

While here are pages of extinction craved.
The one I love is drowned beneath the sea
Of all the soul's sad pleasure, while to me
Thou bring'st the acme of a leisured ease
And thinkest thus my aching heart to please.
The one I love owns but a single claim
To life: that I may wear his name.
While he thou bringest has but one desire—
That I should feed his passion's hungry fire.
The one I love stands forth a signpost clear
The one thou bringest starts the road of fear.
The one I love is mine: as he to me
In single fervour cleaves, so Fortune, see
How I cleave unto him. From Time's first day
This bond existed. Here me as I pray:
Keep this dear servitude from every harm
For haply it existed ere thy charm
Was born. So, Fortune, throw aside reproach,
Give up this mastery that would encroach
On human lives, seek God and gracious be,
And to the strong give not the property
Of being weak, nor give as lawful friend
A woman who loves elsewhere till her end.
Think not that Mejnūn brave is lacking state,
Or that, now maddened, he were sorry mate
For any maid. Who treads disaster's road
As he, in loneliness, has courage showed.
For Ibni Salam, poor unhappy wight,
Knows little yet of cheating Fortune's spite:
From Leylā Mejnūn takes an added fame—
For him contentment stays but in her name.
Yet should it be thou wishest joy of heart,
Know that I with deep affliction smart,
And am the fabled whale in legend told,
And thou the treasure chest of sorrows old.
Much more thy love than mine that rescues me
From parents grim and leaves me but with thee.
For I, offending, ask a pardon clear
For greater wrong and greater passion dear.
So, Fortune, save me now from Father near,
And Mother whom I now begin to fear,
And thus, with one sad grief, the record close,
Lest two calamities the record shows.'

Thus murmured Leylā, sighing as she wept,
And hating all who round about her crept
With bright adornment, moaning loud and long,
Till finally she burst forth into song.

LII

Herein is set forth the Song sung by Leylā on the Occasion of her Marriage with Ibni Salam.

The wheel, O fickle Fortune, is spun in a way
That opposes my every desire;
I ask for the rose, but thy heartless display
Gives no rose but the thorn's burning fire.

Though years to my score I may count but a few,
Not once hast thou met my desire;
But turning and turning, revolving anew,
Thou still bringest unslakéd fire.

No reason I know to humiliate so
A maiden whom many desire:
Time was when all loved me as well thou dost know
Till thy dust came to smother my fire.

My hope was to find ere I passed all my prime,
The soul of my heart's one desire;
But now do I find thou hast used all thy time
To build tortures to set me on fire.

Thy blasphemous hands have in sacrilege torn
The curtain that hid my desire;
The sorrows I hid in my breast all forlorn
Thou hast published and thus fed my fire.

No chance didst thou bring that alone I might live
Still true to my constant desire;
Thou hast brought me to shame as I true promise give
To Loyalty's ravening fire.

To thou, O Fuzūlī, thou wisest of men
The Future itself is revealed;
Thy treasures unprized, have merit but when
The Future is safely concealed.

LIII

Herein follows the Epilogue to Leylā's Song and the Conclusion of this Section of the History of Leylā and Mejnūn.

All those who looked saw great uneasiness
Upon the maiden's brow; they next observed
That all adornment, lustre, beauty's aid
Was quite neglected, put aside in pain,
And, thinking o'er the problem, found the cause,
And that a crueller, sadder grief she had.
The sun, they thought must surely make lament
When separated from a mother dear:
To leave a father desolate, alone,
Must trouble still the gently nurtured mind.

'How right thou art, O jasmine breasted maid,'
They spoke in approbation, 'thus to grieve
At breaking here the lifelong habit formed
Of close companionship with parents dear.
Thou see'st now, when separation comes,
The cruelty that absence always brings.
Let still thy sorrowing be unrestrained
Yet never think that but to thee alone
Comes this unbounded grief. This scorching heat
Of separation's fire has burned before.
Remember, too, the custom of thy folk,
Nor thus exaggerate a proper pain.
Within her father's house no girl may stay
Unnumbered years, nor on her mother spend
The total of her love, yet mindful be
And in thy passing to another sphere
Be not neglectful of thy parents dear.'

These words they spoke, and Leylā, hearing them,
Agreed their justice, but she spoke no word
Of other sorrow, for she saw no cause
Why idle tongues should slander her repute.
For ill befitting one of princely blood
To make avowal of a tender love,
And, thus avowing, shame her modesty.
And thus the Moon, assaulted by the spears
Of ignorant acclaim that tore her heart

Submitted, yet unwilling, to be dressed
For well she knew a thousand shouting tongues
Would rob her of volition. Thus adorned
With sweet embellishment and cunning art
Her face shone forth with such a beauty rare
That Fortune, looking on her handiwork
Cried mercy for a perfect patience found
In Mejnūn's soul, for unadorned the moon
Was but a blight, but now the nimble zeal
Of busy fingers made her beauty shine
That through her veil her glory glittered bright.
And thus, when Night, with stealthy steps and slow
Drove off to darkness all the light of Day,
When all the stars their countless candles lit
And Night's grim darkness in its turn was shed,
Sweet, rose faced charmers gathered all round
Each charmer took a candle in her hand
And joyously in gay procession passed
Five hundred rosy cheeks and ruby lips.
A hundred moons with tiny rosebud lips
The sweet rose water sprinkled on the road
A hundred maids, all rosy cheeked and fresh
Each swung the censor of sweet aloes, thus
With sweetest amber scenting all the way.
Another hundred beauties, singing sweet
With sweetly tunéd instruments conjoined,
Enchanted all who heard. The wine cup passed
And repassed, offered by the tender hands
Of full a hundred maids whose smoky eyes
Languished and fell as still they served the wine.
Nearby, in charge of near a hundred youths,
All rosy cheeked, a hundred trays of gold
Lay waiting to be scattered all abroad
In joyous celebration.
                    Mid the pomp
Sat Leylā in a litter, all alone.
Her eye took in that splendour of the scene,
But saw it dully; apathetic still
She sighed in sorrow, moaned in bitter grief.
Perplexed she went, as straws go with the stream.
Unknowing and uncaring, without joy,
Yet moving still as in a dazed dream,
Till, last, the harem of the palace reach'd

And each companion, every friend, withdrew,
And left her in a private room alone.
And there the rose become a garden sweet
Where thorn and straw were banished out of sight.
When Ibni Salam that Fortune kind
To his fond care had brought the gracious Moon,
That seeker after jewels fine and rare,
Desiring still the greatest gem of all,
With rapid steps made entry in the mine.
And thus, before his almost blinded eyes
He saw a light shine forth behind a veil.
All hidden was her face, but strong desire
Burned fiercely in him and his heart was stirred
By hope of speedy union, as his hand
He raised to lift the still protecting screen
That stayed between himself and his desire.

'O, thou,' said Leylā softly, 'Chief of Tribes,
And now, by chance, the master of my life,
Much talk has passed of all thy attributes,
Of thy intelligence and modesty,
Result of happy breeding. Hear my words,
And merit now the justice that the world
From end to end acclaims thy brightest star.

'Think not that I am rich, for I am poor.
Think not I am thy guest; I am thy slave.
Let not thy slave here suffer cruelty:
Show mercy to this suppliant. See now,
The manner of my suffering in soul
And weakened body, too; and ask my heart
The reason for its sorrowing, and hear
The reason that it gives:
     'Long ages past,
In those dim, far off days when forth to school
I daily went to con my lessons o'er,
It chanced that in my sight a fairy stayed,
A youth of merit, full before my eyes;
And quick, this fairy offspring, djinnie born,
Established firm acquaintanceship with me.
And at my side each moment there he stood
Beseeching me to stay, ere yet I make
A spouse of any human being born

In all the world, and swearing, if I should,
His magic sword with but a single blow,
Would slay us both. My parents magic used,
And sought with every remedy to lift
This chain from off my neck, but naught availed.
My father and my mother vainly tried
To banish this sad evil, then, distressed,
Nor finding any remedy prevail,
My magic love was learned of all the world.
And thus my friends, my sweet companions dear
Turned from me, hating with a sorrowed heart
This maid so ill-bewitched.
                      'This tale is told
And thou, an honoured stranger to our land,
Must sure have heard it said, and though the pearl
O'erprized of all that in the market place
Are offered forth for sale, is now thine own,
By strongest right of purchase, yet, beware,
For here, before me, hand upon his sword,
Stands yet this jealous djinn. Refrain awhile
Nor force not now this union dangerous
To my frail body and to thy dear soul.
Forbear awhile, and put thy trust in God,
That haply, though delayed, a cure may yet
Be found, and thus the door now closed,
May be wide open, while the evil tongues
Of those our enemies censorious
May be for ever silenced, bringing joy
Of satisfied desire to thee and me.'

This story Ibni Salam, simple soul
Believed, and took the tale of djinns as true.
He hoped that union with his love would come
With steady patience: less of life and rank
He thought to have, while yet his rank and life
An obstacle became to bar the road
O'er which this simpleton desired to pass.

There is a custom, old throughout the world,
That he who wishes gain must first have loss:
Who wants his love must first endure the pain
Of torment, just as he who wants the hoard
Of gathered treasure must the dragon face.

When first the lover manifests his love
He early learns the trials he must endure;
And when she sees endurance standing firm,
She quickly ends his torture with her charm,
Restores his fractured head with sweet caress.
But if of sweet endurance he should lack
No shadow of her union on him falls.
This danger now lay clear before the feet
Of Ibni Salam, turning this his day
Of joyous union, to a low despair
With separation crowned; yet not a look
He showed her of reproach, nor ventured near
The Idol of his soul, but nobly stood
And asked a healing for her discontent,
And swore to find the remedy desired.
And from that moment, when he saw the men
Who dealt in magic and enchantment dread,
He begged a chain to turn his grief to joy.

LIV

Herein is set forth the Manner in which the loyal Zayd communicated to Mejnūn the Tidings of Leylā's Union with Ibni Salam.

The Maker of words, who tells this tale
Now ordered his words, each one as a flail.

Companion to Mejnūn was Zayd, a man
For loyalty famous. His beauty outran
The charm of perfection, and captive was he
To a maiden named Zeyneb; so comely was she
Adorned like an Idol, and worshipped by Zayd
Who had suffered the pangs of a heart sorely tried.
The torments of love ever gnawed at his breast
For tongues of the gossips may never have rest.
Mejnūn was his friend, for lovers incline
To find comfort in others who lovelorn repine.

And thus to the love sickened Mejnūn he came
With pale, saddened cheek and with heart all aflame.
His eyes overflowed, his speech all confus'd,

The tale that he brought all his senses bemused—
His heart was aggrieved at the message he brought
That Leylā was married and Mejnūn was naught.
Mejnūn saw his pallor and said:
                              'O, my friend,
Companion with me on a road without end,
Thy speech is unusual, thy manner is strange,
Thy air of sweet gaiety suffers a change—
Come, lighten thy heart, of the misery speak,
Say why thou art restless, say why thou art weak.
'Tis sure that the moon still in Scorprion stays
To lead thee to me in my unhappy days,
Come, open thy lips, tell me all of thy grief.
Perchance that between us we find some relief.'

Zayd with a sigh burning hot from his lips
Struck fire with his breath, as he said:
                              'O, eclipse
Is now thy sad fortune, thy star is now dark,
And Time as it turned, has deceived thee, for mark:
The Idol of Idols, the maid of the heart
The loved and adored one, is now set apart,
And she whom in hope thou hadst hopéd to wed
To false Ibni Salam is now daily bread.
Thy love is a candle within a strange tent,
For thee 'tis a fire whence the flames are all spent.
Sweet love to a stranger is Leylā, and lost
All thy grief and thy sighs on the light breezes toss'd.
No more through the day and the wearisome night
Spend time in affliction, for dead is thy light.'

Mejnūn heard the news and the flame of his sighs
Ascended to heaven and neath the wild skies
O'er arching the desert, he moaned and he wept
Till the small tiny ants and the snakes as they crept
On the ground close beside him, the beast and the bird
To weep on by one his sorrow they heard.
As an overcharged pen Mejnūn shed his black tears
As a letter, twice folded, he bent, never near
To his full stature standing, then quickly he penned
A letter reproachful to Leylā to send.

LV

Herein is set forth the Letter of Reproof sent by Mejnūn to Leylā and his Message of Complaint.

In God's Great Name, the Ancient of the Days,
The ever-new and ever-present God
Who draws aside the veil of secrets hid,
Who makes the Universe leap all contained
From Nothingness, Who sets the Day's Bright Glass
Each Day bright burnished, giving odours sweet
And pregnant with the days gone by:

When Mejnūn thus had sown the seeds of praise
He gave to Sorrow deep Affliction's tongue.
This letter from the Bearer of all Grief,
From him whose heart endured an evil foul,
Who now was left bewildered and amazed
With sorrow, as he sent this reprimand
To her in beauty rich but poor in faith,
Whose loyalty was sadly now forsworn,
Whose cruelty was sadly manifest.

'What aileth thee, that thou hast broke thy vows?
That thou dost break thy promises sincere?
O, Love, who knows no loyalty to vows,
Who, to a stranger, shows a lovely rose,
To me but angry thorn? Wert thou so weak
In loneliness as thus to falsely seek
A stranger to give solace to thy bed?
How dark has grown thy house that thou should'st light
Thy candle for a stranger, burning bright?
Did sad affliction grieve thy weary heart
That thou shoulds't seek a stranger doctor thus?

What fading showed the cypress of thy heart
That thus thou seek'st to water it to life?
What evil wisher to the Garden fair
Of roses sweet brought danger, that thy path
To safety, and the road to heal thy hurt
What fetter of a husband thou should'st wear
As passion strangling necklace round thy throat?
From what dread fear didst thou protect thy jewel?

What cause for this forgetting is advanced:
For this thy action, that another love
Is welcome to thee, while abandoned, I
In every moment swear a testament
Of my condition in my bloody tears
That fall upon the dust before thy door?
Did it so chance my tears were all delayed,
Or failed to halt before thy closéd door?
Or, halting, were their gaping mouths all dumb,
Reluctant still to speak of me to thee?
What is this act disloyal, lacking faith?
What is this nearness to a stranger born?
A new found love is stationed at thy side—
Is then the old love sent to banishment?
'Tis true I gave thee grief and trouble both—
But art thou happy in thy new estate?
Thy promised loyalty had all my trust.
'Tis clear I was deceived, yet did I think
That faith implicit lay in every word
That thy dear lips did make. In ignorance
In happy ignorance I blindly strayed,
Not knowing this defect of purpose firm,
Nor that the Moon so pure could grow defect.
O, Love, that thou, whose speech should be with me
Should'st to thy heart entwine another soul!
That thou should'st be my outward seeming love
And inwardly another to thy soul
Entwine with passion! Or that I, for thee,
Should'st be a byword through the mighty world!
While one of nothing born, of nothing worth,
Should'st steal the only hope that gave me life!
And yet, O Love, no blame should be expressed.
'Tis but by turning, Fortune's Wheel is known.
While yet the rose remains within the bud
A close associate makes with angry thorn,
But, op'ning, all caresséd by the sun,
It finds at hand another, gentler love.
To grow the rose the planter gives his care,
His sweaty labour and his anxious thought,
But when the plant its promise has fulfilled,
And burst into a thousand heady blooms,
The chemist, not the planter, takes the prize,
And from the rose its water sweet distils.

O, thou, desire of my sore wounded heart,
My Idol, grieving much and loving less,
O, thou, whose name was one with loyalty,
The soul within the frame, my light of eye,
Elixir of my brain's great passion black,
The prize still sought within the fool's bazaar,
The very eyebrow of my beauty's sun,
So sweet, so lovely, gentle as thou art—
Know now that I, a sharpened, tempered thorn,
Earth born and back to blackest earth designed,
Wear now a gloomy face, black as the grave,
And use a tongue enslaved to violence.
But should it chance thy heart, oppressed with shame,
Should wonder how I stand, opposed to thee,
Thou knowest well that I have justly told
Of my unworthiness for thee, and how
I held the prize too great for wretched me.
Now I, myself, with but an image left,
Can find contentment sweet in its regard.
'Tis not in reason thou should'st thus forswear
One worthy thee, and filling thy desire.
But ne'er forget that many tongues around,
Besides the tongues of Leylā and Mejnūn,
Talk now of little else but thee and me,
And when they see my constant loyalty,
And know 'tis thou that givest torture thus,
Who, thinkest thou, will then be named disloyal?
Whose deed will then be thought to merit blame?
Think'st thou that good may come of earning ill?
Or finding never charitable word
To bracket with thy name?
      Though contrary
To 'stablish'd custom, throwing off thy love
And binding round thy neck another's chain,
Thy love now giving him: though this is done,
Full many hearts, like mine, in passion burn
And my dread name of Mejnūn shall befall
On each and every one thou smilest on.
And thus I speak: henceforth let every word
Twixt thee and me be ended, and revenge
On thee in yet another love I'll seek—
Brave words indeed! For is another thee
Within the world's wide limits easy found?

Great God on high, amazéd was my soul
When news of this thy marriage came to me!
O, thou sweet fountain, giving water sweet
That nurtures life itself, within my soul
Hidden and cherished, never out of sight,
What magic tied thee to another man?
If Leylā's light for Ibni Salam now
Appears to shine, 'tis but a phantom light,
For but the ghost of Leylā he enjoys.
He lives alone with Leylā's image clear.
He may not say that his companion
Is Leylā dear: her ghost remains with him.
For how can Leylā and the mad Mejnūn
Be parted? How can Leylā find a friend
Apart from Mejnūn? O, Leylā, brightest jewel
Of brightest crown of all, be happy still,
And joyously thy purpose yet achieve.
Collect around thee all thy happy friends;
Dance and rejoice: securely build thy joy.
I suffered pain of waiting with delight
And constant hope that thy remembrance dear
Would fall in sweetness on thy wounded slave.
No word of thine accorded me thy slave,
Yet in this path I have a passage made,
And if thou foundest that my dignity
Was worthy of respect, of wealth or joy,
'Twas only just and courteous to send
Some tidings of thy contemplated act,
That knowledge should to consummation lead.
Now, God be thanked, no pauper slave am I,
And life and money I may spend at will:
Yet, hadst thou thought that I, afflicted sore
Was powerless and crushed beneath the load
Of my distresses, yet apology
For thy desertion was at least my due.
But not a single word, fast penned in haste,
Arrived to gladden me. O, Moon,
O, Rose of all delights, veer not in this sad way!
Think'st thou in this neglect to merit praise?
Within my soul the enemy thou art
Of this my soul, and I, prostrated, lie
Before thee, crying out grief. O, Moon,
Beseeching that the slender statured soul

Who loves and worships thee be not forgot,
Take thou a lover if thou wilt, but yet,
In all thy moments of glad merriment,
Think ye that we, in close embrace entwined
Remain.
  This letter ends with sad quatrains:
Inscribe these lines on costly silk and thus
In reading and inscribing, think of me.'

LVI

Herein are set forth the Quatrains that Mejnūn sent to Leylā.

What is this, thy roaming in the Rose Garden with strangers?
Is it generous to ruin thus the structure of thy promise,
Giving privacy convivial, and granting hundred favours?—
But what of the vow that thou madest with us?

Thou hast listened so intently to claimants so importunate,
And drunk until repletion of the cup that others held;
Thy love was thrown to others, and forgot for this unfortunate—
But what of the vow that thou madest with us?

Thy love, bestowed on others, while warming them has frozen me;
Thy path, that lay in sunlight, thou hast left for darkness black:
Thy life is treaties, promises and vows to others constantly—
But what of the vow that thou madest with us?

What sin or crime lay at our door, that thou, disgusted turned away
We suffered dismal grief while thou in sympathy inclined:
Can this, thy customed friendship, turn the day to night and night to day—
But what of the vow that thou madest with us?

Like Fortune's giddy wheel, thou makest custom of a love unfair,
And, changing, like the wheel, thy name, once honoured, sinks in shame:
To others, oft repeated love thou hast: to me alone the hydra care—
But what of the vow that thou madest with us?

Let not my heart be more dishevelled with the hair lock curling sweet;
Nor my heart bleed on for ever with the passion of thy lip;
No more let tears of sorrow flow a promise-breaker's name to greet—
But what of the vow that thou madest with us?

With hope of sad, sweet union, thou tookst our patience, peace of mind,
But day succeeded day, with every hope left unfulfilled:
My days are passed in greater grief than e'er Fuzūlī brought to mind—
But what of the vow that thou madest with us?

LVII

Herein is set forth the Completion of Words, which recounts the Manner of Zayd's taking of the Letter to Leylā.

> The pen now laid aside, its labour o'er,
> The loyal Zayd took the letter up
> And swiftly, as a pigeon in its flight,
> Sped off in haste to Leylā's country dear.
> Arriving there, he sought by cunning ruse,
> To meet her face to face, by boastful talk
> Of magic, charms and ancient alchemy,
> And slowly Ibni Salam's side attained.
> He heard, with downcast mien the saddened state
> That clung to Leylā's Kismet, of her grief
> And sadly grievéd life. At last he spoke:
>
> 'O, Ibni Salam, Prince of noble blood,
> I here have written words of magic worth,
> A prayer more potent than the doctors' drafts,
> That, as I live, will cure the maid forlorn.'
> Now Ibni Salam heard, and straight believed,
> And close embracing Zayd, entered in
> The chamber of Despair's lone privacy.
> Thus luck helped skill, and Zayd's skill his luck,
> And Leylā's presence saw his journey's end.
> Some moments sat he silent, then erect
> And firmly planted on his loyal feet,
> Stretched forth a hand and held the letter out,
> And paying honour, murmured yet a prayer,
> Bestowed on it a kiss of love, then gave
> The word of Mejnūn into Leylā's hand.
>
> The grieving Leylā, holding in her hand
> The letter, caught the scent of heart's dear love.
> She knew the writing of a stranger hand,
> Yet not of *Amr*,[90] nor the script of *Zayd*.

She knew that Fortune had a blessing sent,
And quickly to its message turned her eyes.
But as she read the op'ning bitter words,
She tore to shreds the garment of her soul.
Now let the ocean of her tearful eyes
Bring forth a million pearls, her bleeding heart
A million rubies from its treas'ry send,
That o'er the words, augmenting still their worth,
The precious jewels may scatter without end!
She read it all and understood its sense,
No gloss were needed for a single line
No single reference was lacking clue;
And then, with soul all pierced with sweet reproof,
She straightway wrote an answer to Mejnūn

LVIII

Herein is set forth the Letter written by Leylā in reply to Mejnūn, and the Manner in which she made her Excuse.

Now flew the reed pen in fair Leylā's hand,
And on the waiting parchment writ her thoughts:

'O, God, Creator, Architect of all,
The Builder of each Treaty, every Vow;
The Giver of the Gifts of Wealth and Child;
Divine Creator out of Nothingness
Of all that has existence, bringing forth
From great Antiquity inventions new;
O, Thou, the Hairdresser of all the World,
Still moulding it to all Thy heart's desire;
Whose Threshold is the far Sublime; O, King,
This letter, written by a wounded soul,
By me, the restive one, must take its way
To him of honour and of noble rank,
To Mejnūn, sick of heart, and sorely hurt.

O, thou, whose carpet is the earth, whose bed
Is tearing thorn, O, thou, the one desire
Of this my grieving heart and tearful eye:
Thy slanders and reproaches tear my heart,

Admitting they are just, while black with shame
My face is hung, dishonoured in thy sight.
Yet know that I, all overwhelmed with shame,
Still suffer pain unceasing. For my guilt
I make admission, yet compassion ask
Of thee who, thus accusing, seek'st excuse.

Thou knowest well that I am but the jewel
Within the market, haggled for by all.
Not mine the choice of market for my wares,
For Fortune blindly still the auction holds.
'Tis she, not I, who blindly makes the choice
Of buyer and of seller else, be sure
That none would purchase Leylā, saving thee.
If now an accusation harsh is made,
Let not thy hatred of me mount, nor yet
Grow wearied of me, for no pearl am I
That quickly purchased, quickly is engraved.
If it be true that Ibni Salam's heart,
Is cheered by me, his candle in the night,
And in day his sun, his sole content
Is found in seeing from afar the light,
For he and I are many leagues apart.
And still if he, afar, can see my beam
And revel in it, drawing near its fire
He finds a torment and a scorching pain.

Think not, my soul, that I in cheerfulness
Pursue my path, for, fettered in a net of grief
I find no power to go to market place,
Nor strength to raise my head from off my breast.
See now my sorrow: when I wish to cry
I first must find a reasonable excuse;
And either think of both my parents dear,
Or long association with my friends.
If grief supplies the impulse to destroy
My garments, then the maker of my robes
Must be at hand to furnish the pretext,
And under guise of anger at her faults
I then may rail and rend my dresses. See
I say, "this skirt is wrong, this pocket bad,"
And thus on false pretext, mask honest grief.
And then, those moments when I seek in vain

Sweet union with thee, I must go forth
And seek the fountain, there to take a bath,
And there, alone, I strip my body bare
And ravel up the hair upon my head,
And gaze upon the mirror of the stream,
And in my dissarray, see Mejnūn there.

Around my neck no second collar rests,
The rubies of lips set forth no speech;
My neck seeks but the collar of thy arm,
My lips enquire of thine of zephyrs sweet.
From grief of thee I languish in my soul
All martyred by thy soul of cruelty.
Thy bloody curtain is my blood-stained shroud:
Though living still, rest me in my grave.
Think thus, that Leylā rests within a grave,
Think not that with a husband joys her life.

Come thou, and make a candle of thy sigh
To light my tomb; embellish it
With all the dust that lies upon thy road,
For I, though singing as a nightingale,
Sing but the dirge of separation's pain.
Though singing thus within a garden fair,
Know that the *bülbül* sings within a cage
Where all the future hides beneath a cloud
Of dark and dreary doubt, as thus with broken wing
And ruined pinion, mournfully I sing.

If now I find companionship with beast
And bird upon the wing, seek no reproof,
For rumour whispers that the bird and beast
Are now blood brother with thee. So am I.
O, sad, deserted lover, never blame
This saddened one who writes these saddened lines.
Wait patiently the day when Fortune smiles
And changes dismal days to happy hours.
Think not that only thou, to Sorrow bound
Art thin with dull Despair's bewilderment.
These quatrains con with understanding eye.
And know that with thee, Leylā sorrows too.'

LIX

Herein are set forth the Quatrains sent by Leylā to Mejnūn.

My garments all are badly torn; the hand of deep disgrace
Has rent my dress: both friend and foe now join to smirch my name:
My soul and body Love's dear name make captive in this place—
Do not these sorrows then suffice, without thy adding more?

I keep my sorrow secret, neither rest nor patience mine,
No friendliness may share my hidden misery:
A captive in a prison though it be no choice of mine—
Do not these sorrows then suffice without thy adding more?

My pallid face assumes the hue of blood embittered tears;
My soul, grief nourished, burns apace in desolation's fire;
The dastard hand of Fortune my heart with sorrow sears—
Do not these sorrows then suffice without thy adding more?

Now sad with wish for union, afflicted with despair,
I know now what my sickness is, from whence my troubles come,
Afflicted with a grief of love that nothing can repair—
Are not these sorrows then enough without thy adding more?

Apart from thee my company is grief and sad distress;
First one by one, then all as one, they give me cruel pain;
So deeply am I fall'n in grief, so cruelly they oppress—
Do not these sorrows then suffice without thy adding more?

Alone before the doctor versed in love did I reveal
The secret of my trouble, how from far eternity
My fate was sure: he knew no art my misery to heal—
Do not these sorrows then suffice without thy adding more?

Fuzūlī, see, this bleeding heart is born of single thrust;
Thou knowest 'tis impossible to render up one's love.
No remedy exists on which to fasten all my trust—
Do not these sorrows then suffice without thy adding more?

LX

Herein the Writer of Words completes this Section of the Story of Leylā and Mejnun.

The sorrow of her heart now in the letter lay,
She said:
        'O perfect sage, how wonderful the day
That brought thee here to send my grief away.
Refreshed and all at ease I feel, my melancholy spent,
Come every day and write a charm: no more I may lament.
A hope is here that in thy spell I am restored to health,
Thy writing is an amulet surpassing any wealth.
I, too, have here an amulet: come, take it as you go,
And whether what is writ is good the sequel well may show.
Do thou interpretation make, reveal its meaning hid,
Correct mistakes, if such there be. Do kindly as I bid.'

These words she spoke to Zayd, gave the letter in his hand:
The style and form were such that wisdom well might understand.
The letter reached Mejnūn the mad, the pearl returned again
A red carnelian, bloody red, by tears that fell as rain.
He understood its meaning, its significance was clear,
The letter gave him pleasure for he knew that Love was near.

LXI

Herein is set forth the Manner in which Mejnūn's Father found him in the Desert, and how he was unable to reform him by Good advice.

When men of letters fell to writing, in this manner they recounted:
Their words, as evidence of truth, the *tugra*[91] now surmounted.
He, the subject of this sorrow, Mejnūn's father, old in years,
Sorrowed for the broken Mejnūn, perplex'd in a flood of tears.
Knew no more in stupefaction that today was but today,
Or that yesterday had followed every other yesterday.
Strength of purpose now had left him, weariness upon him pressed;
Day time found him short of patience, empty nights gave little rest.
Still he stood, yet never doubting, nor committing any crime,
Knowing never cure for Mejnūn found the sages any time.
Thus he stood what time they brought him news that made his passions stir,
With a tale from o'er the border, more his tearful eyes to blur.

'Now hear our message, broken as thou art,
For Leylā's father, he the black of heart,
Yea, he who friends the crowd,
That elephant of ignorance,
But yesterday avowed
Before his chiefs in conference,
That Mejnūn's madness shames his name
And casts aspersion on his fame.

He swears that thy love maddened son
Who from authority has run,
Has brought increasing pain and woe
(They instance Nevfel's anger here)
They think to let his blood o'erflow
And thus regain their honour clear
For while alive thy Mejnūn stays
They feel dishonour clouds their days.

They say he is a viper grown
All poison, and 'tis widely known
That such must be destroyed.
The honour is not ours but thine
That they may find themselves employed
That still our fame may shine
And shelter and relief we find
For Mejnūn and his fate unkind.

And now they think advantage lies
In making sure that Mejnūn dies.
Resolve is quickly made.
And quickly now they think to slay
Thy son and see the reckoning paid
And greet a clearer day.
No stranger, sage, it is thy son
On whom this evil will be done.'

A thousand sorrows now beset the sage;
Fresh tortures now became imperative.
His face a torrent, streaming in full spate,
He quickly the desert set his foot.
From side to side he roamed in eager quest
And speedy, hoping soon to find a sign

To tell him where his grieving son was hid.
From nightly halt to yet another near
He took his rapid way, his only guide
The bloody drops that fell from out his eyes
That sought to find the tears of mad Mejnūn.
When day departed and the darkness fell
And night assumed dominion o'er the world,
No more were halting places clearly shown.
A thousand hardships then beset his path.
Now as he wandered in bewilderment
And sighing in lament, a sudden flame
Far, far away, but bright his eye beheld,
And in the blackened night a guide became,
Reversing night's dim darkness into day.
A fire, he thought it, such as Arabs light:
So he, with stumbling steps, towards the fire
Pursued his path. Arrived, he saw the flame
Was human breath and not a burning pile.
His quest was ended: Mejnūn, sighing here
Had set the world aflame with fiery breath.
Rebellious now upon the flaming world
Had closed his eyes, abandoning his mind
No less than soul and body, seeking now
Nor goods nor dear possessions as a prize.
No wish was left to see a mother dear
Or greet a father: far upon the wind
Had gone his dress of honour, naught remained
Awaiting him but Death, and he for Death
Sat grimly patient.
    When the sage beheld
The sad condition of his tortured son,
He shed his bloodstained tears upon the cheeks
So pallid of Mejnūn, then at his side
In sad compassion slowly sat him down
And stretched his hand to wipe the grieving face.

Bewildered, Mejnūn opened now his eyes
And murmured to the father at his side:

'And who art thou, that here my company
Has sought unasked? If, as a messenger,
Thou seekest me, deliver now thy news.
Recount the tale of my so perfect Moon.

But if no messenger thou art, but one
Who voyages, a traveller o'er the world,
Depart and seek another resting place.'

Now spoke the sage, imploring:
                              'Hear me, son,
In all the world thou art the only one
Who furnishes the treasured purse of life.
I am the casket, closed to further strife,
But thou the pearl, illuminating clear
The night, that is thy grieving father dear.
Thou art the flower I planted in my field;
Thou art my life, to live when all revealed,
I stand within the shadow grim of Death.
O, thou, desired of all my passioned breath,
The very treasure of my treasure chest,
The light of Fortune's eye, this agéd breast
Would swell with pride of thee, my refuge sure,
My pride, my honour and my hope secure.
When Death has called and I resign my throne
Who else should rule but only thee alone?
Thy people, seeing thee, would then my name
Remember, giving thee the same acclaim
That I enjoyed. Thus would I swell my fame.
If drunk and fearless in thy careless youth
Thou makest dusty wilderness a home,
Enjoying fame as maddened lover, truth
May find excuse, for lovers always roam,
And every season brings its special dish.
Succeeding years bring each succeeding wish.
To lusty youth all love becomes an art,
And love becomes the fast maturing heart.
But now thy years of foolishness have sped,
And all thy youthful follies should be dead.
Thy years are such that wisdom now should rest
Upon thy mantle, and within thy breast.
Mature perfection should be close embraced,
And youthful follies rapidly displaced.
See how these follies ill become thy name,
See how accusing voices call thy shame.
If till today, thou dwelt in ignorance
Be wise in time, and seek the conference
Of all thy fellows: take not to the wild

And roam about unknowing, love beguiled.
'Tis wrong amid the beasts to seek thy friend,
For beasts are beasts and will be till the end.
Seek rather thy companionship with men
Of good repute and standing, it is then
The world shall see thee as thou art, who heard
While beast consorts with beast and bird with bird,
A price who, as his friend, the wild preferred?
Some pity find for this unfortunate,
Thy father, hurt by grief disconsolate.
Let not this trouble rest upon my head,
Nor leave my hopes all disappointed, dead.
My limpid mask as white as camphor grew,
Thou art my sun, my morning born anew.
My figure bent, to *dal* from *elif* changed,
Upon thy side as guide, may yet be ranged.
The cruelty of time the passing years
Have reached my very soul, the Helmsman steers
My battered vessel to another land:
Now let me, therefore, take thee by the hand
And make surrender of my name and place
And thus departing, let me see the face
Of my successor, chiefest of my race.

'How may continual drunkenness confer
A blessing? How may idol worshipper
Find good in idol worship? Drunken man,
Thou knowest not thy many faults to scan,
But when the moment comest that, calm of mind,
And sober for awhile, thy thoughts unkind,
And thy irascibility will shame
Thy breeding and thy rightly honoured name.
Thou worshipper before the Idol's shrine,
Who, mid the Idol's temples wouldst recline,
When once this veil of drunkenness is torn
From off thine eyes and sanity is born
Within thy soul again, what angry blame
Wilt thou accord thyself, how then will flame
The fires that will consume thee with thy shame?
If beauty thou desirest, give thy heart
To one whose beauty is alone, apart,
Of firm stability and purpose fine,
Not subject to whatever sun may shine.

And thus bestowed, though world should turn to dust,
And earthquakes crumble its abhorréd crust,
Thy love may still her skirts above the wave
Lift high and thus thy reputation save.
But this, thy falcon, never stays at rest,
Nor on one hand remains: for ever pressed
To render homage to Nevfel's decree,
And now with Ibni Salam makes her free.
Thus Ibni Salam's heart companion finds
That lights the torch for strangers, and entwines
Her heart to others. Be ashamed, my son,
Of melting passion for a girl unwon.
Melt not thy soul with this lamenting sad,
Nor in futility remain thus mad.
Throughout the world stability is known:
Suppose thy love at last became thine own?
Still seek no union with her, for the wife
Divorced, and lover wed, brings strife.
Abandon now this path nonsensical,
Recall the name of God so mystical.
No mention make of others. He, the Source
And Final Goal of Ultimate Resource.
Direct thy steps to Him, He is the End:
He is the Maker, and thy life to spend
In easy idleness, when He has made
The world His workshop, sadly is repaid.
Each his own and necessary place
Must labour in His workshop for a space,
And those whose work constructive is of worth,
The Master will repay, not as his birth,
But as his labour only merits praise.
Come now, leave idleness! Fill out thy days
That meet thee in this workshop of the world.
Rest not, with all thy talents yet unfurled!
'Tis time for me to render up my throne,
To render up the life I still would own,
And go from here, perchance in dignity,
And pass the gates of long Eternity.
Now, therefore, come, consider my estate,
Give not my wealth and my possessions great
Unto a stranger: troubles have I known,
This fortune thus amassed made many groan.
'Tis thine in charge: let not distracted grief

Rob thee for others in a moment brief.
How well I know thy love cannot remain
In this sad state, ever angry pain,
For Fortune yet may smile, and then awake,
Thy passion spent, no further search will make.
My fear is here, that my condition changed,
When I, beyond the world, in death am ranged,
And all my wealth be passed to nothingness,
And thou art left alone in friendlessness,
(For lack of money spells the lack of friend)
'Twas ever thus and will be without end)
A man of wisdom looks beyond his years
While Hope's strong pillar counteracts his fears.'

The father in his wisdom finished thus,
While Mejnūn listened to his sage advice
And to his phrases found himself inclined.
His madness to forswear was in his mind.
He thought to cut the chains of madness clear
And not rest captive in a passion drear,
And thus abandon Love's consuming fire,
And set aside his passion's one desire.
But once again, the Sov'ran of his mind
The *Firman*[92] showed, and to it he inclined.

'O, thou, whose sole possession in this world is only me,
What hast thou in this body and this soul now never free?
No more desire to have my soul, leave now its dwelling place
They call my body, where the soul has rested for a space.
Surrender me, and, severed from my body and my soul
Know thou another as thine own: let others make thee whole.'

Now like the crimson rose tree his blood in passion boiled,
Now like the bosky nightingale, these twisted notes uncoiled:

'O, thou, who buildest all in righteousness,
Whose preaching to me bears the mark of health,
So well I know the worth of thy advice,
So well I know thy bitter words are true.
Thou speakest only for my proper good,
No evil hides within thy accents plain.
And, should I listen, this I know full well,
That though my ear inclines towards thy speech,

What value lies in listening, when forgot
Is every word? Say not, in fond appeal,
"Have knowledge from my words", for, in my mind,
No knowledge now remains of I myself,
So far beyond myself my spirit flies.
Within, without and all around me now
Love holds me captive, and the thieving wind
Has flown afar with pace and patience too.
Where e'er I think to turn my errant step
Toward the sweet appeal of vanity,
Love bars my way with unrelenting: "No!"
Now where am I? For how, by giving Love
Can love eternal vanish from the soul?
The cruelty of slander stabbed my breast.
Come, now, abandon me, as now I see
I have abandoned thee. Hear now my word:
Approach me not with Counsel's honey tongue,
And seek not ways to rectify my course.
My dear despair brings increase of my pain;
It grows as fire fanned high by merry wind.
Suppose a bottle breaks to thousand shards,
Does any skill exist to make it whole?
Make not these offers of a household fine,
Mark rather all the swiftly running time,
And if thy passing leaves it far behind,
What virtue comes if I, the wanton, take
Thy offer of possessions; gathered wealth,
Is all thou hast to give. Think now, thy son,
Is but as thee, and once the owner proud,
He yet may die and leave the golden hoard
To others in their turn.'
     Thus spoke the King
Of all the Land of Sad, Unhappy Love,
And, sighing deeply, to his father spoke
Avowing all his trouble, when his frame
Was seized with trembling, and a mighty fit
Of passion tremored all his body o'er.
The sleeve that clothed his arm was filled with blood
While on the sage a stark amazement sat.
But Mejnūn spoke again:
    'Be not amazed.
The fairy Idol opened now a vein,
The surgeon with his lancet cut her arm,

So here the stigma of the wound appears.
For, though we own two bodies, yet the soul
Is one and jointly owned, between us now
Duality is merged in single state:
No soul is mine but hers, and hers is mine.
Think not that she is she and I am I.
Two bodies live with but a single soul.
If she is glad, then gladness is my share;
If she repines, then sorrow clouds my day.'

And now, at last, the saddened father knew
The quality and merit of the love
That held his son in chains. He knew the sense
Of Justice for a true Perfection.
He knew that none of falsehood and deceit
Was here, that never cunning twist could void
The passion burning in his Mejnūn's soul.
No more he tried to offer fond advice,
No more he censured Mejnūn with disgrace,
But now resigned, he left contention all
And sadly bade farewell, and went his way.

LXII

Herein is related the Manner in which Mejnūn's Father gave up Contention, and how he bade Farewell to Mejnūn with the greatest Reluctance and a keen Feeling of Longing.

O, thou, the thread on which the jewel of my desire is hung,
O, thou, my mirror of belief, whose birth with joy I sung,
For but an instant hear my words, and have compassion sweet:
'Tis but a moment I shall speak! My words with patience greet.
Heed what I say for shortly, I, the broken one, set out
Upon a journey far and long. Forgive: and never doubt
That at my hand, in every way thy life was well endowed.
Now fare thee well, my only son, leave not thy head unbowed:
Let no reproach befoul thy lips, think not that, weak or faint,
I did thee wrong. In all thy life I make me no complaint.
Thy life has brought no happiness, I knew no joy in thee;
With bird and beast thy bosom friend—what pleasure there for me?
A last request is all I make. Mark now, my last command:
Observe a mourning spell for me, 'tis all that I demand.

Each instant moan and beat thy breast, make lamentation brave.
And make a pathway with thy tears all round about my grave.
I ask no joyous merriment, no dancing gay nor song—
Indeed, if merriment I asked, 'twould be a grievous wrong,
For thou would'st say: "No knowledge, I, of arts of simple joy.
True mourning do I understand, and all my days employ
In weeping and lamenting." Now thy course is clearly shown:
Make habit of thy grieving: Its merit make my own.
My purpose is that friend and foe, intoning soft the prayer,
May make *namaz*[93] for me, and thus with prayer perfume the air.
That friendlessness may not disgrace, that all thy sorrow share,
And each and every understand that I have left an heir.'

The wretched father thus composed his will and testament,
Then turned his steps towards his home and his last sacrament.
Oppressed with sorrow, vexéd too, for nothing left to live,
The candle of his life burned out, it had no light to give.
No cure, no balsam could be found: one parting word he said:
'Mejnūn!' and then, incontinent, turned over and was dead.
No trust is found within the world, with every passing breath
Forget not that affliction ends with grim embrace of Death.
This world is but a treasure house where sweets and joys abound;
It knows not any trouble for no basis firm has found.

LXIII

Herein is set forth the first Epilogue to this Part of the Story of Leylā and Mejnūn.

Is there not in store, O, Saki, tulip coloured, crimson wine?
Is there not a cup to empty, easing this exhaustion mine?
Grief has left me quite exhausted, left me in an evil hour:
Bring forth wine of ruddy redness, crimson as the judas flower.
Make not long delay in finding means to banish grief from me,
Nor uncompleted leave thy task, for now I rest my grief on thee.
This world is as God Of Beauty, never think it all disloyal,
Though it charms thee, yet it needs thee, more than thou canst need its coil.
In ignorance thy days are spent, the world desires thy knowledge great,
A guest within the world, thou leavest sorrow keen before its gate.
With merriment and pleasure Fortune always blesses thy estate.

When going from the world and bowing low before the throne
Of the ever mighty God, make thy *surme*[94] of the stone
That the winds have ground to dust, thus until the Judgement Day,
Thy custodian will be in every grain of scattered clay.
Thus the world becomes thy mansion given over to decay,
Keeps thee, brings thee and delivers thee to the long eternal day.
Whosoever gains a knowledge of this subtle purpose clear
Feels no more disgusted at the blindly rolling sphere.
None of torture may he suffer while he draws his living breath,
Nor will shrink with face affrighted at the coming on of Death.

Now it chanced that on a hill top Mejnūn sat still shedding tears,
When a hunter came upon him with a thousand sland'rous spears,
Crying to the maddened one:
      'Void of shame on every side
People blame thee, thy dishonour now by every tongue is cried.
Hast thou never trace of honour; art forgetting now thy name?
People murmur, unbelieving that thou feelest not thy shame.
Extravagance in just reproof will never sorrow's pity know,
The pity is in being thus so pitiless, with heart of snow,
Within his lifetime never once thy father tasted joy of thee,
At least remember him now dead: some shade of duty try to see.
For love of thee the sage thy father, passed from here beyond the
   grave—
What shame is thine that took the gift, but never thought nor mem'ry
   gave!
Does naught of delicacy stay within thy nature falsely named?
By God above, in this thy life full surely art thou deeply shamed.'

The voice at last put fire in Mejnūn's heart,
And lamentation new began to start
The while he hit his head upon the stone
Like wine the tears gushed, seeking to atone.
He asked to see the tomb, and sought to find
A sign while running swiftly, as his tears unkind.
And when before his father's tomb he stayed
A grieving candle of his body made.
His trouble fanned his sorrow's fiery heat,
His heart gave fire, his tears with every beat
Of pulse poured forth. His breast a tablet stone
Engraved with scratches of his nails; alone
In sorrow then his breast upon the grave
He pressed in anguish. Sadly did he rave

The while the earth upon the tomb became
A cover as of petalled flowers, the same
As in a garden full of roses blew.
Renewing then his mourning, weeping slow,
He spoke at last in solemn accents low.

'O, thou, the architect from whom I sprung
Whose praise and strong approval was a boon,
'Gainst whom rebellion earns a penalty—
The injury of thy averted face:
I spurned thy guidance, took it not as sent
As from a Godhead in the lofty skies.
A hundred times my wailing cries go forth
For opportunities so blindly lost:
'Tis pity that, headstrong and obstinate,
I held not in thy path so wisely shown,
Or that, through many endless days and months
I spurned thy offered close companionship.
Thou badest, with a father's voice: "Do good!"
The evil that I chose now grieves us both.
Thy bounty thrown aside, my portion lost,
I strayed afar, mistaking of my course
And tortured thee with disappointment's pain.

'O, my prosperity, depart not now!
O, thou, my candle, suffer not thy light
To be extinguished, when in grief I fell
And sorrowed deeply, thou in all the world
Stayed close to me, a dear, compassionate friend.
My bosom friend, so close in my complaint,
Companion to my story, so ill starred.
But what has chanced that now thy strength has failed
Before my grief, now sadly needing thee?
Wert thou affrighted by my salty tears?
That fell a raging whirlpool from my eyes?
Did I indeed supply fatal cause
That crushed thee in this wretched, sad defeat?

'O, thou, the source of all that gave me life,
My sole salvation from thy pleasure comes.
See how my shameful deeds I grow to learn:
See, now, I know them shameful still, and vile.
In this sad world thy misery was great,
And mine alone the fault; yet visit not

In that next world, revenge of misery
Upon my head. See how I here have burned
And twisted in thy fire of torment fierce,
By thy dear hand thrown headlong into grief.
Thy one desire was but for rest and peace:
Thou tookst a treasure, held it in thy hand
And then didst let it fall, renounced, but who
Say now, but who will solve thy problems thus?
Who saved thee from this great anxiety?'

All night, till morning Mejnūn wept alone,
A captive, desolate, before the grave,
Until at last the musky night was sped
By Day's white dust, and as the ray came forth,
And pierced the darkness with another day
The rites of grief restored, he took his way
To *Nejd*,⁹⁵ his grave, his home among the heights.

LXIV

Herein is set forth the Epilogue within the Epilogue.

> How well those men who have perfection know
> That Love is Beauty's twin and second face!
> All Beauty is a mirror showing clear
> The world entire, but Love supplies the gloss
> And polish, so the glass may shine
> More brightly: yet, should Beauty pass,
> 'Tis clear that Love no more could manifest
> Its purpose, while if Love should fail and die,
> No ecstasy could Beauty then arouse.
> For, lacking Beauty, what can come of Love?
> 'Tis ever the belovéd that inspires
> The urge towards perfection. Lacking Love
> All Beauty would in misery repine.
> 'Tis Love itself that makes the market firm
> For Beauty: lacking it there is no joy,
> And lacking Beauty Love may ne'er appear.
>
> In every grade of all society
> Mejnūn, a brightly burning candle, gave
> Adornment, while his heart in passion flamed
> A burning fire for Leylā: his the cup,

The happiness increasing cup of wine
All purified: for Leylā was his wine.
Whate'er perfection Mejnūn proudly claimed
'Twas Leylā with her love and beauty both
That filled his cup—Mejnūn was Leylā's joy
And Beauty unto Love was strangely drawn.

It chanced one day, alone and wretched, ill
And broken hearted, o'er the wilderness
Mejnūn was roaming when, upon a stone
A tablet such as the engravers use,
The sad and sorrowful scratched forth the face
Of Love and Leylā. Thus two faces showed.
The people round an explanation sought
And asked solution of the riddle strange.

'In error am I fall'n', said Mejnūn.
'We two demand no double picture thus.
We stand as one, in singleness as truth
Stand firm and steady with a single face.
The men of learning know that with us twain
No trace of dualism may be found.'

'But,' answer made his interlocutor,
'Does not a deep disgrace lie hidden here?
That Love should vanish and that thou shouldst live?
If from this tablet Leylā be erased
'Tis shame indeed: nay, rather from the stone
Erase thyself and let thy Love remain.'

Reply made Mejnūn:
                    'In the way of love
'Tis fit and proper that the face of Love
Should be by lovers veiled: two parts exist,
The body visible; the soul concealed.
The loved one, so belovéd, is the soul,
The lovers are the bodies, coarser grained.
No fear may rest in the belovéd's heart
The lover in the world should gather fame,
Or when the lover in the market place
Sheds forth his tears, the great betrayal makes
And all may mouth the dear beloved's name.'

LXV

Herein is set forth a slight Sample of Mejnūn's Condition at this Time and some of the Attributes of his Perfection.

Mejnūn was the Shah of the Kingdom of Affliction,
The beasts of the wilderness all gathered round his name:
The shy gazelle he made to give her tribute by exaction
Of something of her musk, the fox he taxed the same
By holding of its furry coat an unopposéd claim.
A Chief both just and generous, all things that ran or flew
Partook of justice equally: no beast could longer rue
Its fate, for Mejnūn shed his blood to give it still its food,
And satisfied its hunger. While he reigned all things were good,
The wilderness became subdued, the cat with savage pard
Consorted with each other, while the stag earned wolf's regard.
The lion became the comrade of the agile mountain goat
Which gladly gave its udders to the roaring thirsty throat.
Within his shadow now the ant made fast its small abode
And winter store of grain amassed from every tear that flowed.
At times the torrent of his tears was high in mighty flood
And then a thousand beasts were drowned; at times his burning blood
Flared out in sudden heat and then a thousand beasts and birds
Were scorched unto extinction, with little loss of words.
The nails upon his fingers now became an angry spade
That o'er his head the grieving earth and angry mountain made.
The thirsty dust within his hair accumulated fast
And slaked its thirst with all the rears that from his eyelids passed.

The vegetation burgeoned 'neath his heavy uttered sighs,
While roses in the garden of his madness 'gan to rise.
If with the stag he kept his state, by water of his tears
The antlered horn was fertilized; both fruit and leaf appears.
Each instant in his hand he took the lowly crawling snake
And then that pleased unfortunate, Mejnūn, complaint would make:
And say: 'Now in my hand I hold her musky hair
As fragrant as the hyacinth, Desire's great cable fair!'
His soul he branded like the pard with thousand burning brands
And like the lion, his finger nails as claws sprang from his hands.
The leader of the lions and the leopards he became,
And lion and leopard each agreed to glorify his name.

LXVI

Herein is set forth the Prayer in which Mejnūn prayed earnestly and how the Arrow of his Prayer reached the Target of Acceptance.

    It fell that, when the light destroying Night.
Had cast its veil upon the light of Day;
When greedy sky had swallowed up the sun,
That ruby rare, it spangled o'er its face
A thousand limpid pearls, the gleaming stars
That, as a flag with thousand crescents decked
Replaced the ruby flag now darkly furled;
And when th'astronomer of lunar spheres
In each unfolding petal opium caught,
When, one by one, upon her honoured robe
Heav'n's bride sewed on her rare and hidden pearls,
And when the Moon, a stately vessel, sailed
Within the whirlpool of the Milky way,
Its waiting eye; when all the land of Sham
O'erturned his ink horn, spreading blackness dark
O'er all the world; when Venus' inky locks
Now masked her lovely face, the lurking star
That waited for the sun's withdrawal, oped
Its waiting eye: when all the land of Sham
Was conquered by the warlike spear of Mars,
And Night usurped the name and place of Day:
When Jupiter put on his garments black
Of mourning at the sun's withdrawal sad,
The turning heavens as a mirror grew
And Saturn looked, and loved the face he saw.
The stars, secure of place, became the nails
That fastened up the carpet of the sky
Lest, unsecured, it fall. Then, o'er the field
The dweller of the Zodiac came forth:
The tender sweet gazelle, the fleecy lamb,
With Taurus and the spermaceti whale
That filled the world anew with amber fresh,
The Belt of Gemini, enwrought with jewels
That coloured all the heaven's vasty space,
With Cancer banishing the morning breeze,
Its purity from darkness drawing gain;
When Leo now divorcéd from the Sun
Became a candle belching acrid smoke,

When Virgo dressed her hair with ivory
And poured the limpid amber o'er the musk;
When Fortune made a scale of Libra just
And measured pearls for earthly bankers' joy;
When, like a fiend, her halter Scorpion
Let out in wicked curls and tied secure,
When Sagittarius bent his mighty bow
And shot his arrow heads of piercing stars;
When Capricornus, shedding every hair
Made blacker still the heavens' swarthy face,
Aquarius sent his fortune's piercing blight
O'er all the sky with thousand bitter drops;
When Jonah's brightness in the vasty whale
Was darkly swallowed up, lucent dawn
Burned in the sky and filled it all with flame,
And sent its dusky cloak within the house
(The twenty-fifth of all the lunar host)
Where dwelt Aquarii, now rising too
The light that kindled on Leonis' brow:
The *Hak'a* gave embellishment to grace
When *Han'a* crowned the diadem of all,
When Arietis, Virginis as well
With Bootis and Corona closely set
With great Australis, turned away their eyes
And unto Heaven turned the shining face
So that the Archer, Sagittarius,
Might even change with Sarfa (Mansion twelfth
Of all the Moon's great houses)
Then ready Aldeberan in its pride
And all the Pleiades with shiny pearls
To paint in beauty all the vasty sky
And set afoot the motion of the stars
And make them back and forth advance, retreat
And keep their complex ordered journeying:—
Mejnūn, dismayed, dishevelled and confused
Was quite bewildered by the starry maze,
And oped his tearful eye against the sky
And matched the skies with all his tearful stars.
To every star he showed his sorrowed state,
And told his hopeless wishes thousandfold.
First among all to Mercury inclined
And told the planet of his heavy grief:

'O, thou, the Minister of Numbers strange,
The sage of all who, mathematical
Solution seek, the auditor of mind
Examiner of all who Fate forecast,
Transcriber of reality's great charm,
The index of the Heavenly Symbol. Thou
The *Kassam*⁹⁶ of all aim and motive, Thou
Ordainer of all offices of rank,
Know Thou that my account is heavy grown,
And bankrupt is my heart's affliction now.
No Counsellor but Thou is worthy praise,
Note, therefore, all my great affliction sore,
And in a letter to the Sultan write
That haply with the magic of thy pen
A charm be found for all my maddened state.

But quickly Mejnūn found that Mercury
Had little understanding of his case,
And thus another song he 'gan to sing
From Mercury slow turning in distress.
And this, his second plaint, he made to Mars
Well known as Fortune's Executioner.

'O, Thou, the Lord Supreme of Valour's Court,
To whose dread sword the world obedient
Remains in deep subjection, owner thou
Of all the triumph and the victory known;
Thou Crown of all the lusty men at arms:
Know then, that I am weak; my foe is strong.
I friendless, while my enemy is cruel.
Be gracious to me, help a feeble soul
Drive forth calamity from friendlessness.
Draw now thy sword, repel the enemy,
So I may dwell serenely with *my friend.*'⁹⁷

But Mejnūn quickly saw success was hid
Too far on high for Mercury or Mars
To grasp its mantle, then, of sword dismayed,
And disappointed in the arrow, too,
He took his way unto the Throne of God,
And turned his eyes upon the Throne of Grace,
And to his God made hansel of his grief.

'O, Thou, Great Helper of the Sword, and Guide
To every moving pen, with Mars as slave,
And as thy servant mighty Mercury,
O, Thou, the Summit of the hilltop capped
With hope, the Giver to the world of hope
And every form of human happiness:
Be merciful to me, the destitute,
And mis'ry laden wretch who now appeals
That of Thy mighty clemency he gain
A healing for the heart's afflicting pain.
'Twas Thou who gave to Leylā lovely grace
And beauty that my heart was struck to fire;
'Twas Thou who gave her world calamity
And made me overwhelmed with sore distress;
From Thou the beauty came to light the world;
Thou gav'st the fire that over me she flung
That burning me, has burned up all the world:
'Twas Thou that gave me mourning misery,
That put this passion cruel in my blood,
Thus making Leylā cruel as passion's fire.
'Twas Leylā planted this affliction sore,
'Twas Leylā robbed me of my ease of mind
With but a single glance: she has no choice,
Her conduct and its consequence ordained,
No change may come, for Thou hast ordered all.
'Tis so with me and so with her remains
Her helplessness within her own desires,
'Tis but in Thee the wound may be assuaged,
So grant Thy healing kindness, Gracious God.
Thou, of Thy Goodness, give me healing, Lord,
Nor let me look abroad for aid or help.
Thou knowest well from whom has come this grief—
Who else but Thou shouldst be my comrade now?
To many sages scattered o'er the land
I told my sorrow, seeking for relief,
Yet, while they diagnosed my sorrow's cause,
They still were mute and told no remedy.
I knew the Sage supreme was only Thou,
In knowledge of affliction without peer,
Affliction sore and healing come of Thee.
Thou art the Judge, and Thine the will Divine.
Thou, therefore, let my grief intensify
And thus increase my pleasure in my pain

And make my yearning day by day increase.
Before my eyes bring pictures of her lips,
Her beauty's great perfection give my soul;
For ever make her manifest in me,
And being gracious, make two faces one.
Make reputable my valour in my grief,
Let my affliction offer nourishment
To my repining soul, and thus if it should be
That she should chance to light another soul
Grant but that I in singleness may live.
Should Destiny ordain that ne'er her face
That face so dear, may shine before my eyes,
Then banish light from these my bloody orbs.
Or should I find small pleasure in my grief
Take all my strength from this my wounded frame.'

LXVII

Herein is set forth the Epilogue to Mejnūn's Prayer.

O, Lord, in Thee perfection still resides,
In Thee Mustafa's great degree abides,
And Truthfulness, the Prophet's Dynasty
And Purity itself, is born of Thee.
From Thee comes guidance that the saints may scan
A model hast Thou made for every man.
No stranger to Thy privacy is nigh
To which that friend within Thy presence high
Is now become an inmate. Now the fear
Of Thy dread punishment and mighty strength
O'ershadows all with dread calamity.
Reversed we see Thy kindly equity,
Thy bounty and the sweetness of Thy truth,
The torment and the torture that the youth
Of Life's sweet citadel is heavy pressed:
Thy loyalty and love the lovers' blessed
Each loving the belovéd; for Thy gift
And blessing sweet bestowed on Leylā's name
For truth of grief, and Mejnūn's awful pain
Beset with sad affliction and distress.
O, Thou, Who greatly did Fuzūlī bless
With happiness of poverty and death
Of knowing, hear the prayer I make
And grant it for Thy own dear honour's sake.

LXVIII

Herein is set forth the Epilogue to this Section of the Story of Leylā and Mejnūn.

With so much zest and fervour prayed Mejnūn
A guerdon asking for his troubles deep,
That darkling night was quickly sped away.
The rose of day's bright garden burst its bud
And brightened all the world with roseate beam.
The nightingale, the bird of dawning sweet,
Uplifted then its chanson of delight,
What time the dusky rook, with sable wings
Flew off, dismayed with glory in the east.
The land o'er all the earth in glory shone,
The stars were harvested and gathered in,
While yet the sky, a vasty dome of blue
Enclosed the magic mirror of the sun
And flung her harvest of the hidden pearls
Before her feet in selfless ecstasy.
The morning of purity and truth.
The joy of all the world, the op'ning rose
Slow gathered power anew, as in the cup
Of purity, the sky's o'erchanging dome
For Jamshyd made an orgy of delight.
Now like the tulip, Mejnūn mounted high
Upon the mountain, and with tearful eye
Beheld the view in grieving ecstasy.
And as he looked, afar upon the plain
He saw his own companion, faithful Zayd,
Approaching his retreat, upon his face
The light of joy shone visibly, his eye
Expressed the heady joy of beauty found.
No sorrow marred his brow, no anxious thought
Was shadowed on his face. Mejnūn beheld
And gazed in blank amazement at his friend.

'O friend sincere, what pleasure may be found
To give thee this unwonted air of joy?
Hast thou at last attained the final wish
And found thy union with Love's desire?
What newfound dignity now holds thy head

Erect in pride and happiness achieved?'
And Zayd opened now the secret store
Of treasure found, and thus addressed Mejnūn:

'O thou, young bird of paradise supreme,
O, thou, *aphelion*, exalted high,
Know thou that yesterday, the Land of Love,
The land that knows thy cypress statured joy
So near thy heart, was my abiding place.
Encroaching on her secrecy with aid
Of strongly working charm, the harem strict
I entered, saw the Moon's supremest light
Fast in eclipse, enchained, all lustreless
The mirror of her face, the coral lip
Was blanched to whiteness, none of freshness left,
Nor in her cheek one spark of radiance.
Her tears, sweet pearls of sorrow, sadly fell
And mingled with the pallor of her lips,
Thus casting precious jewels on her face.
She looked and saw me, moaning in her grief,
And oped the secret of her heart and said:
    "O, loyal one, O Zayd, loyal friend,
    Thy road, perchance has been with gloomy Nejd,
    Where haply thou met my Idol dear.
    Should this be so, and if indeed Mejnūn
    Thine eyes have seen, then tell this suppliant
    Who lives in sorrow miserable days
    Of his condition, how his months and years
    Pursue their wretched course in loneliness.
    Say who he knows as his companion dear
    And how he bears him in his lonely grief.
    And if, by God's good will, thy stony path
    Should bring thee near his secret harbourage
    I charge thee in the name of God to shed
    Thy pity on the lovesick wretched maid
    Who sorrows here. My sad estate explain
    And ask from me, the sadly sickened one,
    How fares the Lord of all my waking days,
    And how he bears the torment of his grief,
    And overpowers the overpowering loss
    Of all he loves. Say to him, sweetly sad,
    That Leylā heard that he in mournful rage
    Had gone afar from men, and hearing thus,

Her garment tore, and long lamented deep
To hear that from this freshly verdant world
His father, cypress straight, had ta'en his leave.
Tell Mejnūn how I share his mighty loss,
A loss he sorrows not alone, for I
Have lost the only friend I had
Who truly wished to see me Mejnūn's mate.
'Twas cruel of heaven thus to grudge a friend
The one among a hundred thousand foes
Most prized and cherished, yet, and yet, what cure
What remedy may be for cruelty
So viciously inflicted from on high?
No slender grief is this, its mighty shade
Fast stifles life and kills where e'er it falls.
Yet still is patience left, and patience now
Is all that may remain. Mark now my state,
Within a fortress fettered fast, and bound
To deep humiliation and to shame.
No more the candle's innocence may share
My secret, now my shadow is my foe
'Gainst whom I guard myself with painful care.

"And should I tell my shadow of my pain,
The candle stands a gleaming, spying foe.
No freedom rests, no letter may I write,
No tactful confidant is at my side.
Dishevelled now I rest, a rosebud lone,
Though sweet my tongue to whisper words of joy.
My heart with blood of sorrow quite o'erflows.
But thou, my King, who reignest King of Light,
For choice of friends thy freedom yet remains,
Another's rede o'er thee has little power.
The course is ever left within thy hand.
'Tis thus I ask thee, why, neglectful still,
No news of thy condition comes to me?
Thou sendest not thy heart's outpouring verse;
No sample of thy sweetly written words
In letter dear enshrined thou sendest here.
'Tis grievous fault, thus, careless, to neglect
The kindly thought that sends a letter forth.
Thou knowest well the fault that herein lies.
Correct it now and, kindly, as of yore,
Set forth in verses all thy troubled mind,

Expression of thy pallid cheek and tears
Blood red from reddened eyes, and send to me,
The soul that sorrows for a kindly word,
That I may store within my treasury
The jewel of thy hand, repeating o'er
In oft repeated ecstasy the words
Thy hand has writ, that in this dreary world
The workshop of the sadly given life
Thy thoughts may always dwell within my mind
As dear embroidery on precious silk.
And so, upon my steadfast, aching soul
Thy words may be embroidered in the thread
Of grief, and my soul at last find ease."
'These words spoke Leylā softly, then in pain
Repeated this sad ode to tell to thee.'

LXIX

Herein is set forth the Ode recited by Leylā in which she manifested the Condition of her Heart.

O, why does his pen still refuse
On the white waxen block to diffuse
The thoughts that his mind now withholds?
Why sends he now never a line,
Why must I in loneliness pine,
While he every kindness withholds?

My friend every kindness withdraws,
My foes slander all, without pause,
Yet he every kindness withholds.
Say, why is his gentleness lamed,
Why leaves he my foes unashamed,
While he every kindness withholds?

These eyes will no longer aspire
In a letter to read Love's desire
While he every kindness withholds.
For letters ne'er cured lovers' pain
No writing can bring back again
Each kindness that now he withholds.

My life is with feebleness fraught,
No letter the swift pigeon brought
For he every kindness withholds.
Now, seeing the fire of my sighs
The pigeon no more round me flies
While he every kindness withholds.

Fuzūlī! How potent a charm
Were a letter! What infinite harm
He does, who all kindness withholds!
No moment of peace knows the heart
So far from its Idol apart
While he every kindness withholds.

LXX

Herein is set forth the Epilogue to this Section of the Story of Leylā and Mejnūn.

When Mejnūn heard the tidings that were brought by loyal Zayd
His Fortune grew submissive and rested by his side:
He trusted to his own good luck, and light his spirit grew
And quickly sprang a confidence that love was his anew.
The water of his blood red tears he sprinkled on the ground
And fast the garden of his heart a verdant greenness found.
His face became aglow with light, his soul began to sing;
His wounded heart was opened to enjoy his new found Spring.
And thus he spoke with happy words to his companion dear
And Zayd the well belovéd now received this message clear:

'O faithful comrade, dearest friend,
O, dear companion till the end,
Encompasses my savage breast
And gives to all my passion rest;
Such happy tidings do you bring,
And joyful news of Leylā sing,
Take now my praises to her door
Submit salaams and prayer, before
My supplication at her feet
Within the dust is laid, and greet
My lovely jasmine with the fire
Of all my secret heart's desire.

And tell the pearl whose lip is sweet
Whose image still my soul's great heat,
Who joys my heart and lights my eye
And comforts still my lonely sigh;
That now and always fervently
I thank my God that Love I see:
That living hopes and Passion lie
In her, my Idol, till I die.
Such loyalty within her vow
Lies fast concealed, that ever now
A cure is found in every sip
I take from her dear honeyed lip.
Slow knowledge came, O dearest Moon,
Of thy great love, and late or soon,
I thank my God and proudly bless
The name that God may still caress.
The tidings of thy kindness came
And left me restless, scarcely sane:
Thy kindly words my mind bereft
Of friendly reason. Naught was left,
So now thy words intoxicate,
My strength is gone, inebriate,
Endurance flies on speedy wings
Thy honeyed speech this weakness brings.
 'If wantonness another road
Should open to thy net, or goad
Of cruelty should urge the way
Thy soul abhors, upon that day
Thy honeyed words would bitter grow
And sour the wine from Jamshyd flow.
Between us then would torment reign,
Instead of kindness, gnawing pain.
 'We know that Beauty is compact of jars,
Of torture and tormenting pain that mars
Its sweetly dear perfection, so in thee
I see thy sweet tormenting loyalty
To me thy worshipper. So short of thine
The beauties of all other maidens shine,
That were they all on sacrificial pyre
Consumed, if still thy beauty's magic fire
Remained, the world would joyously acclaim
Thy beauty fair and far beyond a name.
No maiden born can reach thy dizzy height

Of loyal love: should passion then requite
The loving heart with gift of loving life
The gift were all too small to tip the scales
To equity. But how thy passion fails
In loyalty! Belovéd as thou art,
This faithlessness now shown within thy heart
Proves thee a lover, not belov'd alone—
A double nature has thy story shown.
And though the world may call me lover mad,
I know myself unworthy, resting sad
And lonely with an empty, worthless name
Imperfect still, unworthy of thy fame.
'Tis thou, companion sweet, intelligent,
Who makest perfect love so evident.
Unique of all the world, admired by all,
The life of all for whom all lives may fall.
If every maid thy loyalty enjoyed
No more unique wert thou, for eyesight cloyed
With Beauty's surfeit, soon would Beauty spurn:
No more for common prize would fondly yearn.
But thou alone in Beauty reign'st a Queen,
Who, lacking Beauty, scarcely had been seen.
Thy sweet remembering has made me glad.
May all thy days be joyous: mine all sad!
Thus may my days be gladdened in distress,
And mercy let remembrance still express.
   'O, thou of cypress stature high
O, thou white jasmine breasted, nigh
In beauty to the blushing rose
Whose flushing petals zephyr blows,
Compact of all the loot that came
Of Patience' store and rose's name,
Thou Queen Beauty in the land
Of *Cyrus*,[98] Moon of Night's black hand
The comforter of all who grieve
The peace of those who joy receive,
Since thou, with mercy falling sweet
Hast stretched the arm, my soul to greet,
Since love for me is clearly shown
Abandon now that pathway sown
With sorrow, take the better way
Forswear the Night: embrace the Day!
   'Forget the past and let my soul survive.

                Nor die in yearning: no more let me strive
                To pass the limit of distresséd grief,
                No more let misery be all my brief.
                Turn but a look towards this barren place
                And haply glance upon this wretched face.
                Thy suffering with me makes of thee a friend,
                Companion with me till all sorrows end.
                If still I err and no companion thou,
                Then, live for ever, seeing then, as now,
                That I, the friend of all affliction deep
                Will stand apart, while thou may'st sweetly keep
                Thy seat secure among the wantons wild,
                Successful, with thy happiness up-piled,
                While I, within a corner, waste anew
                And feed a troubled heart on troubles new.
                Yet is this fair within the way of Love?
                Is this true loyalty from God above?
                If all thy words of loyal love be true
                How then explain the crooked path I rue?
                Come! Let us lift this grief of parting drear
                And kindle now the fire of longing clear?
                Let all thy paths, by night no less than day,
                Be joined in union as well they may.
                Thou knowest well that thou alone art mine,
                Let not thy heart to other men incline.
                Should Ibni Salam barrier impose
                And thus our way of union should close
                Send speedy tidings: black shall be his fate.
                His throne shall crumble with a sigh of hate.'

When Mejnūn finished telling all his heart's o'erwrought desire
The loyal Zayd started for the country of his fire;
The message of the moth before the candle murmured clear:
The tidings of the nightingale he made her garden hear.

LXXI

Herein is related the Manner of the Death of Ibni Salam and of Leyla's Freedom from that Affliction.

                See how the wheel of Fortune still revolves,
                O Saki; see the bubbles in the cup
                Rise up and burst upon the ruby wine

That mirrors all the world: this alchemy
So quickly changes earth to gleaming gold.
Is not advantage here, and greater found
Than that which frees from trouble of the world?
The world is but a dream, a shadowing
Of all imagination may present.
Think not thy dreams give birth to happiness
Nor in imagination rest content,
For time and its conditions ever change,
And men of wisdom spurn its changing state.

    It chanced that, mourning for a sorrow hid,
The *wailer*[99] raised a cry, like those who mourn
The dead, lamenting still that Fortune made
A target for the bitter, burning sighs
Of Mejnūn, out of Ibni Salam brave.
From Leylā and from Mejnūn both fell tears
To wash away the obstacle, the will,
Of Ibni Salam, powerless and sad
Enduring grief of painful longing sweet.
So evil is the pain of emptiness—
An evil guide that leads to Death alone.
His longing sadness and his bitter grief
Soon worked on Ibni Salam's cypress frame,
Till, like a rattan, thin and quickly bent,
He dwindled in despair and 'gan to lose
The charm that kept him company of old.
He sank and weakened in a sad decline
That ways and deeds of yesterday forgot
His name: his couch at last was left his only friend,
And he its frail and feeble ornament.
'Tis sad, indeed, to tell in numbers true
How he, the exquisite, now lay abed
In sickly feebleness that daily grew
From weakness unto weakness: never cure
Was known, for none could know his grief.
No healing could be found to ease his pain.
At last, despairing, knowing life was void
Of all allure and comfort, knowing well
The joys that life had wantonly denied,
He gave his spirit in the hands of God
And entered into Paradise sublime.
    A common fate was his, to gain the world

And then to have it pass. Who knows it not?
It is, indeed, the custom of all life
Should rise in Spring and into Autumn sink.

    Now Leylā found a newer cause to weep.
His death now gave her openly excuse,
And thus the grieving maid had new lament,
And tore her weeping face with sharpened nails,
And rent her garment in a thousand shreds,
Disclosing unto all apparent cause
For every lamentation, burning now
The house wherein she dwelled: her lovely robes
She gave to pillage and destructive fire.
Her fragrant hair, as soft as musky rose
She soiled and tangled in a frenzy pure.
Her sighs and moanings knocked against the skies,
And, like the sky, of deepest black her garb.
Upon her lovely head were ashes cast
(A custom this, they say, of Arabs old,
That when the husband dies wife laments
If wife be left, a heavy year or two,
Bewailing and lamenting every day.)
This custom matched the Idol's grieving wish:
It gave her cause ostensible to weep,
And made her house the home of mourning wild.
Each day, from dawn till eve, she cried her fate.
At last, when many days had sadly sped
She left her home and took her heavy path
Unto the house wherein her father dwelt,
And there continued still to weep her loss,
With bitter, heartfelt tears in ceaseless flood.
Unending were her tears, both soon and late,
And in her heart the weeping Moon would cry
To God for mercy on the dead man's soul,
On Ibni Salam, he who, unaware
Had made her love to flourish in distress,
Who lifted high dissimulation's veil
And caused her secret sorrow to be known.

    Now Zayd, hearing of her sudden loss,
Again across the desert made his way
And saw again the sickened, sad Mejnūn
Among the wilderness of savage beasts

Still standing all alone in misery.
Saluting, Zayd let his news be known,
And told how Ibni Salam fell, the prize
Of Time inexorable, and slowly said:
    'Thy rival, Ibni Salam, unto Death
Has gone to join his peers: hear now the news
I bring thee gladly of thy rival's death.'

    But Mejnūn sighed anew, bewailing deep
And mourned aloud the new disaster come
On him who suffered much, that marvelling
Unhappy Zayd gazed long at him and failed
Of understanding of his new found plaint.

    'Sure, when a lover hears that Death has slain
His rival to the hand that he adores,
'Tis fitting then to joy, not fall to tears
And weep the fate that makes thy pathway clear.'
    So thinking, Zayd sought to find the cause
And asked the reason for his friend's distress.

    'O, loyal friend', said Mejnūn, 'have I now
No sense of shame and honour in my soul
That I should find an all unhallowed joy
In that which leaves me lesser than before?
Who gives his life attains to his belov'd,
While he who gives it not stays ever lost.
The dead was never foe to me, but friend,
For he and I both loved that Idol pure,
And thus a common love gave common cause.
Now he, in sweet surrender of his life
Attains perfection, holds his right degree,
While I remain deficient still of grace
And needs must weep. Now, therefore, do not blame.'

LXXII

Herein is set forth the Ode recited by Mejnūn upon the Death of Ibni Salam.

    Who is the only lover? He who gives
    His life and dying, thus for ever lives.
    The craven, shunning death and holding fast

To every fleeting breath so quickly past
No goal may claim
Of every lover's aim
Before his love his very soul to cast.

Perfection comes of selflessness divine,
Of immolation at the lover's shrine.
Who keeps his love must stand by all confessed
No lover, though by passion sore oppressed.
No lover he
Who dumbly still may see
With life enduring rage still unsuppressed.

Who is the only lover? He who finds
In death alone the union that binds
His soul and that he loves in perfect peace.
Who thus so wisely gives lest passion cease,
And finds the grief
Of separation, be it long or brief
The one and only way of sweet release.

Observe the moth, ye lovers, understand
Their age-long custom, found in every land;
How, burning in unsatisfied desire
Self immolation seeking at the fire
Of every flame.
Let lovers do the same
And gladly burn on love's own funeral pyre.

So die in love, for, dying fettered, bound
To love a heady joy is found
A death so timed brings forth the perfect ease
Of Hızır's Fountains: living streams that please:
The fount of life
The end of strife
The perfect cure for Love's distressed disease.

No charm or posset holds the sov'ran worth
Of curing Love's sweet passion on the earth.
Abandonment is named the only spell
Abandonment of life and love as well.
Thus losing life
And leaving mortal strife
In death thy love and thee may ever dwell.

Yet cease this idle talk of leaving life
And losing thus thy passion's dearest strife.
'Tis but Fuzūlī knows the secret road
'Tis he who sets it forth in happy ode—
This quality
Of winning loses instability
Forgets the tribute that to life is owed.

LXXIII

Herein is set forth the Account of the Adventure that befell Leylā after the Death of Ibni Salam, and of the Calamity that came upon her in this Abode of Trouble.

Time passed and Leylā mourned in her distress
While dwelling in her father's open house
She lived, still holding fast her deep set grief,
Renewing still each sigh as sigh she spent.
Whene'er it chanced she heard of sad distress
Afflicting one she knew, she gathered round
The saddened one, with all her grieving friends
And sang aloud the wailing song of grief.
'Twas Ibni Salam furnishing excuse
That Leylā seized to mourn for Mejnūn mad.
Her lips pronounced the name of him who died;
Her heart sang loud the name of him she loved.
The name she spoke aloud was diff'rent far
Both in degree and kind from that her heart
Rejoiced in naming secretly, with pride
Lamenting with a true pretence of grief.
And thus the fairy-born, disconsolate,
In grief illicit sat with licit cause.
Her grief was sore; it far o'ershadowed all
The grief of those who wept in company,
And slowly, one by one, they softly strayed
To other brighter paths, till all alone
One night with but a candle Leylā stayed.
And then the candle, with a heaving sigh
She straight extinguished. Darkness fell around
   'Tis proper', murmured Leylā, 'thus to dwell
In darkness in the gloom of blackest night
That needs no candle, while my flaming sigh
Suffices.'

         Still she stayed alone and wept
Confessing weakness to her pain and grief:
         'O Grief and Sorrow, leave me now in peace!
For but this single night be gone from me!
In solitary loneliness my course
I still maintain. Seek ye another mate,
And turn your face to others in distress.'

But seeing grief and sorrow could not end,
And frantic still, she turned to blackest Night.

         'O, dusky Night, as black as all my fate,
Swart as the fortune grim that dogs my step,
And causing my bewilderment of life:
Time was when ne'er a fleeting moment passed
When thou in easeful sloth might careless rest.
In ceaseless wandering every fleeting day
Was greatly filled. What change has now been wrought,
That ceaseless still thou holdest single place
Forswearing thus thy ever roaming state?
Is it, perchance, that thou hast found the goal
And final resting place that thou hast sought?
Or in the darkness hast thou lost thy way,
Bereft of progress in the circling gloom?
Thy garment black shows mourning as thy friend—
For whom, O Night, for whom, then, grievest thou?
My pain and sorrow overpower the sea;
Calamity's great torrent overwhelmed
My head, erstwhile held high. A target I
For Fortune's arrow. In the mill of fate
A stubborn grain am I now sadly found.
The wide expansive world is now a house
Wherein I mourn incessantly. No rest
No patience left, nor knowing how the end
Will come, or when, or in what manner dressed.
The very stars have faded into night;
The sky's dread scorpions, with venomed sting
Now scourge me, while the mirror of my dawn
Is rusted o'er; the sky forgets the morn
And all the blessings that it used to show.
And thou, O, Morn, say what has chanced with thee,
That now bereft of strength, in dumb dismay
No more may boast thy sweet accomplishment.

If still thy heart be glad, then gladly smile.
If love is now attained, be merciful.
Make now the cock companion to my plaint;
Let now the kettledrum with noisy throb
Accompany my accents of distress.
Give golden speech to every nightingale
That in the bosky thicket sweetly sings,
And show a sign of lovely morning's breath
That ushers forth a new and lovely day.'

Thus pleaded Leylā heavy in her grief,
Repeating o'er the sorrows of her heart,
And slowly learned that neither morn nor night
Could find a cure to bring her blissful ease.
Then turned she unto Him Who gave the gifts
Of morning and of evening to the world,
And, faltering in unaccustomed words
Began her dismal story to unfold.

'O, Thou, Who know'st the heart's most secret thoughts,
To Whom each sad condition is revealed,
My grief and sorrow still endure; no end
Is found. To whom shall I complain?
My grief is limitless and I am weak,
Companioned thus with never ending woe.
O, Lord, give either strength in suffering,
Or give me pain more suited to my strength.
If now I rend my robe of patience, then
The Way of Judgement full of danger lies:
Yet if I make surrender to my grief
I find it far beyond my feeble power.
Should I, in love, from chastity depart,
And know Mejnūn in intimate embrace,
I fear, unchaste, to trample underfoot
My chastity against Thy stern decree.
If then, in passion, strictly yet I guard
My honour, as a city fair is held,
I fear the smoke of Mejnūn's fiery sigh
May bring increase to sorrow that I bear.
The faithful still desire a good repute—
To flout it is a danger to be shunned.
This way and that way torn, O Lord, assist
My erring mind to reach conclusion firm.

'Tis Leylā, dazed with many miseries
And captive to affliction's bitter pain,
Who, knowing not a final resting place
Nor sure of any refuge, saving Thee,
Who prays Thee look in charity and love
As thus she holds the cup of ignorance
And let Thy kindness hide her many faults.
They say Mejnūn, matured by suffering
Is madly fall'n in love with suffering me,
But, lacking head or foot, unworthy I
With beauty gone, of his undying love.
An atom of a thorn am I, as dust upon the road
The dust of dust upon the way.
And e'en my soul
That in my body still is housed, is Thine.
As trustee only do I keep my store
Of treasured beauty granted but by Thee.
'Tis thou hast given such beauty as I own.
O mighty Lord, now help me in this trust
That I may guard until the Judgement Day
What Thou hast given, then at Thy approach,
When near Thy awful Presence I attain,
I still may keep my brow serene and clear
And hold my face unsullied, without shame.'

LXXIV

Herein is set forth Leylā's Prayer in the Difficulty of Decision.

O Lord, for the Truth of Perfection, found in the Courts of the Great.
For God, Divine in His Goodness, Consummate in all His Estate,
For Truth of the Prophet Mustafa, with countenance constantly bright,
Whose lustre has given the world its all illumining light:
My body submerge in the ocean of love
For the sake of the truth that was sent from above
To furnish for Moses Thy sweet guidance clear
And urge him to follow the laws of Hızır.
Change now, I beseech Thee, my desolate eve
For glory of Morning my sorrow relieve
With daybreak of union, bringing the breath
Of love to my spirit now closing in death.
Let not all my woe and affliction bring ill
Let love that is Thine all encompass me still.

'Tis I who have strayed from the path clearly shown,
Exhibit Thy guidance; Thy counsel make known
For the sake of the guide at Thy hand ever near
Show now the dear pathway that runs straight and clear,
Still letting my heart all its sorrows endure
With those yet approved in a pasion still pure.
Like Fuzūlī, may Thou my devotion to prayer
Complete and inspire, leaving little for care.

LXXV

Herein is set forth the Epilogue to this Section of the Story of Leylā and Mejnūn.

As thus, in weakened state, the Moon made prayer
And added supplication of despair,
She sounded suddenly the journey bell
And summoned forth the camel driver well
Accustomed to migration's dreary round,
With never solace in seclusion found.
Upon the camel's back in cradles laid
Was fastened many a moon aspiring maid,
While Leylā, wretched in a litter lay
Still weak and lonely, trying still to pray,
And praying, adding yet a grievous load
To that great hump the camel ever owed
To devil's handiwork. Her wailing knell
Choked into silence all the tinkling bell:
And heady wine of love, demanding yeast
From saddened eyes, made drunk the savage beast.

LXXVI

Herein is set forth the Manner in which Leylā related her Secret to the Camel, and the Way in which she set forth her Supplication.

The grunting camel, ugly and mis-shaped,
Bereft of beauty, owned a cheerfulness
That prompted Leylā to express her grief
In words as fragrant as the morning dew:

'O, thou, with hair sweet-scented as the rose,
With face so like the rose, with nature sweet
Though Nature still conspires to work thee ill,

With pricking thorns and naked pad on stone,
With head unguarded from the fiery rays
The sun pours down in torrid frenzy, thou
Who sweetly knows a hundred unions gone,
A hundred passions with a sacred love,
Say now, what moves within thy smitten brain?
Tell of the scars of love upon thy breast.
From whence came all the cruelty and pain
That makes thee groan, lamenting every step,
Thus filling every moment with lament?
Thy path is still the path all lovers take,
If thou art yet a lover, I thy friend
And dear companion, understanding all
That causes tears of love's dear torment born.
Though now, all weeping with the grief of love
Thou still within this caravan abid'st,
No choice is thine, no more than choice is mine.
Thy leading rein is held in alien hand
And chance selects thy road as chance has made
Of me a haply found companion sad.
Now therefore, let thy mercy understand
And see my yearning with a kindly eye;
Bring forth compassion, build a stately deed
And make thy way to where my Mejnūn lives.
This saddened soul take now to that dear Moon,
Take now this sorrow to its healing fount.'

She paused and straight a visitation strange,
A rare unconsciousness upon her fell.
Insensible to all her living state,
The light that gave her life an instant fled.
And down she sank deep in a fainting trance.
The group of friends about her hurried on
Unknowing that she lay as dead, so deep
The darkness that had gathered all around.
The very camel driver knew it not
And held his path in stolid ignorance.

Some time had passed before returning sense
Brought back the fairy-faced to see the world
Where all was black and where confusion reigned,
Where neither friendly voice nor camel grunt
Was borne upon the chill and darksome night.

With opening eyes she sought to pierce the gloom
In vain endeavour, seeking for the train.
Now trouble piled on trouble on her head
Set down its heavy weight. Upon her feet
She swayed, unsteady yet, but moving o'er
The darkened desert, venting feeble cries
In hope to reach her distant, moving friends.
Now north, now south, in all directions sped
The maid forlorn. Her cries shook all the air,
But ne'er a trace of guide or road was found.
The caravan had vanished. She alone
Of all its host, she with jasmine breast.
The cypress statured, gently nurtured maid,
Stayed all alone within the desert dark
Where never moon may brightly lucent rise,
Controlled by heaven's still revolving sphere.
So now, the caravan, with Leylā gone,
Lost all its light in deep abysmal gloom,
And soon the sun, fast rising o'er the plain,
All solitary, as was Leylā now,
A litter spread upon the camel cow
Of finest gold entwinéd in its rays.
And now, with ever growing light of day
The maid of jasmine cheek pursued her road
Unto the land where Mejnūn in his grief
Full sorely sorrowed. Looking all about
A sadly woeful figure she espied,
And paused to ask of him a halting place,
As she, o'er all the desert knew no road.
With honeyed voice and accents sweetly soft
She asked his name. In magic waves the sound
Sped forth and reached the saddened slave, whose head
Was bowed in deep dejection. As he heard
He raised aloft his abject humbled head
And answered softly:
     'I am Mejnūn called.'

'O false conceited arrogance', she said,
'Let not the ant speak as the dragon dread;
Nor carrion claim with overweening pride
That he the nightingale is ever named;
Nor let the thorn, in stupid boast proclaim
Himself the rose.'

    Then Mejnūn made reply:
'Unique among the pearls that deck the world,
Is't true that thou thy Mejnūn knowest not?
Say now, what signs are put to mark his brow:
From what fond sign would recognition come?
What would'st expect to see?'
         'So fairy-faced',
Said Leylā softly, 'are his features clear!
So excellent his cypress slender frame!
But thou, bewildered slave of mourning drear,
With broken features, body bent and mean,
No sign compares with him, the world's belov'd,
Mejnūn, the greatest of the great, while thou,
A broken, headless footless wreck I see.'

'All they who love,' said Mejnūn, 'suffer too,
Though suffering should dwell with man alone,
While woman's lot should be all happiness.'

'A nimble finder of excuse art thou,'
Then Leylā made reply. 'A chanter, too,
Of all the fetters of my aching heart.
Suppose, indeed that grief thy face cast down,
Suppose thy figure bent by cruelty,
They say that Mejnūn owns intelligence,
They say his style is pure, his verses sweet.
But where, in thee, is heart inspiring air?
What heart inspiring poems spring unthought
From golden lips that all accord Mejnūn?'

'The greater knowledge, greater speech is lost,'
Mejnūn replied in sadness. 'Tearful eyes
Are witness all-sufficing to express
The state, and witness make of love's distress.
The apt arrangement of the chosen word
Is proof most eloquent of lover's joy,
For only comfort seeks release in verse.
The lover, fallen deep in sad distress
As I am deeply fallen, never needs
Excuse or pardon for his speechless state.'

'And yet I doubt thee,' Leylā still maintained.
'Now prove thy claim that Mejnūn is thy name,
And if thy love be Leylā, now set forth
In verses all the glory that has passed
And make the vanished moment live again.'

LXXVII

Herein is set forth the Manner in which Mejnūn made his sorrowful Condition known to Leylā by telling the story of his past Experience.

When Mejnūn, sorrowing, these phrases heard,
And knew that still she hungered for a word
That cunningly would 'stablish both his claim
To be himself and all his love aflame,
He gathered all his deep extensive grief
And shortly answered her in accents brief.[100]

'O, thou, who, in the garden of my pain
Spread'st tears as copious as the clouds their rain,
Nor giving light upon the falling thread
Of all the anguish gathered round my head,
Ask not, nor wonder how my time is spent,
Nor of the sorrow love has sadly sent.
Shall I recount in saddened words again
How love's repining brings unending pain?
Should I neglect the counsel of my friend?
And blame that those that wish me ill still send?
For many days I suffered torment's pain
And daily went to school in sun and rain.
Each day was spent in torment till the night
Closed down upon the world and hid its light.
Time passed and sland'rous wicked tongues increased
The evil tales that, started, never ceased,
Till, at the dictates of the family ties
Love parted from me, though Love never dies.
My story gained a credence o'er the earth,
The while my parents sought some cure of worth
To end the throbbing of my fevered brain,
And still the passion making me insane.
The doctors' treatment humbly I withstood
But doctors' cures held nothing that was good.

Afar to holy Kaaba was I sent
To make a pilgrimage, but all was spent
In vain endeavour. Never opened door
To cure my sickness, friends could see no more
Despairing of the healing of my mind,
And in abandonment they showed them kind.

'Now all alone to Nevfel did I make
A supplication that he nobly take
His sword on my behalf; but from his aid
No nearer did I reach to win my maid,

'And then came woe! Came Ibni Salam bold,
And brought me torment never known of old.
The tidings brought by Zayd I still believed
And true his every promise I conceived.
In hope still unfulfilled my days have passed,
While evil fortune ever evil cast.
To reach conclusion, all my virile frame
Deep into ruin fell, while still the name
Of Mejnūn earned no joy at Fortune's hand,
Found naught of pleasure. Life was barren sand.'

Now separation spurred his aching heart
And in this ode put all he knew of art.

LXXVIII

Herein is set forth the Ode recited by Mejnūn to Leylā.

No instant brief did Fortune's changing wheel
Revolve in harmony with my desire,
Nor yet did union sweet
Afford divine elixir of content
To send my sorrows into banishment.
With Love I ne'er could meet
Though from her hand
I suffered deep distress of aching heart
That none but lovers ever understand
Nor never feel the smart.
For she alone who knew my aching heart
Found naught to ease

Did nothing that could please
Nor stilled a single cry as tears, like rain,
Fell fast from grieving eyes.
The vale of absence held my wretched life.
To exile I surrendered all my days.
I sought my Moon in many lonely ways
While she I sought came never once a prize
To ease my thoughts with union, still my strife.

O friend, if friend ye be, blame not the sight
Of this my collar torn from off my coat.
For all who see the rose in steady light,
In tearing robes leave sanity, and float
All rudderless. Perfection's Sov'ranty
Is found when, as the King of Poverty,
Thou art enthroned—
A conquest never owned
By mighty *Hakan* or the great *Fağfur*
Who ruled with love intense and passion pure.

What purpose lies in spilling all my blood
With evil sword, O Fortune?
Why then, O Fortune, spill in mighty streams
The life blood of my soul: the lovers' dreams
Hold more than merely suffering and pain:
Mean more than bleeding hearts that bleed again.

My love a promise made and swore that friend
And guardian she would be till life should end.
Yet when the hour of friendship came,
I called her name:
I clearly asked that she compassion send.
With vows forgot
And promises remembered not,
She left me in a lone and weary state
All day disconsolate.
None know the dungeon of affliction deep
Wherein intelligence shall ever creep
Still hoping for release,
Save him who roamed at ease
Within the wide dominion of the mad.
'Twas not alone Fuzūlī told the sad
Uneasy secret of his love: all those
Who taste of love their secret must disclose.

LXXIX

Herein is set forth the Manner in which Leylā came to know and recognize Mejnūn, and how, at the Price of her Soul, she became a Purchaser of his Goods of Union.

When Leylā came to knowledge that the wretch
Who stood before her was indeed Mejnūn,
A flood of tears, o'erspread her pallid cheek,
And, weeping sore, she murmured in distress:

'O light of both my eyes, a stranger still
To me, yet close and kindred to the beast;
In thee I see my own belovéd, now
I know 'tis thee. Thou doctor to my soul!
Thy name alone my tongue unceasing cries
All yesterday, all night and every day.
Thy thought and image dwells in constancy
Unshaken in my lonely pining heart.
Forgive my lack of recognition mad
For I am drunk with sorrow, lawful faults
Those faults that drunkenly are born
For thee, unknowing even of thyself
How yet may others certainly be known?
The moment all thy perfume struck my brain
That moment all the moonbeam of thy face
Fell sweet athwart my eyes, my soul, beyond
Itself in wild bewilderment of love
Grew stranger to itself, while countless pain.
This fragile body sorely was distressed.
An ocean wide of deep astonishment
All differentiation left my sense
Twixt thee and all a hundred strangers found.
Bestow excuse, O Idol of my soul,
Be not censorious, vex me not with rage,
For, lacking thee, my heart in many shards
Lay ruined. Now thy sweetly dear return
Inspires my heart anew with hundredfold
Of thanks and blessing: in my garden fair
My rose of hope with too much hoping died
Of sad satiety.
        O Lord, what dream is here?
What trick imagination plays, that sees
The light of all my hope? My life is bright

Again with happiness, from heavy sleep
My luck at last has risen into day.
O, heart, that vainly used to sigh and weep
In empty hunger for a union,
Now see prosperity so near at hand,
Now know the birthing of the joy of love,
And now, with God's dear aid, refrain from tears
Forgetting all the weeping that has passed.
And thou, dear eye, so pale of many pearls,
So weary, seeking ever for Mejnūn,
See now, the jasmine breasted is at hand.
Now scatter pearls of joy before his feet
And then my soul, with waiting sore oppressed,
Desiring deeply to behold thy love,
Know now that love is here: thy body leave
Forsake me now: to love for ever cleave.'

Her story told, then Leylā, fairy-born
Set forth this poem burning with desire.

LXXX

Herein is set forth the Gazel composed by Leylā.

Dread Fortune never joyed my heart
Before it wounded deep,
Nor gave me gladness till her art
Had tested every way
To turn to darkest night my brightest day,
And on my head let every sorrow creep.

With cruelty she broke my fragile heart,
A hundred pieces fell
About my feet, each shard a fiery dart
And in the meadow green
Of all the world no happiness was seen:
She changed my springing heaven into hell.

Thank God that now at last my aching heart
Its guerdon late receives,
And Fortune, playing still her part
Still leaves without regret
The heart that joy nor passion may forget
My heart, with joy at hand, no longer grieves.

The peoples of the world small patience know,
Nor hold that little long;
For time, spite every sorrow still will show
Solution ere the end,
And patience at the last will surely send
Reward to still the sadly grieving song.

In this the passion dear of love I make
A gain from union
Fuzūlī, he who gladly lets him break
His life for this
Dear love, in life has nothing done amiss
As close to love he holds communion.

LXXXI

Herein is related the Manner of the bewildered Mejnūn's utter Astonishment, and the Manner in which he, in his Turn was completely unaware of Leylā's Identity.

Mejnūn, amazed, in accents all confused,
In stumbling words expressed bewilderment
In her and all she spoke.
                         'O, thou,' he said
Who sadly makest all thy secret known,
And now with words, make'st this, my fallen head
To rear itself again, erect and strong,
Say swiftly who thou art, make known the name
The people use for thee: recount thy aim
And purpose in this wilderness so vile.
Thine elegance revives my drooping soul:
It springs anew from all thy language sweet.
'Tis clear thy nature, as thy words, is soft
And sweet, thy accents gladden all my soul.
'Twould seem that thou and I acquaintance hold
Yet name the land that proudly gave thee birth,
And tell the path thou blindly followest.
If thou art tulip rare, then name thy mount:
If iris, where the garden of thy growth?
Thy speech is sweetest music in my ear,
And o'er my heart's distress fond music showers.
Such conduct from a stranger never yet

Was known by stranger. Dear familiar thought
As thine was never void of interest.
Conciliation has deliberate birth,
'Tis never born upon an idle wind.
So why and wherefore comes thy kind intent
To cast the soothing shadow o'er my head?
Were sanity my handmaid, trav'lling near
My person, resting ever close at hand,
Then knowledge would not 'scape my scattered wits;
Had grief not emptied my insensate heart
Were but my eyes uncurtained of their tears,
This unawareness would not hold its place.
But now my scattered wits no answer give.
I pray thee, tell me who and what thou art.'

LXXXII

Herein is set forth the Ode recited by Mejnūn to Leylā.

Now all intoxicated, knowing not the world,
In deep despair now asking who I be,
Who Saki? What the wine
That all unknowing, red and white, is whirled
In single cup confused,
Though asking Love with tearful eye to see
The wishes of this lovesick heart of mine,
Should Love be kind, yet still with mind bemused
With mingled thoughts, I never find the art
To tell the single thought within my heart.

What is this union in disunion found?
How name the distancy that lovers know?
That separates while yet above the ground
They dwell in sorrow?
No skill nor knowledge he who knows the cause
Of all the world and all its mystery;
Say rather, he whose life without a pause
Is passed in sad unknowing misery,
Is he who rests him skilled in every art
Though knowing not the springs that move his heart.

Thy cry Fuzūlī echoes o'er the earth
And grieving thus the mighty world entire
Perchance brings pleasure to thy cruel breast,
Perchance affliction is our only worth.
If this be so, what cause may rouse thy ires,
Why make these quarrels ever without rest?
If truly Love's affliction gives thee joy,
Why then these mazy methods still employ?

LXXXIII

Herein is set forth Leylā's Reply to Mejnūn.

Then Leylā spoke:
    'O soul's companion dear,
Desire of this distressed and wounded heart,
See now the news that kindly Fortune brings
That all thy dearest wishes are achieved;
See now, the cup o'erbrims with friendship's wine.
See now the news that kindly Fortune brings
That thy desire divinely is fulfilled,
And now, at last, thy passion profit earns.
See now, again, the news that Fortune brings
That every hope is now at last attained;
With God's assistance all thy purpose gained.

'I am thy Leylā, once thy soul's desire,
Thy one desire in sad exhausted state.
This beauty made thy yearning in distress:
This union, now at hand, was all thy need.
The day has come when love is granted thee:
Make no delay, nor fail in duty clear.
Beware neglect, spurn not this proffered gift,
This union call a sweet propriety
God-sent from Heaven. Come without delay,
Nor spurn, nor long retard occasion found.
My heart is vowed to union with thee
While all my soul was ever thine in trust.
It lies before thee, do not now neglect
The maid thy Fortune places in thy power.
Come, pay the vow; take now the trust fulfilled.
If sick thou art, in me a doctor find.

If deep in love thou art, know me thy love.
Come, dwell with me in rapture of desire,
And for a fleeting moment be my mate.
Give lustre to the eye, bold narcissus,
With all the tulip of thy comely lip:
Endow the sweet fresh basil with new grace;
Enhance deep exotic turquoise with the rose
That in the ruby glows make limpid sweet
The food that loving hearts may all desire.
Match now the judas flower and blushing rose,
Let Life's sweet waters reach to far Hızır.
If now all changed, and thou art passionless,
Unwounded by a grief and trouble sore,
By showing now a counterfeited sign,
Bring not to thee and me sad sorrow's pain.
Display sagacity's intelligence,
Avoid disgrace to each and every known.
O, lovely rose, what shame is deeply found
If thou and I in colour do not match!
That I should tender thee the sun, my face,
While thou no slightest warmth should'st manifest!
What shame that stretching thus my virgin cup
Before thee, saying: "Come, and deeply drink!"
Thou restest still in slothful lethargy,
Not springing to thy feet with hot desire!
'Tis rare to find the lover make the loved
And most adored a cheap coquette of love:
Or yet a rose to make a proud display
Before the amorous nightingale, while he
In shameful sloth ignores the proffered gift.'

    The heart adoring Idol now began
To draw near Mejnūn, telling o'er this ode.

LXXXIV

Herein is set forth the Ode recited by Leylā as she drew near to Mejnun.

Mad am I made for love alone of thee;
'Tis thou hast caused this madness in my veins,
How then explain thy standing now aloof
In silence cold,
Nor seeking any proof

Or reason why desire o'ersteps the reins
Of all decorum, setting virtue free
Of all the rules a hundred sages told?

No word of censure could my reason find
If publicly thou provedst thee unkind.
Excuse were easy found.
But from the public to the private state
Should make a change from furnace heat to ice,
And yet, though on the ground
I kneel, in privacy, what angry fate
Still holds in hand the ever loaded dice
That leaves thee cold and careless in thine ease,
And holds me still in unfulfilled disease?

If ignorant, unknowing of my state,
Or knowing not thou wert my only mate
Thy mercy were withheld,
Then bare of hurt were all thy actions cold.
But knowledge rests with thee, the tree is felled
And every branch repeats the message old:
How then construe deliberate intent
Or how in frigid coldness find content?

They say that oftentimes the nightingale
In battle fights that he may win the rose;
Yet haply should he see the flower that blows
In blushing beauty and forget the tale
Of love he sang,
Who then could understand his troubled mind?
This fairy near me hears the words that rang
About my head for many ages passed,
Yet still without a reason stays unkind.
Fuzūlī, say, what crime has overcast
This maid, that, fallen in a deep disgrace,
With supplication spurned, she hides her face?

LXXXV

Herein is related Mejnūn's aloofness and his Refusal of Leylā, and the Manner in which he proved the purity of his moral Qualities.

'O lovely Idol, fairy faced and sweet,'
Spoke Mejnūn softly, 'see, it is not meet
To strike the match beneath the weakly straw.

Thy image only, pure without a flaw,
Gives more and fiercer heat than may consume
My feebleness; yet may I not resume
My fiercely burning passion, but withstand
The guerdon of thy sweetly proffered hand.
Beware, sweet jasmine breasted maid, beware,
Nor closely bring thy cheek's sweet mirror rare,
For this thou see'est, incorporeal
Has now no use for mirror to reveal
An image pure and holy; time has passed
When in my eyes the light of love was cast.
O maiden, when thou sought'st to hide thy face
And closed thyself within a secret place.
No more I have the power of sight in me,
No more thy place before me can I see.
Love, builder of a settled firm estate
Declared that we have union, I thy mate
But not below on this our mortal earth,
But spiritual our state, of greater worth.
Mere thought of face and figure, form divine,
In me is now outgrown, God save that thine,
The fairest seen in all the mighty land
Should move me from the rock on which I stand.
The pleasure born of captivating cheek
That sweetly sickly sadness all may seek,
Is parted from me.
                'God forbid, indeed,
That I again its pleasure sadly need.
Long ages past my soul departed hence
And left my body, soulless, empty, whence
Thou understandest, in my body now
There dwells another soul: come witness how
Within my body now, and quite secure
Thy soul resides in every passion pure.
The blood within my heart, the light of eye
Art thou, and should I explanation try
Of this my freeing of myself of thee,
Thy passion soon would vanish as in me.
Yet still in me thy sadly lovely face
Is manifest in this and every place,
Now I myself am naught, for this my heart
Beats currently with thine: 'Tis thou who art.
Transfigured now in every heaving sigh.

But consolation comes: if I am I
Tormented thus, then what art thou, my dear?
If thou art thou, then make the riddle clear
And name my name, the name I dread to hear.
Now swollen as I am with radiance
And filled o'erflowing with thy brilliance,
'Twere evil now to look for sign outside
Thyself, or seek for other joys untried.
When all thy passion was a tender child
And Fortune still my teacher, never wild,
It fettered still my heart with heavy chain
And taught old *Abjed's*[101] lesson once again.
But now, when long maturing years have sped
No more I need the lesson of Abjed.
Perfection knowing of the letters writ
By those in love, we no more study it.
Since written love found its perfection grand
To write of love is all I understand.
My name alone is fallen in disgrace;
Seek not my footsteps: come not near my place.
Rest still behind thy veil of chastity
And keep thy name still sweet in purity.
The world now calls me Mejnūn, meaning mad,
Entrusting me alone with passion sad.
Beware lest close thy name the legend cling
And all the world at thee the insult fling.
They say that Leylā treads a shameful road,
That only Fate to Mejnūn truly owed.
Know now that I am Mejnūn, O my dear,
So maddened that on earth I have no peer;
Nor seek to change that sweet condition clear.
With Mejnūn, keep thyself apart, not near.
  'O sympathising fairy facéd friend
I am alone Mejnūn: now apprehend
That I alone to madness have a claim,
For I alone am worthy: Leylā's fame
Should not be sullied naming Leylā mad
Change not thy way of life, no more be sad.
This sympathy and suffering makes me glad.
Let all thy life be passed behind a veil
That modesty may be thy habit pale
And hidden. March not as the sun
And shine in every corner thou hast won.

Show not thy beauty in the common mart
Nor let the chaste with fiery blushes smart.
Remember too, whatever manner thine
Is witness to this conduct sad of mine,
For I upon the road of Love am dust,
Yet all acclaim me pure and free from lust.
Be merciful to me, O Idol loyal,
Let not the wagging tongues of slander spoil
Thy fair repute; keep still thy custom strict
And follow still my softly spoke edict,
Thus keeping honour free from injury,
Thy purse of fame quite free from penury.'

Approaching as he spoke this counsel fair,
Mejnūn recited now this poem rare.

LXXXVI

Herein is set forth the Poem addressed to Leylā by Mejnūn.

No union does the heart require
With insubstantial flesh,
In Love's dear image is the fire
That may the heart refresh.
Outside the lover's heart, the truth
That love may live brings but bewilderment:
True love is absolute, it knows no truth,
Admitting never slight impediment
To sweet perfection.
And thus the honest man, although he see
The fairest of the fairest face
Will never sink bewildered, knowing he
Attains perfection
Only when from Beauty he is free,
Perfection cannot live in Beauty's place.

And as a mere idolator to find
A love supreme in Beauty's outward shape,
Is but to show the lover wholly blind
And deep in ignorance,
No rage holds fast to that impermanance
That soon, with time, may vanish and escape.
Well knowing that a friend within the heart
Revolves not in the compass of the eye,

Nor moves his resting place,
But steadfast still remains in happy grace
As permanent in stationary art
As is the lofty mansion of the sky.
'Tis thus that stern philosophy's decree
Ordains the tablet of the heart to be
Of all the world's dark, sinful lusting free,
For he who in a single God believes
Embroiders not his vision with designs,
Nor in the realm of spirit may he lose
His love of images, not yet receives
The pearl of truth and want only consigns
Its preciousness to those who idly choose
To trample in ecstatic pleasure sweet
And crush its heart beneath their careless feet.

He who sees the inner light
Is fettered not by beauty bright
With many-sided charm.
'Tis but Fuzūlī, lacking vision clear
With naught of understanding of its harm
Who rests him fettered still by Beauty near.

LXXXVII

Herein is set forth the Manner in which Leylā gave her Approval of Mejnūn's Conduct, and her sure and certain Knowledge of the Soundness of his Belief.

Then murmured Leylā:
     'O, thou perfect soul,
Who near to God might walk in chastity,
The Miraj of Perfection, Apex high,
How often did I humbly make request
To know of all thy sweet condition pure!
'Tis now, I grow to know thee as thou art!
'Tis now, great God be bless'd, I see the heights
Now reached and held by thy nobility.
And now my acclamations loudly rise
Extolling all thy nature pure and fine.
Though but a form of earth, as all are here,
How right and lovely sweet contentedness

And passion calm, all anger swept away!
I doubted once thy love, and mused at times
Lest insincerity were there enthroned,
And thus in testing thy conduct o'er.
But now, in God's eternal glory bright,
I know thy mind and know that union
In thy clear sight is worthy but of blame.
At first this saddened, now it gladdens me,
And frees me from the tie that was unchaste,
When I, so selfish, dwelt in ignorance,
By ignorance intoxicated oft.
In vain adornment would I curl my lock
And deepen still the mole upon my cheek,
Thus spending precious hours in useless art
In idle thought that thou, in union
With this my curl and that my painted mole
Still pined in deep desire. But now the light
Of understanding of thy holy thought
The *Miraj* of thy dear perfection's truth
Makes bright the deep recesses of my heart.
Though dedicated once to healing cure
And gladdening the hungry searching eye,
With knowledge now my lock and cherished mole,
My dusky eye and rosy reddened cheek
No more in day or night adorn my soul.
If haply for a moment thy dear gaze
May fall upon them and in falling find
Some little comfort for thy great distress,
And in attaining this, thy dearest wish,
Some merit I myself might hope to win.
But if thy spirit finds my beauty rare
Of little worth alone to ease thy soul,
Then what shall mean my beauty rare to me?
The lovely pearl, in body meanly housed,
My soul, the only currency of worth,
Still housed within my fleshly treasury,
I once did think to spend at thy desire,
To scatter all about thee and rejoice
In prodigality so madly found;
And scattering, attainment gladly find
That sweetly sought for union with thee;
And in that union my freedom find
From all my lonely desolation drear.

But since desire no more may hope to reach
Fulfilment, wherefore let my name in vain
Be marred? If now existence in the world
I have forsworn, and chosen now to tread
Extinction's path, I seek no more to live,
Nor wait until the passing years grey o'er
My wasted features growing old and wan.
'Tis now the hour is ripe for furbishing
The mirror and of every attribute
Attaching to my person I am free,
And stand alone in independence clear.
My heart is filled with all of sorrow's tears:
My heart is captive as the folded bud.
The time arrived when, swollen as the bud
That bursts its folded petals in its pride,
I burst my bonds and sought the union
With love, as buds seek union with the sun.
'Twas written that I fold my carpet up
And end my relation with myself,
That in extinction, covering I find
For all my body, and before my face
Lift high the masking veil extinction brings.
That still my lovely cheek, though undesired
Of thee, may yet from other eyes be bid,
For beauty, if intelligent, must share
The sweet desires to which her love inclines.
If now my lover joys not in my grace,
And needs no more my loveliness of face,
'Twere ill becoming to find sweet content
In less than he demands.'
      Thus Leylā spent
Her words in understanding, then this ode
She spoke and all her comprehension showed.

LXXXVIII

Herein is set forth the Ode spoken by Leylā in which she demonstrated her perfect understanding of Mejnūn.

Though lovely, she who never makes a gift
Of all her beauty to her lover dear
Remains imperfect, lacking still the clear
Bright spirit of perfection. Little shrift

Is due to Beauty that attracts no Love:
Incapable of being loved is she
Who still attraction holds not: for above
Its mere possession is the power of lovely face.
For ever kept in secret hidden place
Where those who value not may never see,
Where those, that lack the knowledge mystical,
God's handiwork find all unmagical.
That man who seeks a sweet communion
With beauty, but with flesh needs union.
But he who knows of sweet perfection found,
Twixt union and separation finds
No difference, for he knows how each is bound
To each, afar and near the spirit binds
While on his loved one every lover spends
The riches of his life, forgiving all
The cruelties that from his loved one fall.
All beauties haply seek to gain their end
By sweet coquettish airs, the lover true
Knows well reality stays not in new
Sweet scented lock, or freshly painted mole.
No beauty of itself may make him whole.

Fuzūlī, see how in the world so wide
Thou roamest, still ascetic, still untried
Within thy ignorance all unaware
Of how they end, all those who true love dare.

LXXXIX

Herein is set forth the Epilogue to this Section of the Story of Leylā and Mejnūn.

The Moon had scarcely closed her poem sad
When 'fore her eyes the camel driver rode,
A camel cow with quickly running man
As swift as morning breeze came o'er the plain.
And thus the rose-cheeked, jasmine breasted maid
Was 'ware her absence was no longer hid,
That swiftly now the desert suffered search.
She knew that dark suspicion ever dwelled
Within the rival's heart, knew, too, that grief

Apportioned to the heart afflicts the soul.
Full well she knew that not an instant lost
Since her withdrawal and the search began
And thus, ere yet the thorn could reach the rose
The rose unto the garden bade farewell.
Before Mejnūn her absence had embraced
She fled, with quickly moving, tireless feet,
While he, the seeker, seeking now the Sun
Retarded now his hot impatient haste,
Enjoyed the satisfaction in the heart
That comes of goal achieved, and turned his thoughts
To easy finding of a halting place.
Then joyful, with the royal falcon caught
He left it in its nest. The gardener
Rejoiced again to have his sapling near,
While Mejnūn, left again in loneliness
Again to sorrow turned his every thought,
Again found friendship with the snake and ant.
With strength exhausted, full of restlessness,
He had no choice nor will, but turned his steps
Once more unto the desert's dreary waste.

XC

Herein is set forth the Miraj of Mejnūn's Virtues and an Expression of the Degree of the Goodness of his Moral Qualities.

The King of Kings in all the land of Grief and sore Distress
Mejnūn, by name, still cherishing his sorrow and his pain,
So pure in soul that over all the world
His like had ne'er in any former age
Been known of man: that prosp'rous City of God
Preserved his seat, a reverence deeply was paid
In sacred trust by every spirit's dear shade.
The hatred early bestowed by the wickedness Adam begat
Left him now all alone, committed to solitude sad.
Whene'er the beast in his hand he clasped, ferocity wild
Departed and gained as a friend this human, fashioned of clay;
The beast and the bird in its flight his outward associates grew
While angels hymning their songs his inner spirit embraced.
So kindly his every mood, so gentle his every thought
He found him free of the crowd, absolved from the pain that it brought.

This roamer throughout all the world knew nothing of heat or of cold
He knew the esteem of the world, he counted possession as naught.
His body became full of light, no eating or drinking defiled
The purity found in his soul. Such purity had he acquired
Through unreality's cloud his eye like an arrow had sped
And scattering every doubt had left only truth clear revealed.
For rank or degree his respect had slight as his confidence grown
His aim through Creation to find the divine Creator sublime.
In subtle distinction of thought he balanced the meaning of words
With voice no less gentle than sweet, his style so sweet, manner straight,
Each instant he lifted his voice and chanted in grieving tones
The birds of the air spread their wings and poised them aloft on the breeze.
Sometimes a *gazel*[102] he composed, sometimes a *kaside*[103] sweet
Yes, he so hardly oppressed, so battered, by cruelty sang,
In anguish, heavenly songs that chanted each saint in his turn
That many a well belov'd friend he gained with his voice raised in song.
They brought to completion his words, again and again sang his praise
And thus in the regions of man, this stranger bereft of his joy
A new and especial renown from his music gained a new fame.
His voice and his mind in their chains, his beauty fettered to grief
Had riveted prisoner made of those who a competence owned.
For all who attain to his state, perfection's high apex attain
Alone may be worthy of praise, alone may perfection claim.
In manifestation of this Mejnūn in an ode set it down
Repeating in musical voice these verses written in heat.

XCI

Herein is set forth the Ode recited by Mejnūn.

> The world which seems a prosperous City fair
> Is but a waste to those beyond the world:
> Yet mid the waste, mid all its foetid air
> The mighty treasure of all health is curled.

> So wise the image worshipper, so high
> In self esteem his imitation stays:
> That we who know Reality's sad sigh
> Know how in ignorance he spends his days.

Those lacking knowledge deem the world a drink
Of easeful comfort: we, the doctors, know
For we have filled the cup e'en to its brink,
And drunken, knowing blood will only flow.

We know possession of the world's estate
Proves nothing fruitful, be he young or old.
Time was they thought that Suleyman the Great
Owned all—But Suleyman has long been cold!

Fuzūlī! Thou hast named as things apart
And separate: the wineshop and the place
Of worship: we who thought thy wit and art
Were great, now hide the shamed, deceivéd face.

XCII

Herein is related the Manner in which the Spring of Leylā's Life reached its Autumn.

Now Saki, let the merriment of wine
Brim up and fill each overflowing eye:
Let beaded cup make still incessant round
For on a mirthful journey now thy course
Is firmly set: let not endeavour fail:
Make full the pleasure of the men of worth;
In orgy pass the tulip covered cup
To all who seek the madness of its bliss.
But, more than all, let it o'erbrim for me,
Now resting still half drunk, with heavy chains
That fetter still my soul to angry grief.
The orgy of the men of mirth is sweet
Were all its aim concentred on one goal;
So beautiful the carpet of delight
Were perseverance in its laying found.
The writer of the history of time
Who tells in words the state of every day,
To this sad story, now approaching close
Its ending, this conclusion sadly makes:
That Leylā, finding naught of comfort left,
Nor knowing union with her only love,
Now parted sadly from the mad Mejnūn,
And ceased relation with the busy world,
And gave her soul no further second's thought.

The season came when *Day's* all plundering hand,
(The hand that still controls the passing time)
The carpet of her rosary sublime
All folded up, while fields and gardens all
Became a gloomy house of mourning dark,
Enlivened only with the crow's harsh cry.
The tulip wept and let its petals droop
As Leylā's petals drooped in spirit too,
And like to Mejnūn, withered in his pain
The branches of the judas tree were shrunk.
The lightning injured all the stately trees,
They quivered, growing thin and pale of face,
The candle of the hyacinth expired,
And with the tulip fell in lonely death.
The *sırsır*,[104] roaming cold and fatal wind,
O'er all the vineyard spread a darkness drear,
While still the rose in fear of wind's assault,
And tulip, from the cruel morning breeze
Left all their clothes upon the vineyard bare
And lost their rubies on the mountain high.
Each river now, cold blooded as a snake,
Distilled a poison from each tremoured wave;
The rain that fell from heaven to the earth
Fell down in drops as sharp as head of spear.
So heavy o'er the vineyard lay the curse
Of cruel juggling with the season's change
That water turned to iron twixt eve and dawn,
And armour made of mingled links and spears
That matched the strength of all the vineyard's iron.

One day when thus the season was unkind,
To ease her of her load of heavy grief,
Distressful Leylā to the garden passed
And saw no sign of rose or tulip left.
She saw how every kind of leaf and fruit
Had vanished from the legion of the trees,
That joy of meadow green had passed away,
That now at last, in full maturity,
Defeat of joy had reached its apogee.
From living nature all of strength had gone,
No lustre rested in the faded leaf;
She saw the garden as the House of Death

And all her soul burned up with tenderness.
And now in anguish of her burning heart
She told her grief to all the garden bare:

    'O, frozen garden, with thy frozen sigh
Tell all thy sorrows to one sad as thee.
I, too, am thin and wasted, like to thee,
My rose has died and left me pale as thee,
And sorrowful, without admittance sad
To that propriety, his presence dear,
His very garden now lies closed to me.
Yet still a vital difference is found
Twixt thy estate and mine. Though captive now
In Winter's grim embrace, her icy arm
Will melt in time with Spring's restoring fire,
While I have never hope of union.
Thus claim I greater sorrow, deeper care
Than that which now oppresses all thy life.'

Thus far she spoke when heavy weariness
And sorrow growing more than she could bear
Made Leylā, weeping, turn her pallid eye
To heaven, seeking now its kindly grace.

XCIII

Herein is related the Manner in which Leylā made known to her Mother the Terms of her last will, and the Manner of her Departure from this World with the Name of her Beloved on her Lips.

Now to her God her secret Leylā told
Relating all the prayer within her heart:

    'O Thou, sweet Fowler in the mighty field,
Whose vastness only Judgement Day can yield;
O King upon Uprightness' Golden Throne,
Whose great Omnipotence we all must own;
See how I burn with fire and deep dismay:
See how my life is vexed each living day!
See now how weary of my body grown,

How unacceptable to love I'm known,
Still resting as a candle in the night
Of Love's dread Separation, angry spite
That leaves me now in anguish and despair,
That closes life in misery and care.
The world's great cruelty has made me burn
In torment, while my days still weary turn,
And thus to welcome death I fondly yearn.
    'So foolish was I, thinking in my pride
That, still enduring, then, before I died,
My soul at last the union of peace
Would sweetly know, and all my torture cease.
But I, the sun resplendent, in the ray
Of light, great constellation of the day
Know now that all my body is a screen
That hides me from the love that lovers mean.
Thus, mighty God, my supplication hear,
And show the path to sweet extinction clear.'

So pure the maiden's prayer it soared aloft
And soon was answered, as a change was seen
O'er all her temperament and easy health.
Her troubles grew and weakness mounted high
With growing fever, sapping energy
Destroying all her fairy hue of face
As waxen candle held too close the fire:
A beaded perspiration dewed her brow
And shrunk her beauty as the lovely rose
Is shrunk by drying out the precious drops
To make rose water in the precious phial.
Such frailty besieged her body tall
That last upon a couch she lay unseen,
And all who sought to speak, approaching near
Her litter, but with difficulty saw
That bed had occupant, so wasted thin
And fairy frail she lay, awaiting Death
That now his many reins about her spread,
And one by one each sign of safety slew.
Thus Leylā, knowing now that joyous peace,
Sweet peace of death, was hourly drawing near,
Resolved, as final sign of living love
To tell (all shamefulness apart and set aside)
Her mother all the secret of her heart.

'O, Mother, cure of many troubles sore,
The light of all my candle of desire,
The hidden arrow of my sorrow now
I still endure although it pierce my soul.
The road to Death lies ready at my foot,
And duty to a mother now I pay.
Know, therefore, how, though many moons have gone,
Thy daughter, Leylā, to the sword of love
Has fall'n a glad and mourning victim sad.
'Tis love that sets my fevered blood aflame.
No other fever courses in my vein.
The pain of love's affliction all explain.
Yes, I, thy daughter, weak and wretched grown,
Confess the misery that love has brought
From loving of the moon-faced Idol pure,
And turning all to nothing with desire
For him alone! My every thought was spent
In anxious supplication for his love.
Yet never once, no, not a single day
Was born that gave the hoped for union,
And now my heart, in anguish of desire
All unfulfilled, has nothing left to hope,
And thus its *Kismet* waits with open arms.
Think not that, I, alone, dishevelled, sad,
Thus grieve in loneliness. He too, is sad
With love's dear sorrow, moist of cheek and eye,
And addict, like to me, in love's embrace
Stays deep in sorrow; more, his scattered wits
All crazed, in vales of deep calamity
Now tarry unrelieved.
            'Say I am mad!
Perchance 'tis true; but he in madness held
Has changed his name from Qays to Mad Mejnūn.
His days in simple grief sought only me,
Each day in darkness closed, all unfulfilled.
His great desire, while deep enduring shame
The shame of love he never could attain
Enrolled him 'mong the legends of the world,
A byword and a scoof for all who heard.
Yet not in vain his sighs and deep laments:
Would not his fiery sighs consume my heart?
Now sits an added trouble on my brow,
As deep in shame I part from all this earth.

'O, mother dear, companion of my life,
Dear sympathizing friend and helpmate near,
As now I leave to join another world,
And bidding dear goodbye, depart unseen;
When, lacking then a daughter, heavy grief
Becomes thy portion, when abroad you go
And wander grieving o'er the barren sand
And spiteful rocks that in the desert grow;
When such becomes thy conduct, chance may yet
Bestow the path that leads to Mejnūn's land.
Should this befall, my bitter grief recount.
Be mindful, reaching him, that all of grace
Within him dwells; fall humbly at his feet,
His favour ask, soliciting a prayer
For me, the guilty Leylā, now embraced
Within the arms of Death, cold comforter.
Make known to him, O mother dear
That Leylā, the unfortunate, has died
For love of him, his name upon her lips.
Say: "Leylā, in thy love found sense of word,
Nor knew no contradiction of her course."
The words of this poor addict then recall
And say: "O, thou, that talk'st of loyalty in love,
Thy intimacy has an inmate now;
Thy friend at last is happy, free and glad:
Come now and join her, never make delay
Nor show thee negligent while still she waits.
If thou, indeed art loyal, now take the path
That leaves both world and patience, seeking me.
Now came that we, as lovers true, may find
Our heart's desire, where never strangers scold.
The path to sweet security I take
Where never slander or ill-wishing friend
May mar our bliss. All this I tell thee now,
In God's Great Name, start now, if thy desire
It be to live with me in perfect bliss."'

Then Leylā closed her last sweet dying thought
And started on her last long voyaging.
Her friend and lover lingered on her lips,
And seeking still for union, gave her soul.
Yet mourn her not, for none within the world
But still is mortal; Fortune's turning wheel

Holds none of constancy: the world itself
Is but a seven-headed dragon fierce
That still rejects the sweet anxiety
That holds its friendships in too great esteem.
In every act of grace the world conceals
A thousand cares, each drop of honey sweet
The world distils is mixed with deadly bane.
Time still revolves, as well *the sage* does know
Who set in verses all the Destiny
Of those who gain the world, then swiftly go:
And gave in numbers of his wisdom's store
To guide and help each luckless living soul.

XCIV

Herein is set forth the Ode composed by the Sage to explain the Philosophy of Life.

The world in which thou sufferest the fetters of the heart
Is bitter grief and drudgery, let not the spirit smart
That finds itself a-wandering, a-seeking for a place
Of deadly self-extinction, for it is a lovely place.
Remembering the loneliness that dwells within the grave,
Beware of all disgust, nor yet as madman savage rave;
Still follow in the road that all mankind has had to tread:
Each handful of the earth may hold a human dead,
Each building thou constructest rests ever insecure:
If in the world thou buildest it, it never will endure.
In long Eternity erect thy mansion that its term
Exist in long eternity, on sure foundations firm.
Death saves the soul from danger and from all pollution's fear
Its alchemy an elegant elixir makes appear.
Perfection of the love of man is found alone in Death
Tread now the path of wisdom shown with every fleeting breath.
Indeed it is the *Seal's design* to cause this great effect
And show the image to be true beyond all known defect.
In time of Spring the garden enter where the tulips blow
Nor let despite obstruct thy gaze that on the earth they grow.
Each atom has a double state, of *Jam*[105] and *Jamshyd* made,
For Jam the cup that Jamshyd fills, his reckoning full paid.
The peoples of the world remain to self a wretched slave,
Nor comprehend the value of the sorrow that it gave:
'Tis but Fuzūlī who retains the knowledge heaven gave,
Who thus to separation takes an easy passage brave.

XCV

Herein is set forth the Epilogue that follows the Death of Leylā.

    Leylā, the Rose of the Garden fair
    Faded and dropped in the cold Winter air:
    Her Spring was forgotten as fast under foot
    Her life, by life trampled, now withered its root.
    Her mother, distressful, uncovered her head
    O'erwhelmed by the tears that her reddened eyes bled,
    Her *camphor*[106] she poured on the *saffron*[107] alone
    And bitter of heart uttered dolorous moan.
    Thus sighing and moaning she wept in distress
    Her sorrow was great such as none could suppress.
    The road of funeral mourning she took
    While multitudes gathered, averting the look
    That doubled the cause of its sorrowing state,
    With honour and reverence, mourning her fate,
    In sad stony silence they built her a tomb
    Her body now turning to earth's dusty womb,
    While high in the Apex of Heaven her soul
    Achieved its own unity, found itself whole.
    Thus Leylā in spiritual unity found
    That in Death she and Love were in happiness bound;
    So back to Creation, the Great Ocean, she
    Returned as the raindrops return to the sea.

XCVI

Herein is set forth the Manner in which Mejnūn was informed of the Death of Leylā, and how, full of Longing, he departed from this World.

    All those who gathered from the troubled field
    Ill-omened roses of calamity
    And strewed the flowers of grief o'er all the world
    While scribbling in the books of history
    The sorrows of the ages, thus set out
    This tale of Leylā's end.
                      The loyal Zayd
    Unfortunate and deeply sorrowing friend
    The news received and straightly took the road
    That led to Mejnūn, whom he thus informed:

'O, Mejnūn! Broken toy of Fortune's spite!
Thy actions all are vain, no more the right
To hope thy fierce appeals may win thee peace.
Let now thy supplications ever cease.
The market closed, roll up thy carpet plain,
Now sever thy connection with the chain
That linked thee still with her who now in death
Has parted, naming thee with parting breath.
For love of thee thy Leylā gave her life,
No more content to live in ceaseless strife.
Now Mejnūn lives alone; the Moon is dead:
A sacrifice to thee is she to whom
Thou madest sacrifice. Now beauty's joy
Has ta'en the road that all must needs employ,
The joyful road that leads to heaven's grace,
Enjoying now a prosp'rous holy place.'

Now Mejnūn, hearing all this heavy news
Drew such a sigh from out his burning heart
That all its clamour in the higher world,
Where Leylā held her seat, was clearly heard.
Yes, Leylā, his belovéd, heard his cry
But naught of hope remained that love could yet
Awaken love from heavy sleep of death.
One moment only, loud his shout was heard
Then swooning and insensible he fell
Unconscious on the ground: then heaven's tears
The Autumn of his days bedewed with grief,
While still to Zayd torrents of reproach
Were heaped in anguish.
                    'Saki, what is here?
Thou, Saki, full of grief and earthly fear,
What sin is mine that in thy tyranny
Thou makest now a feast of cruelty?
Explain thy purpose, why destroy my life
Why now destroy my heart with torment rife?
So merciless thy action; killing now
The luckless and unfortunate! O thou,
Great goblet holder of the poisoned cup,
That holds the torture that I still must sup,
Within my soul thy cruelty is fire
That burns with passing of my soul's desire.
Why gainst the ant betray such venomed spite?

Gainst steel the bottle yet must lose the fight.
Beware that unredeemed act insane,
Do now a noble act and balance pain.
Replace this sin with blessing, to the land
Where love resides, where lovers understand
The pains of love, make me a candle clear
That by the tomb of love is ever near.'

    Now Mejnūn started, hand entwined with Zayd,
To seek the tomb where Leylā lay interred,
And God defend us! when he reached the place
And saw the spot that held the rosy-cheeked,
He fell to earth and close embraced the tomb.
He rent his breast and tore a bloody niche
That matched the niche that decked her resting place,
Upon his head, as dust upon the grave,
He poured the barren desert's angry sand,
While on the tomb his bloody bitter tears
Fell streaming till the stone was crimsoned o'er.
His tears now watered all the barren earth
And stored themselves beneath its barren crust,
While some, more restless, lay as lucent pearls
All scattered broadcast o'er the Idol's tomb.
And then, to all his tears he made address
In these dull accents:
                    'Separation's night
Knows thou, its star of darkness. Know thy task
Is now to shine and glitter in the sky
From which the sun is banished ever more.
The Moon has now a constellation won
So far aloft that e'en the morning breeze
No more may reach to fan her lofty seat.
If aught of generosity remain
Stay not above, but enter now the earth
And make enquiry of her resting place.
Discover where now rests the peerless pearl,
Uncover Fortune's sad calamity
And make it known: hear now my holy prayer,
Make supplication, kissing both her feet,
And tell her this, the secret of my heart!

    'O candle of my life, why now refrain
Why now, 'gainst me, the hardly used of Fate,
Conceal thyself from these my seeking eyes?

The world once held the wine cup of regret;
We both did deeply drink. While yet the fumes
Of mad intoxication in us both
Did rise apace, yet from the orgy fierce
Thy path was quickly ta'en. Within the night
A candle rare, illuminating life
Wert thou, attracting all the fire
That came to thee of pleasures sweet of love.
And yet, though fiercely burning the days,
Thy patience wearied, all thy strength was sped,
And all thy dear endurance was consumed.
No more for nights of sleeplessness thy strength
Remained, for now thy hazel eye
To sleep was all inclined, and sleeping now
Companion to my troubles on the road,
O Moon, can fellow traveller desert
His road companion, seeking other paths?
O Earth, let now thy boast address the skies
That now this purest pearl, companion dear,
Now rests within thy hard and stony breast.
O snake, raise not objection to her lock
That curls around her yet lamenting heart.
And thou, O Ant, no molestation make
Of that, her mole, for still the desolate
And grieving soul is tied with heavy chains
To that dear blemish of her lovely face.
O Life make now an end to all thy coil,
For dark within the eye the dreary world
Now love is lost. With love the world was sweet:
With love's departure all is nothingness.
O, soul, a sad farewell now quickly take
Nor seem with sickly man to strive afresh;
Abandon strife, for now I welcome death
And ask him graciously to banish pain,
Destroying all my grievous suffering.
Yea, save me from the suffering of grief
And give the world glad tidings of my end.
And give my mirror of corroding rust,
Rend now the curtain of my great esteem;
Lift now the barrier that yet remains;
Confer the favour of a close approach
To that still lovely Idol of my soul.
My love proposes blessed union dear,

In privacy, where never strangers lurk
With venomed tongues and evil slandering.
'Twere grievous fault should I decline to go,
And thus, O Death, 'tis meet to grant thy aid.
For God's dear sake let not thy succour lag
In giving help, for all prosperity
Each every day averts her lovely face.
O Lord, I need no body now, nor soul,
If Love be not: I need no more the world.
Absolve me now of life's bewilderment
Let all humiliation fly afar
Nor let me more in misery endure.'

With moaning thus he quite forsook himself
While still this poem poured from out his mouth.

XCVII

Herein is set forth the Ode recited by Mejnūn as suitable to the Occasion.

Consumed with desolation lies my soul
Still seeking union with love's dear cheek;
While Love's dear countenance
Of healing all compact
In weary search I pass my endless days
Each moment knowing an affliction deep
Of separation sore.
A nightingale sad moaning in the brake
No more than I
In vain endeavour thrills the midnight hour;
Yet I, the fair rose garden of desire
Solicit still while in the fettered care
That sees my constant weeping sad appeal.
No more in this sad market that the world calls life
My goods a purchaser
May find howe'er I try.
Then hear my plea and in another world
A market let me find,
And vanished from all earthly misery
With weakened body, wounded soul at rest,
In sweet extinction from the troubled world
I peace and mart may both securely find.

Yet, wishing still for death within the night
Of desolation,
How pursue my course? My cup of grief
O'erflows its plenty,
And thus to ease excess
A dear companion at my side I need.
A permanency marks the union
Of love divine: within the mortal world
I may not linger while my love awaits
Its promised union.
For mark, Fuzūlī, how my wish to die
In sweet contentment, knowing no other road
Save that the sweet necessity inspires
The parting as it now inspireth me.

XCVIII

Herein is set forth the Epilogue that follows on the Death of Mejnūn.

The secret of his heart now clearly told
Decree came granting Mejnūn all his wish.
The Grace of God to rescue swiftly came
Fulfilling all the purpose of his soul.
He plucked the roses in the garden bright
Of hope: from Death's decanter drank the wine,
Embraced his Idol in her darkling tomb
And spent his soul in service of its alms.

'O, Leylā,' soft he murmured in release
Of all his hold upon his parting life,
And thus this sad unresting lover left
The world and all its grief for Paradise.

If justly one may think, conclusion plain
Is reached, that love may do no more than this:
And this, the highest point that love may reach,
Can but instil a marvel in the breast.
At times it seems that Love within the hand
Retains the soul in careful watch all day,
That when revolving time has swiftly sped
An auth'rization granting to the soul
Permits a journey to a better land.

While yet his Idol dwelt within the world,
The world remained his only resting place.
But, Leylā gone, he followed without thought
Spontaneously from this too dreary world.
His sad condition Zayd sadly saw
And, loudly mourning, rent his collar off,
And wailing in an agony of grief,
His outcry reached the apex of the sky.
He wept so grievously that mighty crowds
Fast gathered round his sighs' consuming flames,
And, crowding still, they looked with awestruck eye
At him who darkly lived and starkly died,
And saw him sunk upon the waiting tomb
While still his love made scattered pearls of love.
And all, in common sympathy, bewailed
His passing, and a burial decreed
With fine ablution bathing all his limbs,
They made him fitting for his resting place.
Then slow they opened up the tomb of love,
And laid him there with tender loving care:
Beside his fellow sufferer at last
The man of sorrows to his love was joined.

His spirit now in sympathy supreme
Was joined to hers he sought above the skies,
While on the earth at last his body joined
The body he had worshipped unto death.
Now fell the barriers to great desire
At last the seeker found his search fulfilled.
The tomb a double resting place became
Of two great shahs, and in one mansion now
A single constellation held two moons.
In awe inspiring love a sign was made
And placed upon the entrance to the tomb,
That all who passed the story sad could read
And make their passion known to all the world.
While still in circumambulation slow
The crowds made circuit of the holy place,
It grew in honour as the years unrolled
And came to be a lovers' pilgrimage.
See now the sweet reward of love divine
If but clear understanding opes the eyes!

XCIX

Herein is related the Dream of Zayd concerning Leylā and Mejnūn.

Now close to the tomb of the martyrs dwelt Zayd
Where signs of his loyalty grew on each side.
Full many a gift did he make to that tomb
New building erecting while yet there was room
While ever the warmth of his heart did incline
To harbour the candle that brightly it shine.
When slowly infiltering, sand of the plain
Had sullied the tomb, then his tears, fell as rain
And eyelashes proudly became as a broom
And swept up the garbage and tidied the room.
Each instant he mourned with his tears ever fresh
Time passed and the faithful companion distressed
In body now frail as in spirit oppressed
Against the fair tomb for a moment released
Relaxed into slumber with forehead uncreased.
And sleeping he saw through the eye of a dream
Within a glad garden two beauties supreme,
Their faces he saw with all pleasure aglow,
No fear, grief or trouble did either face show.
Each countenance spoke of all joy and delight
No stranger a-gossiping saddened the sight.
A thousand sweet angels attended each moon
As faithful loyal servants. Now Zayd in a swoon
All drowned with his slumber said:
                                    'Say who are these
Bright Moons? Are they princes? Recount their degrees.
What Garden of Paradise this here I lie?
What people are these that with happiness cry?'

   The answer he had, showed the garden of joy
As the sweet field of paradise lovers enjoy,
While mid all the huris and beautiful boys
Sweet Leylā and Mejnūn did gladly rejoice.
This valley of peace the dear lovers enjoyed
And loved with a pleasure that time never cloyed.
The Garden of Paradise mansion became
Of them who in love and in death loved the same.
While fairy faced huris, with minist'ring grace
Assisted by beautiful youths every trace

Of hardship of labour withheld from the eye
And laughter encouraged with never a sigh.
Thus clearly is shown that if God's great decree
Is followed implicitly, all may be free,
And patience in trouble that mutilates life
May yet earn a Paradise empty of strife.

When Zayd awoke from his slumber of peace
His dream in a torrent of words found release,
And telling the story the people around
In pilgrimage sought for the sanctified ground.

C

Herein is set forth the Epilogue to the History of Leylā and Mejnūn.

O saki, see my sad position changed,
Bereft indeed of strength to utter words.
Henceforth thy cup withhold. No more thy wine
In sweet libation pour, for I am drunk
With joy and sorrow. Let thy mercy sweet
Incline, for all my days in slumber wrapped
I lately passed, not knowing how 'twill end.
The capital of all my life is spent.
My hand is empty; none of profit stays
Of all the dealings of my lengthy life.
See, Saki, how this cruelty endures
And makes this alteration in my state,
But causing yesterday a weary flood
Of glist'ning pearls to flow from out my eyes,
I railed at Fortune, told her she was cruel
No moment was I free from grief and woe.
Thy turning wheel revolves against thy friends,
And tortures all perfection found in man.
Had Mejnūn nurtured been in ignorance
Thy hair had all grown grey obeying him:
His foreman then, thy instantly expressed
Approval, would have gained: but Mad Mejnūn,
For reason he was born a man of skill,
And prudence knew, possessing insight clear,
Was sadly lowered from the rank of those
His equals, sinking still, with honour gone,
And all esteem departed in disgrace.

Had Leylā been, indeed a shameless one,
Or loveless and disloyal as thyself,
Thy time had not been spent in torture cruel,
Thy wheel had spun more closely thy desire.
But since the maid, all virtuous, virtue loved,
And understanding in perfection claimed,
Thou mad'st her life a wretched misery
By ever holding out the hand of grief,
And breeding deep bewilderment and pain.
And if, O Tyrant, I were man of lies
Thy helping hand would not in darkness lie,
A happy end I yet might find in thee.
Thy wheel would quickly turn and bring me rest.
But since I claim a decent dignity,
And hold me fast to honour, thou, in hate
Thy pleasure take'st, bestowing misery
And sorrow every weary lagging hour.
Thus, knowing naught of honour, claiming none,
Thy wheel still turning passes slowly on
Unchecked.
   Now Fortune my reproof had heard,
And thus made answer:
      'Thou of little mind,
Who talkest, still unheedful of the truth
That deeply lies where few can drag it forth,
Unskilled thou art, not knowing every point
Of wisdom; still in sweet accord I turn,
And tell thee this so-called blind cruelty
Is loyalty and deep philosophy.
The fault is thine: thy actions all are wrong.
The teacher of the spirit of thy sect
Is merely air: in poetry thy boast
Still, wearing falsehood wicked as a badge.
That sweet perfection, called by thee Mejnūn,
Through thee found knowledge and ability;
'Twas thou that called him mad, and madman named;
His cruelty and torment came of thee.
While Leylā, Moon of all Perfection named
I hid behind the curtain's heavy veil,
Her, madest thou, 'fore people a disgrace,
The butt of all a thousand slanders foul.
Then, too, 'twas thou that charged a cruelty
To Nevfel brave, then, changing thy attack,

Staunch Ibni Salam to thy venomed words
Accused of tyranny, was basely dead.
Thou therefore stand ashamed, absurd thy plaint,
For where is Ibni Salam, where Nevfel?
A story in thy verses thou would'st tell,
Thus finding just excuse for idle speech,
And now, with idle words exhausted, speed
With all the living dead and calumnied,
The dead themselves thy victims now are made
And thus the grave no more protection yields.
The time is near when all the public mind
Of this thy crime will stand it firm convinced,
And accusation sternly will be made.
Think carefully and find an answer clear
For this thy spirit's torture growing near.

CI

Herein is set forth the Poet's Answer to the Criticism of Fortune.

O Parrot, in a plot of idle words
Still chattering, a feeble critic still,
Of sad Fuzulī's sadly written words,
Be not deceived if yet the changing skies
Should slander thee and name thee liar foul.
Spend not thy substance calling poems bad,
Nor yet fatigue thy critic soul in vain.
The merchandise that makes the poet's store
Is never easy found, for words are jewels
Close guarded in the heart's dear treasury.
That still to all the herd is closely locked.
The door once opened, personality
With all its attributes made manifest
The poet only knows. The soul remains
For those who have the wisdom to observe
A lonely word, and only foolishness
Can deem the soul may show a difference.
And thus, invoking God's so dreaded Name.
Fuzūlī asks what evil may be found
In words that make the dead to live anew.
Or where the sin that makes the world rejoice
In telling o'er the sad unhappy tale
Of Leylā fair and Mejnūn nobly mad?

CII

Herein is set forth the Explanation of the Writing of the Book, and the Date when the Door that led to this Result was first opened.

> O travelling pen, split reed, now worn to naught,
> O fellow traveller not vainly sought,
> With growing effort, keeping still thy pace,
> Thou reachest now thy final resting place.
> God's sweet compassion on thee in thy need,
> For all thy proffered help was help indeed,
> And now the ancient building lives again,
> And prospers, sadly born of grievous pain.
> With silvered tears the outer walls are built,
> The inner spread with ambergris and gilt.
> The treasured jewels of sweet affliction rest
> Within its fast securéd chest.
> Each window opens as a channel clear
> Through which the blood is cooled in passing near.
> A garden sweet is now in beauty made
> Within its bosom thousand tulips laid,
> While of the thousand, each one fiercely burns
> As still the heart's consuming blood fast turns
> To sweet abundant streams that succour bring
> While all the lovely eyelashes may sing
> In cloudy unison, bestowing tears
> To see how Death all earthly sorrow clears.
>   That day that saw the end of my desire,
> That tempted me thus feebly to aspire
> To join with Leylā Mejnūn's mighty name
> In magic verses, that the world might claim
> A masterpiece of love made manifest
> In showing still these lovers, nobly blessed,
> Saw love at last, as constant as the sun,
> In life though parted, dead they ruled as ONE.

CIII

Herein is set forth the Poet's Hope for the Acceptance of his Apology by Men of Loyalty, and a Request for a Prayer of Forgiveness from Men of Intelligence.

> See now my weakness, worn and wan with strife,
> All, overcome by sorrow born of life,
> And rather marvel that the Day and Night

Still leaves me words to utter and to write.
And yet, expect not words of sober sense,
Nor thoughts all born of heaven's excellence,
For, as my body, so my words are weak:
Say not it profits little those who seek
The pearls of pleasure; poetry's bright art
And Love's Perfection sorely bruise the heart.
'Tis this the critics constantly forget
Artist and lover pay what never yet
The critic paid. And yet a patron dear
A purchaser for all the thoughts that here
Lie deep within my breast would ope the gate
To all the words my soul would operate.

    Yet this now written, feeble though it be,
Has not been lacking joy, at least to me:
Let not the cult of criticizing skill
Now blind the eye with jealousy, for still
In spite of all aggression's fierce attack
Of all the jealous criticizing pack,
I still reply: if thy ability
Is equal to thy great humility,
Go, write an equal to my verses here;
Show critic's art comes of creation clear.
Speak but of goodness, failing this, my friend,
Remain in silence. Here my words have end.

NOTE: Probable date of completion of the poem as indicated by letters of this chapter is AH 963, that is AD 1556.

NOTES ON PART I

Chapter One
1. This is the opinion of an eminent Turkish literary historian, Fuad Köprülü, cf. *Islam Ansiklopedisi*, sv. Fuzūlī.
2. See Bibliography, pp. 343 ff.
3. For the problem of the date and place of Fuzūlī's birth see my shortly forthcoming article.
4. *Divan*, ed. K. Akyüz et al., Istanbul, 1958, pp. 45–6.
5. *Divan*, ed. Gandjeī, Napoli, 1959, p. 72.
6. These names appear in a work of Fuzūlī's, published recently, under the title *Matlaʿ al-iʿtiqād* (see Ch. II).
7. See article indicated in Note 3.
8. *Persian Divan*, p. 214.
9. *Divan*, p. 6.
10. Preface to the *Persian Divan*, pp. 11–12.
11a. *Ibid.*
11b. Cf. A. Bausani, *I persiani*, Florence, 1962, pp. 182 and 184.
12. Translation of Shāh Ismāʿīl's verse (ed. cit., p. 5): 'The tenor of thy word is the True (God), thou thyself art the sign of the True. He who would say that thou art separate from the True is a misbeliever.'

    Fuzūlī says (*Persian Divan*, p. 177): 'Thy knowledge is manifest in the Lord and in thee is manifested the Lord. What sin of ignorance separateth thee from the Lord!'

    Probably the qasida on pp. 231–4 of the *Persian Divan* is also dedicated to the Shah.
13. *Divan*, pp. 87–9. The Turkish qasidas, pp. 89–91 (according to the title of the Leningrad ms. this qasida is dedicated to the 'shāh' and to Ibrāhīm Khān, cf. ed. Baku, IV, 1961), 109–10, and 351, and the *tarjīʿ-band*, pp. 438–92, *ibid.*, are dedicated to the same person.
14. Biography of Sādiqī, cf. A. Karahan, *Fuzuli*, Istanbul, 1949, p. 243.
15. *Persian Divan*, pp. 227–31.
16. *Ibid.*, pp. 241–2.
17. *Divan*, p. 46.
18. *Ibid.*, p. 44.
19. *Shikāyet-nāme*, ed. Baku, II, 1958, p. 300.
20. Cf. A. Karahan, *op. cit.*, p. 243.
21. *Divan*, p. 50.
22. *Ibid.*, pp. 37–40 and 41–4.
23. Cf. A. Karahan, *op. cit.*, p. 132.
24. For Shiite criticism to the first three caliphs, see A. Laoust, 'La critique du Sunnisme dans la doctrine de al-Hilli', in *Revue des Études Islamiques*, 1966, XXXIV, pp. 40–8. Documents belonging to a period only slightly later than Fuzūlī show a moderate attitude on the part of the Sunnites who speak with veneration of the twelve imāms, and on the part of the Shiites who affirm that their conception is not in fact

bound to the vilification of the early caliphs (whose names however 'never appear in Shiite mouth'), and only a few ignorant Shiites consider the curse a duty. Cf. B. Scarcia Amoretti, 'Una polemica religiosa tra 'ulamā' di Mašhad e 'ulamā' Uzbechi nell'anno 997/1588–1589', in *Annalli* of the Istituto Universitario Orientale of Naples, New Series, XIV, Part II, 1964, pp. 647–71. (Papers presented to L. Veccia Vaglieri.)
24b. *Divan*, pp. 41, 43, 52.
25. *Leylā and Mejnūn*, ed. Onan, v. 380.
26. Cf. H. A. R. Gibb, 'Luṭfī Paşa on the Ottoman Caliphate', in *Oriens*, 15/1962, pp. 287–95. A. Bombaci, 'L'Impero Ottomano', in *Nuove questioni di Storia Moderna*, I, Milan, 1964, pp. 563–4.
27. Qasidas in *Leylā and Mejnūn*, cit.
28. *Shikāyet-nāme*, cit., p. 300.
29. Cf. A. Karahan, *op. cit.*, p. 229.
30. Cf. *Leylā and Mejnūn*, ed. Onan, v. 479. The reference to Baghdad is already in Hātifī's poem *Laylā and Majnūn*, which Fuzūlī had in mind (see Chapters IV and V).
31. *Divan*, p. 105.
32. *Ibid.*, p. 107.
33. *Ibid.*, p. 53. See A. Karahan's explanation, *op cit.*, pp. 82–3.
34. *Divan*, p. 95.
35. *Ibid.*, p. 98; *Persian Divan*, p. 221. See also *ibid.*, pp. 60, 238 and 239.
36. *Persian Divan*, pp. 51, 60, 239; *Divan*, p. 95.
37. *Divan*, p. 93; *Persian Divan*, pp. 51 and 239.
38. *Persian Divan*, p. 221.
39. *Divan*, p. 66. Six Turkish qasidas are dedicated to the pasha, *ibid.*, pp. 54–6, 56–8, 64–6, 66–8, 68–71, 71–3, the *terjī'-bend*, *ibid.*, 59–64, and the qasida, pp. 227–30, of the *Persian Divan*.
40. *Divan*, p. 72.
41. *Ibid.*, p. 68.
42. Cf. *Persian Divan*, pp. 119, 120, 145, 153.
43. *Ibid.*, pp. 207–10.
44. See Farišta, translated by J. Briggs, Vol. III, London, 1829, pp. 228 seqq.
45. *Divan*, p. 69.
46. *Ibid.*, pp. 78–80. The editors of the *Divan* believe that this qasida is dedicated to Muhammad Khān Tekelü, Safavid governor of Baghdad from 1524 to 1534, without the motive being apparent. The indication of the taking of the water to Karbalā' would lead us to think of the Ottoman Governor Baltajī Mehmed Pasha who was in fact the person who carried this out. That the person should appear with the title of 'beg' and not 'pasha' is not surprising for the same title is often used by Fuzūlī for other Ottoman governors, such as Üveys and Ja'fer.
47. *Ibid.*, p. 80.
48. See article already mentioned, Note 3.
49. *Divan*, pp. 82–5.
50. *Persian Divan*, pp. 72–6.

51. *Persian Divan*, pp. 97–100.
52. Cf. A. Karahan, *op. cit.*, p. 69.
53. *Persian Divan*, p. 561.
54. *Divan*, p. 327.
55. *Ibid.*, p. 165. Cf. *Persian Divan*, p. 51.
56. *Persian Divan*, p. 51.
57. For the date of death and the plague in Baghdad see A. Karahan, *op. cit.*, pp. 108–10, 279–81.
58. A. Karahan, *op. cit.*, p. 224.
59. A. Karahan, *op. cit.*, p. 228.
59. A. Karahan, *op. cit.*, p. 228.
60. *Ibid.*

Chapter Two
1. H. Mazıoğlu, in *Fuzûlî-Hâfiz*, Ankara, 1956, p. 19, demonstrates Fuzūlī's imitations of the lines of the Turkish Azerbaijan poet, Habībī. A. Gölpınarlı in *Fuzūlī Divanı*, Istanbul, 1948, pp. XLII–LIII, demonstrates the imitations of the Central-Asian Turkish poet Navā'ī. H. Mazıoğlu also demonstrates the imitations of the Ottoman poet Nejātī, *op. cit.*, pp. 26–7. It is also probable that the use of a riddle in the preamble of a qasida (see above) was suggested to Fuzūlī by Nejātī (*Divan*, ed. A. N. Tarlan, p. 46). For Fuzūlī's couplet quoted last by Mazıoğlu on p. 26, No. 2, a comparison can be made with Nejātī, ghazal 50, couplet 6; the figure of the mountain beating its breast with stones which we shall see in Fuzūlī's *Leylā and Mejnūn* is also found in a couplet of Nejātī (ghazal 410, couplet 6). In both cases, however, perhaps both poets repeat commonplaces. For Khayālī see the following note. In *Leylā and Mejnūn* Fuzūlī mentions the Ottoman poets Sheykhī, Ahmedī, Khalīlī, Nizāmī of whom only the first two are famous (vv. 415–16, ed. Onan).
2. Cf. A. Karahan, *Fuzuli*, Istanbul, 1949, p. 240. For a comparison between the poetry of Fuzūlī and that of Khayālī see A. Gölpınarlı, *op. cit.*, pp. LXI–LXVI.
3. *Hadīqat as-su'adā*, ms. British Museum, Preface.
4. *Divan*, p. 481.
5. *Hadīqat as-su'adā*, cit.
6. Such is their position in the editions of *Külliyyāt*, Istanbul, 1328, of A. Gölpınarlı, of H. Arasly, of A. N. Tarlan. In the edition of K. Akyüz *et al.* the traditional order has not been followed.
7. Cf. A. Bombaci, 'The Turkic Literatures, Introductory Notes on the History and Style', in *Philologiae Turcicae Fundamenta*, Vol. II, Wiesbaden, 1964, p. LIV.
8. *Divan*, p. 492.
8b. *A History of Ottoman Poetry*, Vol. III, London, 1904, pp. 92–3.
8c. *Ib.*, p. 97.
9. In the Baku edition, Vol. IV, 1961, pp. 25–9.
10. These are 40 in the edition of K. Akyüz (where the section 'Kasa'id'

includes 42 compositions; two of these are one 'terkīb-bend', n. XII, and one 'terjī'-bend', n. XV). The qasida on pp. 70–1 of the *Külliyyāt*, Istanbul, 1328, is by the Ottoman poet Fighani and not by Fuzūlī. See A. Karahan, *Kanunî Sultan Süleyman Çağı Şairlerinden Figani ve Divançesi*, Istanbul, 1966, p. XVI.

11. From the title, the qasida n. VI, ed. Akyüz *et al.*, would seem to be in praise of 'Alī, this is in fact the contents of the preamble, but it rather is dedicated to a high-ranking Shiite, Muhammad Najafi.
12. See A. Karahan, *Islâm-Türk edebiyatında Kırk Hadis*, Istanbul, 1954, pp. 167–72.
13. *Persian Divan*, ed. Mazıoğlu, p. 31.

Chapter Three

1. Of the various editions published in Cairo of the *Dīwān Majnūn Lailā* of al-Wālibī, I have kept in mind that published in AH 1358/AD 1939. On al-Wālibī see I. Krachkovski, *art. cit.* in the Bibliography, p. 7. Besides the source there cited see also al-Amālī, II, 126.
2. About the pseudoepigraphic nature of the *Dīwān* of al-Wālibī, besides the subjects dealt with by I. Krachkovski, *loc. cit.*, it can be added that at one point it is said: *wa-qāla Abū 'l-Hasan al-'Alawī: sa'altu al-Wālibī*, etc., 'Said Abū 'l-Hasan al-'Alawī: I interrogated al-Wālibī, etc.' (*ed. cit.*, p. 30). The work therefore at least in the form in which we have it is not by al-Wālibī.
3. To the later monographs mentioned by I. Krachkovski, *loc. cit.*, pp. 7–8, must be added the *Bast sāmi' al-musāmir fī akhbār Majnūn Banī 'Āmir* of Abū 'Abdillāh Shamsuddīn Muhammad ibn 'Alī ibn Tūlūn al-Dimishqī al-Sālihī, of which I know the Cairo edition without a date, ed. 'Abdul-Muta'āl al-Sa'īdī, Professor of al-Azhar.
4. Translated into English verse by A. J. Arberry, Cairo, 1933. See R. Rubinacci, ' "Maǧnūn Lailā" di Ahmad Šawqī' in *Annali*, Istituto Universitario Orientale, Naples, New series, Vol. VIII, Naples, 1957, pp. 9–66 (with Italian translation).
5. Would seem to be identifiable with the person mentioned in the story of al-Tabarī (Pars III, p. 281) (cf. *Kitāb al-Aghānī*, p. 15, Note 1, see Bibliography).
6. *Murūj adh-dhahab*, ed. C. Barbier de Meynard, Vol. 7, Paris 1873, pp. 356–60.
7. Cf. *Kitāb al-Aghānī, cit.*, pp. 77 and 80.
8. On the difficulty of distinguishing between authentic poetry of Majnūn and that attributed to him, see I. Krachkovski, *loc. cit.*, pp. 47–8. A scholarly edition of the *dīwān* of Majnūn (by 'Abdassattār Ahmad Faraj) where this attempt has not been carried out, has recently been published in Cairo (no date).
9. *Kitāb al Luma'*, ed. R. A. Nicholson; Leyden, London, 1914, p. 360.
10. *Ibid.*, p. 368.
11. Some lines in which the lover is identified with the beloved are referred

both to Majnūn and to al-Hallāj, cf. H. Ritter, *Das Meer der Seele*, p. 408 (*cit.* Bibliography).
12. *Ibid.*, p. 433.
13. *Ibid.*, p. 438.
14. *Ibid.*, p. 479; cf. also C. A. Nallino, *Raccolta di scritti editi e inediti*, Vol. II, Roma 1940, p. 369.
15. Cf. H. Ritter's above-mentioned book. See Index, *Macnūn*.
16. A. S. Levend, *op. cit.*, in Bibliography, pp. 103–6. I read: *mu'nisi hijrān ve yarīdur khayāl*, whereas A. S. Levend, p. 105: *Munisi hicrān diyārıdur hayāl*.
17. A. S. Levend, *op. cit.*, p. 106–7.

Chapter Four
1. Dastgirdī's numerical calculation is based on a line in the introduction: 'These four thousand lines and more (*akthar*) were composed in four months and less.' According to Dastgirdī: 'Four thousand lines and more are at the most four thousand and fifty or one hundred, while the poem contains 4,650.' Thus six hundred lines must have been added. It seems to me, however, that nothing prevents the word *akthar* from indicating also some hundreds of lines. Besides it must be kept in mind that in the introduction to the line quoted another 350 lines follow which must be subtracted from the total number mentioned in the line itself because they were presumably written afterwards.

Dastgirdī's method of identification of the added lines is purely arbitrary. He eliminates not only whole groups of lines but entire sections: the chapter on the virtues of Majnūn, the story of Zaid and Zainab, the last meeting between Lailā and Majnūn, and Zaid's dream. When he therefore finds that he has eliminated more than was necessary (1,030 couplets), he then admits that among the lines eliminated there were also lines from Nizāmī, but he then leaves the reader to make his choice. According to the Persian scholar the lines must have been added between AH 780 and 800, i.e. AD 1349 and 1398.

Bertels (see *op. cit.* in Bibliography) considers the argument based on the numerical calculation as valid, but has his doubts about the criteria of 'taste' used in the judgment of what is and what is not authentic in the lines. He observes that a definitive judgment presupposes a deep stylistic analysis which has not yet been carried out. He observes moreover that the eliminated lines are in fact contained in all the texts which we know even the most ancient manuscripts. He is none the less prepared to consider the episode of the last meeting as spurious and he calls it 'limp and arid' (*vyalo i sukho*) and maintains that it is the work of an interpolator who wanted to enliven the rather dull tone of the poem with a scene which the lovers of *havas-nāma* would certainly have enjoyed. Perhaps he was obeying the command of someone in power who was annoyed at the excessive chastity of the poem. Finally, he does not justify it within the unfolding of the plot. It is impossible to discuss his ideas at length here. I note only that the aesthetic judgment depends on impression, that the passage which is substantially chaste is no less so than others which are accepted as authentic, that the episode is absolutely indispensable for the solution which the poet gives to the story of the two lovers, which results from what will be said later and which is clearly seen by Bertels without however founding it on the text.

The period of the insertions arbitrarily indicated by Dastgirdī is however contradicted by the existence of manuscripts dated between 1361 and 1366 containing the parts which were in doubt.

A. S. Levend and R. Gelpke in their writings indicated in the Bibliography have accepted Dastgirdī's opinion without questioning it critically.

2. An anecdote in which Majnūn is seen sitting beside Laylā in a fresco on a wall appears in 'Attār, cf. H. Ritter, *Das Meer der Seele*, Leiden, 1955, p. 417.
3. See A. Bausani, *op. cit.*, in Bibliography, p. 10.
4. *Mathnavī*, 5/2016–2019. See also the *Rabāb-nāma* of Sultan Valad quoted by H. Ritter, *op. cit.*, p. 412.
5. *Mathnavī*, 3/567 sqq.

Chapter Five
1. I read *jem'iyyet-u* with the Baku edition.
2. The three quatrains in the Onan edition are placed before the prose Preface, in the Baku edition they come after. In both cases references to mss. are missing.
3. Cf. H. Ritter, *Das Meer der Seele*, Leiden, 1955, p. 183.
4. See H. Ritter, *op. cit.*, pp. 248 sqq.
5. *Gulistān*, 5/18.

Sofi Huri's translation to which this essay is an introduction is extremely free and at times inexact by the standards of the scholar rather than the poet. The passages quoted above have therefore been re-translated more literally for the purposes of this Introduction by its author. (Follow the Onan edition numeration.)

NOTES ON PART II

1. To those who do not consider Fuzūlī a mystic, I have nothing to say. The great poet has revealed to me his mystical nature and no one can convince me to the contrary.
2. Divan Mejnūn Leyli, Mahmud Kamel Ferid, Cairo.
3. Canonical law of Islam.
4. Mystical order.
5. Symbolizes the general opinion that a male and a female could not be thrown together for a long time and not be inflamed by human love.
6. The customary formula inscribed at the head of each Chapter of the Qur'an, and pronounced before reading the Qur'an, in Divine worship, and before beginning any important act.
7. I.e. Had I not come into the world as a human being, I wonder what I would have been?
8. Apex: Mi'raj.
9. Kef: The letter 'K'.
10. Nun: The letter 'N'. These two letters, K N, together make the word 'Kun' meaning 'Be!', i.e. The creative word.
11. Tambourine: The tef.
12. Flute: The ney, the flute made of a hollow reed.
13. Laulaka: 'but for thee' (the world would not have been called out of non-existence), from the Qur'an.
14. Compass: The compass which is so arranged that its needle points always to Mecca.
15. Night of Power: the 27th of Ramazan when the Qur'an descended from heaven.
16. Yasin: Chapter 36 in the Qur'an.
17. Taha: Chapter 20 in the Qur'an.
18. Miraj (Lit. an ascent): The Prophet's miraculous journey to heaven. It is said to have taken place in the twelfth year of his mission, in the month of Rabiulawwal.
19. The mountain Tur: Mount Sinai.
20. Night of Power: The 27th night of Ramazan.
21. Burak: The name of the courser, the flashing steed, that carried Mohammed on his night journey (Miraj) from Mecca to Jerusalem, and thence to heaven, in an instant.
22. Behrem: The planet Mars. Also name of an angel.
23. Jupiter: Birjis.
24. Nimrod: Nimrod was the impious King of the Chaldeans and a rebel against God. He cast Abraham into the fire upon his refusal to worship idols. He built the tower of Babel. Legend has it that he was finally killed by a gnat!
25. Khalil: Abraham.
26. Ebubekir, Ali, Osman and Omer are the names of the four friends of the Prophet Mohammed.

27. Damascus.
28. Sakiname.
29. Ebi-Nüvas: a great poet.
30. Harut: Name of an angel, who, with another named Marut, visited the earth, being led into sin by the woman called Zuhera; the two angels are confined in a pit at Babylon, there to await the day of judgment.
31. Gazel: An ode.
32. Mesnevi: Poetry composed of distichs corresponding in measure, each consisting of a pair of rhymes.
33. Shahinshah: King of kings.
34. Tuğra: A Sultan's monogram.
35. Mukarnas: The throne of Solomon.
36. Uwais: Sultan Uwais, second of the Ilkanian kings reigning over Iraq, Arabia and Azerbaijan. 756–776 Hajira.
37. Emaret: The territory of a chief.
38. Irem: An earthly, but fabulous paradise, somewhere in the deserts of Southern Arabia, constructed by genie for Sheddad the son of 'Ad mentioned in the Qur'an.
39. Selman: Selman Sawaji, Persian poet, found favour with Emir Shayb Hasan Büzürg, founder of the Ilkanian state. Later tutor to his son Uwais. Wrote eulogies of the Ilkanian dynasty.
40. Meze: Savoury titbits that accompany drinking in Middle Eastern Countries.
41. Rum: Ottoman.
42. Naz.
43. Saz.
44. The Gardener of the Garden of Speech: often referred to throughout the poem, means the poet's fire, or muse.
45. Jamshyd: Name of a Persian King to whom the invention of wine is attributed in Eastern mythology.
46. Sunnet: Circumcision.
47. This concept would be strange to Western thought. She had a mole on her face and moles were considered special marks of beauty. This mole was so lovely that it could have served as an eye if she had lost her two normal eyes.
48. Noon is the letter 'n' which is the first letter of 'nergis', and its curve is meant here.
49. Lam is the first letter of 'lale', 'tulip', and the letter is meant to resemble his curl.
50. The word stands for Melamet. The doctrine of a sect of dervishes who court public reproach by the neglect of the rites and duties of outward religion, hence the condition of a person who has reached a stage when he takes no care for public opinion, conventions, etc. Melamet is here used to indicate 'blame'.
51. 'Lam' 'ye' Leylî. More commonly written today 'Leylā'.
52. Narcissus: The reference here is to the eye of the narcissus which is

conceived of as staring boldly and brazenly out of the white face of the petals.
53. Unca: A fabulous bird of enormous size, said to live in the Caucasus in solitude.
54. Like the candle that is lighted in the Mosque where all may see it.
55. Painted gauze: A lantern which revolves by the smoke of the candle within, and has on the side of it figures of various animals.
56. Elif: First letter of alphabet: a straight vertical line.
57. Noon: Curved letter with dot in middle.
58. Mim: A crooked letter, sometimes likened to the mouth.
59. The inkstand: The inkstand referred to is the old Arabic type of inkstand held in the hand. It was in the form of a stick with a reservoir at one end. It was generally made of brass.
60. Saz: Musical instrument.
61. Reed pen: A pen made of a reed which had black rings along its stem.
62. Fağfur: The Emperor of China.
63. Chosroes: The title of several kings of Persia.
64. Dal: A letter in Arabic alphabet.
65. Khusrev: Name of the hero in Nizami's famous lyric poem called 'Husrev and Şirin'.
66. Shirin: Heroine of the same poem, Khusrev's belovéd.
67. Sikker: Another lady in the same lyric poem.
68. Aries, Capricorn: Zodical signs, meaning kid and lamb. This is a play on words.
69. Harem: The thought sequence is: Harem ... something intimate ... Something holy ... hence the Kaaba.
70. Trav'lling chair: This would be in the nature of a basket to be fastened to the back of a camel.
71. Mihrab: The niche or heart of a mosque.
72. Kible: The direction of Mekka; the place where the Muslim turns in worship of God.
73. Siyadet: A being a descendent from the Prophet Muhammed.
74. Saadet: Prosperity.
75. Zemzem: The sacred well at Mekka.
76. Mejnūn, forgetting he is a man, identifies himself with the beast.
77. Pearl: Alternative text has pigeon.
78. Kevser: A river in Paradise.
79. Billah: By God.
80. The pigeon is to circle her house as pilgrims circle the Kaaba Stone.
81. Box: Symbol of a graceful figure.
82. Karin: One's intimate friend; also, a demon, an obsession. Here is a play on the word Karin.
83. Leylā sings two songs: One for the night when she is alone; the other for the day when she has to take care to keep her love hidden from her parents.
84. The second song begins here.
85. Abir: A kind of perfume made of musk, saffron, etc.

86. Shalvar: Gaily coloured baggy trousers.
87. Rastik: Cosmetic used for blackening the eyebrows.
88. Zekat: Alms.
89. Nikàh: Marriage ceremony.
90. Amr and Zayd: Anybody.
91. Tuğra: The official seal used by the Sultans to indicate authenticity.
92. Firman: Imperial edict. The meaning here is the command of Love, that he should follow and not forsake.
93. Namaz: The daily cycle of prayer followed by devout Mohammedans. Five prayers daily, at stated times.
94. Surme: Kohl.
95. Nejd: The wilderness wherein he wandered. The Central Highlands of Arabia.
96. Kassam: The Distributor; e.g. God.
97. My friend: i.e. Leylā.
98. Cyrus: Persian King.
99. Wailer: i.e. the professional wailer.
100. Note: Mejnūn has not yet recognized Leylā.
101. Abjed: The Arabic Alphabet arranged in its ancient form.
102. Gazel: Lyric poem.
103. Kaside: Laudatory Ode.
104. Sirsir: Tempest.
105. Jam: Short for Jamshyd.
106. Camphor: White hair.
107. Saffron: Pale face. The line means that she let her white hair fall over her pale face.

BIBLIOGRAPHY

Chapter One
A general bibliography of Fuzūlī has been compiled by M. Cunbur, *Fuzūlī hakkında bir bibliografya denemesi*, Istanbul, 1956. See also:
C. Öztelli, 'Fuzūlī biblyografyasına yeni katmalar', in *Türk dili*, VIII, 1959, pp. 333–6. Ja. S. Misćuk, 'Ob odnoĭ rukopisi divana Fuzūlī, in *Tjurkologičeskie issledovanija*, Moscow–Leningrad, 1963, pp. 233–6; and
A. Ateş, 'Fuzulinin el yazısı, in *Türk dili*, V, 1957, pp. 545–7; S. Płaskowicka Rymkiewica, 'Zycie i twórczość Fuzulego' in *Przegląd Orientalistyczny*, No. 7 (21), Warsaw, 1937, pp. 3–77.
On his life the following monographies are fundamental:
A. Karahan, *Fuzuli, muhiti, hayatı ve şahsiyeti*, Istanbul, 1949 (Istanbul Üniversitesi Edebiyat Fakültesi yayımları, No. 410, Türk Dili ve Edebiyat Bölümü: Doktora Tezleri, No. 2) and H. Araslı, *Böyük Azerbayjan Shairi Füzuli*, Baku, 1958. Finally see the article by A. Karahan in *Encyclopédie de l'Islam*, 2nd edition, Vol. II, Livraison 37; Leiden, Paris, 1964, pp. 958–61.
For quotations from Fuzūlī's writings see Bibliography, Ch. II.

Chapter Two
For the *Divan* I use the edition of K. Akyüz, S. Beker, S. Yüksel, M. Cunbur, Ankara, 1958. Previously the *Divan* was edited by A. Gölpınarlı, Istanbul, 1948 (2nd edn., 1961), and by A. N. Tarlan, Istanbul, 1950.
I have also consulted the Baku edition edited by H. Araslı: *Mehemmed Füzuli Eserleri*. I–II, Baku, 1958 (Azerbayjan SSR Elmler Akademiyasī. Nizami adīna Edebiyat ve Dil Institutu).
For the poem *Beng u Bāde*, *Külliyyāt*, Istanbul, 1328, pp. 81–99; Baku edition, Vol. II, Baku, 1958, pp. 235–64 and for the letter to the Nishānjī *Külliyyāt*, pp. 100–3; Baku edition, Vol. II, pp. 299–303.
The *Persian Divan* (qasidas, ghazals and miscellaneous compositions) has been edited by H. Mazıoğlu, *Fuzûlî, Farsça Divan. Edisyon Kritik*, Ankara, 1962 (Ankara Üniversitesi Dil ve Tarih-Cografya Fakültesi yayınları, No. 135. Türk Dil ve Edebiyatı Serisi No. 20).
The *Matla' al-i'tiqād* and the Arabic qasidas were published at Baku in 1958. The former also in Turkey in 1965.
For the *Hadīqat as-Su'adā* I consulted the British Museum manuscript.
A general Bibliography of the works of Fuzūlī can be found in the book by M. Cunbur and in the article by A. Karahan quoted in the Bibliography of Chapter I.
A full analysis of Fuzūlī's writings can be found in H. Araslı's book also quoted in the Bibliography of the first chapter. For the *Divan* see H. Mazıoğlu, *Fuzûlî—Hâfız. Iki şair arasında bir karşılaştırma* (*Doktora Tezi*), Ankara, 1956. For the humour in Fuzūlī see A. Bombaci, 'Il Bello al bagno. Un indirizzo giocoso della lirica persiana e turca' in *Annali dell'Istituto Universitario Orientale*, Naples, New Series, Vol. XIV, Part I, 1964, pp. 33–48 (papers presented to L. Veccia Vaglieri).

Chapter Three
Texts
Ibn Qutaiba: Ibn Qotaiba, Liber poesis et poëtarum, quem edidit, M. J. De Goeje; Lugduni Batavorum (Leiden), 1904.
Kitāb az-Zahra: Kitāb al-zahra (The Book of the Flower). The first half. Composed by Abū Bakr Muhammad Ibn Abī Sulaimān Dāwūd al-Isfahānī (AH 297/AD 909). Edited from the unique manuscript at the Egyptian Library by A. R. Nykl in collaboration with Ibrāhīm Tūqān, Nablus Palestine, Chicago, Illinois, 1932 (The Oriental Institute of the University of Chicago, Studies in Ancient Oriental Civilization No. 6).
Kitāb al-Aghānī: Kitāb al-Aghānī, ta'līf Abīlfaraj al-Isfahānī, al-juz' al-thānī, al-Qāhirah, 1346h.–1927m. (Dār al-kutub al-Misriyyah, al-qism al-adabī).

On the legend of Majnūn, I. Krachkovski's article is fundamental, 'Rannaja istorija povesti o Medjnune i Leile v arabskoi literature', in *Sbornik statei pod redaktsiei*, A. K. Borovkova., Akad. Nauk SSSR, Moscow–Leningrad, 1946, pp. 31–67, translated into German by H. Ritter under the title of: 'Die Frühgeschichte der Erzählung von Macnūn und Lailā in der arabischen Literatur', in *Oriens*, Vol. 8, Leiden, 1955, pp. 1–48, with a *Nachtrag* on pp. 49–50. (Now in Y. Krachkovski, *Izbrannye sochinenija*, II, Moscow–Leningrad, 1955). For the figure of Majnūn among the Persian and Arab mystics see H. Ritter, *Das Meer der Seele. Mensch, Welt und Gott in der Geschichten des Feriduddin 'Attār*, Leiden, 1955, 'Analytischer index', s.v. Macnūn, pp. 730–1. For Majnūn among the Turkish mystics see A. S. Levend, *Arap, fars ve türk edebiyatlarānda Leylā ve Mecnun hikâyesi*, Ankara, 1959, pp. 103–7.

Chapter Four
Edition of Nizāmī's *Laylā and Majnūn*: Nizami Gandjevi, *Layli i Madjnun Kriticheskiy tekst. A. A. Alesker-zade i F. Babaeva. Predislovie A. A. Alizade*, Moscow, 1965 (Akademiya Nauk SSSR. Institut Narodov Azii, Pamyatniki literatury narodov vostoka. Teksty. Bol'shaya seriya. XVII). See Note 2 for the preceding edition of V. Dastgirdī (Teheran, 1333/1954). A partial free translation in English by J. Atkinson, London, 1936; Turkish by A. N. Tarlan, Istanbul, 1943 (not consulted); Russian by P. Antololsky, Moscow, 1957 (not consulted); German (free and incomplete) by R. Gelpke, Zurich, 1963; English of the same in collaboration with E. Mattin and G. Hill, London, 1961.

For Hātifī's 'Lailā and Majnūn' I have consulted the manuscript from the Biblioteca Apostolica Vaticana, Valle 56.

The most complete analysis of the poem is in E. E. Bertels' 'Nizami Monografiya', in *Izbrannye trudy. Nizami i Fuzuli*, Moscow, 1962, pp. 230–74. See also the *Nachwort* in R. Gelpke's translation.

I have not been able to consult M. Ghunaimī Hilāl's book, *Alhubb al-'udhrī wa-hubb al-mutasawwifah 'au Lailā wa-'l-Majnūn fī 'l-'adabain al-'arabī wa-'l-fārisī*, al-Qāhira, 1954.

On Nizāmī's style see H. Ritter, *Über die Bildersprache Nizāmīs*, Berlin-Leipzig, 1927, and the Introduction by A. Bausani to the translation of the Nizamian poem, *Haft Paiker: Nezami di Ganje, Le sette principesse*, Bari, 1967.

The Persian imitations of Nīzāmī's Lailā and Majnūn have been examined by E. E. Bertels, *op. cit.*, pp. 275–300, and by A. S. Levend, *op. cit.*, in the Bibliography of the third chapter.

Chapter Five
I follow N. H. Onan's edition: *Fuzuli, Leyla ile Mecnun*, Istanbul, 1955 (Türk Kültür Eserleri: 1). I have also consulted the Baku edition edited by H. Araslī: *Mehemmed Füzuli. Eserleri. II Jild*, Baku, 1958, pp. 11–233.

A careful German translation has been published by N. H. Lugal and O. Reşer: *Des türkischen Dichters Fuzuli Poëm 'Laylâ—Magnun' und die gereimte Erzählung 'Beng u Bâde' (Haşiş und Wein) nach dem Druck Istbl. 1328 übersetzt*, Istanbul, 1943.

INDEX

Abbasid caliphate, 16, 60
Abjed, 305, 342
Abū 'Amr ash-Shaybānī, 48
Abū Bakr, 13
Abū Bakr al-Wālibī, 50
Abū Hanīfa, 1, 16
Abūlfaraj al-Isfahānī, 48–50, 66–7
Abū 'l-Mahdī, 52
Abū Miskīn, 51
Abū Nuwas, 18
Aghānī, see *Kitāb al-Aghānī*
Ahmad Ghazzālī, 62
Ahmadnagar, 19
Ahmad Shawqī, 50
Ahmedī, 150, 335
Ahmed Sanjakbey of Mosul, 43
Akhbār Majnūn, 49
Akhsatan I, 64, 76
'Alā'uddīn, Qadi of Baghdad, 43
Alexis, St, 72
'Alī, 11–18, 40, 45, 336
Āl-i Osmān, 138
'Alī Shēr Navā'ī, 26, 84
  See also Navā'ī and Nevai
Amālī, al-, 336
'Āmirites, 60
Amoretti, B. Scarcia, 334
'Amr, 249, 342
Anatolia ('Rūm'), 12, 18, 21–2, 62, 86, 103
Anbiya, 138
Anīsu 'l-qalb, 20, 44
antinomianism, 33, 35
Arabic literature, 22, 44, 46, 49–50, 54, 58, 60, 64, 67–8, 79
Araslī, H., 42
Arberry, A. J., 336
Aries, 187
Ariosto, 61
Ash'arite school, 16
'Āshīq Chelebi, 17, 21
'Āshīq Pasha, 63, 89
Asma'ī, al-, 48
astronomy, 13
'Attār, 62
'Awān ibn al-Hakam, 48
Ayās Pasha, 18–20, 38, 41, 43

'Aynulqudāt, 62
Azerbaijan, 11–12, 64, 86, 150, 340
'Azza, 62

Babel, tower of, 339
Babylon, 143, 340
Baghdad, 11–13, 15–18, 20, 22, 38, 40, 63, 66, 139, 152, 334
Banū 'Āmir, 47–8, 51–2, 60–1
Banū Harīsh, 52
Banū Murra, 52
Banū 'Udhra, 54
Basra, 17, 19, 152
Bausani, A., 333, 338
baxt (bad luck), 73
Bayat tribe, 12
Bāyezīd Chelebi, 43
Bāyezīd II, 84
Bedouin(s), 14
Bedouin code of honour, 50
Bedouin poetry, 54
Behrem, 136, 339
Beng u Bāde, 14, 17, 42
Bertels, E. E., 337–8
Bombaci, A., 334–5
Buddhism, 22
Buhlūl, 11
Burak, 135–6, 339
Burhān Nizāmshāh, 19
Bursa, 150

Capricorn, 187
Chosroes, 64, 176, 341
Chosroes, Palace of, 11
Constantinople, 20–1
Ctesiphon, 11
Cyrus, 280, 342

Dal, 180
Damascus, 340
Dastgirdī, 65, 337–8
Deccan, 19
de Troyes, Chrétien, 61
Dhū 'l-faqār, 14
dialogue poems, 42
Divan, 23–30, 333–4

347

Ebi-Nüvas, 141, 340
Ebubekir, 138, 339
Egypt, 234
enigmas, 45
Euphrates, 15

Fağfur, 176, 296, 341
Fakhruddīn Gurgānī, 79
Farišta, 334
Fārs, 66
Fātima, 40
Fazlī (Fuzūlī's son), 20, 45
Fighānī, 336
Firdausī, 78

Gelpke, R., 338
Gharībnāme, 63
ghazals, 23-30, 34-5, 44
Gibb, E. J. W., 34, 38
Gibb, H. A. R., 334
girizgāh, 39
Gölpınarlı, A., 335
Gülshehrī of Qīrshehir, 62, 67, 84, 89

Habībī, 335
Hadīqatu 's-su'adā, 44, 46, 335
Hak'a, 270
Hakan, 296
Hallāj, 11. See also Mansūr al-Hallāj.
Hamadan, 62
Hamdī, 84, 84 n.
Han'a, 270
Haqīrī, 84
Hārūn ar-Rashīd, 18, 48-9, 60, 141
Harut, 143, 340
Hasan, 45
Hātifī, 81-2, 84, 86-8, 93-4, 97-8, 101, 105-6, 111, 334
Haythām ibn 'Adī, 48
Heine, Heinrich, 54
Herat, 23, 26, 81, 90
Hicaz, 234
Hijaz, 52, 82
Hilla, 15
Hindustan, 139
Hishām Ibn al-Kalbī, 48
homosexual love, 26-7
Husayn, 11, 14-15, 45
Husayn Baiqara, 18
Husayn Vā'iz Kāshifī, 20, 44

Ibn 'Arabī of Murcia, 25, 48
Ibn Da'b, 48
Ibn Mu'tazz, 54
Ibn Qutayba, 49-50, 67, 79
Ibn Salām, Ibn Selām, 65-6, 74-5, 78, 82, 87, 89, 95, 98-100, 102, 215-7, 234-7, 240-3, 249, 251, 259, 281-4, 286, 295, 330

Ibrāhīm, Grand Vizier, 16
Ibrāhīm ibn Sa'd az-Zuhrī, 60
Ibrāhīm Khān, 14, 333
Ilkhanian dynasty, 340
Imāmī Shiites, 12
Imām Kāzim, 15
Imams, the twelve, 40, 333
India, 21
Iran, 145, 234
Iraq, 11, 22, 340
Irem, 148
'Isā ibn Da'b, 60

Ja'fer Pasha, 18, 334
Jāhiz, al-, 54
Jalāluddīn Rūmī, 62, 82
Jāmī, 23, 37, 43-4, 81-2, 84, 89-90
Jamīl al-'Udhrī, 49, 54, 60
Jamshyd, 156, 274, 319, 340, 243
Javād, 15
Jebel Nubad, 116
Jelāirids, 11
Jelali, 150
Jem, 84
Junaid, 11

Kaaba, 50, 56, 65, 73, 82, 87, 89, 94, 107, 118, 179, 191-3, 199, 295, 341
Kaaba Stone, 190, 192, 341
Kaabe, 186
Karahan, A., 333-6
Karbalā', tragedy of, 20, 44
Karbalā', 11, 14-16, 18, 20-1, 334
Karīma, 55
Karin, 204, 341
Kevser, 198, 341
Khalil, 138, 339
Khalīlī, 335
Khāqāni, 44
Khayālī, 22, 335
Khouri Boutros Roumi, 115
Khusrav of Delhi, 44
Khusrev (Husrev), 185, 341
  see also Cosroe
Kible, 191, 341
Kirami, 141
Kitāb al-Aghānī, 48-55, 57-9, 336
Kitāb al Luma', 336
Kitāb ash-shi'r wa ash-shu'arā, 49-50
Kitāb as-zahra, 50, 54-9
Köprülü, Fuad, 333
Koran, 25-6, 55, 80, 194
Korasan, 141
Krachkovski, I., 48-50, 59-60, 336
Kūfa, 11
Külliyyāt, 335-6
Kuthayyir, 49, 62

Laoust, A., 333
Laulaka, 132
Levend, A. S., 337-8
Lutfī, 37

makhlas (*nom de plume*), 23
Manichaeism, 22
Mansūr al-Hallāj, 62 see also Hallāj.
Mantiquttā'ir, 62
Ma'rūf, 11
Mas'ūdī, al-, 53
Mathnavī, 62, 82, 338
Matla'al-i'tiqād, 46, 333
Mawlana Djalal Al-Din Rumi, 116
Mazıoğlu, 335
Mecca, 16, 144
medicine, 13
Medina, 16, 51, 144
Mehmed Pasha, 20, 334
Melamet, 159, 172, 179, 199, 340
menqibet qasida. 40
Merv, 14
Mesopotamia, 11-12, 20, 44
Mevlā (Lord), 63
Mihrab, 191, 341
Mi'raj, 134-5, 138, 307-8, 339
Moguls, 21
Mohammed, 339
Mongols, 11-12
Moses, 143, 289
Muhammad Najafī, 336
Muhammad ibn Dāwūd. 50
Muhammad Khān Tekelü, 14, 334
Muhammad (theologian), 62
Mukarnas, 145, 340
Munāzil, 55
Muqtadir, al-, 49
Mustafā, 289
Mustafā Jelālzāde, 20
mysticism, 13, 50
   Islamic/Muslim, 21, 24
   Majnūn as model for, 61-3, 67, 71
mystic poverty (*faqr*), 34

Najaf, 11-12, 14-15, 19-20
Najd plain, 17, 47, 51-2, 56, 79
Nallino, C. A., 337
Narcissus, 160, 340
Navā'i, 18, 23, 26, 84 n., 335 see also 'Alī Shīr Navā'ī and Nevai
Nawfal ibn Musāhiq, Naufal, Nevfel, 51, 65, 67, 75, 78, 82, 87, 89, 95-97, 98, 101-2, 109, 217-26, 255, 259, 295, 329-30
Nejātī, 335
Nejd, 275, 342

Nestorianism, 22
Nevai, 141
Nevfel, see Nawfal
Nikâh, 234, 342
Nimrod, 138, 339
nishānjī (Ottoman Secretary of State), 17, 43
Niyazi Misrī, 116
Nīzāmī of Ganja, 18, 47, 50, 61-2, 64-83, 95-8, 91-112, 141, 150, 335
Nizāmshāhī, 19
Nizāmulmulk, 19
Nizārites, 60
Nu'mān, two mountains of, 58

'Omar ibn al-Farīd, 62
Omer, 138, 339
Osman, 146, 339
Ottoman Dominion, 15, 17-19, 29
Ottoman school of literature, 22, 84

Padishah, 143-5
Persian Divan, 333-6
Persian literature, 22, 24, 30, 32, 35, 38, 42, 44, 49, 64, 68, 107
Petrarch, 79
Phaedrus, 24
Platonic love theory, 24, 60

qasidas, 23, 37-42, 44-6, 62, 333-5
Qays ibn Dharīh, 49, 53-4, 60
Qays Ibn Mulawwah, 47
Qays of Lubna, 62
qismat (destiny), 73
Qutbshāhī of Golconda, 19

rajaz, 46
Ramadan ritual fast, 35-6
religious poetry, 45
Rind u Zāhid, 45
Ritter, H., 60-1, 337-8
Rubinacci, R., 336
Rubinstein, 54
'Rūm' see Anatolia
Rustaveli, 61
Rustem Pasha, 20

Saadet, 191, 341
Sa'dī, 99
Sādiqī, 333
Safavid dynasty, 12, 14-16, 23, 38
Saki, 139-40, 142-3, 149, 165, 186, 201, 263, 281, 300, 313, 321, 328
Sakiname, 340
Salām, 66, 70, 76, 88
Salīm, 66, 70, 76, 87
Sāqī-nāme, 45
Sarah, 52

Saria, 117
Seljukian invasions, 12, 22
Seljukian period, 67
Selman, 148, 340
shāhid (witness), 25-6
Shāhidī, 83, 89
Shahinshah, 144, 340
Shāh Ismā'īl, 12-16, 19, 22, 42, 333
Sham, 139, 269
Shayb Hasan Büzürg, 340
Sheddad, 340
Sheẏkhī, 335
Sheyshi, 150
Shī'a, the Twelver, 19
Shiblī, 61-2, 71
Shiism/Shiites, 12-17, 19-21, 38, 45-6, 333-4
Shikāyet-nāme, 333-4
Shīrīn/Shirin, 64, 185, 341
Shirvan, 139
Shirvan, Shah of, 18, 64, 141
Sikker, 185, 341
sipāhī corps, 29
Siyadet, 191, 341
Söhbetü 'l-asmār, 42-3
Solomon, King, 146
Sufism, 24-5, 30, 62, 71
Süleymān the Magnificent, 15-22, 40-2, 44, 102, 144-6, 313
Sunnet, 156, 340
Sunnites, 12-13, 15-16, 46, 333
Symposium (Plato), 24
Syria, 52, 58

Tabarī, al-, 336
Tabrīz, 13, 20-1, 84
Taha, 133, 339
Taimā', 52
taqiyyay, 16
Tarika, 117
Tauba, 49
Taubād, Mount, 58
tawhīd, 39
Thaqafite, 51
theology, 13
Tihāma, 52
Timurid school of literature, 22

trilingualism, 22
Turan, 145
Turcoman Shiites, 13
Turcoman tribes, 12
Turcomans of White and Black Sheep, 11
Turkish literature, 22-4, 30, 32, 35, 38, 42, 49, 62, 84, 107
Tur mountain, 135, 339
Twelver Shī'a, 12

'Udhrite Arabic ideal of love, 24, 30, 54, 56-7, 60, 67
'Umar ibn Abī Rabī'a, 49, 54
Umayyad dynasty, 16, 47, 60
Unca, 161
'Urwa ibn Hizām, 49, 54, 57, 60
'Uthmān ibn 'Umāra, 53
Üveys Pasha, 18, 41, 102, 334
Uwais, Sultan, 148-8, 340
Uzbek Khan Muhammad Shaybānī, 14

Vīs and Rāmīn, 79

Wālibī, al-, 54, 66-7, 336
Ward, 51
Washsha', al-, 49
wine, 32-3, 45, 142, 149
  see also Saki

Yasin, 133, 339
Yemen, 58
Yemenite tribes, 54, 60
Yunus Emre, 116
Yūsuf Amīrī, 42

Zāhirite theological school, 24
Zayd, Zeyd, 66-7, 70, 88, 89, 109, 242-3, 249, 254, 274-5, 278, 281, 283-4, 320-2, 326-7, 337
Zaynab, Zegnels, 66-7, 88, 242, 337
Zekat, 232, 342
Zemzem, 191 341
Zeyd, *see* Zayd
Zeyneb, *see* Zaynab
Zubayr, az-, ibn Bakkār, 49
Zuhera, 340

UNESCO Collection of Representative Works Indian Series.

This book has been accepted in the Indian Series of the Translations Collection of UNESCO.

© UNESCO 1967, 1969

First published by George Allen & Unwin Ltd., London, 1967.

For Product Safety Concerns and Information please contact our EU representative GPSR@taylorandfrancis.com
Taylor & Francis Verlag GmbH, Kaufingerstraße 24, 80331 München, Germany

www.ingramcontent.com/pod-product-compliance
Lightning Source LLC
Chambersburg PA
CBHW080934300426
44115CB00017B/2810